C0-DKO-371

Medieval Muslims, Christians, and Jews
in Dialogue: The *Apparicion maistre
Jehan de Meun* of Honorat Bovet

MEDIEVAL AND RENAISSANCE TEXTS AND STUDIES

VOLUME 283

Medieval Muslims, Christians, and Jews in Dialogue: The *Apparicion maistre Jehan de Meun* of Honorat Bovet

A Critical Edition with English Translation

by

Michael Hanly

Arizona Center for Medieval and Renaissance Studies
Tempe, Arizona
2005

© Copyright 2005
Arizona Board of Regents for Arizona State University

Library of Congress Cataloging-in-Publication Data

Bonet, Honoré, fl. 1378-1398.
  [Apparicion Maistre Jehan de Meun. English & French]
  Medieval Muslims, Christians, and Jews in dialogue : The apparicion Maistre Jehan
de Meun of Honorat Bovet : a critical edition with English translation / by Michael
Hanly.
      p. cm. -- (Medieval & Renaissance Texts & Studies ; v. 283)
  Includes bibliographical references.
  ISBN 0-86698-326-0 (alk. paper)
  1. Schism, The Great Western, 1378-1417. I. Hanly, Michael G. II. Title.
III. Series: Medieval & Renaissance Texts & Studies (Series) ; v. 283.

PQ1551.B7A7813 2005
841'.1--dc22
                                        2005002641

This book is made to last.
It is set in Garamond
smyth-sewn and printed on acid-free paper
to library specifications.

Printed in the United States of America

Cover Image: BNF fonds français 810 (manuscript P1), fol. 6v
Jean de Meun introduces the Prieur to the Physicien, Sarrazin, Juif, and Jacobin

CONTENTS

To my parents,

Richard F. Hanly and Eileen Monahan Hanly

ABBREVIATIONS

Manuscript sigla

P1   Paris, Bibliothèque nationale de France, MS fonds français 810

P2   Paris, Bibliothèque nationale de France, MS fonds français 811

L   London, British Museum, MS Lansdowne 214 fols. 201r–216v

V   Vatican City, Biblioteca Apostolica Vaticana, MS Reginensis latinus 1683, fols. 39r–87v

Libraries and Archives

ASV   Archivio Segreto Vaticano, Vatican City

BAV   Biblioteca Apostolica Vaticana, Vatican City

BNF   Bibliothèque nationale de France, Paris

BL   British Library, London

Printed Sources

CCSL   *Corpus Christianorum Series Latina.* Ed. F. Bossier, et al. 168 vols. Turnhout: Brepols, 1953–2003.

CPPMA   *Clavis Patristica Pseudepigraphorum Medii Aevi.* Ed. J. Machielsen. 4 vols. Turnhout: Brepols, 1990–1994.

Friedberg   *Corpus juris canonici.* Ed. Emil Friedberg. 2 vols. Berlin: Tauchnitz, 1879–1881.

Mommsen   *Corpus juris civilis.* Ed. Theodore Mommsen, Paul Krueger and Rudolf Schoell. 3 vols. Berlin: Weidmann, 1904–1908.

Mommsen/Watson

    The Digest of Justinian, Latin text ed. Theodore Mommsen and Paul Krueger. Trans. Alan Watson. 4 vols. Philadelphia: University of Pennsylvania Press, 1985.

PG   Patrologiae cursus completus, Series Graeca. Ed. J. Ed. J.-P. Migne. 161 in 166 vols. Paris: 1857–1866.

PL   Patrologiae cursus completus, Series Latina. Ed. J.-P. Migne. 221 vols. Paris: 1844–1864.

SATF   Société d'anciens textes français (Paris)

NUMERATION PROCEDURE

Verse lines are indicated with Arabic numerals, e.g., 1–12.

In the Introduction and Notes, Prose lines are signaled with the addition of the word "Prose" (e.g., Prose 1–5). In the Text, they are indicated by bold type (e.g., **1–5**).

Manuscript sigla are indicated by bold type (e.g., **P1**).

Latin glosses are indicated by the sigla of the manuscript in which they occur, followed by a period and the number of the note in order of its appearance; for added ease of identification, they are always enclosed in brackets, e.g., [P1.29].

ILLUSTRATIONS
(appearing after page xv)

ACKNOWLEDGMENTS

This edition would not have been completed without the financial support of several institutions and the generous help of a number of scholars, and I must offer my heartfelt thanks to them all. I first examined the principal manuscripts in Paris in 1993–1994 while conducting research for a larger project, supported by a Fulbright research grant and a fellowship from the National Endowment for the Humanities. I studied another manuscript in Rome during a sabbatical leave from Washington State University in 1997–1998, under a Fulbright research grant. Washington State University provided travel and research stipends at different times during this period. Many thanks to the staff at the following institutions: the Bibliothèque nationale and Archives nationales, Paris; CNRS-UMR 8589 "Laboratoire de médiévistique occidentale de Paris," Villejuif (Paris); the Huntington Library, San Marino, California; the Archivio Segreto Vaticano and Biblioteca Apostolica Vaticana, Vatican City; and the Burgerbibliothek, Bern, Switzerland. Thanks as well to my friends and colleagues in the Englisches Seminar at the Universität Bern, who welcomed me and provided office and library support during a sabbatical in 1997–1998, and during other summers since then. I am also grateful to Mouton de Gruyter Publishers for their permission to use material from a previously published article as part of my introduction here ("Bovet and Islam"): "'Et prendre nom de Sarrazin': Islam as Symptom of Western Iniquity in Honorat Bovet's *L'apparicion maistre Jehan de Meun*," in *Cultures in Contact: Essays in Honor of Paul Beekman Taylor*, ed. Margaret E. Bridges, special issue of *Multilingua* 18 (1999). 227–49 (Berlin and New York: Mouton de Gruyter).

My colleagues at CNRS in Paris have been enormously helpful. Gilbert Ouy, whose pioneering work on Bovet spurred my interest in this author, made available his extensive notes and manuscript photographs and wielded his legendary paleographical skills several times on my behalf in the Salle des manuscrits at Richelieu. Ezio Ornato, Monique Ornato, Carla Bozzolo, Nicole Pons, and Evencio Beltran generously welcomed a stranger into their midst and helped with every aspect of this edition in its early stages; I learned as much during lunchtime discussions at the CNRS cantina as I did in libraries and archives. Hélène Millet, who graciously collaborated with me on a 1996 article dealing with Bovet, provided crucial insights into this author's career and into the historian's craft. Gabriella Parussa and Richard Trachsler offered erudite assistance with the English translation and with historical details.

I am grateful to François Avril of the Bibliothèque nationale for his generous help with the illuminations in the two Paris manuscripts and with other iconographical lore. William Carey of Ad Fontes Academy and George Mason University offered bibliographical expertise. Riccardo Famiglietti explained some confusing medieval French administrative procedures, and helped with my translation. Laurent Mayali contributed solutions to a number of canon-law conundrums. The late Fr. Leonard O. Boyle, O.P., took the time to straighten out several perplexing juristic references and to offer welcome encouragement. I thank my friend Efem Nevole for his translations from Czech. Rick Emmerson helped with questions on prophetic writings, and along with Stephen Barney, Piero Boitani, Warren Ginsberg, Paul Strohm, Tom Bestul, and Paul Beekman Taylor offered practical advice and crucial letters of support. Elizabeth A. R. Brown helped decipher some difficult passages in the Paris manuscripts. Ralph Hanna steered me in the right direction on manuscript terminology. Jean-Pierre Brunterc'h of the Archives nationales guided me in all my manuscript work there, and found me some elusive printed records. My work at the BAV and ASV, finally, would have gone nowhere without the expert assistance of Christine Grafinger, the kindest person within the Vatican walls and a master of the collections on both sides of the Cortile della Biblioteca. Thanks as well to her colleague Fr. William Sheehan, C.S.B., for his welcome and his suggestions.

I wish to thank my colleagues Nick Kiessling and Al von Frank at Washington State, who for many years have helped me in many ways, from their support of my professional advancement to their careful reading of drafts of various writings. My thanks as well to Bob Bjork, Roy Rukkila, Juleen Eichinger, and the staff at ACMRS, especially to the peerless copy editor Dr. Leslie S. B. MacCoull and to the two anonymous readers of my manuscript—their learned and meticulous commentary saved me from countless errors and greatly improved the overall quality of this edition.

I owe special thanks to one scholar in particular. One of the greatest challenges in preparing this edition was the confrontation between my almost complete ignorance of canon law and Honorat Bovet's many citations of Gratian et al. in the marginal glosses. Realizing that I would have no chance on my own, I began to send email queries to my friend and mentor Henry Ansgar Kelly, who would reply promptly with a solution to the enigma du jour. This work proceeded in fits and starts, but by the time we finished several years later, a host of mystifying citations had been unraveled, and I had learned, through Andy's generosity, a great deal about the methodology and decipherment of canon law. He claimed ceaselessly that he actually *enjoyed* working through these puzzles, and his enthusiasm was inspirational. I can't thank Andy enough for his patience, brilliance, and long hours of toil.

Many friends put me up or put up with me during research trips leading to this book: Aldo and Carmen Roncoroni in Bern, Béatrice Hertig and Jürg Glauner in Basel, Eileen and Michael Hands in London, Monique Mourier in Lyon, Howard and Françoise Appel in Les Bouilladoires, Liudmilla Sinkevitch-Austin and Luciana Gabbrielli in Rome, Mary and Jacques Seneschal in Brovès-en-Seillans, Monika and Christian van Reck in Segur de Calafell, and Nadine Aouizerate in Paris. Hans Schmid and Frank Versaci asked me to speak at several meetings of the Swiss-British Society of Basel, Willy Elmer invited me a number of times to teach as a visiting professor at the Universität Basel, and Jürg Rosenbusch welcomed me to his home in that lovely town. My friends Scott Dean and Craig Morris cheerfully endured my endless talk about Bovet. Thanks to Michael Muller for his confidence. Love and thanks as well to my brothers and sisters and their spouses—Marty and Jan, Rich and Chris, Tim and Terry, Eileen, and Cathy and John; to my awesome nieces and nephews Angela, Ray, Collin, Marie, Matt, Alanna, Kendall, Brenna, Johnny, Clare, and John Keenan; and to our dear godchildren, Nathan Dean and Laura Muller.

My greatest gratitude goes to my lovely Ines, whose patience and sweet encouragement come back to me in every line of this book. She is my muse; whatever I am or do is better because of her. Fiona and Olivia, beautiful and bright, fill our house with their music, love, and gladness. I am triply blessed.

ILLUSTRATIONS

Figure 1. BNF fonds français 810 (manuscript P1), fol. 1r
Honorat Bovet offers his poem to Jean de Montagu

Figure 2. BNF fonds français 811 (manuscript **P2**), fol. 1r
Honorat Bovet offers his poem to Valentina Visconti

Figure 3. BNF fonds français 810 (manuscript **P1**), fol. 6v
Jean de Meun introduces the Prieur to the Physicien, Sarrazin,
Juif, and Jacobin

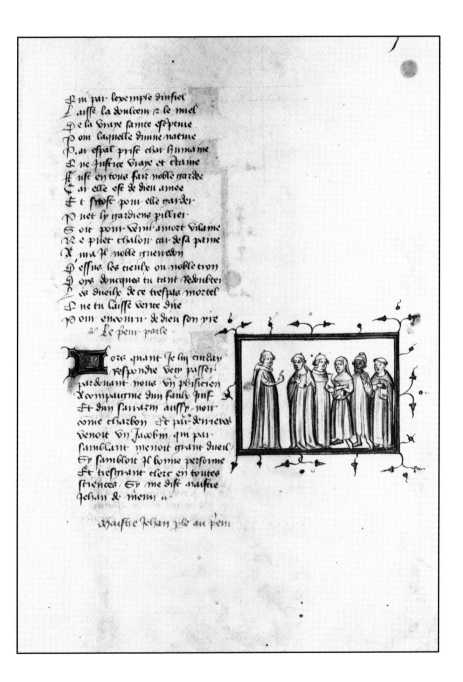

Figure 4. BNF fonds français 811 (manuscript **P2**), fol. 5r
Jean de Meun introduces the Prieur to the Physicien, Juif,
Sarrazin, and Jacobin

Figure 5. BNF fonds français 810 (manuscript **P1**), fol. 9v
Jean de Meun addresses the Juif

Figure 6. BNF fonds français 810 (manuscript **P1**), fol. 10v
The Prieur addresses the Sarrazin

Figure 7. BNF fonds français 811 (manuscript **P2**), fol. 8r
Son Physicien parle a Madame d'Orliens

INTRODUCTION

The Poem

Honorat Bovet composed his reformist dream-vision *L'apparicion maistre Jehan de Meun* in the summer of 1398, and over the ensuing months offered presentation copies to four of the most powerful people at the court of France: Duke Louis of Orléans, brother of King Charles VI; his wife, the Duchess of Orléans, Valentina Visconti; Duke Philip of Burgundy, Louis's uncle and rival at court; and Louis's political ally, the royal councillor Jean de Montaigu. Two of those four presentation copies have survived to this day. No original records mention the text's contemporary reception, however, and with the exception of two fifteenth-century copies of a much-revised version of the manuscript dedicated to Philip of Burgundy, it was ignored for more than four hundred years. In 1845, Baron Jérome Pichon edited and published the poem for the Société des Bibliophiles Français; it was edited again in 1926 as a doctoral thesis by Ivor Arnold.[1] While both editions present accurate transcriptions of Bovet's poem as well as some useful explanatory notes, they are both long out of print and hard to find; this in itself might be justification enough for a new edition of this underappreciated work. But even were these editions readily available, they would need to be replaced, primarily because of their almost complete omission of the seventy-five Latin glosses that accompany the two authoritative manuscripts of the *Apparicion*.

---

[1] Jérome [Baron] Pichon, ed., *L'Apparition de Jehan de Meun ou le Songe du Prieur de Salon par Honoré Bonet, Prieur de Salon, Docteur en Décret [1398]* (Paris: Silvestre, 1845); Ivor Arnold, ed., *L'apparicion Maistre Jehan de Meun et le Somnium super materia scismatis* (Paris: Les Belles Lettres, 1926). The publication of Pichon's edition was funded by the Société des Bibliophiles Français; only 117 copies were printed, including 17 on vellum for members of the society. Arnold's edition was certainly produced in greater numbers than Pichon's, and can be found at larger research libraries in the United States and in Europe. It was printed, however, on the brittle high-acid paper of the time, and many copies are in poor condition.

This substantial body of annotated comments—composed by the author himself and sometimes penned in his own hand—simply cannot be overlooked. Nevertheless, neither of the previous editors found it necessary to grant these comments more than passing notice. Pichon (xi) mentions "un commentaire latin, dont nous avons reproduit dans ce volume tous les passages importants," but his erudite notes include only three references to Bovet's glosses. For his part, Arnold sums up the importance of these comments in a note early in his edition (3 n. 1): "À cet endroit, et ailleurs, dans les deux manuscrits, on a ajouté en marge du texte un commentaire latin. Une grande partie de ce commentaire consiste en citations plus ou moins exactes des auteurs classiques et de decrétales, qu'il n'y a aucun intérêt à reproduire." At various junctures in his edition, Arnold refers in footnotes to individual glosses, and at times even reproduces their texts. But like Pichon, he truncates these glosses even while including them, omitting the citations of authority that conclude almost every marginal comment.[2] Such a dismissal is surprising for a critic who knows this writer as well as Arnold does, for it overlooks the essential fact that Bovet's education and his most important professional accomplishments were as a canonist. It stands to reason, therefore, that Bovet would make significant use of that wealth of knowledge in his works of literature. In his most famous composition, the *Arbre des batailles* (ca. 1386–1387), the author adumbrates his method in the *Apparicion,* claiming that Scripture, canons, and laws are the foundation of his literary enterprise:

> Si vous supplie, mon tres excellent et souverain prince, que rien que je dis en cestui livre ne vous soit ennuyeux, mais vous plaise le avoir pour agreable. Car ce que j'ay mis en lui prend son fondement sur la sainte Escripture et sur les decrets et sur les lois et sur naturelle philosophie qui n'est aultre chose que raison de nature.[3]

Bovet's marginal commentary attaches a learned apparatus to a simple story, and its directives situate the text in the *De regimine principum* tradition. The glosses were designed to lead the poem's first four recipients past the literal level of the dream vision and on to the moral or tropological level. If these first readers of the *Apparicion* were as clever and as ethical as the author presumed, their attention would necessarily shift from an analysis of the external events described in the narrative to an interior examination—

---

[2] For a striking example of the quantity of material that is lost through such abridgements, see marginal gloss [P1.36] at l. 1393 in the poetic text (hereafter "Text") (note 129). Arnold (57 n. 1) omits everything after the word *reprobatur,* so more than half of the aggregate comment.

[3] Ernest Nys, ed., *L'Arbre des Batailles d'Honoré Bonet* (Brussels: Muquardt, 1883), 2.

a measuring of their own actions against the just behavior demanded of
Christian rulers by God.

What level of learning could Bovet have expected from his dedicatees?
Valentina Visconti is reputed to have been fluent in French, German and
Latin, and to have possessed some literary manuscripts.[4] Her husband Louis
of Orléans shared her love of books and appears to have been more devoted to learning than most nobles of his time, as demonstrated by his
competence in Latin. Buonaccorso Pitti, the Florentine ambassador to
France, once observed that Louis was the only member of the French delegation able to follow the Latin conversation between his Italian colleagues
during a diplomatic meeting.[5] It is not known if Jean de Montaigu possessed any serious erudition, but he was renowned in any case for his able
statecraft, having been instrumental in continuing Charles V's enlightened
policies.[6] Philip of Burgundy, finally—to whom Bovet dedicated a revised
copy, now lost, of the *Apparicion*—was renowned more as a patron of the
arts than as a scholar, but he did own several manuscripts on learned topics,
such as French translations of Aristotle and Livy, and a *Gouvernement des
princes*, along with Bovet's *Arbre des batailles*.[7] Bovet, nevertheless, begins his
introduction to the Burgundy revision (here represented by a later "Artois"
redaction, manuscripts **L** and **V**; see "Manuscripts" below) by claiming he
has written this text in French since his lordship understands no Latin (see
Appendix 2).

It can safely be said, therefore, that Bovet's program, as represented by
the seventy-five *Apparicion* glosses, seems pitched to a level of sophistication—not to mention morality—beyond that which could have been rea-
sonably expected of any of the figures to whom he dedicated manuscripts.
His dissemination of the work to four known recipients cannot be seen as
taking part in the same trend in late medieval literary patronage described
by Deborah McGrady in a recent article, in which dedication copies of
Christine de Pizan's works are seen "not circulating as gifts offered to an
individual who can lay claim to them," but rather "as artifacts associated
primarily with their creator, who masterminds their continued distribu-

---

[4] Émile Collas, *Valentine de Milan, Duchesse d'Orléans*, 2d ed. (Paris: Plon, 1911), 48.

[5] Léon Mirot, "Bonaccorso Pitti: aventurier, joueur, diplomate et mémorialiste," *Annuaire-Bulletin de la Société de l'Histoire de France* 60 (1930): 183–252, here 209.
The meeting took place in Paris in December 1396.

[6] Françoise Autrand, *Charles VI: la folie du roi* (Paris: Fayard, 1986), 189–203.

[7] Georges Doutrepont, *La littérature française à la cour des Ducs de Bourgogne* (Paris:
Champion, 1909), 121, 271.

tion."[8] Bovet shows no signs of literary ambitions, of being a seeker after fame, in the manner of Christine; his motivation for writing seems, by all available evidence, to have been purely ideological—even if subsequent events proved his strategy impractical. Since the political effort represented by the *Apparicion maistre Jehan de Meun* ultimately failed, and might even have put an end to Bovet's career at court, his program appears to have been grounded in a misplaced belief in both the good will and the intellectual ability of the most powerful French nobles. Nevertheless, the extant manuscripts containing the text and glosses reveal the singular perspectives on law, war, schism, and international relations of an experienced diplomat and would-be reformer at a particularly critical moment in European history.

My goal in this edition has been to offer a clear, fully annotated text of the *Apparicion* that restores Bovet's marginal comments to their original position of authority alongside the poetic text. In doing so, I have drawn upon the useful notes of Arnold, and sometimes Pichon, and acknowledge them when I do. I have had to go, however, far beyond the scope of their modest commentaries in order to do justice to the complexity of the material presented in this text, since Bovet's dream vision—a rather simple affair on the face of it—presents an imposing body of historical, scientific, and theological lore. A literal page-facing translation, finally, has been provided with a view to making the text's sometimes-daunting Middle French tetrameters and prose passages accessible to non-specialists.

Honorat Bovet, Prior of Selonnet (ca. 1345–ca. 1410): Life and Works

Extant documents offer few details about Bovet's life, and the biographies offered in editions of his works do little more than repeat the scattered facts that can be gleaned from them. His name and title, furthermore, have been the subject of a good deal of confusion in the past. Most early editors and scholars rendered his name as some variation on "Honoré Bonet"; later research altered his patronymic to "Bouvet." A recent article contains the most thorough biography on this author, along with a justification of the decision to call him "Honorat Bovet";[9] I offer here a basic nar-

---

[8] Deborah McGrady, "What is a Patron? Benefactors and Authorship in Harley 4431, Christine de Pizan's Collected Works," in Marilynn Desmond, ed., *Christine de Pizan and the Categories of Difference* (Minneapolis: University of Minnesota Press, 1998), 195–214, here 198.

[9] Michael Hanly and Hélène Millet, "Les Batailles d'Honorat Bovet: Essai de biographie," *Romania* 114 (1996): 135–81. Gilbert Ouy, "Honoré Bouvet (appelé à

rative sketch of his career, followed by a more detailed chronology. Born in
Provence sometime between 1345 and 1350, Honorat Bovet first appears in
extant documents as a law student at Montpellier, having previously joined
the Benedictine order in the orbit of the monastery of l'Ile-Barbe near
Lyon. That first document records a petition to acquire a better position;
this anxiety over his livelihood dogged Bovet his entire life. In 1371, he
abandons his first post in order to be appointed Prior of the Benedictine
priory of Selonnet in the same diocese (Embrun, today in the Département
d'Alpes d'Haute Provence). He holds this position until the end of his life,
often attempting to improve upon it, and for long periods as an absentee; as
he suggests in the text of the *Apparicion*, local wars in Provence reduced this
ecclesiastical position to one of "petite value," and moreover convinced
him his life would be in danger there (Prose 163–165). Original documents
frequently confuse this small village with that of the better-known city near
Arles, and refer to Bovet as "le prieur de Salon."

Bovet next appears in 1382, on a list of supplicants to Duke Louis of
Anjou, seeking to collate his existing position with another. His licentiate in
canon law is mentioned in that document. In the same year, now referred to
as Doctor of Decrees, he represents the University of Avignon before the
court of Anjou, which claimed dominion over Provence. He apparently
caught the attention of his opponent in this affair, Jean le Fèvre, chancellor
of Anjou: after carrying out a similar mission before the Angevin court in
1385, Bovet was engaged by Marie of Anjou for a diplomatic assignment on
behalf of her young son, Duke Louis II, and remained in their service for
several years. In 1386 Jean le Fèvre, chancellor of Anjou, convened an assembly at Avignon to celebrate Bovet's achievement of the doctoral degree.
With twenty years of political and legal experience to draw from, Bovet
then turned his attention to the throne of France.

Like his contemporary Philippe de Mézières, he saw an opportunity for
peace in the majority of Charles VI, believing him to be the fulfillment of
prophecies that claimed society would be healed by a person of royal blood.[10]
Between 1386 and 1387 Bovet completed his major work, *L'arbre des Batailles*,
which he dedicated to the young king and most likely presented to him in
1389. A wide-ranging treatise on history and warfare largely adapted from the
Tractatus de bello, de represaliis et de duello of the Bolognese jurist Giovanni da
Legnano, the *Arbre des Batailles* also includes an original "historical interpolation" that discusses contemporary matters such as the question of the Ange-

---

tort Bonet), prieur de Selonnet," *Romania* 85 (1959): 255–59, presents groundbreak-
ing documentary evidence regarding Bovet's name and heraldry.

[10] *Arbre des Batailles*, ed. Nys, 2.

vin succession to the throne of Naples in 1380. Bovet's intent, expressed in his prologue, was that "[the king's] youth be informed of several significations of the Holy Scriptures," but he appeals to a broader lay audience as well by rendering Legnano's text in the vernacular. Bovet's work was very popular in the fifteenth century, and was imitated by Christine de Pizan in her *Livre des faits d'armes et de chevalerie*, where she refers to Bovet as her "master";[11] it is now considered a milestone in the development of international law.[12] The immediate effect of the *Arbre des Batailles* was the favor of King Charles, who awarded Bovet a pension at this time, and apparently commissioned him to accompany Pierre de Chevreuse, the reformer general for Languedoc, on a tour of the province in 1390.

It is not known when Honorat Bovet would have completed his duties in Languedoc, but a document from 1391 shows him being sent to Armagnac in service of the crown. By March 1392, he claims to have returned to Paris, in time to have taken part in the peace conference at Amiens between the English delegation including the Dukes of Lancaster and York, and the French side including the Dukes of Burgundy, Bourbon, Touraine and Berry. As a Doctor of Decrees and authority on the legal technicalities of the Schism, Bovet possessed the necessary qualifications to represent the Clementist viewpoint to John of Gaunt, leader of the English contingent. Although the extant registers for the conference bear no record of a meeting between the two, Bovet's Latin prose dream vision *Somnium super materia scismatis* of 1394 describes an interview with Gaunt in detail that bespeaks much more the recollection of an actual occurrence than an imagined exchange. The *Somnium*'s major theme is a plea for restraint in the face of mounting support for the *voie de fait*, the forced abdication of the Pope of

---

[11] Christine describes her vision of Bovet: "... un tres sollempnel homme d'abit, de chiere et de maintien d'un pesant ancien sage auttorisié juge. ..." This figure claims he has come to assist her in the writing of the book: "Chiere amie Christine ... suis cy venu pour estre en ton ayde. ... Et ... est bon que tu cueilles sur l'arbre des batailles qui est en mon jardin aucuns fruiz et que d'iceulx tu uses" (BNF MS français 603, fol. 49r). One manuscript of the *Livre des faits d'armes et de chevalerie* (Brussels, Koninklijke Bibliotheek MS 9009–9011, fol. 181v) contains a miniature depicting the tonsured, black-cloaked Bovet appearing to Christine as she lies in her bed. The illumination is reproduced in Lucie Schaefer, "Die Illustrationen zu den Handschriften der Christine de Pisan," *Marburger Jahrbuch für Kunstwissenschaft* 10 (1937): 119–208. Many thanks to Renate Blumenfeld-Kosinski for bringing this illumination and this article to my attention.

[12] See N. A. R. Wright, "The Tree of Battles of Honoré Bouvet and the Laws of War," in *War, Literature and Politics in the Late Middle Ages*, ed. C. T. Allmand (New York: Barnes & Noble, 1976), 12–31.

Rome through armed intervention. The narrative records several lively, largely familiar encounters with most of the period's Christian heads of state,[13] including an account of a meeting with the Duke of Lancaster. In this episode, the narrator—who is rather transparently Bovet himself—persuades the Duke that the election of Boniface IX, the new pope of Rome, was worthless, and that his predecessor's claim to the papacy had also been tenuous. The conference appears to have been a success, finally, even if the problems in the Church persisted for another generation.[14]

After a mission to the court of Aragon,[15] Bovet returns to the court of Paris probably in late 1393, and later writes that he must spend more than a year at this time convalescing after a serious illness.[16] He then composes the *Somnium super materia scismatis*, in which he laments, among other things, his precarious position at court and constant shortage of cash.[17] Charles VI had been experiencing recurring periods of insanity since 1392, an affliction that created turmoil at all levels of government after 1392 and apparently left

---

[13] One of these is the King of Aragon, mentioned in note 15 below.

[14] Hanly, "Courtiers and Poets: An International Network of Literary Exchange," *Viator* 28 (1997): 305–32, here 319.

[15] In the *Somnium* (ed. Arnold, 73–74), the King of Aragon refers to the Prior of Salon's long sojourn at his court; Noël Valois ("Un ouvrage inédit d'Honoré Bonet, Prieur de Salon," *Annuaire-Bulletin de la Société de l'Histoire de France* 27 [1890]: 193–228, here 210–11) argues that Bovet might have been part of the delegation sent by Duke Louis II of Anjou to negotiate a marriage with the infanta Yolande. The *Somnium* was edited without apparatus or notes by Ivor Arnold in the same volume that contains his edition of the *Apparicion* (see note 1 above); Patsy D. Glatt is currently preparing a new, critical edition of the work with an English translation.

[16] ASV Armarium 54, vol. 21, fol. 73v, letter of 2 November 1394: "Fui infirmus usque ad mortem, et duravit infirmitas anno et ultra; nec sum adhuc perfecte curatus" (I was sick unto death, and the sickness lasted a year and more, nor am I even now entirely cured). This passage appears in a letter by Bovet which, along with copies of three other letters, were added—most likely by an amanuensis—to the copy of his *Somnium super materia scismatis* now conserved at the Archivio Segreto Vaticano. They have been published by Valois, "Un ouvrage inédit," 216 (see note 15 above).

[17] In the *Somnium* (ASV Arm. 54, vol. 21, fol. 78r; ed. Arnold, 78–79), the narrator describes an unhappy episode at the court of Hungary. He wishes to approach the table for dinner, but is refused, "quia nec habebam denarium neque bursam, quoniam pro habenda annua pensione, quam dudum rex michi sua gratia dederat, meum servitorem transmiseram ad dominos generales" (because I had neither money nor purse, since, in order to have the annual pension that the king of his grace had long ago given to me, I had sent my servant to the general lords [perhaps the "Grand Conseil" of the king]). Humiliated, he has to wait for an almsgiver, and has only water to drink and the hard ground for a bed.

Bovet without a patron at court.[18] But if Bovet was worried about his status among the leaders of government in this time, his last two extant works suggest that his sense of mission triumphed over his drive for self-preservation. The *Somnium* injudiciously depicts Duke Philip of Burgundy, the most powerful man in France, as a hedonist.[19] Before 1390 Bovet had tried to ingratiate himself with Burgundy by presenting him with a copy of his *Arbre des Batailles*,[20] but his dedication of a manuscript of the *Apparicion maistre Jehan de Meun* to that prince in 1398[21] seems a futile gesture, since he had clearly aligned himself by that time with the unstable and unpredictable Charles VI and with Louis of Orléans, a young man yet incapable of mounting any serious challenge to Burgundian primacy in the power vacuum at the court of France.[22] The last straw could well have been provided by the *Apparicion* itself, abounding as it does in criticism for the corrupt and incompetent French chivalry in the wake of Nicopolis, a campaign that had been led by Philip's heir, Jean sans Peur. The Duke of Burgundy cannot have been moved to sympathy for Bovet's plight at the reception of this censorious poem. And so for the remainder of the decade the Prior found himself in the predicament described by his narrator in the *Somnium*, that of being entrusted with diplomatic tasks and yet having neither a stable posi-

---

[18] See note 2 (at l. Prose 14) in the Text for more details on the ramifications, for Bovet and for his ally Jean de Montaigu, of the king's sickness.

[19] In the *Somnium* (ed. Arnold, 100), the "Duc de Bourgogne" admits to the narrator that he enjoys his luxurious lifestyle: "Venacio nobis hactenus placuit; gaudebamus mimos et ystriones audire; non respuebamus aliquando pompas et delicias corporales" (Up to this time, hunting has pleased us. We took delight in listening to mimes and players. We did not at times reject bodily pomp and pleasure).

[20] Bovet's narrator in the *Somnium super materia scismatis* (ed. Arnold, 101) claims to have known the Duke of Burgundy a long time, and in the opening to the Vatican manuscript of the *Apparicion maistre Jehan de Meun* (see Appendix 2, line 5) mentions the gift of a copy of the *Arbre des Batailles*, which the duke appreciated. This gift is corroborated by Burgundian records in Dijon (Archives départementales de la Côte d'Or MS B1479, fol. 146r) and Paris (BNF MS Colbert 500, no. 127, fol. 151r).

[21] The dedication to Philip of Burgundy is preserved in the two mid-fifteenth-century "Artois" copies of the poem; see "Manuscripts" below.

[22] The two manuscripts of the *Apparicion* at the Bibliothèque nationale display the strongest evidence for Bovet's intimacy with the Orléans party: MS français 810 (**P1**) contains dedications to Duke Louis of Orléans and to Jean de Montaigu, a leading "Marmouset" and thus also an enemy to Burgundy; MS français 811 (**P2**) is dedicated to Louis's duchess, Valentina Visconti. See "Introduction," note 52, below.

tion nor a steady income. He left Paris permanently before the end of the century, and died sometime before 1410.[23]

Chronology

ca. 1345–1350
> Born in Provence, in the viscounty of Valernes, near Sistéron, to a family that has left no records of nobility.[24]

before 1368
> Takes vows as a Benedictine monk at the Abbey of l'Ile Barbe in the diocese of Lyon.[25]

1368
> A bull of Urban V at Rome mentions Bovet—a student in canon law at Montpellier—as petitioning to leave l'Ile-Barbe and join the congregation at Cluny. (20 February). Bovet claims to have been in Rome at the time.[26]

---

[23] Christine de Pizan refers to Bovet as a guiding spirit in her *Livre des fais d'armes et de chevalerie,* usually dated at 1410; see note 11 above.

[24] Several members of the Bovet family are mentioned in the accounts of the viscounty of Valernes (See M. Z. Isnard, *Comptes du receveur de la vicomté de Valernes, 1401–1408* [Digne: Chaspoul & Barbaroux, 1904]), and all are not necessarily of the same family. Honorat's family, nevertheless, shows no evidence of noble lineage, and is therefore unknown to genealogists.

[25] The document (n 22864) cited in the following note points out that Bovet, in February 1368, is already described as a member of the Benedictine order.

[26] Michael and Anne-Marie Hayez, and Pierre Gasnault, eds., with Janine Mathieu and Marie-France Yvan, *Urbain V (1362–1370): Lettres Communes (analysées d'après les Registres dits d'Avignon et du Vatican),* vol. 7 (Rome: École française de Rome, 1981), no. 22864, 464 [20 February 1368]. Bovet is granted the priory of Voisey (Haute-Marne), affiliated with the Cluniac priory of Vergy (Côte-d'Or), a position being contested at that time by another claimant. Had Bovet been successful in this claim, his obedience would have been transferred from Ile-Barbe to Cluny. However, in the next extant document bearing his name, from 1371 (see following note), Bovet is still described as being in the congregation of Ile-Barbe, thus indicating that Vergy had gone to the other claimant. This letter also records the fact that Bovet was studying canon law at Montpellier at his parents' expense (*expensis parentum suorum studet*).

In his *Somnium super materia scismatis* (ed. Arnold, 76), Bovet's narrator encounters the King of Cyprus, and observes that he had met his predecessor, Peter I (Pierre de Lusignan, d. 1369), while in Rome during the time of Pope Urban VI (" . . . quon-

1371

Bovet, now having earned a bachelor's degree in canon law, has up to this point held the office of Prior of Sainte-Marie de Bayons in the diocese of Embrun; he is at this date transferred to the position of Prior of Selonnet in the same diocese. Both positions were attached to the Benedictine Abbey of l'Ile-Barbe (3 July).[27]

between 1371 and 1391

Composition of a history of the counts of Foix, for Count Gaston Phébus of Foix (d. 1391).[28]

1382

Louis of Anjou presents a list of supplications to Clement VII at Avignon, including Bovet's request to collate his position at Selonnet with one at another priory. (14 May)[29]

---

dam regem Petrum Chipri alias videram, tempore Urban justi pape, in Roma . . ."). The King of Cyprus was indeed in Rome from March through May 1368 (Nicolae Jorga, *Philippe de Mézières et la croisade au XIVe siècle* [Paris: Bouillon, 1896], 371–76), so even though Bovet's claim is not confirmed by original documents (see notes 34 and 36 below), it seems quite plausible that he was in Rome at this time.

[27] Hayez, Anne-Marie, ed., with Janine Mathieu and Marie-France Yvan, *Grégoire XI (1370-1378): Lettres Communes (analysées d'après les Registres dits d'Avignon et du Vatican)*, vol. 3 (Rome: École française de Rome, 1993), 643, n° 14876, section *De regularibus, An. 1 (1371–72)*. Another document in the same collection (1, 568, n° 5904, in the section *De beneficiis vacantibus,* An. 1 [1371–72], Rome: École française de Rome, 1992) records a request made by Bovet on 3 July 1371 for the reservation of a monastic position at Bayons (also in Alpes d'Haute-Provence) pending the examination of the current tenant's request for transfer.

[28] Michel de Bernis (alias "Miguel del Verms"), *Chronique des Comtes de Foix en langue béarnaise,* in J. A. C. Buchon, Panthéon Littéraire. Choix de Chroniques et Mémoires sur l'Histoire de France (Paris: Mairet et Fournier, 1841), 575–600. For discussion of this curious document, see Hanly and Millet, "Les batailles d'Honorat Bovet," 150–53.

[29] Noël Valois, "Honoré Bonet, prieur de Salon," *Bibliothèque de l'École des Chartes* 52 (1891): 265–68, 481–82, cites and edits (266) this section from a long roll of petitions, ASV *Registrum Supplicationum Clementis VII antipapæ,* An. IV pars I, fol. 141v. The pope gave blanket approval to the whole list on this date, but Bovet apparently failed once again to acquire another income. The document stipulates that the combined income from the new position and Bovet's present position (at Selonnet) not exceed 300 pounds per year, and clerics were in general not allowed to have two cures of souls at the same time without special dispensation. Nevertheless, even though Bovet had been prepared to resign the one position in order to gain the new one, the attempt failed, through some sort of incompatibility.

1382

Representing the Nation of Provence at the University of Avignon, Bovet, now Doctor of Decrees, presents the oration "Leva in circuitu oculos suos et vide" before Duke Louis I of Anjou, adoptive heir of Queen Giovanna of Naples (8 April).[30]

1385

Bovet delivers the oration "Omnis lapis pretiosus" before Marie of Anjou and her young son, Duke Louis II of Anjou (2 May).[31]

1386

Jean le Fèvre, Chancellor of Anjou, presides over a ceremony recognizing Bovet's Doctorate of Decrees at the University of Avignon (23 October).[32]

1386–1389

Composition of L'arbre des Batailles, dedicated to Charles VI; Bovet probably gives him a presentation copy during his stop in Avignon en route to Languedoc (1389).[33]

---

[30] BNF MS fonds français 5015 (Journal of Jean le Fèvre, Bishop of Chartres and Chancellor of Louis I of Anjou), fol. 13v: ". . . et fist un docteur religieux de Saint Benoist prieur de Salon la proposicion 'Leva in circuitu oculos tuos et vide' ("Lift up thine eyes round about, and see," Isaiah 49:8) et je respondi pour monseigneur 'Oculi mei semper ad Dominum, qui ipse evellet de laqueo pedes meos' ("My eyes are ever towards the Lord, for he shall pluck my feet out of the snare," Psalm 24:15)."
This journal was edited (incompletely) in 1887 by Henri Moranvillé, Journal de Jean le Fèvre, évêque de Chartres et Chancelier des Rois de Sicile Louis I et II d'Anjou, 1380–1388 (Paris: A. Picard, 1887); a second volume containing notes was originally planned, but only a transcription of the text and a seven-page introduction were actually printed in a 300-copy run. The mention of this oration by Bovet appears in Moranvillé's edition (29).

[31] BNF MS fr. 5015, fol. 53v, May 1385: "Le second jour fu faite une harengue devant le Roy et Madame [Duchess Marie of Anjou] par le prieur de Salon, et fu de par les provenceaulx estudians en Avignon, Et prinst son theme 'Omnis lapis pretiosus operimentum tuum'" ("Every precious stone was your covering" Ezekiel 28:13): Journal de Jean le Fèvre, ed. Moranvillé, 105.

[32] BNF MS fr. 5015, fol. 82v, October 1386, Avignon: "Mardi xxiiie jour je fis docteur en decres le prieur de salon et y eust grande et belle compagnie": Journal de Jean le Fèvre, ed. Moranvillé, 323. Le Fèvre (note 30 above) refers to Bovet as "doctor" already in 1382.

[33] Hanly and Millet, "Les batailles d'Honorat Bovet," 156.

1389–1390

Service with Pierre de Chevreuse in the royal reform commission for Languedoc.[34]

1391

To Armagnac with another emissary, Pierre Sanglier, in service of the French crown (October).[35]

1392

Defends Clementist cause in meeting with John of Gaunt, Duke of Lancaster and head of English delegation, at the Amiens peace conference (April).[36]

1392

Granted annual gift of 100 francs by King Charles VI (3 April); renewed in May 1398.[37]

---

[34] In the *Apparicion maistre Jehan de Meun* (ll. 226–229), Bovet's narrator exclaims: "Mais . . . ay je veu tant de choses en la commission qui fu jadis donnee au sire de Chevreuse es parties de Languedoc et de Guyenne, an laquelle je fuz par la voulenté du roy. . . ." For Bovet's participation in this and other political events (including the Amiens conference of 1392; see notes 26 above and 36 below), the only evidence so far unearthed is contained in his literary works; Bovet's name, for example, does not appear in a list of officers in D. F. Secousse, *Ordonnances des rois de France de la troisième race* (Paris: Imprimerie Royale, 1745), 7:328–329 n. There is, nevertheless no good reason to mistrust his claims regarding these missions. Documentary support for Bovet's statements is provided in Hanly, "Courtiers and Poets," 318 n. 82.

[35] Paris, BNF, Pièces Originales 2626 Sanglier, dossier 58,417 n 7, 23 October 1391, records a payment to Pierre Sanglier for "un voyage que le roi notre dit seigneur et son conseil lui font faire hastivement en compaignie de messire Honoré Bongnet, docteur en decrez, prieur de Sallon, ou pais de Gascongne, devers le comte d'Armignac . . ." (cited by Eugene Jarry, *La vie politique de Louis de France, duc d'Orléans (1372–1407)* [Orléans: Herluison, 1889], 80, n. 1).

[36] Although no original documents corroborate his account, Bovet, in the *Somnium*, provides a detailed description of an interview with John of Gaunt. Once again (see notes 26 and 34 above), we have no reason to question his veracity, and the lack of archival confirmation did not trouble Noël Valois (*La France et le grand schisme d'Occident* [Paris: Picard, 1896; repr. Hildesheim: Georg Olms, 1967], 2:320–22) or Edouard Perroy (*L'Angleterre et le grand schisme d'Occident: Étude sur la politique religieuse de l'Angleterre sous Richard II (1378–1399)* [Paris: Monnier, 1933], 358–59), both of whom accept without question the facticity of Bovet's claim.

[37] The original copy of the grant document has not been found; a seventeenth-century copy, BNF MS fr. 21145, fol. 93, is cited by Ouy, "Honoré Bouvet," 256.

between 1387 and 1392

    Bovet spends several months doing diplomatic service in Aragon during the reign of King Juan I.[38]

1393–1394

    Serious illness.[39]

1394

    Composition of the *Somnium super materia scismatis* (June–October), dedicated to Charles VI; copy sent to Pope Benedict XIII (2 November); four letters composed the same day are contained in the Vatican manuscript of the *Somnium* (ASV Armarium 54 t. 21, fols. 73r–90r).[40]

1398

    Composition (July–September) of the *Apparicion maistre Jehan de Meun.*

1398

    Bovet is consulted (between July and December) by Simon de Cramaud, titular Latin Patriarch of Alexandria and driving force behind the withdrawal of France's obedience from Benedict XIII, on the subject of presenting appeals to papal condemnations, a strategy necessary in the wake of the subtraction.[41]

1399

    Bovet is elected, *in absentia*, to the office of Abbot of the Abbey of l'Ile-Barbe (5 October).[42]

1400

    In Prague (2 February) as emissary from the court of Charles VI to the Holy Roman Emperor, Wenceslas IV; between May and August, Bovet delivers oration entitled "Da nobis auxilium de tribula-

---

[38] Ed. Arnold, *Somnium*, 73–74. See note 15 above.

[39] See note 16 above.

[40] The four letters are those edited by Valois; see note 16.

[41] This matter is the theme of the long Latin gloss I catalogue as [P1.9] that Bovet appends to the opening of manuscript **P1** (fols. 2v–3r); it appears in this edition as Appendix 7. See also Text, note 17.

[42] For the details of this election, see Nicholas A. R. Wright, "Honoré Bouvet and the Abbey of Ile-Barbe," *Recherches de théologie ancienne et médiévale* 39 (1972): 113–26.

tione," defending France's decision to withdraw its obedience from Benedict XIII.[43]

1401

Bovet's election as Abbot of l'Ile-Barbe is invalidated by decision of a court in Lyon (28 February).[44]

1401

Embassy on the part of Benedict XIII at Avignon to Louis of Or-léans in Paris (4–15 December).[45]

1404

Established once again in his homeland, Bovet is named to a life term as an important financial officer, "maître-rational de Provence."[46]

1406

Bovet is included in a list of members of Louis II's royal council (25 October).[47]

1408

Another list of royal councillors describes Bovet as still being in the service of Louis II.[48]

1409

At Aix-en-Provence, the assembly of Provençal clergy names Bovet to represent that body at the proposed Council of Pisa (22 January).[49]

---

[43] This discourse was published by K. Höfler, ed., *Geschichtsschreiber der Husitischen Bewegung in Böhmen,* Fontes rerum Austriacarum: Österreichische Geschichts-Quellen, Erste Abteilung [Scriptores], 6. 2 (Vienna: Kaiserliche Akademie der Wissenschaften, 1865), 174–87, and more recently by F. M. Bartos, *Autograf M .J. Husi,* Bibliothecae Clementinae Analecta 4 (Prague: Statni pedagogicke Nakladatelstri, 1954). Many thanks to Efem Nevole for his translation of Bartos' work from Czech.

[44] See Wright, "Honoré Bouvet and the Abbey of Ile-Barbe," 117–18.

[45] Noël Valois edited selections from this letter by Louis of Orléans (15 December) in *La France et le grand schisme d'occident,* 3:254 n. 1: ". . . venit ad me prior Sellionis cum pulcerrimis litteris vestris . . ." Valois does not identify the "prior Sellionis" mentioned here.

[46] Fernand Cortez, *Les grands officiers royaux de Provence au Moyen Age* (Aix-en-Provence: Secrétariat de la Société d'études provençales: A. Dragon, 1921), 97.

[47] Marseille, Archives départementales des Bouches du Rhône, MS B9, fol. 138.

[48] See Cortez, *Les grands officiers royaux de Provence au Moyen Age,* 97.

[49] Johannes Vincke, *Briefe zum Pisaner Konzil* (Bonn: Hanstein, 1940), 129, n 72, cites a document that lists various procurators from the dioceses of Provence

1409

> Representing Provence at the Council of Pisa, Bovet, procurator
> for the abbeys of l'Ile-Barbe and Boscodon, votes to depose the
> two rival popes (between 14 June and 7 August).[50]

1410

> Christine de Pisan, in her *Livre d'armes et de chevalerie*, describes a vi-
> sion in which the ghost of Bovet appears to her.[51]

Structure of the Poem

The *Apparicion maistre Jehan de Meun*, over its 1543 lines of verse and 299
lines of prose, stages a panel discussion on various topics of importance to
the court of France in 1398, a time of domestic instability and external
menace. The poem presents the views of four speakers and their moderator, with occasional interjections by "The Prior," Bovet's dreaming first-
person narrator. This "panel" consists of representatives of what in Paris at
the end of the fourteenth century were "marginalized" social groups: a Physician, a Jew, a Muslim called the "Sarrazin" (see detailed description in the
section "Bovet and Islam," below), and a Dominican Friar or "Jacobin."
Jean de Meun, himself a controversial figure at the time (and at the center
of the "Querelle de la Rose" in the next decade), both moderates the "debate" and offers critical commentary consistent with that of the other
speakers. The poem in outline:

Prose 1–Prose 12	Dedication to Valentina Visconti
Prose 13–Prose 33	Dedication to Jean de Montaigu
Prose 34–Prose 81	Dedication to Louis d'Orléans
Prose 87–Prose 92	Prieur's introduction to the vision
1–60	Jean de Meun's opening harangue of the Prieur
Prose 95–Prose 112	Prieur's excuses

---

named to participate in the Council, among them "Honoratum Beneti priorem de
Gollone decretorum doctorem."

[50] See Hélène Millet, "Les français du royaume au Concile de Pise (1409)," in
Crises et réformes dans l'Église de la réforme grégorienne à la préréforme (Actes du 115e Congrès national des sociétés savantes, Avignon, 1990 (Paris: Éditions du CTHS, 1991),
259–85, esp. 280. Millet cites BAV MS Vat. lat. 4000, fol. 102v.

[51] See note 11 above.

61–80	Jean de Meun's challenge
Prose 115–Prose 119	Appearance of the Physicien, Juif, Sarrazin, and Jacobin
81–89	Jean de Meun addresses Physicien
90–228	Physicien's speech
229–245	Jean de Meun addresses the Juif
246–292	Juif's speech
293–298	Jean de Meun addresses the Sarrazin
299–898	Sarrazin's speech (with brief interruptions by Jean de Meun)
899–902	Jean de Meun addresses the Jacobin
903–1525	Jacobin's speech (with brief interruptions by Jean de Meun)
1526–1529	Jean de Meun addresses the Prieur
Prose 151–Prose 297	Prieur's prose exposé of corrupt social practices
1530–1543	Consolatory poem for Valentina Visconti, Duchess of Orléans

Manuscripts

The four extant manuscripts of the *Apparicion maistre Jehan de Meun* fall into two distinct groups: two copies roughly contemporaneous with the composition of the text, and two dating from the mid-fifteenth-century that represent a version of the text revised by another author. The two earlier texts, upon which this edition is based, are conserved at the Bibliothèque nationale de France in Paris. Full descriptions of all four codices appear below.

The two Paris manuscripts, BNF MSS français 810 (**P1**) and 811 (**P2**), are presentation copies executed under the supervision of the author. Manuscript **P1** was produced for Jean de Montaigu, councillor for Louis d'Orléans and member of the "Marmouset" party.[52] Manuscript **P2** was offered to Valentina

---

[52] See Autrand, *Charles VI*, chap. 10, "Le temps des Marmousets," 189–203, and John Bell Henneman, *Olivier de Clisson and Political Society in France Under Charles V and Charles VI* (Philadelphia: University of Pennsylvania Press, 1996).

Visconti, Duchess of Orléans; the dedicatory introduction to that manuscript appears in this edition at the opening, Prose lines 1–12.

Description of the Manuscripts

• Paris, Bibliothèque nationale de France, fonds français 810 (P1)

Honorat Bovet, *Apparicion maistre Jehan de Meun*, 1398

1r: Dedication miniature, bearing arms of France and of Montaigu (fig. 1)

1r–1v: Dedication to Jean de Montaigu (edition lines Prose 14–Prose 34)

1v–2r: Copy of dedication to Louis d'Orléans (edition lines Prose 35–Prose 82)

2v–3r: Latin treatise on papal schism inc. "Pro evidencia materiarum" and exp. "ulterius non procedam." (Appendix 7)

3v: blank

4r–35v: *Apparicion maistre Jehan de Meun*

36r: 14-line consolatory poem for Valentina Visconti (Prose 1530–1543) (fig. 7)

36v: blank

    fols. 1–36: Parchment, 355 x 250 mm. 34 lines; writing block 215 x 115 mm. One gathering of five, one of eight, and a final one of five. Collation: 15, 18, 15. Binding: red calf with gold tooling, bearing the arms of Napoléon I (1804–1814). The dedication indicates its original ownership by the royal councillor Jean de Montaigu, executed by the Bourguignons on 17 October 1409; it is not known when it passed into the Louvre library. Manuscript is in very good condition overall. According to the text of the manuscript's dedication (ll. Prose 21–24) it was presented to Montaigu on 1 January, 1399 (n. st.), "ce jour des estreines" (Mod. Fr. *étrennes* = New Year's gifts; see Text, note 4, below). Parchment is of good quality, rarely wrinkled but in some places displaying hair follicles. The ink is medium brown, paling occasionally to a light gold shade. Decorated initials in blue, red, and gold appear throughout. Forty Latin marginal glosses in a contemporary hand, indexed to relevant passages in the poetic text with small red pointers. Seventeen illuminations (generally square, 80 mm) depicting various characters from the narrative appear in the manuscript. Plates are found in Richard C. Famiglietti, *Tales of the Marriage Bed from Medieval France (1300–1500)* (Providence, RI: Picardy Press, 1992), #16: fol. 1r, and Sandra Hindman,

Christine de Pizan's "Epistre Othea": Painting and Politics at the Court of Charles VI
(Toronto: Pontifical Institute of Mediaeval Studies, 1986), #65: fol. 9v); a
series of pen-and-ink illustrations depicting the miniatures appear in the
edition of Pichon (1845).

No quire signatures or catchwords. Text is ruled throughout in plummet. No apparent prickings; these could have been trimmed off at the most
recent (early nineteenth-century) rebinding. Hair faces hair, flesh faces flesh,
throughout. Two sets of Arabic numerals in top right corners throughout,
except for 1r; neither appears to be older than 17th century. The smaller,
likely earlier numbers are fainter and further outside the position of a larger
numeral; numeric pairs are always consistent. Fol. 1r at top right bears two
earlier catalogue numbers, 835 and 7202 (the previous catalogue number
from the Bibliothèque royale). The manuscript is almost completely free of
later scribbling; fols. 11r, 21v, and 34r contain comments of up to six words
in a small 17th-century hand. Curiously, however, there is some evidence of
vandalism: the faces and, in two places, the entire bodies of characters depicted in the the miniatures (see description, below) were smudged beyond
recognition; the damage appears to have been done while the paint was still
fresh. The scribal hand for the poetic text is a tidy Gothic secretary or bastard secretary;[53] that of the glosses is a medium-quality Gothic semi-cursive.
The textual hand is extremely regular and legible, whereas the much smaller
marginal hand, while still mainly legible, is moderately abbreviated and
shows less evidence of patient care.

Description of illuminations in manuscript **P1**

   1r: Dedication miniature: Bovet, kneeling, presents book to Jean de
         Montaigu; arms of France and Montaigu at top (fig. 1)

   4r: Jean de Meun and Prieur in garden; following line Prose 92 "dire
         en ryme"

   6r: Jean de Meun and Prieur in garden; following line Prose l. 112,
         "escripre nouvelles choses"

   6v: Jean de Meun facing Prieur, Physicien, Sarrazin, Juif, and (ton-
         sured) Jacobin; following l. Prose 119, "Sy me dist maistre Jehan
         de Meun" (fig. 3)

---

[53] Paulin Paris, *Les manuscrits françois de la Bibliothèque du Roi*, vol. 6 (Paris: Techener,
1845), 245, terms it *"lettre de notes*, c'est-à-dire en caractères cursifs et liés"; Geneviève
Hasenohr, "Discours vernaculaire et autorités latines," in *Mise en page et mise en texte du
livre manuscrit*, ed. Henri-Jean Martin & Jean Vezin (Paris: Editions du Cercle de la Librairie-Promodis, 1990), 289–316, here 292, calls it a "bâtarde pointuel."

7r: Jean de Meun and Physicien, who holds a pitcher; both have black skullcaps; following l. Prose 121, "Sy prist a dire a ces iiii dessus nommés:"

9v: Jean de Meun faces Juif, who wears a red and white badge; following l. Prose 125, "et ly commença a dire bien rigoureusement" (fig. 5)

10v: Jean de Meun faces Sarrazin, whose head is lightly smudged; following l. 292 "trouvoit en plaine voye" (fig. 6)

16v: Jean de Meun faces Sarrazin; following l. 680, "trop blasmer Françoys"

17r: Jean de Meun faces Sarrazin; following l. 699, "traitter contre Crestiens"

18r: Jean de Meun faces Sarrazin (figure completely effaced from waist up); following l. 736, "Sy en ma voye n'ay debat."

19v: Jean de Meun faces Sarrazin (figure completely effaced from waist up); following l. 830, "Laissiez moy tenir mon chemin."

21v: Jean de Meun (head effaced) faces Jacobin; following l. 898, "Et la sienne tenir celee." Rubric "Maistre Jehan parle au Jacobin" (Prose 140) also within border of miniature.

23r: Jacobin faces Sarrazin; following l. 1014, "Au Sarrazin mieulx que sauray."

26v: Jean de Meun (head lightly smudged) faces Jacobin (also lightly smudged); following l. 1255, "Car n'en sauroye mieulx parler."

27v: Jean de Meun (head again lightly smudged) faces Jacobin; following l. 1303, "Je ne vous en vueil plus parler."

29v: Jean de Meun faces Jacobin; following l. 1423, "Et puis leur doint saint paradis." Rubric "Maistre Jehan parle au Jacobin" (Prose 147) also within border of miniature.

31v: Jean de Meun (head smudged off) faces Prieur (tonsured, bareheaded); following l. 1525 "Tenir en bonne charité"

• Paris, Bibliothèque nationale de France, fonds français 811 (P2)

Honorat Bovet, *Apparicion maistre Jehan de Meun*, 1398

i: paper flyleaf containing early catalogue number ("N 7203") in post-medieval cursive hand fol. 1r:　　　blank

fol. 1v:　　　miniature; Bovet dedicates his book to Valentina Visconti. Her arms—France/Visconti—appear at top. (fig. 2)

fol. 2r:　　　dedication text; "A ma dame d'Orliens" to "vie et longue" (Prose 1–12)

fol. 2v:　　　blank

fols. 3r–7v:　*Apparicion maistre Jehan de Meun*, lines Prose 83–123, 1–228

fol. 8r:　　　miniature; depicting Valentina Visconti and a female attendant (left) and a Physician (at right); in center appears a 14-line consolatory verse for the Duchess (fig. 7)

fols. 8v–33v:　*Apparicion maistre Jehan de Meun*, line Prose 124–end.

fol. 33v:　　　at bottom, an *ex libris* and the signature of Charles d'Orléans:
　　　　　　　"Ce livre est a Charles duc d'Orlians etc. Charles."

　　fols. i, 1–33: Parchment, 365 x 280 mm. 34 lines; writing block 215 x 115 mm. Gatherings of four, three, four, five, and a final, single folio. Collation: 14, 13, 14, 15, 11. Binding: red calf with gold tooling, bearing the arms of Napoléon I. The manuscript was quite likely presented to Valentina shortly after its completion in late 1398; after her death (1408), it passed into the possession of her son, Charles d'Orléans, whose *ex libris* and signature appear on the final leaf. The manuscript is in very good condition overall. Parchment is of good quality, perhaps more consistently than **P1**; only occasional appearance of hair follicles. As in **P1**, the ink is medium brown, paling occasionally to a light gold shade. Decorated initials in blue, red, and gold appear throughout. Thirty-five Latin marginal glosses in a contemporary hand, indexed to relevant passages in the poetic text with small red pointers. The manuscript contains eleven illuminations, generally smaller than those in **P1** (usually rectangular, 80 x 55 mm) depicting the six characters from the narrative. Plates are found in Hindman, *Épistre Othea*, #66, 67: fols. 1v, 8r; the pen-and-ink illustrations in the edition of Pichon mainly follow the miniatures from **P1** but include a few from **P2**, notably the two illuminations depicting Valentina Visconti (fols. 1v, 8r, Pichon pp. 2, 14).

　　The physical description of manuscript **P2** is remarkably similar to that of **P1**; the two are clearly the product of the same Parisian atelier, and were quite likely executed at the same moment in 1398 (see the section "Illuminations," below). As in **P1**, there are no quire signatures or catchwords, and the text is ruled throughout in plummet. There are also no apparent prickings; hair faces hair, flesh faces flesh, throughout. Also consistent with the practice in **P1**, there are two sets of Arabic numerals, probably seventeenth century, in top right corners throughout, except for fol. 1r, which at top right bears two earlier catalogue numbers, 835 and 7202 (its former number, from the catalogue of the Bibliothèque royale). The manuscript contains only one annotation posterior to the execution of the manuscript: at fol. 3r top, in a cursive sixteenth-century hand, appears (inexplicably) "quatre cents nonante deux." The scribal hands are very similar to those of **P1**: the poetic text is a tidy Gothic secretary or bastard secretary; that of the glosses is a usually regular Gothic semi-cursive. As is the case with manuscript **P1**, the textual hand is neater and more readable than the smaller, moderately abbreviated marginal script.

Description of illuminations in manuscript **P2**

    1v: Dedication, 14.5 x 14 cm: Valentina, seated, greets kneeling Bovet, who presents her with the book (fig. 2)

    3r: Jean de Meun, with book, faces seated, contemplative Prieur; the two figures are quite similar; following l. Prose 92 "dire en ryme"

    4r: Prieur faces Jean de Meun; following l. 60, "Tant qu'il treuve sa bourse vuide."

    5r: Jean de Meun faces Prieur (in skullcap), Physicien (carrying pitcher), Juif, Sarrazin, and Jacobin (tonsured, bareheaded); in margin, right of l. Prose 115, "Lors quant je lui cuiday respondre . . . Jehan de Meun" (fig. 4)

    5v: Jean de Meun faces Physicien; following l. Prose 121, "Sy prist a dire aux quatre dessus nommés:"

    8r: "Belle Susanne" ("Son physicien parle a madame d'Orliens"), 195 x 85 mm (fig. 7)

    8v: Jean de Meun faces Juif; following l. Prose 126, "Maistre Jehan parle au Juif"

    9v: Jean de Meun faces Sarrazin; following l. Prose 128, "Maistre Jehan parle au Sarrazin"

    19r: Jean de Meun faces Jacobin (hooded); following l. 898, "Et la sienne tenir celee."

    21r: Jacobin faces Sarrazin; following l. 1014, "Au Sarrazin mieulx que sauray."

29r: Jean de Meun faces Prieur (the figures are identical, right down to their hat buttons); following l. Prose 149 (not found in **P1**), "Lors maistre Jehan regarda vers moy et sy me prist a dire"

Date of the Paris Manuscripts

The date of both Paris manuscripts can be determined fairly precisely by their reference to historical events. One is the Western defeat by the Seljuk Turks at Nicopolis, which took place in September of 1396 and was made known to the court of Paris by Christmas of the same year. Bovet's *Sarrazin* (ll. 632–660) criticizes his interlocutors for having forgotten all the Christians captured at Nicopolis, an accusation implying that a certain amount of time has gone by since the battle. A speech by the Jacobin (ll. 1310–1328) and an appended gloss ([P2.30], Text, note 123), furthermore, refer clearly to an event of 27 July 1398, the announcement of the French clergy's withdrawal of its obedience from the intransigent Avignon Pope Benedict XIII. The narrative alludes to a notorious current affair, that of the two Augustinian friars who had been engaged to cure the king's madness. Upon realizing that their restorative efforts had failed, they began to blame others in the court, including Louis of Orléans; he retaliated, however, and they were imprisoned, probably late in 1397, and beheaded in Paris on 30 October 1398. At the time of Bovet's writing, during the warm summer season,[54] these unfortunates would already have been in custody;[55] in the dedicatory passage to Philip of Burgundy found in manuscripts **V** and **L**, moreover, Bovet observes that the two have already been dealt with as they deserved (Text, note 48). The composition of the first redaction of the *Apparicion* can therefore be dated fairly cerrtainly between July and September 1398. As noted in the description of **P1** above (and in Text, note 4, below), finally, in the dedication to Louis of Orléans copied into that manuscript, Bovet claims to be offering the book on "cestuy benoyst jour des estreines" (l. 22), which means 1 January 1399 (n. st.).

Glosses

As noted above, the marginal comments are linked to specific lines of text, and sometimes to individual words in lines, by small abbreviations in red ink that appear alongside the gloss and once again next to the word, or at the end of the line, being cited. The practice is one widely employed in

---

[54] See Text, lines Prose 14–15 and note 3.
[55] See glosses [P1.31] and [P2.10], attached to l. 226 in Text, note 48.

manuscripts equipped with significant commentary, notably glossed canon-law codices.

P1 contains 40 marginal glosses; **P2** contains 35. **P1** provides a more thorough commentary on the earlier part of the text: by line 126, **P1** is presenting its 23rd gloss, at which point **P2** has only had 6 (at line 106). By contrast, at this point **P2** begins to catch up, and by line 1392 contains 31 glosses, one more than **P1** (30 at line 691). This is because **P1** contains no marginal comments at all between folios 9v and 25v (and thus no glosses to the speeches by Sarrazin and Juif); in **P2**, there are no such long outright gaps, simply a paucity of glosses in the early sections of the manuscript.

Distribution of glosses to text by speakers in **P1**:

Dedication 11, Prieur 5, Jean de Meun 11, Sarrazin 0, Juif 0, Jacobin 5, Physicien 9

Statistics on distribution of glosses to text by speakers in **P2**:

Dedication 2, Prieur 4, Jean de Meun 2, Sarrazin 11, Juif 1, Jacobin 10, Physicien 5

Illuminations

The illuminations in the Paris manuscripts appear to be products of the same Parisian atelier, one that was quite active in the last decade of the fourteenth and the first decade of the fifteenth century. They were executed by two different illuminators, and if neither one is a particularly brilliant example of late medieval manuscript painting, both are representative of the design and perspective of the era. The figures drawn in MS français 810 (manuscript **P1**) are arguably superior to those in MS français 811 (manuscript **P2**), and, as François Avril suggests (personal communication, 12 July 2002), appear to be the work of the artist responsible for the illuminations in a deluxe copy of the *Légende du Saint-Voult* executed ca. 1410 and now conserved at the Biblioteca Apostolica Vaticana (Vatican City, BAV, Codex Palatinus Latinus 1988). Dr. Avril judges the miniatures in the Palatine manuscript the best work produced by the artist known only as the "Saint-Voult Master"; the work is certainly of much higher quality than that found in **P1**. The images in the *Apparicion* manuscript, nevertheless, are clearly the work of the same illuminator, and were probably produced in the atelier of the so-called "Coronation Master."[56] Avril kindly provided me with a list of

---

[56] *Bibliotheca Palatina: Katalog zur Ausstellung vom 8. Juli bis 2. November 1986, Heiliggeistkirche Heidelberg* (Heidelberg: Braus, 1986), vol 1: Textband, 315–16; vol. 2: Bildband, 213–15.

manuscripts that, according to his analyses, contain the work of this illuminator; my independent (if inexpert) examination confirms his suspicions.[57] The figures in a manuscript now conserved at the Walters Art Gallery in Baltimore, moreover, appear to be the work of this same artist: a study by Lilian M. C. Randall presents an illumination in a contemporary French manuscript that is clearly the work of the **P1** painter.[58] Randall identifies three different illuminators in the codex, the first, "Hand A," being the well-known Perrin (or Pierre) Remiet (a.k.a. Remy Perrin; see below). "Hand C" is the Saint-Voult Master: here, as in **P1**, it is some rather mediocre work. This performance causes Randall to comment on the artist's "heavyhanded approach to figure style" and to conclude that "the miniatures by Hand C are characterized by a rigid figure style and preference for deep tonalities that further rob his compositions of any sense of animation."[59] A manuscript in the Bibliothèque municipale de Soissons, Guyart Desmoulins's *Bible Historiale* (BM 210–212), also contains illustrations by both Remiet and the Saint-Voult Master, a fact suggesting that they worked in the same Paris atelier. Michael Camille notes that this text contains four miniatures by Remiet and the work of several other painters, including "the Master of BN fr. 810."[60]

Manuscript **P2**, very similar in layout, size, and scribal hand to its sister volume, probably comes from the same atelier, although its illuminator's work has not survived in such abundance and is therefore not as easy to identify as that of **P1**. Baltimore, Walters Art Gallery MS W. 138, *Grandes Chroniques de France* fol. 232r, contains an image of Charles V with Queen

---

[57] These are: Paris, BNF, MSS fr. 20105, St. Augustine, *Cité de Dieu* (Raoul de Presles translation), fol. 1r; fr. 31, Livy, *Des excellens Fais des Rommains* (Pierre Bersuire translation) fols. 1r, 58r 75r, 170r; fr. 52, Vincent de Beauvais, Le miroir historial (Jehan de Vignay translation), fols. 7v, 9v, 10r, 15v, 53r, 56v, 57r, 66v, 73r, 74r, 76v, 80r, 81r, 97r, 101r (where a monk looks exactly like manuscript **P1**'s "Prieur"), 142v, 143v, 172v, 174v, 175v; fr. 338, Guiron le Courtois, *D'Heli Borron*, fols. 140v, 141r, 143v, 144r, 153v; and lat. 14247, Nicholas of Lyra, *In Vetus Testamentum*, fols. 1r, 2r, 107v, 129v, 179v.

[58] Lilian M. C. Randall, ed. *Medieval and Renaissance Manuscripts in the Walters Art Gallery*, vol. 1: *France, 875–1420* (Baltimore: Johns Hopkins Press, 1989), figure 149, p. 334. The two-volume work is manuscripts W.125 and 126, the *Bible historiale* of Guyart des Moulins, a book once owned by Jean de Berry.

[59] Ibid., 200, 201.

[60] *The Master of Death: The Lifeless Art of Pierre Remiet, Illuminator* (New Haven, CT: Yale University Press, 1996), 253. On the Soissons manuscript, see also Edouard Fleury, *Les manuscrits à miniatures de la Bibliothèque de Soissons, étudiés au point de vue de leur illustration* (Paris: Dumoulin, 1865), 130–39.

Jeanne de Bourbon present, in which her hair and facial expressions strikingly resemble the feminine fashions depicted in the "Belle Susanne" illustration on **P2** fol. 8r.[61] The ivy-leaf filigree ornamentation surrounding the miniature in this manuscript, furthermore, is almost precisely the same as what is found in **P2**.

The appearance in more than one manuscript of illuminations by Remiet and the **P1** master, finally, strongly suggests that the presentation copies of the *Apparicion* were products of this famous Parisian workshop. The fact that these books contain the work not of the "star" but rather of a "staff" painter—and not even that artist's best work, at that—intimates, as well, that Bovet was not able to offer the atelier the sums of money it expected for truly deluxe products. His penury notwithstanding, Bovet's association with this atelier—artists charged with the illustration of several French translations we associate with Charles V's intellectual agenda (i.e., the works by Presles, Vignay, and Bersuire among the BN manuscripts listed by François Avril, above)—links him with other reformist thinkers and writers of the 1390s, most notably Eustache Deschamps, and the members of the Marmouset party.[62] Consider, as well, Geneviève Hasenohr's research showing that Deschamps and Bovet, both of them (apparently) jurists, produced manuscripts that participated in the development of a peculiar bilingual mise-en-page adapted to their intellectual projects.[63] If we lack the extant correspondence that could firmly connect him to these figures who lived in the same places and embraced many similar political notions, the illuminations in Bovet's manuscripts make the case that they had more in common than the obvious.

The "Artois" Manuscripts

Some time not long after presentation copies of the Apparicion were offered to Louis of Orléans, Valentina Visconti, and Jean de Montaigu, a revised version was executed for Philip of Burgundy (see "Date of the Paris Manuscripts," above). This copy is now lost. What we now possess is two manuscripts containing a revised and greatly expanded version of what was

---

[61] Randall, *Medieval and Renaissance Manuscripts,* fig. 157, p. 213.

[62] For this suggestion, see Jean-Patrice Boudet and Hélène Millet, *Eustache Deschamps en son temps* (Paris: Publications de la Sorbonne, 1997), 141.

[63] Hasenohr, "Discours vernaculaire et autorités latines," 289–90. The manuscripts she analyzes are BNF fr. 20029, Deschamps's *Lai de fragilité humaine* (1383), and fr. 810, our manuscript **P1**, along with fr. 578, the *Enseignement moult piteux* of Jean de Remin (1366). Deschamps is known to have studied law at Orléans, but it is not known what degree he earned there.

originally offered to Duke Philip. In an introductory comment found only in the Vatican manuscript (Appendix 1), the anonymous redactor, a scribe of Artois, informs us that his master, likely the bishop of Arras,[64] "Prestre de la plus noble eglise / Qui soit dedens Artoys," had instructed him to copy and correct a manuscript of Bovet's Apparicion. He takes it upon himself, however, not only to correct what might have been faulty but also to versify all of the prose passages in the book he was given to copy. This exemplar must already have been quite different from the original version of the poem presented to Philip, which, I contend, would have differed from the Paris manuscripts upon which I base my edition in only a few essential elements: it would have begun with an original dedication to Duke Philip of Burgundy (see Appendix 2); it would have omitted all the marginal glosses found in **P1** and **P2**; it would have added a 62-line exemplum featuring the Angevin King Charles of Naples (after l. 1365 in the edited Text; see Appendix 3).

The two extant "Artois" manuscripts—based upon a copy of Burgundy's version already at several removes from the archetype—differ from the two Paris copies, however, in much more than these details. As the exasperated Ivor Arnold wrote seventy-eight years ago in the introduction to his edition (*Apparicion*, xxxv), "le copiste a réussi à gâcher complètement l'original, l'allongeant en même temps de quelques cinq cent vers." Even this assessment of the Artois scribe's enlargement is too modest. The text of the *Apparicion* in **L** and **V** is roughly 2800 lines long, compared with the Paris manuscripts' 1842 (1543 lines of verse, 299 of prose). The reviser not only gives way to prolixity at almost every juncture of the verse text, but even takes pains to versify the prose passages found in Bovet's original version, a decision leading to enormous expansion of the text. To make an accurate comparison of the two versions, we must account for the fact that the prose lines in the present edition contain about twice as many words as the verse lines (in **P1** and **P2**, the prose sections are rendered in the same short-lined format as the verses)—for example, the edition's 45 lines of the "Datiller et Courge" story (Prose 198–243) is rendered by **P1** in 94 and by **P2** in 88 lines, roughly twice as many. Even accounting for this variance by doubling the 299 prose lines in the edition (which number includes rubrics like "le prieur parle" and single words like "Amen"), however, we come up with a total of 2138 lines, meaning that the **L** and **V** reviser has increased the length of the text by almost one-third. There is no reason to believe, furthermore, that any of this

---

[64] Arnold, xxxiv n. 5., suggests that the personage referred to here could be Martin Poiré (1407–1426), a Dominican and confessor to Jean sans Peur, Philip's son and successor as Duke of Burgundy. He cites Noël Valois, *La France et le grand schisme d'Occident*, 1:118.

expansion, aside from the Burgundy introduction and the "Charles de Napples" exemplum (see Appendix 3), is the work of Bovet.

Three parallel passages (see Appendices 4–6) provide examples of the great alterations the text underwent at the hands of the Artois redactor. The first, Appendix 4, shows the scribe expanding a simple prose introduction by more than 30%, from 33 to 50 words. Appendix 5 represents an even greater inflation of another straightforward prose introduction, from 22 to 46 words, more than 50%. Appendix 6 provides a much milder example of expansion, barely 14%, from 135 words in the prose original to the redactor's 157. I include it here, finally, to indicate the scale of the versifier's work. These efforts take the Artois redaction quite a distance from the sense of Bovet's original text, which is the very soul of restraint, a thinly veiled rant against an inveterate political enemy. Manuscripts **L** and **V** represent a drastic revision—a bowdlerization, if you will—of the work of Honorat Bovet, and must therefore must be eliminated for all but the occasional emendation of the Paris copies.

• London, British Museum, MS Lansdowne 214 fols. 201r–216v (L)

Apparicion maistre Jehan de Meun, revised version with dedication to Philip of Burgundy. Paper, 197 x 275 mm. Red initials at the head of each line. No visible ruling or pricking. The text was repaginated, in pencil, subsequent to the publication of the description in *Catalogue of the Lansdowne Manuscripts in the British Museum,* ed. Henry Ellis and Francis Douce (London: Taylor, 1819), 80; a flyleaf, containing a list of contents, was at that time given the number "1," the original folio 1 given the number "2," and so on. The manuscript was also rebound at some time, and bears signs of excessive trimming (e.g., top fol. 80r). Two columns, forty-five lines each, 2725 lines in all. A crabbed, unlovely Gothic cursive hand. The Lansdowne catalogue (80) notes that the manuscript was executed for the renowned bibliophile Charles de Croy, Count, then Prince of Chimay, godfather to the Emperor Charles V, about the year 1455. Charles's name appears with both titles in two different texts in the manuscript; Chimay having been elevated from county to principate in 1486, at least part of the book belonged to him before that date. Since the manuscript is a compilation of six different texts executed by several different scribes, the various papers employed bear a number of different watermarks, all of which confirm this approximate dating. In the section containing the text of the *Apparicion,* there appears a Gothic letter "P," closest to Briquet 8523 (30.5 x 44 mm, Colmar 1447–1450 or Basel 1449–1452) or 8527 (29.5 x 40, Quiévrain [Belg.] 1463–1466, Colmar 1469–1470); another "Lettre P gothique à fleuron à 4 feuilles" appears as well, a watermark closest to Briquet 8588 (30 x 43, Lille? 1445), and 8591 (Colmar, 1452; Douai, 1456–1457; Basel, 1456–1465).

Contents of the manuscript:

fols. 2r–84v: French translation of the first four books of the *Annales Hannoniae* (*Annales du Hainaut* of Jacques de Guise, d. 1399)

fols. 85r–193r: French translation of Geoffrey of Monmouth's *Historia Regum Britanniae*

fols. 194r–195r: *Les Merveilles de l'Isle de Bretaigne que nous disons Engleterre*, exp. "Le livre del a grant Bertaigne, d'Engleterre et de Merlin, lequel est a Monseigneur Charles de Croy, Prince de Chimay."

fols. 196r–200r: Jean Chapuis, *Sept articles de la Foi* or *Le livre de la Trinité*, which in the Middle Ages was known as the *Codicille maistre Jehan de Meun* (see note 65 below).

fols. 201r–216v: "*L'apparition de maistre Jean de Meung*, poeme, par Honoré Bonnor, Prieur de Salon."[65]

fols. 217r–275v: "La Signification des Lunes." On last folio: "Ce livre traicte des cronicques d'Engleterre et de pluiseurs autres livres petis. Lequel est a Monseigneur Charles de Croy comte de Chimay. CHARLES."

• **Vatican City, Biblioteca Apostolica Vaticana, MS Reginensis latinus 1683** fols. 39r–87v **(V)**

Apparicion maistre Jehan de Meun, revised version with dedication to Philip of Burgundy. Parchment, 306 x 214 mm. Writing box 156 x 106 mm. Thirty

---

[65] Ivor Arnold, "Notice sur un manuscrit de la traduction des *Annales du Hainaut* de Jacques de Guise par Jean Wauquelin (British Museum Lansdowne 214)," *Romania* 55 (1929): 382–400, notes a similarity in the contents and order of texts between the London manuscript, **L**, and the other compilation containing the later version of the *Apparicion*, manuscript **V**: "Ces feuillets [Lansdowne 214, fols. 201r–216v] contiennent un remaniement de *l'Apparicion maistre Jehan de Meun*, ouvrage d'Honoré Bonet. Au fol. 216v, après le texte on a écrit les mots suivants: 'le Codicille de Maistre Jehan de Meun comenchant par la Trinité.' Il est donc évident que ce text et celui qui précède auraient dû être reliés en ordre inverse; et c'est de cette façon en effet qu'on les trouve reliés dans un autre manuscrit qui contient ces deux textes, le manuscrit Regina 1683 du Vatican" (384).

lines, single column; a spacious, handsome mise-en-page. No miniatures. Ernest Langlois examined the manuscript in the late nineteenth century, and concluded that a number of illuminations had been removed from the text[66] (fols. 52–55 and 60–76 have all had upper-corner repairs in parchment). However, although the entire upper corners of fols. 52–76 have indeed been excised, it seems unlikely that miniatures would have been been painted in such a location. Red calf binding with arms of Pope Pius IX (1846–1878). Langlois notes that the manuscript was seen by a Monsieur Fauchet, who saw fit to make a number of inconsequential comments in the margins of the *Apparicion*.

The text is copied in a tidy *cursiva bastarda* of (probably) the mid-fifteenth century. The entire manuscript contains 113 folios; the first leaves are missing, which accounts for some lacunae in other texts. The manuscript is ruled (in red) throughout at 30 lines per page; after Chartier's *Lay de la Paix* ends at 38r, 38v is lined but blank, then on 39r, starting near the foot of the page (line 25 of 30) begins an original 66-line introduction/dedication to the Bishop of Arras (see Appendix 1). The text ends on fol. 87v at line 7 [not counting the "Explicit l'apparicion mastre / Jehan de Meun" that appears three lines below end of text]; the entire poem, therefore, occupies 2863 lines.

Contents of the manuscript:

fols. 1r–20v: Pierre de Nesson (1383–1442/3), *Les Vigiles des morts or Paraphrase des neufs leçons de Job.*

fols. 21r–32r: Pierre de Nesson, *Le lai de guerre* (imitation of Alain Chartier's *Lai de la paix*). Missing opening.

fols. 33r–38r: Alain Chartier, *Le lai de la paix.*

fols. 39r–87v: *Apparicion maistre Jehan de Meun*, revised version.

fols. 88r–113v: *Codicille Maistre Jehan de Meun* (see note 65 above)

Selection of Base Text

The rationale for considering the text found in the Paris manuscripts rather than that of the London and Vatican manuscripts as authoritative is

---

[66] Ernest Langlois, "Notice des manuscrits français et provençaux de Rome antérieurs au XVIe siècle," in *Notices et extraits des manuscits de la Bibliothèque nationale et autres bibliothèques, publiés par l'Institut national de France, [faisant suite aux Notices et extraits lus au comité établi dans l'Academie des Inscriptions et Belles-Lettres]*, vol. 33 (Paris: Imprimerie Nationale, 1890), part 2, 208–17.

straightforward: the Paris copies were executed during the author's lifetime and even under his supervision (as shown by his indisputable authorship of the glosses), while the other two were copied roughly a half-century later, and present a verbose revision of the poetic text stripped of its marginal apparatus. This, of course, is not to suggest that **L** and **V** are useless: they present material not found in **P1** and **P2** that can only be by Bovet, ranging in length from couplets (see "Date," above) to the 38-line dedication to Philip of Burgundy and the 62-line passage amplifying the author's defense of faithful vassals (see Appendix 3). Some of these short passages present readings that correct or explain passages in **P1** and **P2** (see Text, notes 56, 66, 67, 81). If the poetic text of the later manuscripts was even vaguely close in size to that of the earlier, I would have been obliged to collate them against the others and include their readings in the list of variants. But as I have argued above (see "The 'Artois' Manuscripts"), this is not the case. Manuscripts **L** and **V**, therefore, were eliminated from consideration as candidates for base text.

The justifications for the choice of one Paris manuscript over another as base text, finally, are not as obvious. In opting for manuscript **P2**, Arnold[67] concedes that the choice of one manuscript or another was inconsequential, and justifies his selection of **P2** on the rather tenuous grounds that it does not include some minor linguistic oddities present in **P1** that he feels could not have been produced by Bovet. The two Paris copies are quite likely near-contemporaneous copies of the archetype (even if **P1**, offered to Montaigu on 1 January 1399, might have remained in Bovet's possession a longer time). I have opted for manuscript **P1** rather than **P2**, simply because it seems the more important of the two. For one thing, its miniatures are of a higher quality than **P2**'s, and it is more heavily annotated (including a few lines in Bovet's hand). It also contains the dedication to Jean de Montaigu and the copy of the dedication to Louis d'Orléans, two figures who certainly carried more weight at the court of France than Valentina Visconti, the recipient of the other presentation copy. The insignificance of the differences notwithstanding, I have provided a list of textual variants near the end of this volume.

---

[67] "Le choix d'un manuscrit ou de l'autre n'avait pas d'importance; on nous nous sommes décidé pour **V** [**P2**] à cause de quelques erreurs, surtout dans la déclinaison, que présentait **M** [**P1**], qui ne semblaient pas être du fait de l'auteur" (xxxiii–xxxiv).

Versification and Language

In his 1926 edition, Ivor Arnold approaches the *Apparicion* more as a linguistic than as a historical object, and as a result devotes a good deal more space to the language of Bovet's poem than he does to explanatory notes. A full and competent discussion of various topics covers thirty-five pages (xlii–lxxvi), treating "Phonétique" (xlii–lxviii), "Morphologie" (liv–lxvii), "La langue de l'auteur" (lxviii–lxxiii), and "Versification" (lxxiv–lxxvi). I will defer to Arnold's examination of linguistic issues and will comment here only briefly on Bovet's versification and on the essential elements of dialect noticeable in the *Apparicion*.

The *Apparicion maistre Jehan de Meun* represents Honorat Bovet's only extant attempt at poetry, and his decision to convey a political message through verse must have been based on pragmatism rather than any artistic ambition. Knowing his courtly audience's preference for poetry over philosophical treatises, and the era's absorption with the dream vision form, he presents a series of controversial reformist ideas in a popular guise, adopting the dreaming narrator and the rhyming octosyllabic couplets found in the *Roman de la Rose*. Indeed, he is not an expert versifier, and many of his rhymes seem forced at best. Arnold (lxxiv) observes that Bovet "ne travaille aucunement ses rimes," noting that the poem contains only 10% *rimes riches*, only 22% *rimes feminines*. His prosody, furthermore, is faulty: the poem includes a fair number of lines containing either too few or too many syllables. Arnold (lxxv) suggests that this flaw arises from an insufficient mastery of the rules governing the use of the feminine "e." This may well be so. In any case, it seems clear enough that message dominates medium for Bovet.

The author lived in several different linguistic domains during his career (Provence, the Lyonnais, as well as Paris), and the language of his poem reflects diverse dialectical influences. However, as Arnold (lxix) remarks, these regional variants seem less indicative of Bovet's individual dialect than of his participation in a widespread fourteenth-century trend among French poets: he mixes elements drawn from regional dialects with the standard Francien that was becoming the *koine* in the time. For example: Bovet replaces the expected *moy* with the Picard *my* (l. 16) in the service of rhyme, and substitues *no* for *nostre* (l. 1277) and *vo* for *vostre* (l. 429, l. 741) in the service of meter. He substitutes the occasional Provençal form for its Francien equivalent for the same purposes, as well: meter dictates the use of *esclaux* instead of *esclaves* (l. 660), while rhyme brings on *infiel* (l. 63, paired with *miel*) instead of some form of "infidèle" (cf. *anfidelité*, l. 1276). In the same way that the great poets of his age drew from various French dialects in creating a literary language, so did the amateur versifier Bovet exercise poetic license and call upon his rich linguistic background as he struggled to compose rhyming couplets in an eight-syllable line. If the results are not always correct, or pretty, one should keep in mind that his alter ego in the poem, the Prieur, never speaks in verse, and describes himself to the shade of Jean de Meun (Prose 103) as "petite personne et de petit affaire," in no way worthy to follow in the footsteps of the great poet. I imagine it would not have troubled Bovet greatly to be told that the verses of his *Apparicion maistre Jehan de Meun* did not measure up against those of Machaut and Froissart; he clearly considered versifying to be a means to an end. The expense he incurred executing two deluxe presentation copies nevertheless shows he must have thought the result was worth the effort.

Editorial Procedures

In preparing this text I have essentially observed standard editorial conventions as outlined by Foulet and Speer.[68] Abbreviations (except numerals) have been expanded in conformity with forms in full found elsewhere in the manuscript; the *cédille* has been used as in modern French, except in the case of *scavoir*, since the *sc* is read as a grapheme indicating the required sound; capitals and punctuation have been added where necessary; *j* has been distinguished from *i* and *u* from *v* according to accepted usage. The verb "to be able," however, is written as *pouoir* and not *povoir*, following the recommendation of Omer Jodogne.[69] I have added acute accents to indicate the past participles of verbs (to distinguish *regardé* from *regarde*, for example), to indicate the Picard reduction of the feminine disyllabic *-iee* to *-ie*, to distinguish the diphthong *ie* when it is word-final (e.g., *pitié* for *pitie*) and also in cases where pronunciation would clearly dictate the use of the accent (for example, *Crestianté* for *Crestiante*). The *tréma* has been added where it indicates the pronunciation of a vowel needed for purposes of meter (e.g., *seüre*, l. 446). Elision of most monosyllables is noted by the use of the apostrophe (*s'y*, *l'amoit*, *qu'elle*, *n'a*, etc.) where in the manuscript the words are regularly conjoined. I have indicated folio numbers of the base manuscript in the right margin, and have divided the text according to rubrics in the manuscript indicating the speaking parts of characters or narrator.

Bovet's Latin glosses are presented with abbreviations expanded and necessary punctuation added. Numbers for glosses are given in brackets for

---

[68] Alfred Foulet and Mary Blakely Speer, *On Editing Old French Texts* (Lawrence, KS: Regents Press of Kansas, 1979), esp. 62–73.

[69] Omer Jodogne, "Povoir ou pouoir? Le cas phonétique de l'ancien verbe povoir," *Travaux de linguistique et de littérature* 4 (1996): 257–66.

clarity, with the siglum appearing first, followed by the gloss number, e.g., [P1.17]. Manuscript sigla appear in bold type, e.g., **P1**. The *tréma* has been added to the text of the glosses where it actually appears in the manuscripts (e.g., *tÿrannos*, gloss [P1.19]). In glosses containing citations to canon or civil law, Bovet's abbreviated references appear in the gloss text itself either in parentheses, or as part of the syntax of the comment where context demands; whenever necessary, modern canon-law citations—as well as any other citations or suggested emendations—are added to the gloss text in brackets. Parentheses, therefore, indicate Bovet's authorship; brackets, editorial addition. Translations are mine unless otherwise noted, and follow the cited texts, in brackets.

The critical apparatus below (chapter V) indicates variant readings from manuscript **P2** and the occasional preference of a **P2** for a **P1** reading, as well as emendations based on readings from the later manuscript witnesses **L** and **V**.

Bovet and Islam: A Key to the Apparicion

The speakers in Bovet's poem—amplified by the glosses in his Latin apparatus—discuss a wide variety of matters in late fourteenth-century Western Christian society that were ripe for reform. No one issue or dialogue, however, is as wide-ranging and incisive as that of Christianity's conflict with militant Islam, as dramatized by the exchange of speeches between the Jacobin and the Sarrazin. A detailed analysis of this "debate" can suggest ways to interpret the socio-political and religious pronouncements not only in this section but in other areas of the poem as well.

European leaders in the years leading up to 1400 had to be genuinely concerned about the encroachment of a militant Islam into Christian territory. The Serbs had been defeated at Kossovo Polje in 1389 by the Ottoman Turks under Sultan Murad I; Bulgaria fell in 1393, and Wallachia in 1395; and finally, after years of pleading by the King of Hungary and others, a large Western force had been assembled, and then annihilated by Murad's successor Bāyazīd I (Bajazet) at Nicopolis in the fall of 1396. When Europeans thought about the Orient in 1398, therefore, what came to mind was renewed crusade rather than camaraderie, reconquest rather than conversation. If diplomats and writers like Philippe de Mézières clamored for an end to the hostilities between England and France at this time, they saw it largely as a means to an end: peace between Catholic nations had to come before an all-out war against the non-Christian lords of the Holy Land.[70] That such a war against an alien faith might in any case not constitute a *justum bellum*[71] did not trouble the sensibilities of the most influential Western political movers of the day. Bovet's *Apparicion maistre Jehan de Meun,* however, represents a rare exception to this aggressive foreign policy. His speakers call for an end to the rhetoric of belligerence and prescribe a humbling self-examination for European society, both secular and ecclesiastical. The narrative includes a daring innovation: a Muslim nobleman takes his place in the cast of characters, and delivers some of the most controversial and critical statements in the poem.

In making this appeal through literature, Bovet draws upon the two major elements in his professional experience, the courtly and the academic. A diplomat at aristocratic courts since the mid-1380s, he was seeking to persuade a noble audience by couching his matter in a fashionable form, a dream vision in vernacular verse.[72] His juridical training moved him as well to educate and reform his readers while entertaining them, and explains the presence of the Latin marginal apparatus in the two authoritative manuscripts. In brief, Bovet believed that the Islamic menace had resulted from Christian failure and division, and held that only through internal reform of the kind either advocated or implied by his characters could true concord be achieved within and without the Christian West. The epilogue to this optimistic effort, unfortunately, was that both Bovet and his poem seem to have been largely ignored once his presentation copies had been delivered in the fall of 1398; the Great Schism in the papacy continued until 1417, and the Hundred Years War went on until 1453, the same year that Con-

---

[70] The political and literary careers of Mézières and of Bovet are examined in Hanly, "Courtiers and Poets."

[71] Honorat Bovet's previous work had treated the issue of "just war" in his *Arbre des Batailles* (ca. 1387). See Philippe Contamine, *La Guerre au moyen âge* (Paris: Presses Universitaires de France, 1980), who refers to Bovet's works at several points in his discussion (e.g., 230, 240–41). Furthermore, a marginal gloss in the *Apparicion* ([P2.35]; Text, note 140) cites a canon from Gratian's *Decretum* (C. 23 q. 2. c. 2 *Dominus Deus noster jubet*) that deals with the same subject. See also Bovet's arguments against crusade, note 86 below, and the treatment of this issue in Hanly, "Marriage, War, and Good Government in Late-14th-Century Europe: the *De Regimine Principum* Tradition in Langland, Mézières, and Bovet," in *Chaucer and the Challenges of Medievalism: Studies in Honor of Henry Ansgar Kelly,* ed. Donka Minkova and Theresa Tinkle (Frankfurt am Main: Peter Lang, 2003), 327–49.

[72] On the popularity of this genre see Kevin Marti, "Dream Vision," in *A Companion to Old and Middle English Literature,* ed. L. C. Lambdin and R. T. Lambdin (Westport, CT: Greenwood Press, 2002), 178–209.

stantinople finally fell to the Turks. History might not have been any different had the French royal council taken the advice of this obscure monk, but
the poem, a rare example of medieval Christian pacifist narrative, displays a
willingness, quite uncommon in that time and place, to look inward for the
causes of the forces threatening Christendom.

The poem's dreaming narrator is called *le Prieur,* a character anyone at
the Parisian court would have recognized as Honorat Bovet, the Prior of
Selonnet in Provence.[73] The author therefore seems consciously to forgo
the insulation from criticism and reprisal this genre made possible: although
he could have chosen to hide behind a fictitious narrator, he names this
dreamer after himself, and thereby puts his signature to the document. The
Prieur falls asleep in the garden of the Hôtel de la Tournelle, a former residence of Jean de Meun, and dreams that the "grant clerc" himself appears,
commanding the dreamer to relate what he will see and hear (ll. 1–60). De
Meun, himself a controversial figure at the time (and at the center of the
"Querelle de la Rose" in the next decade), assembles a panel of four speakers, all culled from the margins of Parisian society in 1398. Referred to by
the narrator as *Maistre Jehan,* he both moderates the proceedings and offers
critical commentary consistent with that of the other speakers, interrogating
them with approaches ranging from deference to outright hostility. A medical doctor, the *Physicien,* speaks first (ll. 90–228), and complains of the un-
fairness of the treatment accorded his fellow doctors at this time: Charles
VI had been experiencing periods of insanity for six years and, with no cure
in sight, popular opinion had begun to turn against the medical profes-
sion.[74] He is followed by the *Juif,* who together with his fellow Jews has
been banned from the Kingdom of France since 1394, because of imputa-
tions of usury in their money-lending.[75] The Juif, in the briefest of the four
panelists' statements, confesses he has been sent back into French territory
to ask if his people might now return; having toured the country under
cover, he submits sarcastically—or simply realistically—that the Jews, if
allowed to return, would settle for charging less interest than he has lately

---

[73] The confusions over Bovet's name and ecclesiastical titles are discussed in
Hanly and Millet, "Les Batailles d'Honorat Bovet." See also Ouy, "Honoré Bouvet."

[74] This matter is discussed in notes 2 and 35 to the Text. See also Richard C.
Famiglietti, *Royal Intrigue: Crisis at the Court of Charles VI (1392–1420)* (New York:
AMS Press, 1986), for an extended consideration of the king's illness and its politi-
cal ramifications.

[75] See the account in the *Chronicle* of the Monk of St.-Denis: Louis Bellaguet,
ed., *Chronique du Religieux de Saint-Denys, contenant le règne de Charles VI, de 1380 à 1422*
(Paris: Crapelet, 1840), 2:118–22.

seen Christian bankers demanding (ll. 246–292). Seemingly pacified by the Juif's explanations, Maistre Jehan turns to the third speaker, the *Sarrazin*. Since barely eighteen months have passed since Paris heard the news of the defeat of the Western army and the massacre of most of the European survivors at Nicopolis by Bajazet,[76] the astonished de Meun appropriately inquires why and by whose authority a Muslim—the object of such hatred and fear in the West at this time—has entered a Christian country. The Sarrazin replies eloquently, dominating the discussion for the better part of six hundred lines (ll. 299–898). When this speaker has concluded, Maistre Jehan, as "moderator," gives the floor to the final speaker, a Dominican friar or *Jacobin*. His order had been vilified since 1387 when one of its members, Juan de Monzon, began to preach that the doctrine of the Immaculate Conception was heretical.[77] The Jacobin receives the same six hundred lines (ll. 903–1525) to reply to the Sarrazin's proposals and, as we shall see, mostly corroborates the findings of the Muslim despite a vitriolic introduction. The last section is taken up with the Prieur's prose disquisitions condemning various administrative abuses and at least one particularly nasty political nemesis back in Provence. But by far the majority of the lines in this poem are given over to the speeches of the Jacobin and his ostensible adversary, the Sarrazin.

The Sarrazin is depicted as doubly "other" for this place and time: he is not only an object of terror as a representative of the people that had recently beheaded some 3,000 Christian prisoners, but is also visibly alien, being "aussy noir comme charbon" (Prose 116–117). This description merits a brief excursus. For it is odd that Bovet should insist upon the utter blackness of the Sarrazin; such a description seems more appropriate to African Muslims,[78] or—considering the relative value of the adjective to a

---

[76] The battle took place on 28 September 1396; word reached the court of France at the beginning of December, but was not confirmed until Christmas Day. Froissart's *Chronique* (ed. Henri Kervyn de Lettenhove, *Oeuvres de Froissart,* vol. 15 [Brussels: V. Devaux, 1872]) describes the battle (15:309–21) and the slaughter of the prisoners (15:326–28).

[77] William A. Hinnebusch, O. P., *The History of the Dominican Order* (New York: Alba House, 1973), 2:171–76.

[78] Note this passage in *La Chanson de Roland:* Joseph Bédier, ed., *"La chanson de Roland," publiée d'après le manuscrit d'Oxford* (Paris: H. Piazza, 1966, ll. 1913–1918), when one Muslim leader has fled but another brings up his African reinforcements "from Ethiopia, a cursed land":

La neire gent en ad en sa baillie;
Granz unt les nes et lees les oreilles . . .

late fourteenth-century Frenchman accustomed to an almost complete ethnic homogeneity—even to comparatively lighter-colored Muslims from Nasrid Granada. The ferocious Turks who would be so much in the consciousness of Parisians at this moment were not as dark-skinned as the figure here described. Bovet's portrait (which is not pleonastic, the passage in question being a prose interstice) could be said to stem from a lack of experience with Islamic peoples: while the late medieval Arab world encompassed a varied spectrum of skin colors,[79] most people in Bovet's Europe would have had no personal contact either with non-white peoples or with Muslims. On the other hand, Bovet might well have been aware of these distinctions but opted for a color denoting absolute otherness, and inspiring terror (as in *Roland*—see note 78 above). But whatever its source, the effect of this attribution would have been jarring for Western readers accustomed to seeing Muslims only as ignorant idolators. For the Sarrazin's cogent arguments keep him in the center of things, and his creator gives him so much breath that he cannot be ignored. Indeed, certain manuscript evidence, and the oblivion into which both author and poem soon passed, may indicate that this narrative strategy aroused a certain amount of animosity among its readership.[80]

Superficially, the black Sarrazin is the ultimate cultural outsider, an Orientalized figure from Said's "imaginative geography," a stock character one would expect to revile Christian faith and culture from a stereotypical pagan

---

[He had the black people in his domain; they had big noses and ears].

Their color must be considered in contrast to whatever was the "normative" color of the main fighting force of the "Sarrazins d'Espagne" (l. 1083). See following note.

[79] Bernard Lewis, *Race and Color in Islam* (New York: Harper and Row, 1970), provides a context for this Western attitude toward color. He shows that Arnold Toynbee (*The Study of History* [London and New York: Oxford University Press], 3.226) indicates a prejudice on the part of "swarthy whites" toward non-Arabs lighter-skinned than themselves. Presenting a long historical survey (2.§103), however, Lewis refutes this proposition, showing that while Islamic theology largely claimed equality for believers of all color, in the social practice of the Middle Ages and afterwards people of lighter complexion were dominant and those of darker colors discriminated against.

[80] Both Paris manuscripts contain illustrations of the six speakers; in several miniatures in manuscript **P1** (BNF MS français 810), the head and sometimes the entire body of the Sarrazin has been smeared, apparently while the paint was still relatively fresh (see fig. 6). The image of Maistre Jehan (who, after all, opens the door to the Sarrazin's critiques) is defaced in some miniatures as well. See discussion in "Manuscripts" above.

perspective.[81] But if the Sarrazin's color is the opposite of his Western interlocutors,' his cultural critique sounds home-grown: his speeches express
attitudes common to documents of contemporary European political dis-
sent (e.g., the ostentation of ecclesiastical courts, the laxity of the chivalry),
and would not have required a Muslim messenger. Neither does he lecture
upon Islamic theology or philosophy, as do characters in other works that
take part in the genre of "interfaith dialogue," such as those by Peter Abelard, Guibert of Nogent, and Ramon Llull.[82] Instead, the Sarrazin, for all his
alien appearance, functions as an authority not on Oriental civilization but
on Western history and theology, and is thus transformed from a reified
object—whose predictable carpings could be easily dismissed—into a dangerous double-agent in their midst. The character's sophistication and title
force Bovet's readers to ignore his otherness and perceive him as a social
peer; they must endure his dispassionate and enlightened observations, as
unpleasant as they might sound, especially coming from him. The Sarrazin's
color, religion, and Turkish nationality identify him as enemy, and definitely
raise the hackles of French aristocratic readers, but this narrative position
amplifies, rather than diminishes, the force of his critiques.

In a rare study of this poem, Jean Batany observes that the Sarrazin does
not represent the culture and luxury of the Orient, and that the dialogue
therefore seems to be less "Oriental-Occidental" than what we might call
"North-South": between a people with a bad conscience as regards their
"consumer" civilization and a "primitive" adversary who presents himself as a

---

[81] Edward Said, *Orientalism* (New York: Vintage Books, 1978), 55–73.

[82] A work by Guibert of Nogent (R. B. C. Huygens, ed., *Dei Gesta per Francos*,
Corpus Christianorum: Continuatio Medievalis 127A [Turnhout: Brepols, 1996])
advances anti-Islamic polemic depending largely upon stereotypes and misinforma-
tion about Islam, but nevertheless displays at least a fundamental acquaintance with
the tenets of Islam. A dialogue by Abelard (ed. Rudolf Thomas, *Petrus Abaelardus,
Dialogus inter Philosophum, Iudaeum et Christianum* [Stuttgart: Bad Cannstatt, 1970];
trans. Pierre J. Payer, *Peter Abelard, A Dialogue of a Philosopher with a Jew and a Christian*
[Toronto: Pontifical Institute of Medieval Studies, 1979]), however, works from a
more thorough knowledge of Islamic theology, and treats the non-Christian faiths
more fairly. Ramon Llull's *Llibre del Gentil e dels tres savis* of 1277 (trans. Armand
Llinarès [Paris: Cerf, 1993]) stages the meeting of a pagan with three sages, Jewish,
Christian and Muslim, and treats the opposing faiths with respect, offering con-
cepts more identifiably Islamic than are found in his more polemical works. See
now Dominique Iogna-Prat, *Order and Exclusion: Cluny and Christendom Face Heresy,
Judaism, and Islam (1000–1150)*, trans. G. R. Edwards (Ithaca: Cornell University
Press, 2002), 323–57.

"modèle irréductible," and an image of the past of civilized peoples.[83] This argument fits well within his thesis that Bovet's Sarrazin does not present the kind of thoroughgoing Eastern critique, the "appel à l'orient," that would become a vogue among French authors in the eighteenth century. It overlooks, however, some details of the Sarrazin's own résumé. For one thing, he is quite clearly a Turk: near the end of his discourse, he tells Maistre Jehan that when his fact-finding mission is complete, he will return to his master Bajazet ("Puys retourneray a Bazat," l. 735). More important are the professional credentials with which he introduces himself to Maistre Jehan:

> Sire, se vous m'avez mercy,
> Par mon Mahommet je vous dy
> Que je vous diray ce pour voir
> Tout mon chemin et mon espoir,
> Car je suy plus franc trocimant
> Qui soit en Sarrazime grant,
> Car je scay parler tout langage;
> Et sy suy homme de parage
> Et suy bon clerc en nostre loy;
> En tous estas m'enten un poy,
> Et sy scay faire ryme et vers
> Et le droit retourner envers.   (ll. 299–310)

This is hardly a savage, however noble. The Sarrazin's people are indeed presented as possessing the physical strength and military discipline that Bovet wants to argue are lacking in contemporary chivalry. However, in the the tradition of such pro-Arab polemics as those by Abelard and Llull, this Muslim is also depicted as being at least as cultured and sophisticated as his Christian counterparts. The importance of Bovet's Latin glosses in the interpretation of this poem cannot be overstated: they represent the author's urgent appeal for leaders to acquire learning and its product, wisdom, and to practice it in their statecraft. Such hortatory rhetoric is also found, however, in the prose introductory comments in the manuscript dedicated to Louis d'Orléans's associate Jean de Montaigu. The author makes it clear that the Saracen threat and the papal schism are both a result of divine displeasure with Christian dereliction (Prose 28–33). In order to return to God's favor, Western leaders must listen to what this book offers them, text and gloss. Bovet's characterization of the Sarrazin as learned, and especially as an expert in the law, should be read as an encouragement to West-

---

[83] Jean Batany, "Un Usbek au XIVe siècle: le Sarrasin juge des Français dans *l'Apparicion Jehan de Meun*, in *Images et signes de l'Orient dans l'Occident médiéval: littérature et civilisation*, Actes du colloque du CUER MA, février 1981, Sénéfiance 11, ed. Jean Arrouye (Aix-en-Provence: Publications de CUER MA, 1982), 41–88, here 47.

ern nobles who aspire to this level of learning, and as an indictment of those who do not. As a court diplomat and a jurist, finally, the Sarrazin is a Muslim counterpart to Bovet's Prieur. Batany's article provides much information useful to the study of the poem, but makes too much of the cultural issues at work there, and somewhat overstates the author's acuity in foreign politics and religion. It was not the author's object, in any case, to instruct his audience on the subtleties of Muslim doctrine or present a defense of that faith. His purpose was the inner reform of Christendom, and I would venture to say that his interest in Islam was restricted to his awareness of theories that showed it to be a wayward Christian sect, and a symptom of the sickness at the root of his own faith and culture. He adopts the persona of the Sarrazin as a way of intensifying criticisms that are also pronounced by Westerners. To maintain that there is less sociological complexity here than is argued elsewhere does nothing to diminish the boldness or originality of Bovet's stratagem.

Let us look more closely at the Sarrazin's argument. The Muslims are, from the outset, depicted as the results of Christian waywardness. In his opening oration to the Prieur, the shade of Jean de Meun says he has come back to France and found it full of evil and the fruits of that evil, including the war between England and France and the Papal Schism but most significantly and recently the disaster of Nicopolis:

> Quer vecy tres perilleux temps,
> Nombre de xiiii cens ans,
> Au dit commun de maint Crestiens,
> Juifz, Sarrazins et payens,
> Ou vous verrés fieres nouvelles.
> Les premisses n'en sont pas belles,
> Quant l'eglise est ainsy noire
> Et les Sarrazins ont victoire . . .   (ll. 27–34)

A marginal gloss attached to this passage ([P1.14]) recognizes the power of divine indignation in these dire events. Maistre Jehan then directs the Prieur to listen well to the speakers he will hear, and to have the courage to proclaim the truth of their statements to the leaders of France, so as to make themselves worthy once again of God's mercy. The encroachment of Islam challenges Christianity to reform itself, and its representative in this poem will hold up a mirror to Western society to reveal its most notable shortcomings. When at last he turns his attention to the Sarrazin, Maistre Jehan brusquely but not disrespectfully asks him what business brings him to France, and the Muslim replies that he has been sent on a mission by his leaders to learn about Christians, and especially the mighty French:

Pour veoir l'estat des Crestians
Et tout especial des Frans,
Car les Francoys sont entre nous
Sur tous Crestiens nommés plus proux,
Plus nobles et les plus puissans,
Plusfiers, en armes plus vaillans.
Pour ce suy venus en partie
Pour veoir des Françoys leur vie,
Leur fait, leur noble contenance,
Quel foy ilz ont, quel ordonnance.   (ll. 313–322)

Maistre Jehan wishes to know what he has learned, but the Sarrazin is fearful of the Christians' wrath should he disclose the unflattering truth; once the moderator has assured him of his immunity, the Muslim begins to recite a litany of transgressions. The first place he saw on his visit was Rome, which he had heard was the most powerful city on earth; however, they were an evil crew that lived there now, and what is more, says the Sarrazin, they speak very ill of the French, and hold them for schismatics. This is quite surprising, he says, since he thought there was only one law in Christianity:

C'est dont erreur sur les articles
Que vous tenez en vostre foy.
N'estes vous dont tous d'une loy
Entre vous et les diz Rommains?   (ll. 362–365)

The theme of the Lord's disfavor, discerned by Maistre Jehan and accentuated by Bovet's marginal gloss, is given here an incontrovertible physical form by their Muslim interlocutor: once he tells his people about this state of affairs, says the Sarrazin, they will not hesitate to invade Europe, since a divided people cannot defend itself from external aggression:

Par Mahommet, je suy certains
Que quant nostre gent bien saura
Ce descord qui entre vous va,
Ilz n'auront doubte ne paour
De Crestienté mettre en cremour,
Car gent qui a descort en loy
Ne s'aydera par bon arroy,
Ne ja victoire n'aura gent,
S'en une loy ne se maintient . . .   (ll. 367–374)

The Sarrazin goes on to make that point that it was because of a previous schism in Christianity that Islam has now become the master of the Middle East:

Or prenez exemple de Gresse:
Pour ce que pris a loy diverse
L'a laissee Crestienté

Fouler, et sy n'en a pité.
Foulee l'ont les Sarrazins:
Prez tous les Grez sont leurs subgis. (ll. 381–386)

After comparing the unity and severity of Islamic law to the negligence he has witnessed in the Christian countries, the Sarrazin turns to another European dilemma, the war between France and England, and the behavior of the Western chivalry. At first he claims that the war between Christian nations causes great worry among his people, "Car les debaz font vostre gent / Savoir l'usaige de guerroyer" ("Because fighting teaches your people / The warrior's arts"; ll. 410–411). But this is faint praise at best for the Western knights, perhaps intended to placate the chivalric audience in advance of the harsh criticism to follow. For the Sarrazin immediately qualifies that statement, claiming that of all the nations that are engaged in war, the French are the ones they least fear, because their addiction to luxury has reduced their effectiveness in combat. He first considers their extravagant diet:

Vous estes gens, car apris l'ay,
Qui vivés dilicieusement;
Se vous n'avez pain de froment,
Char de mouton, beuf et pourcel,
Perdriz, poucins, chappons, chevrel,
Canars, faysans et connins gras,
Et que demain ne faillist pas
Habondance plus qu'aujourd'uy,
Vous estes venus a l'ennuy . . .   (ll. 420–428)

The Christian knights require not only gourmet dining while in the field, says the Sarrazin, but also first-class lodgings, clean clothes, and vintage wines. Not so for his people:

Mais nous Sarrazins tout envers,
Com scet monseigneur de Nevers,
Vivons autrement, pour certain:
L'eaue clere et un pou de pain
Est grant disner d'un Sarrazin,
Sy n'a cure de noble vin
Ne de char qui soit de saison . . .   (ll. 435–441)

The reference to "monseigneur de Nevers" adds insult to injury: the untried twenty-four-year-old Jean de Nevers, who would later be called "Jean sans Peur" for violence against his own countrymen, was commander of the Christian crusading force at Nicopolis. The son of the fabulously wealthy Duke Philip of Burgundy, he was held captive by the Turks until his ransom in June 1397, and his discomfiture even during a relatively easy imprisonment would be an appropriate and stinging example of laxity among the Western nobility.[84] The Sarrazin's previous claim that Muslims feared the French because they were constantly at war with the English now sounds at best patronizing; in light of the reference to Nevers, it seems openly provocative. Indeed, he continues his address by insisting that soldiers need to drill outdoors more in order to regain their fighting form of yesteryear, thus belying his previous claim that the ongoing war with England made the French a fearsome adversary. French knights are ruined in their youth with too much luxury; they cannot survive without their fine dining and fancy clothes, and the result is the armies of sissies France now puts into the field:

> Pour ce avez tendrez chevaliers
> Et pou redoubtés saudoiers.   (ll. 491–492)

When it comes time to mount one of your crusades against us Saracens, he says, you do not give a thought to the physical capability of the soldiers who will have to endure weeks and months of marching and may well die along the way; indeed, he claims that the knights are so short-sighted as to think no further ahead than the splendor of their departure: "Mais que le partir soit joly, / Vous ne regardés point la fin" (ll. 515–516). In a statement displaying a certain awareness of Eastern military practice, Bovet's speaker observes that Saracens arm themselves lightly and sensibly (l. 535), train incessantly, and subject themselves to all sorts of physical ordeals to prepare them for combat; Christian armor, on the other hand, is extremely heavy, too heavy even, considering the knights' lack of stamina. In what is perhaps the most cutting comment of all, he goes on to argue (ll. 543–590) that Western commanders really ought to consider letting their peasants do the fighting for them; after all, they are in much better physical shape, and are accustomed to hardship and humble nourishment.[85] The only concession

---

[84] See Text, l. 436 and note 59. J. M. A. Delaville le Roulx, *La France en Orient au XIVe siècle: Expéditions du Maréchal Boucicaut*, 2 vols. (Paris: Ernest Thorin, 1886), 1:287, observes that the conditions for prisoners after Nicopolis were not terribly harsh, but nevertheless represented a great ordeal for the Western knights: "La captivité, sans etre, semble-t-il, d'une rigueur extrême, ne laissa pas que d'éprouver beaucoup les chevaliers. Habitués à une nourriture raffinée, au service de nombreux domestiques, ils avaient peine à se contenter de grosses viandes mal cuites et mal preparées, de pain de millet, et à supporter la privation du vin; on vit bientôt les maladies s'attaquer à eux. A Brousse, ils furent rejoints par Bajazet et, sur son ordre, la prison du comte de Nevers fut adoucie." Also cited in Arnold, *Apparicion* 22 n. 1. Bovet deals with this theme as well in his *Arbre des Batailles* (ed. Nys, 255).

[85] The Sarrazin (l. 564) cites Vegetius's *De re militari* in support of his premise that peasants were doughty fighters. But this was not simply a theoretical proposition: Bovet refers as well (l. 559 and note 73) to the recent battle of Aljubarrota

the Muslim makes to aristocratic pride is his insistence that the villeins be led in battle by a good French captain (ll. 555–556). The Sarrazin here holds his people up as a model of what Christian soldiers once were. Bovet's text thereby insists that this is what they must become again if they are to perform their societal function as *bellatores,* defenders of the people.

The speeches in the *Apparicion* are notable for their abrupt changes of subject, and the Sarrazin's long harangue is no exception. His oration gains momentum, and the indictments begin to follow one after the other in rapid pace. He drops the previous topic and takes up that of the evils of picking young men for important offices; young blood is hot, and a good judge needs a cooler head, he says (ll. 623–626), citing Cicero's *De senectute* for support.[86] The implication is clear that this practice usually results from nepotism, a case in point being Philip of Burgundy's son being given command of an army years before he was ready. The Sarrazin then broaches another new issue (ll. 631–640), the neglect of Christian soldiers still being held for ransom after Nicopolis. The Sarrazin accuses the nobles now safe in France of having abandoned the captive veterans of that battle—a delinquency that makes a mockery of Christian charity—and even compounds the criticism by contrasting their habitual opulence with the misery of the forgotten prisoners: "Jamais en lit ne coucheront / Tant qu'en Turquie esclaux seront" (ll. 659–660). While you disport yourselves with hunting and frivolity, he says, your old comrades are busy ploughing fields and herding beasts for the infidels, and probably being beaten for good measure (645–649). A Turkish emissary would definitely have known of the presence of these prisoners in his country, so the Sarrazin's awareness of their plight is certainly "in character." What is incongruous here, and what makes the speaker seem more transparently a mouthpiece for the author at this point, however, is that at the conclusion of this particular speech the Sarrazin is exhorting Christians to take action against Islam. He chides them for their failure to avenge the disgrace inflicted upon them at Nicopolis, and to liberate the prisoners. This comment seems intended simply as a provocation to the chivalry, since Bovet in another work argues at length against crusade.[87]

(1386), where Portuguese peasants under their King Juan repulsed the invading force of King Juan of Castile and won their independence, an analogue to the victory of Swiss farmers over a Habsburg army at Sempach in the previous year .

[86] See l. 630 (and note 75) in Text.

[87] Aziz Atiya, *The Crusade of Nicopolis* (London: Methuen, 1934), discusses the anti-crusade stances of late fourteenth-century writers such as John Gower and William Langland, and includes Bovet in this group, presenting a useful summary of his pronouncements on this topic drawn from his *Arbre des Batailles.* Atiya observes in

Nevertheless, his oration on the whole condemns Christians, and especially the French, who concern themselves neither with charity or mercy, but only with pleasure. He concludes that if the Christian West, and especially the French, would only learn discipline the way his people have, no country could stand against them, and with his last words delivers a challenge:

Par dessourdre et par orgueil
Sont souvent venus a leur dueil.
De ces deux choses pluiseurs foys
Ay ouy trop blasmer Françoys.   (ll. 677–680)

The accuracy and import of this testimony, replies the moderator, are painful to hear, and before the Sarrazin can catch his breath and continue, Maistre Jehan stops him with a Lombard phrase meaning "Hold on a moment, now it's my turn" (l. 684). For rhetoric's sake, he requites the Sarrazin's affront with a promise of vengeance, referring to a prophecy that foretells failure for the Christians in their first Eastern venture, but conquest at their return.[88] But de Meun, here functioning as a figure of prudence and restraint, then coolly asks the Muslim to continue his discourse with a report on the invasion plans he intends to contrive with the Muslims in Spain. At this request, the Sarrazin claims that the time has come for his people to recover the heritage that was wrested from them in the time of Charlemagne, drawing this directive from a prophecy by the Franciscan Jean de Roquetaillade. His commentary on the *Oraculum Cyrilli* (1345–1349) foretells that before the last battle with Antichrist, the true pope will find refuge in France, and that for a

---

Bovet's arguments "a turning-point in the history of crusading propaganda" (123). Bovet wishes to demonstrate that war shall not be made against the unbelievers for two reasons: 1) God has created all the good things on the earth for human creatures, for the evil as well as the good; so since God has given so many blessings, why should Christians take these from them? 2) Scripture ordains that we cannot, and ought not, constrain or force unbelievers to receive either Holy Baptism or the Holy Faith, but must leave them in their free will that God has given them. Furthermore, according to the Decrees, the Christian subjects of unbelieving rulers should obey the rule of their masters irrespective of their religion; and the Pope has no right to issue indulgence for war against the Saracens in lands other that the Holy Land. Kiril Petkov, "The Rotten Apple and the Good: Orthodox, Catholics, and Turks in Philippe de Mézières's Crusading Propaganda," *Journal of Medieval History* 23 no. 2 (1997): 255–70, here 267, also cites Bovet's *Arbre* as an essential statement on changing attitudes toward crusade in the late fourteenth century.

[88] This prophetic text is presented in glosses in both Paris manuscripts. See Text l. 721 and notes 78–79 and 81.

while the forces of good will be routed.[89] The Sarrazin's chosen verses tell-
ingly omit the conclusion to the prophecy—the final battle in which the King
of France and the Franciscans will triumph, after which all Jews, schismatics,
and Saracens will be converted—and this reverse *reconquista* could be the
event he has in mind when he claims Islam is being "summoned" by the
words of Roquetaillade (ll. 721–722).[90]

This statement touches the core of Bovet's political strategy in the
poem: it must be considered in the context of Maistre Jehan's dismayed and
yet not dismissive invitation for the Sarrazin to continue, and of the Jacobin's affirmations to follow. For the moderator, as the voice of reason in
the poem, has asked the pagan to give an honest description of his goals.
That the Sarrazin cannot "see" to the end of the prophecy and therefore
comprehends only partially what was offered in the vision is in keeping with
enlightened Christian assessments of Islam: the people of Muhammad share
much with the Christian Church, but since they long ago began to embrace
error, they cannot now "read" texts properly. However, as Roquetaillade's
commentary claims, the Muslims will eventually be made part of the one
true Church again. Bovet here effectively eliminates crusade as either a
theoretic principle or as a foreign-policy option. For Islam can now no
longer be seen as an alien adversary; it is a part of the Christian flock gone
astray, a heresy, and, more importantly, a schism.

This complex topic deserves a fuller contextualization than is possible
here; for a discussion of some essential concepts, I will turn to Norman
Daniel's seminal study of European perceptions of Islam. He observes that
"From the Muslim point of view Christians are a privileged association of

---

[89] Richard K. Emmerson, *Antichrist in the Middle Ages: A Study of Medieval Apocalypticism, Art, and Literature* (Seattle: University of Washington Press, 1981), 67, discusses medieval identifications of Islam with Antichrist: "During the crusades and
long after the crusading spirit had died, the Saracens were described as Antichrists
and and the forces of Gog and Magog. They were also associated with the other
symbols of Antichrist. To Joachim of Fiore, for example, the Saracens represented
the fourth and sixth heads of the dragon and the persecutors of the church to appear at the time of the opening of the fourth seal (Apoc. 6:7–8)." Norman Daniel,
Islam and the West: the Making of an Image, revised ed. (Oxford: Oneworld. 1993),
observes that "Islam took its place rather dramatically, but inevitably, in the historical sequence as a prefiguration of Antichrist, for as long as political, economic and
military requirements dominated European thought upon the subject" (192–93).

[90] See further discussion in Text, note 81, and in Marjorie Reeves, *The Influence
of Prophecy in the Later Middle Ages: A Study in Joachism* (Oxford: Clarendon Press,
1969), 321–22. See also Martha H. Fleming, *The Late Medieval Pope Prophecies*, MRTS
204 (Tempe: MRTS, 1999).

people who have become diverted from the right way," and cites an early Qur'an annotator as saying that Muhammad "called the Christians deviators because he thougth they adored three gods as well as images." Medieval Christians reversed this Muslim attitude to themselves, and interpreted Islam "as a deviation from the Church, that is, as a heresy . . . The great proportion of Christian truth contained in Islamic belief made this possible, although, as a heresy, Islam would always remain particularly formidable and, in fact, unique."[91] But other historians and theologians took this distinction even further, and classified the Muslim faith as a schism. Many commentators placed Islam in the same category as dissident Christian churches, and felt that "All the separated bodies called for reunion." Daniel (192) cites the position taken by William of Adam, bishop of Sultaniyah, in his work *De modo Saracenis extirpandi*—that reunification with the Greek Orthodox Church would be "the first stage in the reunion of the world"—and refers to other sources who held that "the Arabs had been converted to Christianity before they were 'perverted' to Islam."[92] Dante was the most notable purveyor of this idea, placing Muhammad in Hell and referring to him as "seminator di scandalo e di scisma" (*Inferno* 28.35). Daniel concludes that:

> Thus Islam was conceived in many contexts, not only as heresy, but as a schism belonging with the Eastern Churches, as part of a providential scheme of progressive error developing after the Christian revelation, as constituting the third *law*, that is, with Judaism and Christianity, the third of revealed religions, and as one in a wide sequence of all the religions of the world . . . Islam was always seen to be in a definite relation to the Catholic Church; the mediaevals, though often querulously, looked ultimately to the reunion of all men.[93]

Bovet does not cite and may not have been aware of the essential writings on this issue that Daniel assembles. But the interplay of his characters clearly indicates that he embraced this optimistic belief. The Sarrazin, in answering the call to *jihad*, is playing his role in the scheme of divine providence that will bring the two religions into conflict before reuniting them once and for all. Having hinted at this issue of global import, the Sarrazin will now reply to a few of the moderator's questions regarding domestic matters; bringing to mind the structure of a contemporary dream vision, *Piers Plowman*, the narrative here seems to strive to approximate the rambling structure of dream itself, defying linear analysis. I will briefly review some ideas from this section that find resonance in the subsequent arguments of the Jacobin. The Sarrazin first condemns profanity and the swear-

---

[91] Daniel, *Islam and the West* (1993), 184.
[92] Daniel, *Islam and the West* (1993), 192.
[93] Daniel, *Islam and the West* (1993), 192–93.

ing of oaths (l. 751) and denounces the widespread practice of divorce (l. 769), providing erudite commentary in glosses on both offenses. He next serves as a mouthpiece for one of Bovet's most cherished causes, the abuse of power by royal officers.[94] He delivers a bitter review (ll. 783–816) of the rapacious practices employed by an ever-growing group of lesser administrators ("sergeants"), who "will not let the poor people live." Jailers are next (ll. 817–828): since these officers demand that all food be bought from them, many prisoners are reduced to destitution by the time of their release, an outrage the king would never tolerate if only he knew. Bovet's marginal comment[95] implies that both groups inflict "tyranny" on the subjects of the realm, and that the result is disorder and suffering. As we shall see, it is this same phenomenon, perceived here in microcosm, that is at root of the international and even eschatological problems facing the West.

The Sarrazin begs his host's permission to depart at this point, but Maistre Jehan asks him to remain and answer one more question: what else did you see during your stay in Rome? He recites a catalogue of fancy clothes, silverware and meals that seems to outdo even the possessions of the French chivalry (ll. 838–898). But this time the Sarrazin is really finished; he tells the moderator he has had enough of this interrogation, and would now hear what someone else has to say. Maistre Jehan asks the Jacobin to comment upon what he has just heard. His response, as I have noted, is as long and as varied as the Sarrazin's; we will limit our consideration here to the Jacobin's direct replies to, or affirmations of, statements made by the previous speaker. He begins by complaining of the University's harsh treatment of his Dominican order in the Monzon affair (ll. 903–1014). During this section he compares this limited example of institutional disharmony to a greater one, that of the divisions among Christians, Jews, and Muslims— and the Jacobin points makes it clear that the other two faiths take great

---

[94] Bovet had served on Pierre de Chevreuse's reform commission for Languedoc that followed King Charles VI's royal process through the region in late 1389 (see note 34 above). One of the results was the removal of the king's uncle, Jean de Berry, from his governorship, and the execution of one of his closest and most corrupt lieutenants, Bétizac. This officer was notorious for having grown very rich at the expense of the common people, who cheered his burning at the stake (*Chronicle* of Monk of St.-Denis, ed. Bellaguet, 1:612). It is likely that Bovet has this sort of administrative abuse in mind during this tirade and that of the Jacobin on the same issue (ll. 1338–1385).

[95] See gloss [P2.21] at l. 823 (Text, note 88): "O Deus, quantum peccatum et quanta tirannia regnat in carceribus Francie . . ." (O God, how much sin and *tyranny* reign in the prisons of France . . .) [my emphasis].

comfort from the sight of Christian internal disunity (ll. 989–990). After more than one hundred lines of *apologia*, he finally addresses the Sarrazin.

The Jacobin's first line (1015) does nothing less than insult the Muslim's intelligence and hurl a racial slur: "Tu es esbahy, noir malostru" ("you are shocked, black miscreant"). But since the ensuing statements do not continue in this vein, the remark seems a rhetorical flourish, reminiscent of Maistre Jehan's harsh greeting to the Juif (ll. 229–235) and implied threats to the Sarrazin (ll. 296–298). In all cases rational discourse ensues, and these openings must be seen as representing a slap in the face, a token of the ruinous discord of their time, that comes before the speakers' movements toward civility. I will return to this notion. The Jacobin wants at first to counter the Sarrazin's criticisms of Roman opulence by referring to the splendid court of Pope Gregory XI (ll. 1019–1030), but the tactic misfires, offering more collaboration than resistance to the other's position. It can be seen as the first of a series of statements supporting the Muslim's arguments. The Jacobin then himself lambastes the Roman cardinals for their avarice and ignorance: they refuse to read or learn anything, while Bovet, in text and marginal comments, tirelessly defends learning as requisite to virtuous leadership.[96] He notes their proficiency at amassing stipends and ecclesiastical positions for themselves and their friends:

Les cardinaulx trouverent l'art
Pour ce qu'en eussent leur part,
Et pour eulx et pour leurs amis
Avoir l'Eglise a leur devis.   (ll. 1099–1102)

All of this is fairly conventional, even if notable for the accord it implies with one of the Sarrazin's contentions. The Jacobin will eventually offer direct defenses of those positions: for example, he echoes and reinforces the Sarrazin's condemnation of the avarice and proliferation of royal administrators (ll. 1354–1392), extortion by jailers (ll. 1396–1414), of the negligent upbringing of young knights (ll. 1432–1471), and of divorce in service of dynastic gain (ll. 1472–1493), quite often introducing the topic by exclaiming "As the Sarrazin says . . ." But the next item on the Jacobin's agenda proves to be the keystone to Bovet's whole program: he argues that the West caused the "schism" that not only produced the split with the Greek church, but also gave rise to Islam itself. This is essentially an internal problem, he declares; once the Christian world repairs its own schism

---

[96] See gloss [P1.37] at l. 1393 (Text, note 131): "Vere timendum est quod istis diebus scientia evanescat quia pauci prelati diligunt litteratos . . ." (It is truly to be feared that in this time learning may disappear, because few prelates esteem scholars).

through secular and ecclesiastical reform, the whole Church will become one again, and the Saracen menace will exist no longer.

This argument springs out of the Jacobin's exposé of the venality of the cardinals: the Pope seeks to fill his coffers at their expense (ll. 1124–1125), but they build extravagant palaces nevertheless, sucking the money out of distant dioceses. The speaker then details the geographical scope of this curial rapacity: all churches in the world were subject to periodic inspections, with a view to extracting more contributions out of them (ll. 1131–1133). He next recounts the reaction to this policy in the territories of the "Greek" or Eastern church (ll. 1134–1148): the people are so furious at seeing their money diverted to Rome, they decide to choose their own "pope": "Constantinoble / Avoit pape tout franc, tout noble" (ll. 1143–1144). This is the most curious detail in a difficult passage, for, despite the innumerable episodes of antagonism between Roman Catholicism and the Byzantine (Orthodox) Church since the fourth century, the definitive break—involving the election of a rival pope—did not occur until 1054. Since it is hard to believe that an educated man in 1398 would have been ignorant of this fact, and impossible, given constraints of space and expertise, to examine this matter adequately, I am forced to speculate that the rupture mentioned here could refer to a defiant action by some Constantinopolitan patriarch before the seventh century, the period to which the rest of the events roughly chronicled here appear to take place.[97] Whatever the case, Bovet definitely presents the rise of Islam (see ll. 1156–57) as posterior to whatever "schism" has been described above.

Another discrepancy between Bovet's exemplum and the historical record is that chronicles of the Great Schism of 1054 do not describe excessive financial demands by Rome as a major cause of the split, as is implied in the Jacobin's speech (ll. 1134–1135). Nevertheless, the insertion at this place in the text of a marginal gloss describing evil tyranny indicates Bovet's belief that this general species of abuse caused the breakup: "De ista maligna tirannia et casu orribili, vide in Tholomeo libro XI et ibi plene."[98] Ar-

---

[97] Bovet could have been referring to the Acacian Schism of the 4th century; see A. Kazhdan and T. E. Gregory, "Akakian Schism," in *Oxford Dictionary of Byzantium*, 3 vols. (New York: Oxford University Press, 1981), 1:42–43. Curiously, a note by Pichon related to this material (77 n. 18) refers to the definitive schism between the Roman and Byzantine churches as having taken place in 854 and not 1054, an inaccuracy repeated elsewhere (76 n. 17); perhaps he simply misdates the schism instigated by the patriarch Photius in 867; see Warren Treadgold, *A History of the Byzantine State and Society* (Stanford: Stanford University Press, 1997), 454–61.

[98] Gloss [P2.27] is appended to l. 1134.

nold (48 n. 1) indicates that he did not find any passage relative to this matter in the 11th book of Tolomeo of Lucca's *Historia ecclesiastica*. However, bk. 12 chap. 17 (col. 921) describes the reign and downfall of an infamous tyrant, the Roman Emperor Phocas (r. 602–610), despatched and replaced by Heraclius, the Byzantine emperor (r. 610–641). Heraclius—the emperor whose "tyranny" is later blamed for the eruption of the Islamic "schism" (see below)—is himself given a brief character portrait in chap. 21 (col. 926).[99] But given that these are only two excerpts, whereas the gloss has specified a citation of the entire chapter or book ("et ibi plene"), Bovet could have been referring to another text by Tolomeo: the entire eleventh chapter of book 1 of his *De regimine prinicipum* deals with the benefits of good government and the dangers of tyranny.[100]

The Jacobin then ties this event to one even more ominous for the fourteenth-century West: the birth of Islam. He prefaces the next section by bewailing the West's tendency toward tyranny, a form of madness (l. 1150) that works counter to the Church's aims (l. 1152). He finds that the tyranny of the Roman curia was not only a cause of discord between eastern and western Christianity, but that "the Saracens came as a result" (l. 1156). For the Church of Rome exacerbated the difficulty it had caused, ignoring the just grievances of the Eastern congregations and sending an army to support the tyrant. The result was a loss of credibility for the pope, and a new schism. The leader responsible for this rupture is "the emperor named Justin." As Pichon observes (77 n. 18), the emperor described in this episode (ll. 1134–1192) shows no similarity to the careers of Justin I (r. 518–527) or Justin II (r. 565–578), nor with Justinian I (r. 527–565) or Justinian II (r. 685–695; banished; restored, r. 705–711).[101] The most likely candidate is Heraclius, even though, once again, it is rapacity (l. 1160), along with the people's sense of being despoiled (l. 1165), that is named as the prime cause of their revolt, when in actuality its origins were as much theological and political as economic. Heraclius is duly famous for his campaign against the

---

[99] Tolomeo of Lucca, *Historia Ecclesiastica*, ed. Lodovico Muratori, in *Rerum Italicarum Scriptores*, 25 vols. (Milan: Societatis Palatinae, 1723–1751), vol. 11 (1728). For modern biographies of these figures, see W. E. Kaegi, "Phokas" and "Herakleios," *Oxford Dictionary of Byzantium* (New York: Oxford University Press, 1991), 3:1666 and 2:916–17 respectively.

[100] See James M. Blythe, trans., *On the Government of Rulers: "De Regimine Principum" by Ptolemy of Lucca*, with portions attributed to Thomas Aquinas (Philadelphia: University of Pennsylvania Press, 1997), 99–102.

[101] Pichon mentions "trois Justiniens," and was likely thinking of the split reign of the second while making his count.

Persians (622–630), who in the previous decade had captured much Byzantine territory: Syria, Palestine, and Egypt, and even the city of Chalcedon, one mile from Constantinople. Even though these actions did not involve Byzantine forces, they must be what are signified by the defeats the Jacobin recounts in ll. 1168–1177, since once Heraclius turned his attentions to the Persians, he compiled a perfect record as a commander, and eliminated them as a political force. The imperial treasury being depleted, the emperor's military efforts were supported by the riches of churches in the capital and the provinces, under an agreement with Sergius I, Patriarch of Constantinople. Bovet's mention of an emperor's depredations (l. 1165) and of collusion with a "pope" (ll. 1178–1181) shows he likely has this episode of Byzantine history in mind.

But even if the Jacobin seems to cite the emperor's endless avarice as the root of the problem in this section, at the end of this passage he describes the Islamic "schism" as having been caused, more generally, by "tirannye" (l. 1194), and—according to a historian from whom Bovet may well have drawn for this material—"tirannye" manifested itself in this cataclysmic event not as acquistiveness, but as religious persecution. Since Bovet cites a volume by Tolomeo of Lucca elsewhere (see above), he may also have been familiar with that author's *Historia Ecclesiastica,* and indeed, some of the details presented in that work parallel the account given by Bovet here of the people's abandonment of Christianity and subsequent embrace of Islam. Tolomeo's historical work clearly indicates Heraclius's oppression as the reason for the apostasy of "people of the east" (l. 1163). The passage in question appears in Book 12. Tolomeo first describes Heraclius's persecution of the Monophysite heresy in territories he has recovered from the Persians, and the rebellion this despotism engendered. He finds Heraclius responsible for the resulting break between the eastern and western churches: "Caussa istius erroris fuit Heraclius, quia propter suam tyrannidem post victoriam de Persis habitam nimis premebat Persas . . ." [The cause of this error was Heraclius, because he oppressed the Persians excessively with his tyranny after he defeated them].[102] Bovet refers here to the many Nestorian and Monophysite Christians living in Syria, Palestine, and Egypt: they were thought to have preferred the domination of the fire-worshipping Persians, who largely tolerated their religion, to the oppression

---

[102] Bk. 12, chap. 2, vol. 11, cols. 929–930. Arnold reproduces some of the passages from the *Historia Ecclesiastica* cited here, but with almost no commentary. For the view that Byzantine disunity and mistreatment of the Christian Arabs helped bring about the rise of Islam, see Irfan Shahîd, *Byzantium and the Arabs in the Sixth Century* (Washington, D.C.: Dumbarton Oaks, 1995), 1:529–659, 2:922–948.

practiced by the Byzantines.[103] Their alienation from Roman orthodoxy prepared the way for their swift acceptance of rule by the Muslims, who in their beginning were also tolerant of different religions:

> Sic accidit de illis populis, in quorum regionibus ista inchoata est schisma, quia ex turbatione Imperii, ut rebellio perseveraret, fecerunt schisma, ut non solum recederent ab Imperio, sed etiam a Christianismo, accipientes quaedam contraria legi, videlicet Moysi, et Evangeliis Christi, ut patet in Alchorano. Et attende, quia etiam in Alchorano praedicto continetur, quod quaedam sectae hereticorum multum fuerunt familiares Mahometo, quos mandat honorari, ut sunt Nestoriani.[104]

Tolomeo next describes the battle of Jâbiya-Yarmuk in Syria (August 636), where Muslim forces gained a decisive victory over a Byzantine imperial army led by Heraclius and put an end to Byzantine influence in the region. The sequence of events as he relates them intimates that this particular "schism" led directly to the Christian defeat:

> Caussa igitur, et ratio una, unde ista inchoata est secta, fuit tyrannicus principatus Heraclii quantum ad illas gentes ubi initium habuit. Omnes enim conveniunt quod de Arabia, et de radice Montis Caucasi, progressa est gens perfida contra Heraclium. . . . Sarracenorum autem erant duo Duces qui ducenta millia armatorum instruxerant in acies. Cumque uterque exercitus non procul a se invicem castra posuissent, nocte, quae diem belli praecedebat, subito in castris Graecorum LII millia pugnatorum exanimata reperta sunt; qua de re reliqui metu perculsi, in diversa fugerunt loca, totum Imperium hostibus relinquentes.[105]

---

[103] See, for older accounts, A. A. Vasiliev, *History of the Byzantine Empire, 324–1453* (Madison: University of Wisconsin Press, 1952), 194–209, and Romilly Jenkins, *Byzantium: the Imperial Centuries, A.D. 610–1071* (New York: Random House, 1966), 28–29; now see Treadgold, *A History of the Byzantine State and Society,* 293–303.

[104] *Historia Ecclesiastica,* Bk. 12, chap. 3 (ed. Muratori, 11:930): "Thus it happened among those peoples in whose regions that schism originated that, because of the upheavals in the empire, they started a schism to keep the rebellion going, thereby abandoning not only the empire but also Christianity, accepting various things contrary to the Law [of Moses] and to the gospels of Christ, as is evident in the *Koran.* And note that the foresaid *Koran* also records that certain sects of heretics, like the Nestorians, were very familar with Mahomet, who orders them to be honored."

[105] *Historia Ecclesiastica,* Bk. 12, chap. 3 (ed. Muratori, 11:930): "Therefore the only cause and reason for the beginning of this sect was the tyrannical rule of Heraclius over those peoples where it originated. For everyone agrees that the infidel people came out of Arabia and the foot of Mount Caucasus against Heraclius . . . Now the Saracens had two leaders who marshalled 200,000 in arms, and since both armies set up camp not far from each other, on the night before the battle 52,000 soldiers were suddenly found dead in the camps of the Greeks, and those who were left alive were stricken with fear and fled in all directions, leaving the entire Empire to the enemy." Tolomeo's account concurs in many details with that

Bovet's Jacobin, then, has argued that local discontent with tyrannical policy encouraged the spread of Islam, and given these historical analogues, the point seems well taken. He concludes, "All the harm I am telling you about / Is the fault of tyranny alone" (ll. 1193–1194). This is the situation in which the world now finds itself: the Muslims are nothing less than our estranged sisters and brothers who by all rights should be part of Christianity. The West's excessive greed and aggression caused the rifts between nations, popes, and religions, and perpetuates the decadence in our military and the injustices suffered by our common people. Only a return to the charitable practices—customs the Sarrazin reminds us we once observed—can reunite us with Islam, end the papal schism, bring peace between Christian nations, restore our chivalry to its bygone dignity, and make us pleasing once again in the sight of God. A token of that longed-for healing can be discerned, finally, in the modulations of address between the beginnings and endings of speeches in the poem.

As the Jacobin approaches the end of this most important section of his discourse, he replies no longer to the queries of the intermediary, Maistre Jehan, but to the Sarrazin directly. The courts of these greedy cardinals, he says, will soon be so magnificent as to rival the splendor of "your Bajazet" (l. 1203); it has driven our Church into desolation, and this, concludes the Jacobin, "is the answer I give you, Lord Sarrazin" ("Dam Sarrazy," l. 1234). This respectful address cannot be seen as ironic, the rough words that opened his discourse notwithstanding. Like those of Maistre Jehan we considered above, they can be seen, on the one hand, as creating dramatic tension in the narrative. But what is more important, in theological terms they illustrate the late century's new plague, discord, which can be overcome only through internal reform. When discourses between Christians and "others" in the text begin, it is always with hostility or apprehension; as the speeches develop, however—even if this development is hardly systematic, given the vagaries of the dream vision genre—a certain interrelational progress can be discerned, especially in the case of the Jacobin's address to the Sarrazin, and if the interlocutors are not on intimate terms by the time they finish speaking, they are certainly closer to communicating than they were when they began. The exhortations to reform contained in the discourses of the six speakers become a simulacrum for that reform itself: in proclaiming and externalizing the cor-

---

of the Frankish chronicler Fredegarius (ca. 659); see J. M. Wallace-Hadrill, trans., *The Fourth Book of the Chronicle of Fredegar* (London and New York: Nelson, 1960), 55. For a modern analysis of the battle, see Walter E. Kaegi, "Problems of Cohesion: the Battle of Jābiya-Yarmuk Reconsidered," in *Byzantium and the Early Islamic Conquests* (Cambridge: Cambridge University Press, 1992), 12–146.

ruptions of Western society, the characters, representatives of various groups in the body of humankind, purge themselves of personal *tirannye,* and thereby figuratively heal the little world represented in the text. In the course of his "confession" of Christian abuse and negligence, in which he espouses many principles already voiced by the Sarrazin and underlined by the author in marginal comments, the Jacobin has become a figure of reconciliation, and here foreshadows the reunification of the global Church by hailing Islam's representative in reverent terms.

In conclusion, I offer some thoughts on the personal and political stakes of writing such a poem at such a time. Chivalric romances were the preferred genre among the nobility, and even if Bovet did seek to appease that audience by clothing his arguments in the dream vision form rather than writing a straightforward treatise on the topic—as he had already done in the case of his *Arbre des Batailles*—the rhetorical structure of the text and the identities of the various speakers would have made it quite a controversial item. For despite its basic structure allowing six speakers to discourse on subjects in their expertise—a format usually suggestive of dialogue—the overall mode in the *Apparicion maistre Jehan de Meun* is not dialogue but univocal and unrelenting polemic. If the French speakers (Jean de Meun, the Jacobin, and the Physician) at times will defend Christianity and the West against the attacks of the "Outsiders" (the Juif, the Sarrazin), the speeches by all parties are for the most part quite censorious of the Western clerical and chivalric estates. Their collective disapproval makes the *Apparicion* a pretty audacious piece of work for a mid-level political appointee at that moment. Employment at court always depended on the good will of those in power, and late medieval rulers disliked criticism as much as those in any age. In light of the penchant for bloodshed shown by the royal relatives grappling for power during the king's illness, therefore, Bovet was playing a very dangerous game, one whose riskiest maneuver was the casting of an Oriental nobleman as chief accuser of late medieval Western society. The stratagem was exploited more fully over three hundred years later by Montesquieu in his *Lettres persanes,*[106] but Bovet's enlistment of the Sarrazin in his attempt to reform Christian society is much more daring given the political risks, and more innovative as well, given the general willingness on the part of European society in this era to reduce the Arab world to mere "other." Bovet's Sarrazin has some damning things to say, and, in service of an urgent objective, is given abundant space to say them. If his critiques of the

---

[106] This idea is developed by Batany, "Un Usbek," 47, and Jacques Lemaire, "L'*Apparicion Maistre Jean de Meun* d'Honoré Bouvet et les *Lettres Persanes* de Montesquieu: Points de convergence," Études sur le XVIIIe siècle 5 (1978): 59–71.

West were not necessarily those that would be uttered by a contemporary Muslim, they carry greater weight in the text and context of the *Apparicion maistre Jehan de Meun* as the result of this novel attribution. Honorat Bovet addressed his poetic appeal to a very difficult audience, and hindsight would suggest that such criticisms could hardly have the desired effect. But it seems hard to believe that the man would have written the poem—and paid for two deluxe presentations copies, to boot—if he did not give it at least an even chance of winning over hearts and minds. Given his circumstances, therefore, Bovet's optimism is extraordinary, and even inspirational. When he calls for his fellow Christians to change themselves so that they might be at one again with people of a foreign and inimical culture, he is placing great faith in their intelligence and capacity for change. Although such faith might seem unjustifiable, the poet fills his text with it, and through the voice of the Jacobin (ll. 1415–1416, 1419) hopes out loud that, God willing, "Une refformacion bien noble" would follow this time of division and strife, and that it one day might even come to pass—

Il pourra bien venir un jour.

Honorat Bovet

L'apparicion maistre Jehan de Meun (1398)

Text and Translation

[Dedication to Valentina Visconti, Duchess of Orléans:
manuscript P2—Paris, BNF, manuscrit français 811, fol. 2r]

A Madame d'Orliens.

Tres haulte et tres redoubtee Dame,[1]

A l'onneur de Nostre Seigneur, et de monseigneur d'Orliens, pour
le bien commun et par especial des povres gens j'ay escript une petite
5   chose en la fourme que vous pourrés veoir en cestuy petit livre; et pour
ce que vous vueilliez soliciter le dit monseigneur a mettre et querir les
remedes qui s'appartendront sur le dessus dit escript, je vous en ay fait
copie, laquelle je vous envoye; car vous, en ce faisant, ferez plaisir a Dieu,
et tout le royaume priera Dieu pour vous. Sy vous suppli tres
10 humblement que de petite personne vueilliez prendre en gré le petit
present. Ly Sains Esperiz par sa doulce grace vous garde en honneur et
vous doint bonne vie et longue.

[Dedication to Jean de Montaigu:
manuscript P1—Paris, BNF, manuscrit français 810]

Mon redoubté Seigneur[2]   [fol. 1r]

J'ay escript un petit libel en cestuy chault temps, en la saison
15 de la chace de l'esprevier;[3] car tout ainsy que les grans seigneurs
s'esbatent lors au plus gay gibier de l'annee, aussy les clers, pour fouyr
parresse, negligence et oyseuse vie, se doivent parefforcier de vivre avec
le gibier de leurz livres. Car combien que leur estude soit de grant la-
bour, aussy est il plain de delit et de joye espirituelle et de
20 fruit gracieux. Sy fut envoyé le livre, car aprés Dieu pour luy fut fait, a
monseigneur le duc d'Orleans; et car je ne scay bonnement autre chose
que je vous puisse envoyer a cestuy benoyst jour des estreines,[4] je
[fol. 1v] vous envoye la copie, et vous supplie que le petit present vueilliez
prendre en plaisir et en bon gré, et mettre diligence avec le roy et son grant

Dedication to *Valentina Visconti, Duchess of Orléans:* manuscript **P2**—Paris, BNF, *manuscrit fonds français 811*

To my lady of Orléans:

Most noble and mighty lady:[1]

To the honor of our Lord, and of my lord of Orléans, for
the common good and especially for the poor, I wrote a little
5   thing in the form you see before you in this little book; and in order
that you might seek to encourage his lordship to effect and enforce the
reforms pertaining to the above-mentioned text, I have made you a
copy of it, which I now send you; because you, in so doing, will please God,
and the entire kingdom will pray to God for you. And so I beseech you
10   very humbly that you deign to accept a little gift from a humble person.
May the Holy Spirit by his sweet grace keep you in honor, and grant
you a good life and long.

Dedication to *Jean de Montaigu:* Manuscript **P1**—Paris, BNF, *manuscrit fonds français 810*

My mighty lord:[2]

I wrote a little book in this hot time of year, during the season
15   for hunting with the sparrowhawk,[3] because, just as all the great lords
revel then in the best hunting of the year, clerics, likewise, to avoid in-
dolence, laxity and an idle lifestyle, must strive to live on the "game" of
their books. For as much as their erudition involves hard work, it is also
full of delight and spiritual joy and blessed fruit. And so I had
20   this book sent to you, because it had been made to honor God first, and
then my lord of Orléans; and because I really do not know of anything
else I can send you on this blessed day of gift-giving,[4] I send you now
this copy, and implore you that you deign to receive this little present
with pleasure and delight, and that you entreat the king and his high

25 conseil comment, pour le bien de son ame, de la sainté de son corps
et reliefvement de tout son royaume, vueille prendre et mettre a effect les
choses qui sont a refformer sur pluiseurs excés qui cueurent au jourduy.
Car sans amender nostre vie, j'ay paour que Dieux ne nous aydera, et sy
doubte que les Sarrazins durement ne griefvent Crestianté, se autrement
30 nous ne retournons a la mercy, pitié et misericorde de Dieu; car tout
appertement il est adviz qu'il soit courroucé contre son pueple, par especial quant il nous a osté la tres clere lumiere de sainte Eglise et laissié
prendre tel avancement aux annemis de nostre foy.

[Dedication to Louis, Duke of Orléans]

34 A monseigneur le duc d'Orleans.

35 Tres hault Prince[5] et mon tres redoubté Seigneur,
Combien que vous ayez assez affaire sur les occuppacions mondaines
et sur le gouvernement de vostre terre et de vos subgiez! Car n'est pas
petite la charge d'un seigneur terrien, lequel entre ses hommes doit tenir
justice du fort au fieble, du riche au povre et du grant au petit, sans faire
40 difference des personnes et sans faveur non deue. Et sy fauldra que par
devant Dieu une foys rendés compte de l'administracion qu'il vous a
donnee ou commise en cestuy mortel monde et des consaulx que vous
aurez donnés a vostre seigneur[6] vostre frere pour lui aidier a gouverner son
royaume. Lequel selon vostre conscience je tieng que vous avez
45 conseillié et conseillerez preudomielment et loyalment, car celluy qui mal
conseille son seigneur non est pas sans grant coulpe, ains en sera pugnis
durement par le Roy des roys. Avec tout ce est il bonne chose de veoir
aucuns fruiz de l'escripture; car disoit li bons philosophes Socrotes[7]
que lors seroit ly siecles beneurés quant les roys et les princes
50 sauroient ou quant se mettroyent en estude de scavoir. Et sy a bien grant
temps que ly mondes n'ot princes qui guerez s'adonnassent a estude de
scavoir. Car puys que mourut ly bons roys Robers de Cecille[8] qui fut de
vostre sang et fut moult grant clerc, nous avons eu pou princes qui bien
amassent science, fors vostre pere qui Dieu face mercy; car
55 il l'ama et sy fist il les bons clers; et ly roys de Navarre,[9] derrenier trespassé,
vit pluiseurs choses en science et ama les hommes estudians; et monseigneur
Bernabo de Melan[10] les ama fort toute sa vie et leur fist pluiseurs
[bi]ens;[11] mais combien qu'il leur fist escripre pluiseurs [fol. 2r] beaulx
livres, il avoit son estude plus en or qu'en science; et s'est chose[12]

25   council, for the good of his soul, the health of his body, and the welfare
of all his kingdom, that they accept and implement the measures necessary for reforming the many excesses rampant nowadays. Because
without reforming our lives, I fear that God may no longer help us, and
thus fear that the Saracens may grievously afflict Christianity,

30   unless we return to the grace, the worship, and the mercy of God; because it is quite clearly apparent that he is angry with his people, especially seeing how he has taken from us the bright light of Holy Church
and allowed so much progress by the enemies of our faith.

34   To my lord, the Duke of Orléans.

35   Most distinguished prince, and my very mighty Lord:[5]

How great are your obligations in worldly affairs and in the
government of your land and subjects! For it is not a little thing,
the duty of a temporal lord, who must keep justice among his people,
from the strong to the weak, the rich to the poor, the great to the humble,

40   with prejudice toward none and without awarding undeserved favors.
And thus will you one day be obliged to give an accounting before God
of the administration He gave you or to which He assigned you in this
mortal realm, and of the counsel you will have given to your lord,[6] your
brother, in helping him to govern his kingdom. I believe that you have

45   counseled him and will counsel him honestly and loyally, because he
who gives bad advice to his lord is not without great guilt, and will
therefore be punished severely by the King of Kings. In all of this, it is
a good thing to see some of the fruits of learning, for this is what the
good philosopher Socrates[7] said, that the world would be blessed when
        kings and princes were

50   learned, or when they applied themselves to the acquisition of learning.
And so it has been a long time that the world has lacked princes who
cared to devote themselves to the acquisition of knowledge. Because
since the death of Robert of Sicily,[8] who was of royal blood and was a
great scholar, we have had few princes who really loved learning, one
exception being your father, God rest his soul,

55   because he loved it and loved good scholars as well; and the King of Navarre,[9] recently departed, understood many things and loved studious
men; and my lord Bernabò of Milan[10] loved them very much his whole
life, and did them much good;[11] but even though he had many beautiful
books made for them, his studies were always more on gold than on
        knowledge, and if there is a thing[12] that greatly

60 qui trop empesche estudier science, c'est avarice. Car Socrotes[13] cuidant
vrayement non pouoir ensemble possider avoir et science, son or getta en
la mer, ainsy comme dit nostre decret. He Dieux! quel avoir puet avoir
plus bel que de science et de sagesse, car tous avoirs, toute richesse en
comparacion de luy est comme arene de neant de value! Et dont vient la
65 loenge que l'en donné au roy David, au roy Salamon, aux empereurs
Justinien et Julles Cezar? Par leur puissance d'or? Certes que non, ains
par leur science et par leur sagesse qui seront en perpetuel memoire,
comme tres gracieusement dit Origenes.[14] Sy sont les livres de nature de
feu, que nulz ne se puet approuchier d'eulz que l'en n'emporte
70 aucun prouffit; sont aussy de nature de farine, que qui se met pres emporte aucune chose. Et combien que je n'ay eu ou temps passé vostre
congnoissance ny accointement de vostre noble estat, pour ce que j'ay
entendu que vous amés les livres, j'ay escript une petite chosette que se
tout vault petit, mais que soit au plaisir de Dieu et de vostre seignourie,
75 mes cuers en sera plus appaisiez, car je desire de veoir aucunes choses
que j'ay touchiees en cestuy petit escript. Sy vous suppli pour l'onneur
de Dieu que, se j'ay aucunement parlé oultrecuideement, que le me
vueilliez pardonner, car un homme qui escript doit ce que luy est adviz de
verité sans flaterie[15] escripre.
80 Ly Sains Esperiz vous tiengne tousjours en sa sainte garde et aprez ceste
gloire mondaine[16] et de petite duree vous emmaint a la pardurable.   Amen.
Et sy aura nom cestuy petit libel l'Apparicion maistre Jehan de Meun.[17]

                                                              [fol. 4r]

83 A tous ceulx qui vouldront ouyr parler de verité[18] soit de
par Dieu donnee bonne perseverance de la soustenir et de la dire,
quant lieu sera et proffit, sans aucun offendre non deuement.[19]

86 [Le prieur parle:]

En mon deport aprez soupper, heure bien tarde, alay ens le jardin
de la Tournelle hors de Paris,[20] qui fu jadis maistre Jehan de Meun; ou je
me fu mis tout seul ou quignet du jardin, prins telle ymaginacion
90 qu'elle me tint tant longuement que, se je m'endormy, soit en bonne
heure. Mais vecy venir un grant clerc bien fourré de menu ver, sy me
commença a tancer et fierement parler et dire en ryme:

60 impedes the acquisition of learning, it is greed. Because Socrates,[13] believing that he could not possess both riches and knowledge, threw his gold into the sea, as our *Decree* teaches us. My God, what riches could be better to have than knowledge and wisdom? For all possessions, all riches in comparison with them are like worthless sand! [Wisdom 7:9] And from whence comes

65 the praise that we give to King David, to King Solomon, to the emperors Justinian and to Julius Caesar? From the power of their gold? Certainly not, but rather from their knowledge and their wisdom which will always be remembered, as Origen[14] put it so elegantly. And so books are like fire, in that nothing can come near them without attaining some benefit; they

70 are also like flour, in that he who gets close to it takes something away with him. And even though in the past I neither enjoyed your friendship nor even made your acquaintance, noble lord, because I have heard that you are a lover of books I have written a little thing which is worth very little; but if it should please God and your lordship, my heart will be very

75 much at peace, because I hope to behold some of the things that I have touched upon in this little writing. And so I implore you, for the honor of God that, if I speak at all presumptuously, that you would excuse me, because a man who writes must write what he takes to be the truth without dissembling.[15]

80 May the Holy Spirit keep you always in his holy protection, and after this short-lived earthly glory,[16] may He bring you to eternal life. Amen

And so this little book will be called "The Apparition of Master Jean de Meun."[17]

83 To all those who would hear the truth[18] spoken may God give the determination to uphold and to proclaim it, where the opportunity presents itself, without unduly offending anyone.[19]

86 The Prior speaks:

While relaxing after dinner, at a very late hour, I went into the garden of la Tournelle outside Paris,[20] where master Jean de Meun used to live; and there I placed myself in the corner of the garden, and fell into a reverie

90 that held me there so long that I fell asleep, very quickly at that. Then there came a great scholar, his robes well lined with thin vair, who began to berate me and to speak angrily in rhyme:

93   Maistre Jehan parle au prieur: [fol. 4v]

       "Que faites vous cy, sire moyne,
       Et quel vent ne temps vous y moyne?
       Je ne fis oncques cest jardin
       Pour esbatre vostre grant vin
5   Que vous avez anuit beü.
       Je suy maistre Jehan de Meun
       Qui par maint vers sans nulle prose
       Fis cy le Rommant de la Rose[21]
       Et cest hostel que cy voyez
10   Pris pour acomplir mes souhés.
       Sy en achevay une partie.
       Aprez, mort me tolu la vie.
       Et vous, sire, ne bon ne bel
       Mengiez ceans comme pourcel
15   Sans faire proffit a nully.
       Se Dieux me gart, ce poise m'y
       Quant vous en cest lieu demourez;
       Et se remede n'y mettes
       De vivre plus diligemment,
20   Je vous prise moins que neant.
       Et se je fusse com jadiz,
       Je deisse bien mon adviz
       Au monde plain d'iniquité,
       De tricherie, de fauseté,
25   Se ne laissasse pour mourir:
       De dire le vray sans mentir.
       Quer vecy tres perilleux temps,
       Nombre de xiiii cens ans,[22]
       Au dit commun de maint Crestiens,
30   Juifz, Sarrazins et payens,
       Ou vous verrés fieres nouvelles.
       Les premisses n'en sont pas belles,   [fol. 5r]
       Quant l'eglise est ainsy noire
       Et les Sarrazins ont victoire;[23]
35   Jeunesse sy outrecuidee
       Qui tient viellesse pour foulee.
       Les petis ont tant fol courage
       Qu'ilz portent estat de parage;
       Moisnes et autres religieux[24]

93 Master Jean de Meun speaks to the Prior:

"What are you doing, lord monk,
And what wind or season brings you here?
I never intended this garden
To be the place you can enjoy all that wine
5   That you have drunk tonight.
I am Master Jean de Meun,
Who in many verses and not a single line of prose
Here wrote the *Romance of the Rose*,[21]
And I rented this mansion that you see here
10   In order to fulfill my wishes.
And so I finished one part.
Later, Death deprived me of my life.
And you, sir, you ne'er-do-well,
You sit there eating, like a pig,
15   Doing no good for anyone.
God help me, this weighs on me here,
When you stay in this place;
And if you do not take pains
To live more heedfully,
20   Then I consider you to be less than nothing.
And if I were as I was before,
I would certainly speak my mind
To this world full of iniquity,
Of cheating, of falseness,
25   So as not to let it perish:
I would speak the truth without lying.
For behold, a very perilous time,
The number of fourteen hundred years,[22]
As many Christians,
30   Jews, Saracens and pagans say,
When you will see portentous things.
The omens are not good,
When the Church is so sullied,
And the Saracens are victorious;[23]
35   Our youth who think old age is folly
Are quite presumptuous.
Lowly people have so much foolish bravado
That they take on the rank of peerage;
Monks and other religious[24]

40　　Sont retournés tant glorieux
　　　Que n'a en eulz devocion;
　　　Vecy male conclusion.
　　　Les pueples menus sans cesser
　　　S'estudient de mal parler
45　　De leurs souverains et des clers;
　　　Vecy mal dit, vecy mal vers,
　　　Quant subgiez n'ayment leur seigneur.
　　　Vers eulx n'ont crainte[25] ne honneur
　　　Que les tiennent en leur justice,
50　　Pugnissent les maulx de leur vice.[26]
　　　Se seignourie n'estoit en terre,
　　　Nul homme ne seroit sans guerre;
　　　Le monde seroit trestout nice,
　　　Se es princes n'estoit justice,
55　　Et les grans seigneurs sans doubter
　　　Mettent leur or en maçonner;[27]
　　　Maçonner est de tel nature
　　　Qui plus y met, plus y a cure,
　　　Et se gaste plus qu'il ne cuide,
60　　Tant qu'il treuve sa bourse vuide."

94 Le prieur parle:

95 Lors me tins moult pour esbays, et a grant paine je puis croire [fol. 5v] que
ce fust maistre Jehan de Meun. Mais quant je l'ouys parler par ryme,
je le pensay aucunement, se ly respondy: "Sire, pardonnés moy,
car en verité je ne vous sauray pas tres bien parler par vers; mais
pourquoy me blasmez vous se je me tiens ceans en paix? Car je ne
100 sauroye pas estudier comme vous fistes jadis, et sy ne seroye pas
escoutez par aventure,[28] se je disoie pluiseurs choses comme vous fistes,
car je suy d'estrange pays, petite personne et de petit affaire. Se ne
scay que doy dire au temps present, car ly mondes est trop perilleux
et les cours des princes trop dangereuses. Et s'il vous plaist a
105 souvenir des anciennes dottrines, le grant Valery[29] recita l'oppinion d'un
tressage senator lequelz une foys, quant il vit la chose publique qui
estoit gouvernee petitement, en un conseil ne volu dire son oppinion,
sy respondy: 'Par ma foy, fist il, de parler me suy je souvent
repentis, de taire non jamais.' Et pour ce, a mon adviz, quant ly

40 Are become so vainglorious
  That they neglect all observances;
  That is a bad result.
  The lowly people, without ceasing,
  Devote themselves to speaking ill
45 Of their sovereigns and of the clergy;
  It is a bad song, it is a bad poem,
  When subjects do not love their lord.
  They show neither fear[25] nor respect
  To those who administer justice for them,
50 Who punish the crimes brought on by their evil.[26]
  If there were no seigniorial authority on earth,
  No man would live in peace;
  The world would be in very bad shape
  If princes were not agents of justice.
55 And the great lords, of course,
  Are putting their gold into mansions.[27]
  Of house-building, there is this:
  The more one puts into it, the more cares one has,
  And more gets wasted than he thinks,
60 So much so that his purse ends up empty."

94 The Prior speaks:

95 Then I was totally amazed, and I had a very hard time believing that this was Master Jean de Meun. But when I heard him speak in rhyme, I did not think this any more, and so I answered him: "Sir, forgive me, because in truth I could not recognize you very well speaking in verse; but why do you chide me for sitting here in peace? For I was not able to
100 devote myself to learning as you were in days gone by, and so perhaps I went unnoticed if I said several things as you once did, because I am from a foreign country,[28] a nobody of no means. So I do not know what I am supposed to say in this day and age, because the world is too perilous and the courts of princes too dangerous. And if it please you to
105 recall some ancient teachings, Valerius Maximus[29] repeated the opinion of a very wise senator who once, when he saw that the Republic was being governed poorly, did not wish to give his opinion in the council, and so replied: 'By my faith,' he proclaimed, 'My words have I often regretted; my silence, never.' And for that reason, in my opinion, when

110 mondes est perilleux, se feroit bon taire et deporter le temps.[30] Et
aussy le monde tient pour nice tout homme qui vueille escripre
nouvelles choses."[31]

113 Maistre Jehan parle au prieur: [fol. 6r]

"Ce sont paroles de faulx vilein
Et ne sont pas de bon Crestien,
Qui par l'exemple d'infiel
Laisse la doulceur et le miel
65   De la vraye Sainte Escripture,
Pour laquelle divine nature
Par especial prist char humaine
Que justice vraye et certaine
ust en tous fais noble gardee,
70   Car elle est de Dieu amee.
Et si tost[32] pour elle garder
Puet ly gardiens pariller,
Soit pour venir a mort vilaine,[33]
Ne puet chaloir, car de sa paine
75   Aura il tres grant guerredon
Dessus les cieulx ou noble tron.
Doys doncques tu tant redoubter
Les dueilx de ce trespas mortel
Que tu laisses verité dire
80   Pour encourir de Dieu son yre?"   [fol. 6v]

114 Le prieur parle:

115 Lors quant je ly cuiday respondre, vecy passer par devant nous un
phisicien acompaignié d'un faulx Juifz et d'un Sarrazin aussy noir comme
charbon, et par derrierez venoit un Jacobin qui par samblant menoit
grant dueil, sy sambloit il bonne personne et tresgrant clerc en toutes
sciences. Sy me dist maistre Jehan de Meun:

120 Maistre Jehan dist au Prieur:

81   "Escripvez ce que ceulx diront,
Car certes a nous parleront."

110 the world is a dangerous place, one does well to keep silent and to live through this time.³⁰ What is more, the world takes for a fool the man who seeks to write of new things."³¹

113 Master Jean speaks to the Prior:

> "These are the words of a false knave—
> And not of a good Christian—
> Who by the example of the infidel
> Leaves the sweetness and the honey
> 65   Of true holy Scripture,
> For the sake of which, in particular, the godhead
> Took on human flesh,
> That true and certain justice
> Be preserved in every noble act,
> Because Scripture is beloved of God.
> 70   And although,³² in defending it,
> The guardian can perish,
> Even endure an ignoble death,³³
> It does not matter, because for his pain
> 75   He will have a great reward
> Above the skies on a noble throne.
> Why must you, therefore, so much fear
> The afflictions of this mortal sojourn
> That you refrain from speaking the truth,
> 80   And incur the wrath of God?"

114 The prior speaks:

115 Then, when I was just about to answer him, we saw appear in front of us a Physician, accompanied by a wicked Jew and by a Saracen, black as coal; behind them came a Jacobin who, by the look of him, was in deep mourning, and who appeared to be a good person and a great scholar in all disciplines. And then master Jean de Meun said to me:

120 Master Jean de Meun speaks to the Prior:

> 81   "Write down what these men say,
> For they will surely speak to us."

121 Sy prist a dire a ces iiii dessus nommés:[34]

122 Maistre Jehan parle au phisicien:

> "Dont venez vous, dant phisicien? [fol. 7r]
> Querez vous en ce jardin rien
> 85 Ou n'a sentier, chemin ne voye?
> Quelle aventure vous envoye
> D'aler par nuyt par les jardins?
> Estes devenus malandrins
> Qui vont par nuit pour desrober?"[35]

123 Le phisicien respont:

> 90 "Sire, ne me vueilliez tancer;
> Plaise vous mon excusacion,
> Quer je croy bien, m'arez pardon,
> Se vous me voules escouter,
> Car je me puis bien excuser
> 95 Se je laisse le chemin bel
> Et m'en voys en un cheminel.
> Car puis voy ma science confondre,
> Il fault que je m'aille rescondre;
> Sy n'ose passer par Paris,
> 100 Car, par le Dieu de paradis,
> L'ygnorant gent prent tel propos, [fol. 7v]
> Duquel vraiement ne me los,
> C'un prince n'aye maladie
> Ne prengne desroy par folie,[36]
> 105 Se ce ne vient par traison,
> Par sorcerie ou par poison.
> Et vecy fole oppinion,
> Simple ymaginacion,
> Car un prince est aussy pacibles
> 110 Comme autres homs corruptibles,
> Se c'est par parmision divine
> Aucune gent y est encline
> D'ouyr medecine nouvelle;
> Oncques ne fu bonne ne belle,

121 He then turned to speak to the four named above:[34]

122 Master Jean speaks to the Physician:

> "Where have you come from, lord Physician?
> Are you looking for something in this garden,
85   Where there is no path, no road nor track?
> What adventure is it that sends you
> To roam in gardens by night?
> Have you physicians become bandits
> Who go out at night to pillage?"[35]

123 The Physician replies:

90   "My lord, please refrain from rebuking me;
> May my explanation satisfy you,
> Because I do believe that I shall be pardoned
> If you will but listen to me,
> For I can certainly excuse myself
95   For having left the high road
> And appearing here on this path.
> For now that I see my profession in disarray,
> I must go into hiding;
> I therefore dare not pass through Paris,
100   Because, by God in heaven,
> The ignorant folks are of such a mind—
> They are not praising me much these days—
> That a prince is not ill
> Or has a disorder because of insanity[36]
105   But rather comes from treason,
> From sorcery or from poison.
> This is a fool's point of view,
> Pure hallucination,
> Because a prince is just as susceptible to illness
110   As other mortal men.
> It is by divine sanction
> That some people are prone
> To respond to new medicines.
> We never did anything wrong or wicked,

115 Ains est contre la sainte foy,
Contre les ars, contre la loy,
Contre decrez, contre canons,[37]
Contre tous ce que nous lisons;
Ne oncques Dieux telle phisique
120 Controuva, ne fist tel musique,
Ne tel chançon, ne tel parler
Que on veult aujourd'uy trouver.
Car par art qui est condempnee
Et par tous les sains reprouvee
125 On veult guerir maladie fort,
Soit ce par droit ou soit a tort,[38]
Oultre tout l'art de medecine
Qui sus au ciel prist sa racine,
Laquel Dieux mesmes ordonna
130 Pour l'ayde qui besoing n'a,
Et quelconque sage personne
Honneur et loz et pris ly donne.
Ly Sains Esperiz sy l'a cree
Et l'Eglise l'a honnoree.   [fol. 8r]
135 Or sont venuz meschans devins,[39]
Sorceliers, arquimans, coquins,
Qui vueullent par art d'invoquer
Sans Dieu les malades saner.[40]
Et quant ne puent a ce venir,
140 Pour paix et amour departir
Entre prouchains et parens chiers,
Treuvent cas orribles et fiers
Pour troubler les cuers des menus;
Car des sages ne sont creuz,
145 Mais entre basses gens nicettes
Se font tenir comme prophetes;
Et a l'istance et requeste
Du deable a qui ilz font feste,
N'eussent fait pluiseurs gehiner
150 Et bien durement tourmenter;
Se fust creuz leur faulx raport,
Pluiseurs en fussent mis a mort,[41]
Dont le pueple a esté dolans
Contre nos seigneurs les plus grans,

115 For such practices are against our Holy Faith,
     Against the arts, against the law,
     Against decrees, against canons,[37]
     Against everything we read;
     God never invented such physic,
120 Nor made such music,
     Nor such a song, nor such speech
     That one can find nowadays.
     For by the use of arts that are condemned
     And denounced by all the saints
125 These ones seek to cure a serious illness,
     Whether it be right or wrong,[38]
     Outside the bounds of medicine,
     Which takes its root from the heavens above,
     And which God himself has ordained
130 To help those who have need of it,
     And whatever wise person
     Who gives it honor and praise and reverence.
     The Holy Spirit created it,
     And the Church honored it.
135 But now wicked fortune-tellers have come,[39]
     Sorcerers, alchemists, rascals,
     Who seek, through their powers alone,
     And without God, to cure the sick.[40]
     And when this comes to nothing,
140 They drive out peace and love
     Between close friends and beloved relatives
     By inventing horrible and potent causes [for the sickness]
     To disturb the hearts of the menial folk,
     For the real scholars are not believed,
145 And instead, among these silly common people,
     [These sorcerers] are taken to be like prophets,
     And at the order and request
     Of the devil, whom they celebrate,
     Were several people put to torture,
150 And quite severely maltreated.
     Their false report was believed;
     Several people were put to death,[41]
     Which caused the people to make many complaints
     Against members of the highest nobility,

155 Car cuidoit que leur faulseté
Fust sainte pure verité.
Sy a diffamé maint grans personnes,
Nettes, leaulx, feaulx et bonnes:
Plus chier ameroient la mort
160 Qu'a leur seigneur faire tel tort[42]
Comme de lui tolir santé
Et mettre a chetiveté.
C'est la soutiveté du deable
Qui de mensonges est connestable,[43]
165 Qui tousjours par division
Fait perdre le tant noble don
De paix, d'amour et de concorde,
Pour lequel tout bien se discorde. [fol. 8v]
Par division vient toute guerre,
170 Par division pert seigneur terre,
Par division laissent seigneurs
Les petis, moyens et greigneurs;
Division confont les royaumes,
Les abbayes et les sept sealmes.[44]
175 Oncques l'annemi ne vestit
Cote de maille par qui il vainquit
Ce monde en champ de bataille
Com par division sans faille.
Regardés com par division
180 A mis l'Eglise turbacion;
L'estat grant et merveilleux
A mis en fier cas perilleux.
Regardés Flandres la puissant[45]
Par division descroissant;
185 Par division Lombardie
N'eust jamaiz guerre finie.
Or s'est venue essayer
Se pourra France envenimer[46]
La columpne de Crestienté
190 De noblesse et de bonté,
De biens, de richesse, de foy;
Sur tous autres, a puissant roy.
Et pour ce que tieulx gens inique
Par art de dampnee magique

155 Because they believed this falsehood
To be absolute truth.
And so many great, upright, loyal, faithful and good personages
Were defamed;
They would rather die
160 Than do their lord such wrong[42]
As to deprive him of health
And reduce him to misery.
It is the cunning of the devil,
Who is the commander-in-chief of liars,[43]
165 Who always, through discord,
Causes peace, that noble gift, to be lost,
And love and concord;
Because of this all good is contested.
From discord comes all wars,
170 Through discord lords lose their lands,
Through discord, lords abandon their people,
The little, the middling, and the great.
Discord undoes kingdoms,
And abbeys, and the seven psalms.[44]
175 The Adversary never puts on
His coat of mail—which allows him to conquer
This world on the field of battle—
But through discord; it never fails.
Behold how discord
180 Has thrown the Church into confusion;
Its grand and wondrous standing
Has been reduced to a terrible, dangerous state.
Behold mighty Flanders,[45]
Through discord now declining;
185 Because of discord, Lombardy
Has never seen an end to war.
Now discord has come to see if
It will be able to poison[46] France,
The pillar of Christianity,
190 Of nobility and goodness,
Of wealth, riches, and faith;
It has a king mighty above all others.
And because such villains
Through accursed magic arts

195 Ont accusé les phisicians,
Sages clers et leaulx et grans,
De negligence, de non savoir,
Combien qu'ilz ont menti, pour voir,
Le petit pueple nous maudit;
200 Car non, c'est leur faulx esperit.
Et pour ce me vueil je musser
En ce jardin, tant que passer   [fol. 9r]
Voye leur puante mensonge;
Car leur fait ne sera que songe,
205 Sy passera comme fumiere,
Car mauvaistié a tel maniere
Que s'il florist, ne gette graine;
Tousjours le tient fievre quartaine
Sy ne puet durer longuement,
210 Et ceulx qui sueffrent maintenant,
Diffamé par leur faulseté,
Seront nes et loyaulx trouvé.⁴⁷
Car loyauté est de nature
Qui de l'uile tient la figure:
215 Qui plus le boute en parfont,
Tousjours retourne il amont;
Qui en l'eaue le pense nayer,
Il se haulse plus sans fouler.
Quant verité sera trouvee
220 Et faulseté sera foulee,
Lors yray je par plain chemin
Et vous lairay vostre jardin.
Sy vous suppli bien doulcement
Que laissiez passer ce mal vent,
225 Car certes ces puans varlés
Cuidoient faire que maillés⁴⁸
Se levassent pour desrober
Les riches et les grans tuer."⁴⁹

124 Mais quant le phisicien ot parlé, maistre Jehan regarda vers ce faulx
Juif, et ly commença a dire bien rigoureusement:

126 Maistre Jehan parle au Juif: [fol. 9v]

195   Have accused the physicians,
       Those great clerks, learned and loyal,
       Of negligence, and ignorance—
       Although, in truth, they have lied—
       The common people curse us.
200   But no, that is just their inconstant nature.
       And because of this, I must hide out
       In this garden, until I see
       Their stinking lie has passed on;
       For what they have done will vanish like a dream,
205   Will pass like smoke,
       Because such wickedness
       Unless it flowers, produces no seed;
       The king still has the quartan fever,
       But it cannot last very long,
210   And those who now suffer,
       Defamed by others' dishonesty,
       Will be found innocent and loyal.[47]
       Because loyalty is of such a nature
       That it retains the character of oil:
215   No matter how it is pushed down,
       It always rises back to the surface;
       Although one might think he can drown it in water,
       It rises back higher, unscathed.
       When truth is finally discovered,
       And dishonesty destroyed,
220   Then I will show myself openly, in the street,
       And will leave you your garden.
       I therefore beseech you, politely,
       That you let this ill wind go by,
225   Because those stinking knaves surely
       Thought they could make rioters[48]
       Raise themselves up to rob
       The rich and kill the nobles."[49]

124 But when the Physician had spoken, master Jean looked toward the false Jew, and began to speak to him quite harshly:

126 Master Jean speaks to the Jew:

"Tres ort Juif de faulx desroy,
230   Contre l'ordenance du roy
      Pour quoy venez en ce pays?
      Ne savez vous pas que jadiz
      Par vostrez grans iniquitez,
      Par usures,[50] par vos pechiez,
235   On vous getta hors du royaume?[51]
      On vous trouva sus tant de blasme
      Que l'en vous deust avoir tous ars
      Car vous n'usez de nulz bons ars,
      Ne prouffiz ne utilitez
240   Ne vendront la ou demourrez;
      Par vous n'est terre labouree
      Ne la mer n'en est honnoree;
      En paradis n'avez vous part.
      Oyez! dittes, truant paillart,
245   Pour quoy estes vous venus cy?"

127   Le Juif respont:

      "Loy de Dieu, sire, je vous pry
      Que vous me vueilliez escouter:
      Je suy ça venus espyer,   [fol. 10r]
      Par mandement de nos Juifz,
250   Se nous pourrions estre remis
      Et retourner en ceste terre.
      Nous avons oy que tel guerre
      Y font les usuriers marchans[52]
      Qu'ilz gaignent le tiers tous les ans;
255   Sy font secretement usure[53]
      Tel qui passe toute mesure.
      Car il fauldra grant gage perdre,
      Se cilz ne vient au jour par rembre,
      Et qui gage baillier ne puet.
260   Il aura pelles, se il veult,
      Mais il fault qu'il les pleige bien,
      Autrement n'emportera rien.
      Les pelles on ly monstrera,
      Mille frans les achetera;

"Vile Jew, most wicked:
230 Why, against the edict of the king,
Do you come into this country?
Don't you know that, some time ago,
Because of your great iniquities,
Because of usury,[50] through your sins,
235 You were thrown out of this kingdom?[51]
You were found so guilty
That we should have burned all of you,
Because you never use good arts,
Nor will anything beneficial or useful
240 Come where you dwell;
The land is never plowed by you,
Nor do you ever sail the seas;
You will have no part in Paradise.
So listen! Tell me, wretched scoundrel,
245 Why have you come here?"

127 The Jew replies:

"By God's law, my lord, I pray you,
That you deign to listen to me:
I have come here to see,
By order of the Jews,
250 If we could be readmitted,
And could return to this country.
We have heard about the campaign
Being carried out here by merchant usurers,[52]
That they earn a third in interest every year;
255 And thus they secretly practice usury,
So much so that it passes all moderation.[53]
For a large security will be forfeited
By whoever does not return to pay the debt by the appointed day,
And whoever cannot redeem his pledge.
260 He can have pearls, if he likes,
But he will have to give firm guarantees for them,
Otherwise he'll get nothing.
He'll be shown the pearls,
And be told they cost one thousand francs;

265   Il confessera cel achat,
        Mais il vendra de l'autre part
        Un marchant qui marchié fera
        Et pour huit cens frans les aura.
        Et sy sera mise journee
270   Pour payer la somme nommee,
        Et s'il ne paye celluy jour,
        Oncques ne fut tant mal sejour,
        Car il fault prendre autre terme,
        Mais il fault bien l'interest rendre,
275   Tel que, se je disoye tot,
        Vous orriez envis celluy mot,
        Pirez usures oncques ne vy
        Qu'ilz font aujourd'uy, je vous dy:
        Les courratiers font ce lendit.
280   Ne dittes qui le vous a dit,
        Mais ja ne diront de bon gré
        A nos seigneurs la verité.   [fol. 10v]
        Et pour ce suy je ça venus,
        S'il plairoit au roy et aux dus
285   D'en ce pays retourner nous;
        Et nous serions plus gracious
        De prendre plus petite usure,
        Car celle qui queurt est trop dure.
        Et quant n'ose par nuyt aler,
290   Comme veez, me fault musser,
        Car bien scay que perdu seroye,
        Se on me trouvoit en plaine voye."

128 Maistre Jehan parle au Sarrazin:

        Quant ly Juifz ot tout parlé
        Et ses excusacions finé,
295   Maistre Jehan dit au Sarrazin:
        "Et vous, pour quoy passés par cy ?
        Or dittes par quelle ordonnance
        Estes venus en ceste France."

129 Le Sarrazin respont:

265   He will agree to this purchase,
        But there will come from another place
        A merchant who will bargain,
        And buy them for eight hundred francs.
        And then a deadline will be arranged
270   For repayment of the sum in question,
        And if he does not pay on that very day,
        It will be the unluckiest of delays,
        Because he'll have to agree to a new date of payment,
        While, of course, paying the interest all the same,
275   So much so that if I told you all
        You wouldn't hear it willingly.
        Worse usury have I never seen
        Than is practiced nowadays, I tell you:
        The courtiers are also in on this business.
280   Do not say who told you this,
        But no one ever willingly tells
        The truth to our rulers.
        And it is for this reason that I have come,
        To find if it would please the king and the dukes
285   To let us back in to this country;
        And we would be more cooperative
        In that we would accept a smaller rate of interest,
        Since the current rate is too high.
        And when I dare to go out by night,
290   As you see me, I must hide,
        Because I know well that I would be finished
        If I were to be seen at large in public."

128 Master Jean speaks to the Saracen:

        When the Jew had said everything on his mind,
        And finished his explanations,
295   Master Jean said to the Saracen:
        "And you, why have you traveled here?
        Declare, now, by what authority
        You have come to France."

129 The Saracen replies:

[fol. 11r]

"Sire, se vous m'avez mercy,
300 Par mon Mahommet je vous dy
Que je vous diray ce pour voir
Tout mon chemin et mon espoir.
Car je suy plus franc trocimant
Qui soit en Sarrazime grant;
305 Car je scay parler tout langage;
Et sy suy homme de parage
Et suy bon clerc en nostre loy;
En tous estas m'enten un poy,
Et sy scay faire ryme et vers
310 Et le droit retourner envers.
Et pour ce nos seigneurs de la
Sy m'ont envoyé par deça
Pour veoir l'estat des Crestians
Et tout especial des Frans,
315 Car les Francoys sont entre nous
Sur tous Crestiens nommés plus proux,
Plus nobles et les plus puissans,
Plusfiers, en armes plus vaillans.
Pour ce suy venus en partie
320 Pour veoir des Françoys leur vie,
Leur fait, leur noble contenance,
Quel foy ilz ont, quel ordonnance.
Espaigne doy puis visiter
Pour aucun secret emporter;
325 Mais par Arragon passeray
Ou grans Sarrazins trouveray.
La trouveray je bel acueil,
La trouveray feste sans dueil.
Puys visiteray noble roy
330 De Grenade[54] puissant, ce croy;
La sera fynie ma voye
Des pays esquelz l'en m'envoye."

130 Maistre Jehan parle:

[fol. 11v]

"Sarrazin, je voy tout assert
Que trocymant estes appert

"My lord, if you will allow me,
300   By Muhammad, I say
That I will tell you, in truth, all about
My travels and my wishes.
For I am the most noble emissary
That there is in all of Islam;
305   For I know all languages;
I am of high birth,
And I am good theologian, too;
I understand something about all things,
And I can write poems, as well,
310   And can turn the law inside out.
For this reason, the leaders from my side
Have sent me over here
To see the estate of the Christians,
And particularly the French,
315   For among us, the French
Are called the most courageous of all Christians,
The most noble and most mighty,
Most formidable and valiant in arms.
This is part of the reason I have come,
320   To see how they live, the French—
Their deeds, their noble appearance,
Their faith, their laws.
Then I must travel to Spain,
To deliver certain secrets;
325   But I will also go through Aragon,
Where I will find great Saracens.
There, I will find a warm welcome;
There I will find joyful celebrations.
Then I will visit the noble king
330   Of mighty Granada,[54] this I believe;
There it will come to an end, my path
Through all the countries where I have been sent."

130 Master Jean speaks:

"Saracen, truly I see
That you are a superb emissary,

335   Et hardy et sage parlier.
Mais je vous pry que par entier
Dittes ce que avez veu
Entre Crestiens, ne congneu,
Que en vous cuidiez reporter."

131 Le Sarrazin respont:

340   "Sire, trop me faites doubter
En cest rapport que je feray,
Car se vous voulés bien, je scay,
Ma vie sera tost finee.
Or vy je mal ceste encontree,
345   Se pour ce me faites mourir."

132 Maistre Jehan parle:

"Sire, par saint Denys martir,
Vous n'aurez mal ne vilonnie
En toute nostre compagnie;
Mais dittes quanque vous en samble."

133 Le Sarrazin respont:

350   "Sire, trestout le cuer me tramble,
Mais puis m'avez asseuré,
J'en diray bien ma voulenté.
Sire, je suy passés par Romme,
Celle qui fut jadiz en somme
355   La plus puissant cité du monde.   [fol. 12r]
Or meschante gent le revironde,
Ou j'ay ouy par pluiseurs foys
Parler aux Rommains des Françoys.
Mais c'estoit bien vilainemant;
360   Ilz les prisent moins que neant,
Car ilz les ont pour scysmatiques.
C'est dont erreur[55] sur les articles
Que vous tenez en vostre foy.
N'estes vous dont tous d'une loy

335   And brave, and a wise orator.
           But I ask that you
           Recount everything you have seen
           And learned among Christians
           That you are able to relate."

131 The Saracen replies:

340   "My lord, there is much that frightens me
           In this report that I would make,
           For if you were to order it, well I know
           That my life would quickly end.
           At this point, I have a bad feeling about this encounter;
345   It could be a way for you to kill me."

132 Master Jean speaks:

           "My lord, by Saint Denis, martyr,
           No evil or wicked treatment
           Will come to you from any in our company;
           Tell us, therefore, all that you have gathered."

133 The Saracen replies:

350   "My lord, my heart is pounding wildly,
           But since you have given me your pledge,
           I will tell you everything I like.
           My lord, I went through Rome,
           Which was in years gone by
355   The most powerful city on earth.
           But now wicked people congregate there,
           And I heard them many times,
           These Romans, speaking about the French.
           But it was always quite contemptuously;
360   They consider the French to be less than nothing,
           Because they hold them to be schismatic.
           There is, then, an error[55] in the beliefs
           Held by your religion.
           Are you not all held under one law,

365	Entre vous et les dis Rommains?
	Par Mahommet, je suy certains
	Que quant nostre gent bien saura
	Ce descord qui entre vous va,
	Ilz n'auront doubte ne paour
370	De Crestienté mettre en cremour,
	Car gent qui a descort en loy
	Ne s'aydera par bon arroy,
	Ne ja victoire n'aura gent,
	S'en une loy ne se maintient;
375	Car une loy conjoint les cuers,
	Diverse loy depart les meurs.
	Une loy tient en unité,
	Diverse loy diversité;
	En une loy vit charité,
380	En diverse crudelité.
	Or prenez exemple de Gresse:
	Pour ce que pris a loy diverse
	L'a laissee Crestienté
	Fouler, et sy n'en a pité.
385	Foulee l'ont les Sarrazins:
	Prez tous les Grez sont leurs subgis.
	C'est ung grant debat de desloy
	La ou n'a loy ne bonne foy.[56]
	Pour loy laisse pere son filz, [fol. 12v]
390	Le frere son frere en perilz;
	L'amy son ami mettre a mort
	Lairoit mettre par son accort.
	Regardés dont, sy en ma foy
	Un autre se tient contre moy,
395	Comment lui aideray de cuer?
	Se c'estoit mon frere ou ma suer
	Et n'avoit cure d'amender,
	Je le lairoye bien tuer.
	Ou monde n'a sy fiere guerre
400	Comme de foy; qui veult enquerre
	Ce qu'en dit la vostre euvangile
	Ne nostre maistre Virgile.[57]
	Car entendés bien que vous dit
	Le vostre maistre Jhesu Crist,

365   You and the Romans?
        By Muhammad, I am sure
        That when our people find out
        What discord there exists between you,
        They will not doubt or fear
370   That they can strike terror in Christianity,
        Because people divided in belief
        Will never unite for combat,
        And they will never be victorious
        Unless they obey one law.
375   For a single law unites all hearts,
        And separate laws cause morality to disappear.
        A single law holds all in unity,
        While having different laws brings out differences;
        In one law, there is charity,
380   But in diverse laws, cruelty.
        Now, take the people of Greece, for example:
        Because they chose divergent beliefs,
        They allowed Christianity
        To become oppressed, and there is no pity for it.
385   The Saracens overcame them:
        Almost all the Greeks are their subjects.
        It is a great, iniquitous struggle
        When there is neither law nor fidelity.[56]
        Under the law, a father leaves his son,
390   A brother leaves his brother in danger of death;
        The friend would allow his friend to be executed,
        And by his own accord.
        Look, then, if another of my faith
        Places himself in dispute with me;
395   How can I, sincerely, be of help to him?
        Even my brothers or my sisters
        Who did not take care to mend their ways,
        I would certainly turn over to be put to death.
        In the world, there is no war as fierce
400   As a religious one; whoever wishes should examine
        What is said about it in your Gospels,
        Or in our master Virgil.[57]
        For listen well to what is said
        By your master, Jesus Christ,

405	Lequel tout clerement en prose
	Le vous a dit en test sans glose.
	D'autre debat que vous avez
	Entre vous, de vray me creez,
	Avons nous doleur grandement,
410	Car les debaz font vostre gent
	Savoir l'usage de guerroyer.
	Par Mahommet, nous aurions plus chier
	Que eussiez tousjours paix sans guerre,
	Plus legiers seriez a conquerre,
415	Et que tousjours fussiez amis,
	Car plus tost vous aurions conquis.
	Mais a tout ce que guerre avez,
	Entre nous estes pou doubtés,
	Et les raisons je vous diray:
420	Vous estes gens, car apris l'ay,
	Qui vivés dilicieusement;
	Se vous n'avez pain de froment,
	Char de mouton, beuf et pourcel, [fol. 13r]
	Perdriz, poucins, chappons, chevrel,
425	Canars, faysans et connins gras,
	Et que demain ne faillist pas
	Habondance[58] plus qu'aujourd'uy,
	Vous estes venus a l'ennuy;
	Et se vo lit mol blanc n'avez
430	Pour une nuyt, estes foulés.
	Chemise blanche sur le corps,
	Ou autrement vous estes mors.
	Et se bons vins n'avez en teste,
	Pour non riens est toute la feste.
435	Mais nous Sarrazins tout envers,
	Com scet monseigneur de Nevers,[59]
	Vivons autrement, pour certain:
	L'eaue clere et un pou de pain
	Est grant disner d'un Sarrazin,
440	Sy n'a cure de noble vin
	Ne de char qui soit de saison;
	S'il en trouve, ce soit empron.[60]
	Et quant ce vendra au gesir,
	Il n'a cure de desvestir,

405 Who quite clearly, in prose,
Explained it to you in text, without gloss.
From the other conflicts that you have
Between you, believe me truly,
We have much sorrow,
410 Because fighting teaches your people
The warrior's arts.
By Muhammad, it would be better for us
If you were always at peace rather than at war,
For that way you would be easier to conquer;
415 And if you were always on friendly terms with each other,
That way we would defeat you sooner.
But even with all the wars you wage,
You are but little feared by us,
And the reasons for this, I will tell you:
420 You are people, so I have heard,
Who live like epicures;
If you do not have wheat bread,
Mutton, beef, pork,
Partridge, young hen, chicken, hare,
425 Duck, pheasant, and fat rabbits,
And if tomorrow there's not more
Abundance[58] than today,
You are much troubled;
And if you do not have a soft, white bed
430 For a single night, you are devastated.
There must be white garments on your back,
Or it's death for you.
And if there are no fine wines in the bottle,
The whole feast goes for nought.
435 But we Saracens, on the other hand,
As my lord of Nevers[59] knows,
We live otherwise, for certain:
Clear water and a bit of bread
440 Is a big meal for a Saracen,
So there's no worry over cellared wines,
Or what meat is in season;
If any is found, that is first-rate.[60]
And when it is time to go to bed,
He does not worry about disrobing,

445   Ne daignera fuerre querre,
       Mais qu'il treuve seüre terre.
       De grant cuisine ne lui chault,
       Ne de rost, ne pastes chault,
       Ne saulse vert ne cameline,
450   Ne blanc mengier de pouldre fine.[61]
       Telz choses font un homme tendre
       Que fain ne froit ne puet atendre,
       Et s'il gist en lieu descouvert,
       Sa vertu et sa santé pert.
455   Regardés bien vos loys anciennes
       Qui furent vrayez et certaines
       Pour faire les bons coustumiers
       D'estre en armes fors et fiers.   [fol. 13v]
       Ne vouloyent fussent pansart;
460   Ceulx leur donnoyent feves et lart
       Et l'eaue pure, lit de paille,
       Couchier avec cote de maille,
       Demourance hors des cités
       Pour estre des champs plus privés[62]
465   Et fussent tousjours ordené
       Et pres, quant seroient mandé.
       Car com usage fait bon maistre,
       Et non usage le fait triste,
       Cuidiez vous que pour estuver,
470   Pour doulx vivre, pour deporter,
       Pour penser tousjours en veandes,
       Pour mengier les choses friandes,
472a   [Qu'on deviegne preux chevalliers,
472b   Fors escuiers, fors soudoiers.][63]
       Ce dit Valere de Cathon,[64]
       Chevalier sage, grant et bon:[65]
475   Oncques mauvaiz pain ne blasma,
       Ne bevrage ne refusa;
       Ne lui chaloit de perdre fain
       De mengier paste ou levain;
       Pour son logis ne queroit salle,

445 Or trouble himself with looking for straw,
But only with finding some solid ground.
Fine cooking matters not to him,
Neither roasts nor meat pies
Nor *sauce verte* nor *cameline*
450 Nor blancmange with *poudre fine.*[61]
Such things make a man soft,
One who cannot endure hunger or cold,
One who, if he sleeps outdoors,
Loses his strength and his health.
455 Examine well your ancient laws,
Which were dependable, and sure
To put your men in the habit of
Being strong and fierce in arms.
Those laws did not want them to be paunchy;
460 They provided the men with pork and beans,
And fresh water, and a bed of straw,
Slumber in their coat of mail,
And a place outside the city walls,
So as better to learn the lay of the land.[62]
465 And these orders were always transmitted,
And followed, once they had been given.
For just as good habits make a good leader,
And lack thereof brings him to grief,
Do you believe that it is from taking hot baths,
470 Living the good life, seeking amusements,
Thinking always of meats
And eating gourmet foods
472a [That you become brave knights,
472b Strong squires, strong men-at-arms?][63]
This is what Valerius says of Cato,[64]
A wise knight, great and good:[65]
475 He never turned up his nose at poor bread,
Nor refused any drink;
Nor was it important for him, in satisfying hunger,
To eat meat pies or cakes;
For his lodgings he sought no shelter,

480   Pour ses robes bahu ne malle;
        Mais qu'il se peust garder du froit,
        Couleur de drap ne regardoit.
        Un chevalier de grant bonté
        N'a cure de cel vanité,
485   Car vie vraie et certainne
        Par grant vertu fait vie saine.[66]
        Pour ce disoit vostre Bernart:
        'Estudie, tu qui es cornart,
        Plaisir ou monde pour bontés,
490   Ne pour robes ne vanités.'[67]
        Pour ce avez tendrez chevaliers   [fol. 14r]
        Et pou redoubtés saudoiers.
        Aussy vous tenes vos enfans
        Tant doulx nourris et tant frians,
495   Tant bien vestuz en leur jeunesse
        Que, quant ilz viennent a grandesse,
        Ne scevent passer chaut ne froit
        Ne veande qui doulce ne[68] soit.
        Enfant masle, quant il est tendres,
500   Doit fort mengier pour mettre membres,
        Mais ne doit mengier doulz repast,
        Car tel vie le rendroit gast.
        En jeunesse ne doit aver
        Fourreure de menu ver,
505   Double chapperon, ne barette,
        Ne chose qui a tendrour le mette.
        Nous disons que vous n'estes sages,[69]
        Quant vous voulés faire passages
        Contre Sarrazins ou payens
510   Quant prenez ainsy tendres gens.
        Ne regardés se ilz pourront
        Porter les grans maulx qu'ilz auront
        En chevauchier tant longue voye,
        Qui les plus fors souvent ennoye;
515   Mais que le partir soit joly,[70]
        Vous ne regardés point la fin.
        Pour ce meurent ilz en la voye,
        Ou font a leurs annemys joye;
        Et quant ce vient a la bataille,

480 For his clothes, no trunk nor chest;
As long as he was protected from the cold,
He didn't care about the color of the cloth.
A knight of great worth
Does not concern himself with such vanity,
For an honest and exemplary life,
485 Because of its great virtue, makes one healthy as well.[66]
On which subject said your Bernard:
'You devote yourself, you fool,
To the pleasures of the world, for its gifts,
490 Its gowns, its vanities.'[67]
Because of such behavior, you have dainty knights,
And soldiers who are little feared.
You raise your children, furthermore,
So well-nourished, so genteel,
495 So well-dressed in their youth
That, when they reach maturity,
They can endure neither heat nor cold
Nor meat that is not tender.[68]
A male child, when he is young,
500 Should eat well to grow strong limbs,
But not eat gourmet dishes,
Because such habits would make him sickly.
In youth, one should not have
Coats trimmed with vair,
505 Fancy hats, tall *chaperons* or flat *barettes*,
Nor any other thing that leads to softness.
We say you are not wise[69]
When you want to plan a crusade
Against Saracens or pagans,
510 When you take these tender people along.
You do not look to see if they can
Endure the great discomforts that they will have
During those long days in the saddle,
Which are a challenge even to the strongest knights;
515 But in assuring that the start is splendid,[70]
You never give a thought to the finish.
As a result, these ones die along the way,
Which gives joy to their enemies;
And when they get into battle,

520   Leurs coups sont legeres, sans faille:
      A troys coups ferir force fault,
      Et sont perdus par ce deffault.
      D'une autre chose vous dy tant
      Que vous vous armes trop pesant,[71]   [fol. 14v]
525   Tant que quant estez tout armés
      En pou d'eure estes foulez;
      Se gueres dure la bataille,
      La puissance vous fault, sans faille,
      Et se un homme d'armes chiet,
530   A tart relevera son chief,
      Et pluiseurs meurent estouffez
      Des vostrez, car trop sont armés.
      Ayez doncques vostrez gens dures
      Pour soustenir leurs armeures.
535   Les Sarrazins s'arment legier,
      Sy ont bon courage et fier,
      Et sueffrent longuement bataille,
      Et chevauchent tres bien, sans faille.
      Pour ce qu'ilz ont aprins durté,
540   Sueffrent longuement de bon gré
      Paine, traveil et chaut et froit:
      Aille le vir qui ne m'en croit.
      Vous laissiez les gens de labour
      Qui ne scevent qu'est bon sejour
545   Labourer les vignes et terres,
      Quant voulés faire sur nous guerres,
      Qui vivroient mieulx de frommage[72]
      Que de chappons gent de parage,
      Car n'ont jamais eu nul bien.
550   Vous tenés qu'ilz ne vauldriont rien;
      S'ilz avoient un pou coustume
      Simple cote en leur coste,
      Ilz nous feroient plus grant guerre
      Que tous les gentilz d'Engleterre,
555   Mais qu'ilz eussent ordonnance
      D'un bon cappitaine de France.
      Prenés example de Portugal,
      Se les vilains firent le mal   [fol. 15r]
      Qui naguerez prindrent gent d'armes,[73]

520 Their blows are weak, of course:
After three strokes, their strength must fail,
And they are lost, through this deficiency.
I'll tell you of one other thing:
Your armor is too heavy,[71]
525 Which means that when you are fully armed,
In a short time you are crushed;
If the battle lasts any time at all,
Your strength fails you, invariably,
And if a man in armor falls,
530 He'll be slow in raising his head,
And many of yours die suffocated,
Because they wear too much armor.
Therefore, make your soldiers tougher
So that they can hold up under their armor.
535 The Saracens arms themselves lightly,
So they are courageous and fierce,
And can endure a long time in battle;
And, of course, they ride very well.
For they have developed great stamina,
540 And in battle, they willingly endure for long periods
Pain, fatigue, heat and cold:
Whoever does not believe me, go and see.
You leave behind your peasants,
Who don't know what a pleasant pastime is,
545 To plow in the vineyards and fields,
When you want to make war upon us,
They who would be happier with mere cheese[72]
Than would you aristocrats with capons,
Because they have never had anything luxurious.
550 You feel they would be worthless.
If they had but a small wardrobe,
A simple tunic on their backs,
They would make war against us better
Than all the nobles of England,
555 So long as they were led
By a good French commander.
Take the example of Portugal:
See if those peasants did ill
Who in the past took up arms.[73]

560 Dont maintes dames gettent lermes,
Soit en France ou en Espaigne,
En Lombardie, en Alemagne,
Soit en Chippre, ou soit en Grece.
Ly grans maistres d'armes Vegece
565 Nous dist que les laboureux
Sont pour les armes pourfiteux.
Se lisiez Valere la grant
Il le vous preuve cleremant.[74]
Or les faittez vous reposer,
570 Ceulx qui pourroient mieulx porter
Le long chemin, la longue paine;
Car pour nourreture vilaine
Ne craingnent mal lit ne mal pain,
Ne vent ne pluye ne trop fain;
575 Et tous travaulx scevent porter,
Et ont les braz usez pour donner
Grans coups et longuement tenir,
Car ont usé paine souffrir;
Sy ne fault que les coustumer
580 Tant seulement harnoys user.
S'ilz sont malades ou navrés,
Ilz n'en sont mie sy grevés
Comme sont les hommes gentilz,
Car de nourreture sont vilz,
585 Pour passer tout mal, tout tourment.
Et sy y a moins perdement,
S'ilz sont en la bataille mors;
Et se en prison est leur corps,
Crestiens n'y ont pas tel dommage
590 Ne tel honte com de parage.
Vous avez une autre police   [fol. 15v]
Qui certes me samble trop nice,
Qu'entre vous je voy ces truans
Voulans contrefaire les grans:
595 Se un grans portoit mantel envers,
Incontinent un vilain sers
Aussy se prent envers porter
Pour les biens nobles ressambler.
Se un noble treuve nouvelle guise,

560   Because of them, many ladies weep,
          Whether in France or Spain,
          Lombardy, Germany,
          Cyprus or Greece.
          The great master of warfare, Vegetius,
565   Tells us that peasant workers
          Can serve effectively as soldiers.
          Therefore, read Valerius Maximus,
          Who will prove it to you clearly.[74]
          Now, however, you leave at home
570   Those who could better withstand
          The long journey, the long discomfort;
          Because, as a result of their austere peasant experience,
          They fear neither bad bedding nor bad bread
          Nor wind nor rain nor prolonged hunger;
575   And they can bear any exertion,
          And have the practiced arms for delivering
          Heavy blows, and for great tenacity,
          Because they are accustomed to enduring pain.
          And so all you have to do is train them
580   In how to use their equipment.
          If they are sick or wounded,
          Their state is nowhere near as bad
          As that of the nobleman,
          Because they have had that peasant upbringing
585   That allows them to withstand any adversity or suffering.
          And also, less is lost
          Should they die in battle;
          And if they land in prison,
          Christendom will not suffer such a setback,
590   Nor such shame as the nobles.
          You have another policy
          That truly seems like folly to me,
          Because among you I see these scoundrels
          Who want to counterfeit a noble rank:
595   If an aristocrat wears a coat inside out,
          Forthwith, a lowly serf
          Will turn his inside out as well,
          So as to look like the aristocrats.
          If a noble finds an elegant new style,

600   Un savetier, giponnier nice,
       Un maçon et un vigneron
       Jamaiz n'en feroient pas leur pron,
       S'ilz n'avoient fait robe pareille.
       Un marchandel robe vermeille
605   Portera d'escarlaste fine,
       Sa femme vestue com royne.
       Un qui n'a maison ne cuisine
       Portera martres ou fayne
       Comme fera le filz d'un duc;
610   Et pour ce seront malostruc,
       Car quant leur fauldra telz estas,
       Feront lairecins ou baraz,
       Dont vendront a meschante fin
       Ou reprendront estat meschin.
615   Ancores une autre police
       Avez: que pour tenir justice
       Prenez entre vous jeune gent.
       Jeune gent est toute boulent,
       Et juge convient estre froit;
620   Pesant et meur estre doit,
       Car jamaiz n'aura meurté
       La ou sourmonte voulenté.
       Tulles reputoit chose vaine
       D'ordonner jeune cappitaine:
625   Jeune president, jeune mire   [fol. 16r]
       Font plain gibet, plain cymetire.
       Pour ce disoit il que gastees
       Avoient esté et triboulees
       Pluiseurs choses par jeunes gens
630   Et reformees par anciens.⁷⁵
       On dit entre nous une fable
       Que vostre loy est charitable,
       Mais je vous dy pour verité
       Que nous avons plus charité
635   Entre nous autres Sarrazins
       Que vous n'avez a vos voisins.
       Regardés quel chevalerie,
       Quant noble gent, quel compagnie
       Avez perdue entre nous.⁷⁶

600 Then a cobbler, a silly tailor,
A mason, and a vintner
Will never be satisfied
If they don't have the same garment.
A merchant will wear a vermeil robe
605 Cut from fine fabric,
His wife dressed like a queen.
Someone who has neither house nor kitchen
Will be wearing furs of marten or of sable,
As the son of a duke would do;
610 And on account of this, they will be miserable
For when they have to be like the upper class,
They become larcenous, fraudulent,
And will therefore come to an evil end
Or return to their servile estate.
615 Still another policy
You have: for the administration of justice, you choose
From among your young people.
Young people are always in a boil,
And being a good judge demands a cool head;
620 One should be thoughtful and mature,
Because there will never be maturity involved
Where impulse prevails.
Tully thought it a silly thing
To make a young man a commander:
625 A young president, a young physician,
This makes for full gallows, and full cemeteries.
For this reason he said that
Many things had been damaged and
Destroyed by young folks,
630 And set right again by their elders.[75]
Among my people, we call it a fable
That your religion observes charity;
But I tell you, and make no mistake,
That we exhibit more charity
635 Among us Saracens
Than you do toward your own neighbors.
Consider how many knights,
How many nobles, what an assemblage
That you have lost to my people.[76]

640   Mais quel plainte en faittes vous?
      Je n'en voy nully qu'en souppire,
      Ne qu'en pleur, ne qui en laist rire;
      Tant avez de pitié, non plus,
      Com sy ne les eussiez veus.
645   O Dieux, quant noble chevalier
      Qui en ce temps a l'esprevier
      De ça s'aloient deporter,
      Qui maintenant les fault houer
      Et labourer vos festes toutes
650   Ou endurer xv ou vint soubtes!
      Vostre dimenche et Noé
      Les fault labourer mal leur gré,
      Aler sans chausses, sans chapel,
      Sans seinture et sans coustel,
655   Garder les brebis, les moutons,
      Mengant pou de pain sans oignons,
      Servir les beufz et les chevaulx
      A pluye, a vent, par les chesaulx.
      Jamais en lit ne coucheront   [fol. 16v]
660   Tant qu'en Turquie esclaux seront.
      Qui est entre vous qui en ce pense
      Ne qui cuide faire vengance
      De la grant honte et de la perte
      Que prindrent Crestiens celle feste?
665   Pour ce dy je que charité
      N'est entre Crestiens ne pité.
      Vous n'estudiez que en estas,
      En doulces veandes et plains plas.
      Crestienté ne vit qu'en bobance,
670   Et par especial gent de France.
      S'ilz ne fussent tant sur leur bouche,
      Sur blanc lit sur mole couche,
      Sur delit et sur femenie,
      Tant comme dure payennie,
675   Se tenissent bien ordonnance,
      Ne pourroit durer contre France.
      Par dessourdre et par orgueil
      Sont souvent venus a leur dueil.
      De ces deux choses pluiseurs foys

640 But have you taken any action over this?
I don't see anyone sighing,
Nor anyone weeping, nor anyone ceasing to laugh;
That's how much sympathy you have any more,
As if you had never set eyes on them.
645 Oh God, how many noble knights
Who, in this time of the sparrow-hawk hunt
Used to go out and amuse themselves in this land,
Who now must hoe the soil
And labor in the fields during your season of sport,
650 Or suffer through fifteen or twenty blows!
On your Sundays and on Christmas, even,
They have to work whether they want to or not,
And go without shoes, without a hat,
Without a belt and without a knife,
655 To watch the lambs and the sheep,
Eating a bit of bread with no onions,
To care for the cattle and the horses
In the rain, in the wind, through the wide plowed fields.
They will never sleep in a bed,
660 As long as they are slaves in Turkey.
Who among you thinks about this
Or considers taking vengeance
For the great shame and the loss
That Christians are suffering during this season?
665 This is why I say that you have no charity
Among you Christians, and no pity either.
All you care about is your social rank,
Your tender meats and your full plates.
All Christians do is live like epicures,
670 And especially the French.
If only they were as little concerned with their mouths,
With white beds and soft divans,
With pleasures and with women
As are the rugged Saracens,
675 If they obeyed their own laws,
There would be no one who could stand against the French.
Through disorder and pride,
Many have come to grief.
These are two things for which, many times,

680   Ay ouy trop blasmer Françoys."

134 Maistre Jehan parle au Sarrazin: [fol. 17r]

         "Sarrazin, n'alés plus avant,
         Car tu me fays le cuer dolant,
         Tant as aprins de nostre affaire.
         'Spete un pou et laisse faire!'
685   Ce dist bien souvent le Lombart,
         Car se tout nous advisons tart
         De la vilonnie qu'i[77] avons prise,
         Ne tardera, ce croy, l'emprise
         De celle honte sy vengier
690   Que vous l'acheteres bien chier.
         Car une prophecie disoit[78]
         Que le premier franc qui la yroit
         Seroit pris et sa compagnie,
         Mais celle mesmez prophecie
695   Met un retour de tel vengance
         Que mal en sera vostre pance.[79]
         Mais puis tu vas en Arragon,
         Dy nous laquelle trayson
         Cuidés traitter contre Crestiens."

135 Le Sarrazin respont: [fol. 17v]

700   "Sire, or soyez bien certains
         Que nous avons trop grant plaisir,
         Quant par dela vueulent souffrir
         Entre eulx pluiseurs Sarrazins,
         Sy les ayment comme voisins,
705   Et leur laissent armes porter,
         Estre hostelliers, gens hebergier,
         Viennent de quelconcques pays.
         Ainsy sont seigneurs par advis
         Par dela comme les Crestiens.

680   I have heard the French much censured."

134 Master Jean speaks to the Saracen:

      "Saracen, don't go any further,
      Because you give me a sorrowful heart,
      So well have you informed me about our affairs.
      'Hold on a moment, now it's my turn!'
685   This is what the Lombards often say,
      Because if, indeed, we have been slow
      In responding to the disgrace we endured there,[77]
      I don't think the reprisal will be long in the planning
      That will avenge this dishonor,
690   And you will pay dearly when it comes.
      For a prophecy has said[78]
      The first Frenchman who went there
      Would be captured along with his soldiers,
695   But this same prophecy
      Describes a return involving such vengeance
      That it will make you sick to your stomach.[79]
      But since you are going to Aragon,
      Tell us what treason
      You are intending to undertake against the Christians."

135 The Saracen responds:

700   "My lord, now you are quite certain
      That we are exceedingly happy
      When, down in Spain, they see fit to tolerate
      Among themselves a good many Saracens,
      Where they love them like neighbors,
705   And let them bear arms,
      Keep inns, lodge visitors
      Who come from many different countries.
      In this way they are like lords, and justifiably so,
      In Spain, the same as Christians.

710   Or y voy je seürs et sains
            Et puis bien avec eulx traittier
            Et leur dire tout par entier
            Les entreprinses de nos gens,
            A ce que regardent le temps,
715   S'ilz veoient leur avantage
            Pour recouvrer nostre heritage
            Que Charlemaine nous osta,
            Qui quatre royaumes occupa
            Nobles de nostre seignourie;[80]
720   Car cestuy temps par prophecie
            De Roche Seche nous sommoint[81]
            De recouvrer, s'il vient a point.
            Puis en Granade m'en yray
            Et le roy bien adviseray
725   Et sauray trestout son advis,
            Pour ce qu'il est pres du pays,
            Et combien aura il de gens
            Apris en armes bien lusans,
            Et que tousjours pluiseurs en mette,
730   A chevauchier a la genette.
            Aprés au partir de ly,   [fol. 18r]
            M'en yray en Belamary[82]
            Et aux autres roys qui sont dela
            Tant que vers miedy terre y a,
735   Puys retourneray a Bazat,[83]
            Sy en ma voye n'ay debat."

136 Maistre Jehan parle:

            "Sarrazin, vrayement vous dy
            Que pour tant n'en yrez de cy.
            Vous avez eu compagnie
740   Avec Crestiens en vostre vie:
            De nos fays dittes vo pensee."

137 Le Sarrazin respont:

710 Now I will go there in complete safety
And will be able to do business with them
And tell them everything
That our people are doing,
So that they will be ready when the time comes—
715 If they are conscious of their interests—
To take back our patrimony
That Charlemagne, who held four noble
Kingdoms of our aristocracy,
Took from us.[80]
720 Because this era—according to the prophecy
Of de Roquetaillade—summons us[81]
To reconquest, if that prophecy is accurate.
So, then to Granada I will go,
And I will consult with the king,
725 And I will hear all of his plans,
Because he knows his country well,
And how many people he will have,
Equipped in shining armor and weapons,
And how there are always many on the border,
730 Riding with stirrups up high.
After leaving him,
I will go to Belmarye[82]
And to the other kings who live there,
Down in the southern lands,
735 And then I will return to Bajazet,[83]
If I encounter no fighting along the way."

136 Master Jean speaks:

"Saracen, truly I tell you,
That you're not leaving here yet, in any case.
You have been associated
740 With Christians in your lifetime.
Tell us your thoughts about our behavior."

137 The Saracen replies:

"Sire, puys que bien vous agree:
J'ay bien veuz vos marchans,
D'ommes gentilz, la mer passans,
745 Et sy me suy bien advisés
En ceste voye, quant suy passes
Par la plus belle Crestienté.

[fol. 18v]

S'ay veu mainte noble cité
Et congneu mauvaiz usage
750 Qui bien sont contre mon courage:
Les marchans ne font que jurer,
Sy n'ont honte de parjurer.
Petis et grans sans renoer
Ne sauroient un mot parler.
755 L'un reny Dieu, l'autre la Mere,
Les uns le Filz, autres le Pere.[84]
A chascun mot dit: 'Par ma foy!'
Le Crestien, et 'Par ma loy!'
Et sy vous dy, par Mahommet,
760 Qu'il n'a cuer en ce que promet.
Et vecy un tres grant deffault,
C'est usage qui riens ne vault:
Uns homs vault tant com tient son dit.
Se il a ame ne esperit
765 Et puis vers son Dieu est parjurz,
Quelz homs yert avec luy seurz?[85]
Une autre chose congnois bien
Entre vous que ne prise rien:
Que ne gardes bien mariage,
770 Ains la ou sont plus de parage,
Sourvient souvent melancolie
Telz qu'ilz seront toute leur vie
Sans estre jamaiz bons amis.
Se l'un vit mal et l'autre pis.
775 Et se voisins a femme joyne,
Les autres bien mettront leur poine
D'elle bien tost desmarier,
Ou mariage varier.
Vecy mandement de loy

"My lord, since it pleases you:
I have seen your merchants,
And your nobles, as I sailed the seas,

745 And I have given it a good deal of thought
On this journey, as I passed
Through the most beautiful sights of Christendom.
I saw many noble cities
And observed bad habits

750 That are against my nature:
The merchants do nothing but curse,
And have no qualms about perjuring themselves.
Without blasphemous oaths, neither the great nor the lowly
Would be able to speak a word.

755 One swears by God, the other by the Madonna,
Some the Son, others the Father.[84]
For every other, the Christian adds
'By my faith!' and 'By my creed!'
And so I tell you, by Muhammad,

760 There is no surety behind their promises.
And this is truly a great failing,
This worthless custom of yours:
A man is only as good as his word.
If he has soul and spirit

765 And then perjures himself before his God,
Who will have trust in him?[85]
Another thing I know very well
That you esteem very little among yourselves:
You do not respect your marriages,

770 But instead, among the higher levels of society,
They come quite often to grief,
Such that they will spend their entire lives
Without ever having been good friends.
If one's life is bad, the other's is worse.

775 And if a neighbor has a young wife,
The others will surely take pains
To have her soon divorced,
Or to contest the marriage.
Here is a commandment of the law

780 Que vous ne gardés se bien poy.
De larrecins ne fault parler,
Car les larrons sont ça la mer. [fol. 19r]
Vivent soudoyers de leurs gages?
J'ay veu que plus grans dommages
785 En pays plat font qu'annemis.
Encorez font les sergens pis
Qui povre gent ne laissent vivre:
Dehors portent chapeau de bivre
Et se font servir comme roys,[86]
790 Je l'ay veu bien par pluiseurs foys.
Et sy n'avoy en mal aux dens
Quant veoie les povres gens
Plourer et eulx cryer mercy;
C'estoit pour neant, bien le vous dy.
795 Ancorez avez d'officiers
Tres plus que ne seroit mestiers.
Et s'ilz ont de leur seigneur gages,
Encores vueulent par oultrages
Avoir grant don chasque annee,
800 Soit montee, soit envalee,[87]
Et sy espargnent leur heritage.
Ne leur souffist il dont du gage
Et vivre bien de leur office?
Bien leur souffist l'amour du prince
805 Sans autres grans dons demander,
Car aux autres fault il donner.
Encorez y a plus grant oultrage,
Que se officiers fait mariage
De soy ou de filz ou de fille,
810 Vecy tres grande merville:
Il fault au roy payer la feste.
Par foy, vecy male tempeste!
Et pour l'office par dela
Aura plus que ne despendra,
815 Car chascun se tendroit pour nice,
Qui present ne fist a l'office. [fol. 19v]
N'ose dire des geoliers
Comment gouvernent prisonniers;
Mais on m'a dist par le chemin

780	That you hardly keep at all.
	You should not speak of criminals,
	Because there are so many of them here.
	Do soldiers live within their means?
	I have seen them do more damage,
785	In the countryside, than the enemy.
	And the sergeants are even worse,
	Who will not let the poor people live:
	When they go out, they wear beaver hats
	And are served like kings,[86]
790	I have seen this happen several times.
	And if it doesn't give you a toothache
	To see the poor people
	Weeping and crying for mercy from these men,
	Then it is all for nought, I tell you truly.
795	There are more of these officers,
	Many more, than are needed.
	And if they have a salary from their lord,
	They will still seek, through some chicanery,
	To obtain a fat gift every year,
800	Whether the lord has had a good year or bad,[87]
	And in this way they feather their nests.
	Does not their wage suffice
	For them to live well from their position?
	The love of their lord alone should be sufficient,
805	Without their asking for supplementary gifts,
	Because the lord needs to provide for others.
	And there is an even greater outrage,
	That when these officers get married,
	Or their sons or their daughters,
810	Behold a great wonder:
	The king has to pay for the wedding.
	My word, this is a disaster!
	And the officers here
	Will have more than they need for expenses,
815	Since anyone would be considered a fool
	Who did not grease the officer's palm.
	I do not dare to speak of how jailers
	Oversee their prisoners;
	But I have been told along the way

820   Qu'ilz en ont le vaissel et le vin:
       Ne or ny argent ne emportera
       Le prisonnier quant partira.
       Quant on lui dist qu'il fait pechié,[88]
       Et il respont tost de rechié
825   Que la geole lui vent on chier[89]
       Et qu'il n'y perdra ja denyer.
       Se le roy savoit qu'on y fait,
       Jamais ne souffreroit tel fait.
       Puys tant ay parlé, je vous pry:
830   Laissiez moy tenir mon chemin."

138 Maistre Jehan parle au Sarrazin:

       "Par Dieu, sire, n'empartirés
       Encorez plus avant dirés.
       Puis que par Romme estes passés,
       Dittes ent ce que vous penses   [fol. 20r]
835   De l'estat de dant Boniface,[90]
       Car je pense, par saint Eustase,
       Que vous l'avés bien advisé."

139 Le Sarrazin respont:

       "Sire, je vous dy mal mon gré
       Tout ce que j'ay en mon advis.
840   J'ay veu tant vers et tant gris
       Porter et fines escarlastes,
       Tant grans robes, tant belles chappes,
       Tant grans chevaulx et tant destriers,
       Tant chappellains, tant d'escuiers,
845   Tant de varlés et servitours,
       Tant belles salles, tant beaux atours,
       Tant de vaisselle, tant parement,
       Se n'est c'un songe vrayement
       De l'haultesse et mondiel gloire.
850   Car a paine m'en pourroit croyre
       De cel atour, de l'appareil,
       Car entre nous ne l'a pareil,
       Et que parlons des nostrez roys.
       Ne vivent de lart ne de poys,

820 That their tableware and wine, they get from prisoners:
Neither gold nor silver will he take with him,
The prisoner who leaves the jail.
When someone tells him that this is a crime,[88]
And he always replies at once
825 That the jail cost him a great deal of money[89]
And that he'll never lose a single cent while running it.
If the king knew what went on there,
He would never tolerate such a thing.
But now that I have spoken so much, I beg of you:
830 Let me resume my journey."

138 Master Jean speaks to the Saracen:

"By God, my lord, do not leave us
Before you have told us yet more things.
Since you have passed through Rome,
Tell us what you think
835 About the conditions at the court of lord Boniface,[90]
For I believe, by Saint Eustace,
That you have much pondered on it."

139 The Saracen replies:

"Lord, I tell you against my will
Everything that I have in my thoughts.
840 I have seen so much green, so much grey
Being worn, and fine fabrics,
So many great robes, so many gorgeous capes,
So many horses and so many chargers,
So many chaplains, so many squires,
845 So many valets and servants,
So many beautiful halls, such fine headdresses,
So many dishes, so much ornamentation,
That it can only be a dream, really,
Of magnificence and earthly glory.
850 For I could hardly believe
The sight of all that finery, those special preparations,
Because among my people, there is nothing comparable,
Even if we speak only of our kings.
[In Rome,] they do not live on lard and peas,

855   Ains menguent plus belles veandes,
        Plus coulourees et plus friandes[91]
        Que je visse onc en tisnel.
        Servir de table est sy bel,
        Touailles blanches et plas dorés,
860   Preuves[92] et naux de noble frés,
        Trenchouers d'or ou d'argent fin,
        Les mes triples et le fort vin,
        Gelee franche, blans mengiers
        Viennent par devant sans dangiers,
865   Puis nobles fruiz, frommage gras.   [fol. 20v]
        Ne scay comment portent ly las
        Tant de traveil par vostre Eglise,
        Mais encor dont vient tant grant mise
        Me suy merveillié souvent,
870   Ne qui paye ce que despent
        Tant grande court com il y a.
        Car Bonnifaces ne tient ja
        Tout seul l'estat que j'ay parlé.
        Ilz sont, se je n'ay mal compté,
875   Treize portans chappeaulx rouges
        Qui tiennent l'estat, sans mensonges,
        Plus curieux que roys du monde,
        Plus net servy, hostel plus blonde,
        Et fors que bien pou chevauchier
880   Ilz n'ont paine ne grant dangier.
        Et sy vouldroye bien savoir
        Dont leur vient tant qu'ilz ont d'avoir,
        Car tout un monde seroit las
        De soustenir tant grans estas.
885   Encor vouldroye bien savoirs
        S'ilz sont emperieres[93] ou roys,
        Car s'ilz estoient hommez d'eglise,
        Ce seroit une pompe nice
        En orgueil mettre devocion,
890   Au monde donner achoison
        D'amer delis et friande vie,
        Pompes, haultesses, seignourie.
        Pour quoy me dittes qui ilz sont,
        Dont sont venus, ne que vous font.

855	But eat much finer meats,
	Of better color and more appetizing[91]
	Than anything I ever saw at a banquet.
	The table service is so beautiful,
	White napkins and gilded plates,
860	Tasting-dishes,[92] and serving-boats costing princely sums,
	Carving knives of gold or of fine silver,
	Three main courses and the strong wine,
	Clear jelly, blancmanges
	Carried to table without any trouble,
865	Then fine fruits and rich cheeses.
	I do not know how the poor creatures survive
	All this toil for your church.
	But where does such lavishness come from—
	It often amazes me—
870	And who pays the bill
	For such a grand life as this?
	For Boniface is not the only one to maintain
	This grand estate that I have described.
	There are, if my count is not mistaken,
875	Thirteen wearing red cardinal's hats
	Who maintain this estate, and that's no lie;
	More greedy than worldly kings,
	More pampered, and with such spotless residences,
	And except for the few times they have to mount a horse,
880	They know neither discomfort nor great danger.
	And I would really like to know
	From whence comes all their wealth,
	Because it would make the whole world tired
	To maintain such extravagant lifestyles.
885	And I would also like to know
	If they be emperors or kings,[93]
	Because if they are clergymen,
	It would be a rather silly practice
	To worship Pride in such a way,
890	To inspire the world
	To love pleasures and voluptuous living,
	Magnificence, grandeur, power.
	Therefore tell me who they are,
	And whence they have come, and what they do to you.

895   Vous me faittes tour de Lombart,
       Qui par engin et par son art
       Veult savoir d'autruy la pensee
       Et la sienne tenir celee."

140 Maistre Jehan parle au Jacobin: [fol. 21r]

       "Sire, vous avez bien ouy
900   Les questions de ce Sarrazin;
       Je vous pry que les declairez,
       Car bien croy, faire le saurés."

141 Le Jacobin respont:

       "Le grant Boece dit, pour voir,
       Que tres fort empeche savoir
905   Douleur de cuer et la destresse;
       Car homme qui aye tristesse
       N'aura ja memoire certaine.⁹⁴
       Or suy je venus a grant paine
       Veoir d'un bien loingtain pays,
910   Pour lire, se puis, a Paris.
       Mais on m'a dit que non feray,
       Car nostre mere, sans delay,
       Se je lisoie une lesson,
       Me feroit mettre en prison.
915   Car tous Jacobins sont prive   [fol. 21v]
       Des fays de l'université⁹⁵
       Et quant ce Sarrazin saura
       Que entre nous tieulx debas a,
       Il en aura joye sans faillir.
920   D'autre chose n'a il desir,
       Par especial se sur la foy
       Avions discorde ne desroy.
       Sy devroit on bien labourer
       Comment on puist tost accorder:
925   Ce debat qui tant a duré.
       Cellui par qui vint ne fust né!⁹⁶
       Mal vismes jamais de Mouson
       Tuit cil de la religion,
       Car certes sa melancolie,

895   You're dealing with me like the Lombard,
      Who by cunning and cleverness
      Seeks to know the thoughts of others,
      While keeping his own thoughts hidden."

140 Master Jean speaks to the Jacobin:

      "My lord, you have now heard
900   The questions of this Saracen;
      I beg you to clarify them,
      For I well believe that you know how to do that."

141 The Jacobin replies:

      "The great Boethius says, in truth,
      That they are very great impediments to knowledge,
905   Heartache and anguish;
      For he who experiences grief
      Will never more have clear memory.[94]
      Now I have come in great hardship
      From a very distant country,
910   To lecture, if I might, at Paris.
      But I am told that this will not be done,
      For our mother, the University of Paris, without delay,
      Were I to give a single lecture,
      Would have me thrown into prison.
915   For all Dominicans are denied
      The offices of the University,[95]
      And when this Saracen finds out
      That there are such disagreements between us,
      He will never lack for levity.
920   He desires nothing more—
      Especially if in matters of religion—
      Than that we have discord and confusion.
      We should therefore work hard
      To find a way to reconcile ourselves quickly:
925   This conflict has gone on too long.
      The one who made it come to pass should never have been born![96]
      Ever after, evil has come as a result of Monzon
      To all of his order,
      For surely his bad humor,

930   Sa mauvaistié, sa baverie
       Donné a pluiseurs bons grant blasme,
       Et nous a mis sur tous diffame.
       Mais nostre doulce belle mere
       Devroit regarder nostre pere,
935   Qui de Dieu fut tant bons amis:
       Saint Domenge, qui nous assis.
       Aussy devroit avoir memoire
       Du grant dotteur de haulte gloire,
       Monseigneur saint Thomas d'Aqui;
940   Car longuement son filz fut cy,[97]
       Et escript maint livres notables,
       Je n'en dy mensonges ne fables.
       Le noble saint Pierre Martir[98]
       Ne vouloit pas la foy mentir,
945   Quant pour soustenir la loy fort
       Porta tant maulx et puis la mort.
       Cilz qui ordonna les decretables,[99]
       Tant bien dittees, tant creables,
       Fut de nostre religion;   [fol. 22r]
950   Puis fist somme sur droit canon
       Pour donner a pluiseurs dottrine.
       Jehan d'Alemant, com parle fine,[100]
       Fist un livre de tel emprise
       Qu'il a en grant clart mise
955   Science des loys et des decrés.
       Ne doy laissier qui vint aprés,
       Cellui qu'on fist le "questionnary";
       Ne fut pas petit exemplary.
       Celle Somme des Confesseurs
960   Est ly grans maistres de leurs fleurs:
       Des sains ne fait pas a blasmer.
       Et sy devroit on bien loer
       Le Vincent qui escript tant livres.[101]
       Du roy Phelippe prenoit vivres[102]
965   Pour ce que mieulx peust vaquer
       En science pour tout dottriner,
       Car mains clers sy laissent d'escripre
       Pour ce qu'ilz n'ont bien de quoy vivre.
       La Tripertite, je vous supply,

930 His corruption, his loose talk
   Have given many good people a bad name,
   And have caused every one of us to be defamed.
   But our sweet, beautiful mother
   Should have a look at our father,
935 Who was such a good friend of God's:
   Saint Dominic, who founded our order.
   She should also recall
   The great and glorious doctor,
   My lord St. Thomas Aquinas;
940 Because for a long time he was her son here,[97]
   And wrote many significant books.
   I don't tell any lies or fables about it.
   The noble saint Peter Martyr[98]
   Did not wish to deny his faith,
945 And so for strongly upholding the law
   He endured many wounds and then death.
   He who compiled the *Decretals*,[99]
   So well composed, so trustworthy,
   Was of our order;
950 Then he wrote a *Summa* on canon law
   To bring learning to many others.
   John of Germany like a rare pearl,[100]
   Wrote a book of such magnitude
   That it brought great clarity
955 To knowledge of the law and the decrees.
   She [the University] should not overlook those who came afterward.
   He who wrote the *Questionarius*—
   It was no small leaflet.
   This *Summa confessorum*
960 Is the matchless exemplar of its genre:
   It does not blame saints.
   And so he should truly be praised,
   The Vincent who wrote so many books.[101]
   He was supported by King Philip[102]
965 So that he could better dedicate himself
   To learning, so as to teach everyone,
   For many in the clergy stop writing
   Because they have no means of supporting themselves.
   The *Tripartita*, I ask you,

970   Doit estre misë en oubly?
       Guydon de nostre ordre la fist,[103]
       Et avec cela aprés complist
       Les hystoires jusqu'a son temps:
       Ce n'est pas un livre vileins.
975   Cilz qui fist Livre des Vertus[104]
       Fut grans amis du bon Jhesus,
       Et sy fist Somme de tous vices.
       N'est pas qui l'entent du tout nices.
       Et se je vouloye tout dire
980   Qui ont mis paine en bien escripre
       De l'ordre nous prescheours,
       J'en seroye trop annuyoux.   [fol. 22v]
       Puis nostre 'mere,' passe temps,
       A eu de nous telz 'enfans';
985   Souvent li en devroit souvenir,
       Et, pour faire le desplaisir
       De ces Sarrazins de mal estre,
       Nous retourner au premier estre.
       Car eulx et Juifz ont grant joye
990   Quant voyent que l'en nous desroye.
       Et se Mouson a sommé mal,
       La religion qui est feal
       N'en doit pas avoir turbacion
       A tousjours sans conclusion.
995   Car la mere son filz chastie
       Et puis l'embrace chiere lie.
       Sy lisons es Fais des Rommains
       Que par les bons notables fays
       Des peres, les filz oultrageux
1000 Trouvoyent mercy entre eulx.[105]
       Sy n'est pas grant melancolie
       Se en sy grande compagnie
       Se treuve un homme mauvais,
       Qui face aucuns mauvais fays;
1005 Car avec Jhesu le grant sire
       Ot un traytre qui fut pire.
       Et pour ce vous vueil je pryer
       Que vueilliez au roy supplyer
       Et a tous les duz nos seigneurs,

970 Should it be forgotten?
Bernard Gui, of our order, wrote it,[103]
And later also completed
A history, up to his own day:
It is no insignificant book.
975 He who wrote the *Summa de virtutibus*[104]
Was a good friend of the good lord Jesus,
And also wrote the *Summa de vitiis*.
This is hardly someone with foolish aims.
And if I wanted tell of everyone
980 Who strove to write moral books
In our Order of Preachers,
I would be much too verbose and boring.
In days gone by, therefore, our 'mother'
Has had 'children' like these from among us;
985 She ought to be conscious of this more often,
And, to bring discomfiture
To these wicked Saracens,
She should return us to the first rank.
For they and the Jews are very glad
990 When they see that we are in disarray.
And if Monzon's pronouncements were in error,
The order itself, which is faithful and loyal,
Should not be thrown into turmoil
Forever, with no hope of ending.
995 Because the mother chastises her son,
But afterwards takes him joyfully in her arms.
And we read in the *Gesta Romanorum*
How, through the noble and remarkable deeds
Of their fathers, profligate sons
1000 Found mercy among their people.[105]
It is therefore not too great an unhappiness
If, among such a great company,
One bad man is found,
Who does some wicked things;
1005 Because with Jesus, the great lord,
There went a traitor who did worse.
And for this reason I wish to ask
That you see fit to implore the king
And all the royal dukes, our lords.

1010 Qu'ilz facent traittié gracieux
Comment vers nous soit nostre mere
Comme vers filz doit estre pere.
Aprés cecy je respondray
Au Sarrazin mieulx que sauray."

142 Le Jacobin parle au Sarrazin: [fol. 23r]

1015 "Tu es esbays, noir malostru,
Car tu as telz estas veu
Demener a Romme la grant.
Tu t'es esbays, c'est pour neant,
Car se en temps de unité[106]
1020 Fussez venus en Crestienté,
Tu ne prisasses pas un blanc
Ce que as veu maintenant.
N'a pas grant temps, mouru Gregoire;[107]
Je te dy que toute la gloire
1025 Du plus hault seigneur terrien
Vers son estat estoit pou rien.
La ne failloit pompe ne mise
Que herault sceust a devise,
Richesse du tout sourmontant
1030 Tout prince qui lors fut vivant.
Mais car Dieux veult que soubz la nue
Ne soit estat qui ne se mue,
Il se monstre trestout puissant
Quant les plus hault met au neant.   [fol. 23v]
1035 Se n'y a nul puissant terrien
Qui soit seurs de tenir bien;
Car la on cuide fort ister,
Souvent le fait Dieu trebuchier.
Dont ly plus sages Salemon
1040 Nous aprist faire oroison
A Dieu son pere par amour
Que il nous doint le pain d'un jour.
Il n'y a haultesse, tant soit grant,
Soit seure du temps venant:

1010   That they make a generous truce,
       So that our mother will be toward us
       The way a father ought to be with his son.
       After this, I will reply
       To the Saracen better than I now can."

142 The Jacobin speaks to the Saracen:

1015   "You are shocked, black miscreant,
       Because you have seen such lifestyles
       Being led in the great city of Rome.
       You are surprised, and for no reason;
       For if during the time of unity[106]
1020   You had come into Christendom,
       You would not think anything at all
       Of what you have seen this time.
       Not long ago, Gregory died;[107]
       I tell you, all the glory
1025   Of the highest temporal lord
       Was but a small thing compared to his court.
       There was lacking no pomp or expense there
       That a herald would be familiar with,
       Wealth surpassing by far
1030   Every prince who ever lived.
       But since it is God's wish that, below the skies,
       There be no condition that does not change,
       He shows himself to be the most mighty
       When he causes the highest to be brought low.
1035   There is, therefore, no powerful man on earth
       Who can be sure of maintaining his estate,
       Because the one who firmly believes he will survive
       Often is cast down by God.
       For this reason, Solomon, the wisest of men,
1040   Taught us to offer songs of praise
       To God, his father, out of love for him,
       So that he will give us our daily bread.
       There is no eminence, however great,
       That can rest secure, in the time to come:

1045 En un point met le bas bien hault,
En un autre fait qu'il deffault.
Quant parles de ses grans vassaulx,
Il les appelle cardinaulx;
Et sy sont ilz de science plains,
1050 Ses conseilliers, ses chappellains.
Mais a dire dont sont venu
Quant a l'estat, ne l'ay pas leu.
Ilz furent premier appellé
Les chapelains de la cité.
1055 Et pour ce qu'au commencement
Furent proudommes et bonnes gent,
Se estoit par leur proudomie
Honnoree la compagnie.
Un emperiere leur donna
1060 Rentes, et bien les assigna,[108]
Dont ilz pouoient bien porter
Leur vie, sans riens mendier.
Ly pappes ne leur donna mitres,
Mais sur ces rentes donna tiltres
1065 D'une eglise a chascun d'eulx,
Pour ce qu'on les congnoisse mieulx.
Et sy avoient grant plaisir,   [fol. 24r]
Quant approuchoient d'enviellir,
S'ilz, pour viellesse reposer,
1070 Peussent eveschié empetrer;
Et bien petite la prenoient
Et pour bien contens s'en tenoient.
Et sy furent bien longuement
En cel humble istement,
1075 Tant que par tort des faulx Romains
Fut ostee hors de leurs mains
L'eleccion, vaquant la chaere,
Laquel Romains avoient entiere.[109]
Lors l'eleccion nostre saint pere
1080 Sy fut mise, pour elle fere,
Aux cardinaulx pour pape nommer,
Dont comencerent eulx d'essaucer,
Tant que d'eulx evesques seigneurs
Ont depuis fait leurs serviteurs.

1045   In one place, God makes the lowly to be exalted,
        And in another, causes a deficiency.
        When you speak of those great vassals,
        They are called "cardinals";
        And if they are full of learning,
1050   They are counselors and chaplains.
        But to tell you how they came
        To live in such a manner: I have no idea.
        They were at first called
        The chaplains of the city.
1055   And because of this, at the beginning
        They were worthy men, good people,
        And so it was that by their worthiness
        The entire assemblage there was honored.
        An emperor granted them
1060   Annuities, and really did assign them,[108]
        And in this way they could certainly endure
        Their lives, without any needs or wants.
        The pope didn't just give them mitres,
        But to these revenues he attached titles
1065   For a specific parish to each one of them,
        So that people would come to know them.
        And so they were very happy,
        When they grew older,
        If they could obtain a bishopric
1070   So as to have ease in their old age;
        And they would accept a small one,
        And count themselves very fortunate.
        And so for a very long time they were
        In this humble state of affairs,
1075   Until the dishonest Romans, as a result of their own evil,
        Had the right of election—
        The papal throne being vacant—taken from their hands,
        Which heretofore had belonged to the Romans exclusively.[109]
        Then, the election of our Holy Father
1080   Was given over
        To the cardinals, who would choose the new pope;
        Because of this, they began to exalt themselves,
        To such an extent that, for them, our lords the bishops
        Since then have been their servants.

1085 Sy dirent a nostre saint pere
     Qu'il pouoit toutes choses fere
     Quant prindrent le rouge chappel.
     Ne treuve livre lait ne bel
     Qui le me die clerement,
1090 Sy m'en suy estudiez souvent.
     Mais assez trouveront d'estas
     Qui de richesse sont fourras.
     Sy firent reserver dignités,[110]
     Toutes eglises, tout prevostés,
1095 Tout chanoiniez, tout priorés,
     Et trestout quanque vient aprés.
     Ly pappes le fist voulentiers
     Pour estre seigneur par entiers.[111]
     Les cardinaulx trouverent l'art
1100 Pour ce qu'en eussent leur part,
     Et pour eulx et pour leurs amis
     Avoir l'Eglise a leur devis.   [fol. 24v]
     S'en ont tant pris a toutes mains
     Que par le monde les plus grans
1105 Ont ilz euz pour leurs amis
     Ou pour eulx, tout a leur devis.
     N'alasses en court riens querir,
     Se ce ne fust a leur plaisir;
     Ne dy pas, fussent courratiers
1110 Pour aucuns en prenant deniers.
     Encorez fit il entendant
     Que il avoit a faire tant
     Que pour l'eglise soustenir
     Il pouoit tres bien retenir
1115 De chascun vacant prime annee.[112]
     Et se ly mors avoit laissee
     Grant richesse ne grant avoir,
     Il le pouoit prendre, pour voir.
     Les cardinaulx y ont chascun
1120 Leur part pour service commun.
     Aprés, com vit qu'obeissance
     Estoit par tout et reverence,
     Orez fut lieu de faire un sault:
     "Sur tout," le pape dist, "il nous fault

1085 Indeed, they told our Holy Father
   That they could do anything
   When they put on the red hat.
   I have never found a book, homely or comely,
   That could explain this to me clearly,
1090 And I have often examined the question.
   But those who are wild about riches
   Will find many positions.
   Indeed, they have benefices reserved for them.[110]
   All churches, all provostships,
1095 All canonries, all priorships,
   And everything that comes after.
   The pope does this willingly
   So he can have dominion over everyone.[111]
   The cardinals invented the art
1100 Of always getting their share of the goods,
   Both for them and their friends,
   Of having the Church at their disposal.
   Indeed, they have taken so much, with both hands,
   That they have the most powerful people in the world
1105 As their friends,
   Or on their side—everything their hearts desire.
   Do not go to court to ask for anything
   Unless it be something that would please them;
   Do not tell them that accepting bribes
1110 Makes them brokers to those who give them.
   And yet he [the pope] made it known
   That he had to do so much
   In order to sustain the Church,
   That he could very well retain
1115 The first year of revenue from each vacant office.[112]
   And if a dead man had left
   Great wealth and many possessions,
   He could most certainly take it.
   The cardinals each get
1120 Their share of it for their service.
   And afterwards, when the Pope saw that he was obeyed
   Everywhere, and revered,
   Now was the time to make a leap:
   "Most of all," said the pope, "we must

1125 "Avoir le disme pour iii ans."[113]
    Les prelas furent assez vains,
    Sy commencerent a obeir,
    Mais a tart les virent faillir.
    Lors fut la court en grant haultesse,
1130 En grant pompe, en grant richesse.
    Mais pour faire plus grans maisons
    Fallut prendre visitacions
    Par toutes eglises du monde.
    Mais quant Grece vit ainsy fondre[114]
1135 Leur richesse et aler vers Romme,
    Ilz prindrent conclusion en somme   [fol. 25r]
    De non obeir plus avant,
    Et sy mirent des debas tant,
    Que toute Crestienté sainte
1140 En mena douleur et complainte.
    Encor pour mieulx estre delivrés
    Et que fussent entre eulx sires,
    Vont dire que Constantinoble
    Avoit pape tout franc, tout noble.
1145 Et pour mieulx fonder leur appel,
    Vont tenir article nouvel
    Contre ce que creons deça,
    Lequel soustiennent par dela.
    Et ce fut tout par tirannye,
1150 Dont vient non sens, dont vient folie,
    Dont vient toute rebellion:
    L'Eglise pas ne fit son pron.[115]
    L'en ne pourroit dire la moittie
    Des maulx venus par tirannie,
1155 Car, se j'ay vrayement leu,
    Les Sarrazins en sont venu.
    Car puis les Grieux furent partis
    Par la maniere que vous dys,
    L'emperiere, nommé Justin,[116]
1160 Amoyt or comme noys corbin,
    S'estoit tirans sur tous mortelz;
    Oncques ne fut un plus cruelz.
    Tant greva les gens d'orient
    Qu'il ot leur or et leur argent.

1125 Have tithes for three years."[113]
     The prelates were rather impotent,
     And so at first they obeyed,
     But later one could see that they did no longer.
     The court became greatly exalted at this time,
1130 In great splendor, great luxury.
     Moreover, in order to build bigger houses,
     It was necessary to make inspection tours
     Of all the parishes in the world.
     But when the Greeks saw that this was dissolving[114]
1135 Their wealth, and causing it to flow toward Rome,
     They came to the conclusion, at the end,
     Not to obey any more as before,
     And quarreled so much
     That all of Holy Christendom
1140 Was in anguish and lamentation as a result.
     And finally, to assure themselves of their liberty,
     And to be their own masters,
     They will say that Constantinople
     Had its own pope, sovereign and noble.
1145 And, the better to establish their claim,
     They will adopt a new article of law
     Counter to that which we believe here
     But that they uphold in that region.
     And this was all because of tyranny,
1150 From whence comes not reason but only folly,
     From whence comes all rebellion;
     The Church did not do what it should have done.[115]
     One could not tell you half
1155 Of the evils that come from tyranny,
     Because, if I have read correctly,
     The Saracens came as a result.
     For once the Greeks had taken their leave
     In the manner I have told you,
     The emperor, named Justin,[116]
1160 Loved gold the way a crow loves nuts,
     And was a tyrant over everyone alive;
     There was never anyone more cruel.
     It greatly grieved the people of the East
     That he took away their gold and silver.

1165 Quant ceulx se virent despouilliez,
     Ilz cryerent com hommes fiers
     Contre le tirant seignourie.
     Sy fut moult grande compagnie
     Qui se va mettre sur les champs.   [fol. 25v]
1170 L'emperiere, qu'estoit puissans,
     Vint avant, sy les combaty;
     Mais en la fin en champ perdy,
     Sy s'en fouy en Coustanty,
     Reprist son pueple plus hardy
1175 Et retourna pour eulx combatre.
     Les autres furent pour un quatre:
     Se fut autre foys desconfit.
     Et pour ce le pape requist
     Qu'il lui voulsist secourir tost:
1180 Ly papes ly envoya bon ost
     Au moins pour garder son pays.
     Quant les autres orent apris
     Que ly papes avoit ce fait,
     Ilz commencerent nouvel plait,
1185 Sy dirent que la foy du pape
     Ne estoit bonne ne valable,
     Et ainsy, par despit de ly,
     Firent Mahommet[117] Sarrazin
     Leur cappitaine souverein,
1190 Et il les enseigna tant bien
     Qu'il leur fist lessier nom Crestien
     Et prendre nom de Sarrazin.
     Tout le dommage que vous dy
     Vint seulement par tirannye.
1195 L'Eglise en fut amendrie.
     Or l'ay je dit a ce propos
     Que les papes prindrent ce los
     Et les cardinaulx jusqu'a cy,
     Que de pou en pou, je vous dy,
1200 Ont rungié toute la clergie,
     Tant grevee et tant chargie,
     Qu'ilz puent tenir grant estat
     Plus que ne fait vostre Bazat.   [fol. 26r]
     Oultre cela par Crestienté

1165 When they saw themselves so despoiled,
They cried out like fierce men
Against the tyrannous rulership,
And there was a very large company
That went onto the field of battle.
1170 The emperor, who was powerful,
Took the van, and thus gave battle;
But in the end he lost the day
And fled to Constantinople,
Gathered his more stalwart soldiers
1175 And returned to do battle against them.
The others outnumbered them four to one:
And so he was once again put to flight.
And because of this he asked the pope
To help at once.
1180 The pope sent him an army,
Strong enough to defend his own country.
When the others had heard about
What the pope had done,
They began a new protestation,
1185 Saying that the pope's word
Was not to be trusted,
And so, to avenge themselves on him,
They made Muhammad the Saracen[117]
Their sovereign leader,
1190 And he taught them so well
That they forsook the name of "Christian"
And adopted the name "Saracen."
All the harm I am telling you about
Is the fault of tyranny alone.
1195 The Church was diminished as a result.
Now, I mentioned this matter
That the popes adopted this policy
And the cardinals up to this point
Because little by little, I tell you,
1200 They have devoured the entire clergy,
So afflicted and so encumbered them,
So that they can maintain extravagant lifestyles,
Greater even than does your Bajazet.
Aside from that, throughout Christendom

1205   Les cardinaulx ont empetré
        Les dignités, les benefices,
        Et sy se tiennent bien pour nices,
        Quant trestous ne les puent avoir.
        N'en auroient assez, pour voir!
1210   Et vecy la raison pour quoy
        Ilz puent tenir l'estat d'un roy:
        Car nulz homs mortelz ne scet bien
        L'or qui a court de Romme vient.
        Sy en sont eglises grevees
1215   Et pluiseurs abbayez foulees;
        Pluiseurs conventuelz priorés
        Sont de leurs moynes despoullés;
        Pluiseurs moustiers et hostelz notables
        Sont cheuz et inreparables.
1220   Ne servent pas tant Crestienté
        Qu'ilz deussent pour verité
        Tant occuper des benefices,
        Car s'en pert le divin services.
        Et ceulx qui eglises douairent
1225   Oncques vrayement ne penserent
        Que ce fust pour tenir, en somme,
        Les grans estas de court de Romme,
        Pour acheter bien grans cités,
        Grans baronnies ne grans contés[118]
1230   Aux freres, nepveux ou parens
        Du pape ne des adherens,
        Dont l'Eglise en est vil tenue,
        Mesprisié et confondue.
        Et veez vous la, dant Sarrazy,
1235   La response que je vous dy.
        Mais je croy, le temps est venus
        Qu'ilz ne en seront plus creuz,   [fol. 26v]
        Car ly mondes voit par exprez
        Leurs oultrages et leurs excez,
1240   Sy feront tant princes et clers
        Que, puis qu'ilz ont fait droit envers,
        Ilz retourneront l'envers droit,
        Pour ce que chascun aye droit.
        C'est nature de desmesure

1205   The cardinals have obtained
        Privileges, benefices,
        And so consider themselves foolish
        If they cannot acquire everything.
        They will never have enough, that is clear!
1210   And here is the reason why
        They can maintain the lifestyle of a king:
        Because nobody on earth could fathom
        The amount of gold that comes into the court of Rome.
        In this way are parishes plundered,
1215   And many abbeys looted;
        The priories of many orders
        Have been despoiled of their monks;
        Many monasteries and important religious houses
        Are dilapidated and irreparable.
1220   It has been no service to Christianity
        That they, in truth should have
        Occupied so many benefices,
        Because as a result the Mass and sacraments are lost.
        And those who endow churches
1225   Never truly considered
        That what this gift really did was support
        The great households at the court of Rome,
        And support the purchase of great cities,
        Great baronies and great counties[118]
1230   For the brothers, nephews or relatives
        Of the pope and his cronies,
        As a result of which the Church is seen as debased,
        Despicable, and troubled.
        Behold, therefore, Lord Saracen,
1235   The answer that I give to you.
        But I believe that the time has come
        When they will no longer be believed,
        For the world sees very clearly
        Their misdeeds and their luxuriance,
1240   And since Rome has turned the law upside down,
        Many princes and clergy
        Will turn the law back the proper way
        So that everyone will have rights again.
        It is the very essence of intemperance

1245   Que tousjours revient a mesure.
        Tousjours veons, par saint Lambert,
        Que qui trestout veult, trestout pert.
        Tel avarice tient l'abisme[119]
        D'enfer et sy engendre scisme.
1250   Avarice tous biens decline
        Et de tout mal est la racine,
        Pry vous, maistre Jehan de Meun,
        Que se je n'ay bien respondu,
        Vous plaise le moy pardonner,
1255   Car n'en sauroye mieulx parler."

143 Maistre Jehan parle au Jacobin: [fol. 27r]

        "Par Dieu, sire bon Jacobin,
        Vous estes de Dieu bon amy;
        Mais ja ne vous lairay pour rien
        Se non dittes du phisicien
1260   Sur ce qu'il a dit par avant
        Vostre bon et loyal samblant."

144 Le Jacobin respont:

        "Sire, gent qui sachant ne sont
        A tart ne moy ne autre croiront
        Que li cas soit tant perilleux,
1265   Ne tant fiers, ne tant oultrageux,
        Comme il est entre nous clergaulx;
        Il est tres griefz, tres lait, tres maulx,
        Car est adviz par theologie
        Qu'il approuché ydolatrie
1270   Invoquer l'esperit mauvez
        Pour savoir de Dieu les secrez,
        Et ce qu'est ou seul Dieu sans fable
        Vouloir faire par art du deable.
        Penser guerir de maladie,
1275   Sans Dieu, par art, pres d'erisie
        Vient ou de anfidelité.
        No mere, l'université,
        Monstrera bien endroit de soy,
        Se ce est contre nostre foy.

1245   To return always to continence.
        We always see, by St. Lambert,
        That he who covets everything, loses everything.
        Such greed comes from the abyss[119]
        Of hell, and thus began the schism.
1250   Greed degrades all things good,
        And is the root of all evil.
        I beg you, master Jean de Meun,
        That, if I have not responded well,
        You deign to forgive me,
1255   For I can speak no better."

143 Master Jean speaks to the Jacobin:

        "By God, my good lord Jacobin,
        You are a good friend of God,
        But I will never abandon
        Your good and faithful person,
1260   If you say something about
        What the Physician said earlier."

144 The Jacobin replies:

        "My lord, ignorant people
        Will wrongly disbelieve me and my fellows
        When we say the situation is so dangerous,
1265   So severe, so extreme,
        As it is among us clerics;
        It is most grave, most vile, most evil,
        Because theology tells us
        That it gets very close to idolatry
1270   To invoke the evil spirit
        So as to know God's secrets,
        And to seek to do that which is truly God's alone
        Through the power of the devil.
        To presume to cure sicknesses
1275   Without God, by art—out of something near to heresy
        It comes, from the infidels.
        Our mother, the University,
        Will show clearly and definitively,
        That this is against our faith.

1280   Et dire tout pour verité:[120]
        'Je vueil avoir le chief coupé,
        Se dans troys jours guery nen est
        Cellui qui bien malades est':
        C'est affermer temps advenir,
1285   Ce que nulz ne scet sans mentir
        Fors Dieux, car cilz faillir nen puet
        De savoir quanque savoir veult.
        Les angelz[121] bien voyent, dessus,   [fol. 27v]
        En contemplant le dieu Jhesus,
1290   Les choses qui sont advenir;
        Et aux prophetes par son plaisir
        Revele souvent son vouloir.
        Mais encor retient son pouoir
        Par non advenir dispenser
1295   Et son courroux faire cesser.
        Dont un homme mortel et vain
        Ne puet dire tout pour certain:
        'Tel chose sy est advenir
        Et se sera, nen puet faillir.'
1300   Tel oppinion est tres nice;
        La soustenir est tres grant vice.
        Mais, quant c'est cas tres creminel,
        Je ne vous en vueil plus parler.''

145 Maistre Jehan parle au Jacobin:

        ''Mon maistre le prescheour,
1305   Je vous prie par bonne amour
        Qu'encorez dittes un pou plus
        De ce que a dit par dessus
        Le Sarrazin de nos afferes,   [fol. 28r]
        Sur quoy nous conseil Dieux ly peres!''

146 Le Jacobin respont:

1310   ''Sire, trop est difficulté
        De sur tout quanqu'il a parlé
        Respondre bien parfaittement;
        Car il a tout premierement
        Parlé largement de la scysme:

1280   Moreover, to hold this as truthful, saying:[120]
        'I will have my head cut off
        If in three days this gravely ill man,,
        Is not healed'—
        Would be to claim knowledge of the future,
1285   That which no one knows, unless he lies,
        Except God, because he never fails
        To know whatever He wishes to know.
        The angels[121] above surely see,
        As they fix their gaze upon Jesus, our God,
1290   The things that are yet to come;
        And to prophets, according to His pleasure,
        He often reveals his will.
        But He yet withholds his power
        By not allowing knowledge of the future
1295   And not curbing His wrath.
        Therefore a man, mortal and vacuous,
        Cannot say with complete certainly:
        'This thing will happen in this way,
        And will be so, without fail.'
1300   To have these thoughts is great folly;
        To support them, a great crime.
        But, as concerns a truly nefarious case,
        I wish to speak to you no longer about it."

145 Master Jean speaks to the Jacobin:

        "My lord preacher,
1305   I beg of you, by God's love,
        Once again to say a little more
        About that which he said above,
        The Saracen, regarding our affairs:
        May God the Father counsel us on these points!"

146 The Jacobin replies:

1310   "My lord, it is too difficult—
        Considering all that he has spoken—
        To give a comprehensive response;
        Because, firstly, he has
        Spoken broadly about the schism.

1315 La matiere est un abisme[122]
A mon adviz, sur cestuy fet,
Car il est cler a tout discret
Qu'il n'y a que une seule voye,
De cession; mais pas non l'ottroye
1320 L'un ne l'autre des debatans.
Dont est difficulté sy grans
Que, se Dieux les roys n'enlumine
Et la Vierge de grace pleine,
De les laissier com maulx Crestiens,
1325 Cest scisme durera long temps.
France a commencié de faire
Son devoir pour le fait atraire
A la vraye conclusion.[123]
Or fault, pour avoir union,
1330 Les autres roys faire ainsy
Le cas pareil, ou je vous dy
Qu'il fauldra par voye de fait
Les Rommains, com jadiz fut fait,
Mettre en tel melancolie
1335 Qu'ilz recongnoissent leur folie.
De ce fait cy plus nen diray,
Mais aux autres choses vendray.
Car se li roys donne office
A aucun homme, ou benefice   [fol. 28v]
1340 Dont puet vivre honnestement,
Il est vilain descongnoissent
De demander aprez grant don,
Ou il a noble achoison,
Car d'avoir esté prisonniers
1345 Des annemis, dont grans deniers
Lui fallit payer pour sa rançon;
Lors seroit bonne la raison
Que ly roys luy fist aucun bien,
Puys que pour lui ce mal lui vient.
1350 Hommes d'onneur, chevalereux,
Gentilz, sages, loyaulx et preux,
N'en savoient leur cuer abaisser
De tousjours ses dons demander;
Mais hommes bas, de neant venus,

1315 The matter is an abyss,[122]
In my judgment, as regards this case,
Because it is clear to any reasonable person
That there is only one way,
That of concession; but this course is not authorized
1320 By either one of the rival popes.
The difficulty, therefore, is so great
That if the kings receive no enlightenment from God
And from the Virgin, too, who is full of grace,
To discard those popes as bad Christians,
1325 This schism will last a long time.
France has begun to do
Her duty to bring this matter
To a legitimate conclusion.[123]
What is missing now, if we are to have union,
1330 Is for the other kings to do, in this matter,
The same thing, or I tell you
That it will become necessary, by the way of force,
To put the Romans—as was done in the past—
Into such desolation
1335 That they will become aware of their madness.
I will say nothing more about this matter,
But will turn to other concerns.
For if the king gives an office
To some man, or a benefice
1340 That will allow him to live honestly,
He is contemptibly ungrateful
To ask later on for a larger gift,
Unless he has some benevolent motivation;
When there are those held prisoner
1345 By the enemy, to whom great sums
Must be paid for their ransom—
That would be a good reason
For the king to provide him with some largess,
Since it was on account of him that this disaster came about.
1350 Men of honor, chivalrous,
Noble, wise, loyal and brave
Would not be capable of lowering themselves
To this constant solicitation of gifts;
But lowborn men, come from nothing,

1355   Qui vueulent le bas monter sus,
       N'ont honte de riens demander.
       Puys parle qui en vouldra parler,
       Car ilz l'auront pour flatoyer[124]
       Ou pour la robe desplumer,[125]
1360   Sy se riront des chevaliers
       Qui n'auront robes ne deniers,
       Qui ont porté pour le roy douleur
       Et sont prests de porter greigneur
       Et de mourir com bon vassal
1365   Pour garder le roy de tout mal.[126]
       Les autres, par sainte Marie,
       Le serviront de flaterie
       Et de porter nouvelle guise,
       N'oncques leur peres n'eust la mise
1370   Que il peust payer la façon.
       Aprés vouldront faire maison
       De deux sales de lis tendus.
       D'argent vaisselle comme dus
       Vouldront il avoir tost aprés,   [fol. 29r]
1375   Et s'ilz treuvent rentes assés
       Que vueulent vendre gentilz hommez,
       Les acheteront ces preudommes.
       Le mondez est huy tres puissans,
       Quant des sy bas fait si tost grans,
1380   Car de vray vilain chevalier,
       Ne de droit buzart esprevier,
       Ne de toille franc camelin,[127]
       Ne de goudale sade vin,
       Souloient dire les anciens,
1385   Non se pourroit faire pour riens.
       Se au prince failloit conseil querre
       Ou s'il sourvenoit une guerre,
       De quoy luy sauroyent ayder?
       Ne le me vueilliez demander.
1390   Je n'en diray plus de cecy.
       Mais bien vous dy, pour faire fin,
       Que se les princes chevalerie[128]
       Et les prelas[129] n'aiment clergie,
       Ly mondes ne sera[130] ja bien.

1355   Who wish to climb from the bottom upward,
        They are not ashamed to ask for anything.
        Whatever one might say about this,
        They will get something through flattery,[124]
        Or for picking the feathers out of a great man's robe,[125]
1360   And for this they will laugh at the knights
        Who have neither robes nor money,
        Who suffered hardship in the king's service
        And who are prepared to suffer even greater ones,
        And to die like good vassals
1365   In guarding the king from any harm.[126]
        These others, by holy Mary,
        Will serve him with flattery
        And by wearing new fashions—
        Their fathers would never have had the means
1370   To pay the tailor to make such things.
        Later, they will want to build houses
        With two halls and canopied beds.
        Silver dishes just like dukes
        They'll want soon afterward,
1375   And if they find some property
        That noblemen wish to sell,
        Then they'll buy it up, these gentlemen.
        The world today is quite powerful
        When such lowly folk become so great so quickly,
1380   For base peasant to become a knight,
        Or a mere harrier, a sparrowhawk,
        Or burlap, fine *camelin*,[127]
        Or beer, sweet wine—
        As the ancients were wont to say,
1385   These things cannot be made for nothing.
        If a prince needed to call his councillors
        Or if war were to break out,
        Then how would such newcomers be able to help him?
        Do not ask me.
1390   I will say no more about this.
        But I tell you, in conclusion,
        That if the princes do not devote themselves to the art of war,[128]
        And the prelates[129] to learning,
        Then the world will never be[130] sound again.

1395　Or nen vous en diray plus rien.
　　　 Ly Sarrazins dit des geoliers
　　　 Qu'ilz despouillent les prisonniers,
　　　 Mais cecy est chose certaine
　　　 Que les vendre est du demaine,
1400　Et sy n'est pas petite rente
　　　 Que les geoles soient en vente.
　　　 Ce c'est offendre charité,
　　　 Et ly roys n'est bien informé;
　　　 Il les puet prendre en sa main,
1405　Et mettre tel qu'il soit certain
　　　 Pour bien les droiz royaulx lever,
　　　 Sans les dis prisonniers grever.
　　　 Des sergens et des officiers
　　　 S'il n'y a plus qu'il n'est mestiers,　　　　　[fol. 29v]
1410　C'est dommage de povre gent,
　　　 Car chascun veult estre si grant,
　　　 Puys qu'il est officiers du roy,
　　　 Qu'il fault pour cert avoir de quoy
　　　 Tenir estat, comment qu'il soit.
1415　Dieu vueille, tost viengne par droit
　　　 Une refformacion bien noble
　　　 Pour releesser le povre pueple,
　　　 Et ordonner nombre menour.
　　　 Il pourra bien venir un jour.
1420　Dieux doinst grace au roy puissant
　　　 Et a son conseil notable et grant
　　　 De garder en paix les subgis,
　　　 Et puis leur doint saint paradis."

147　Maistre Jehan parle au Jacobin:

　　　 "Pour Dieu, beau sire gracious,
1425　Encor n'en partirez de nous,
　　　 Ains direz aucune dottrine
　　　 Que jeune gent non soit encline
　　　 De vivre ainsy tendrement,　　　　　　　　　[fol. 30r]
　　　 Et ainsy habondeusement
1430　Ne vueulent vivre chevaliers;
　　　 Et soyez leurs vrays conseilliers."

1395 Now I will tell you nothing more about this.
The Saracen says of jailers
That they despoil their prisoners,
But this much is certain:
That the jail revenue belongs to the crown,
1400 And that, truly, it is not small sums
That are raised in the jails.
It is against the law of charity,
And the king is not well informed:
He could take the matter in hand,
1405 And put a person [in charge] who would, in all certainty,
Levy the royal rights properly,
Without harming the aforesaid prisoners.
The police and other officers,
If there are more of them than there are positions available,
1410 It is a great affliction for the poor people:
For each one wants to be so great,
Since each is an officer of the king,
That there must be means, you can be sure,
To preserve his comforts, however he gets it.
1415 God willing, soon will come, under the law,
A just and equitable reformation
To gladden the hearts of the poor people,
And decree that fewer royal officers will serve.
It could truly come one day.
1420 May God give grace to our mighty king,
And to his distinguished and exalted council
That they keep his subjects in peace,
And afterward give them holy paradise."

147 Master Jean speaks to the Jacobin:

"For the love of God, my fair and gracious lord,
1425 Once again, do not leave us,
But proclaim your teachings,
So that young people may not be so predisposed
To live so luxuriously
And so extravagantly,
1430 As knights ought not to live;
Be, then, their true counselor."

148 Le Jacobin respont:

"Sire, tenez tout pour certein
Que je ne suy point phisicien,
Mais bien ay tant livrez veuz
1435 Que, se les ay bien entenduz,
Qui vit trop dilicieusement
Non puet bien vivre longuement,
Car celui donne nourreture
Qu'il ne puet souffrir chose dure:
1440 Un pou de froit le met a mort,
Un pou de chault a desconfort.
Et quant Françoys menguent souvent
Et sy boivent a l'avenent,
Nature ne puet digerer[131]
1445 Ne tant boire ne tant mengier.
Françoys ne se scevent garder
Quant ilz se vueulent estuver,
Car, s'aprez estuve vient froit,
De deux choses fault l'une soit:
1450 Ou qu'il prengne mal dont mourra,
Ou goute pour temps qui vendra.
Encores, aprez le grant chault,
Se ly vins frois et fort deffault,
Un Françoys pense estre perdus,
1455 Mais il s'en trouvera camus,
Car ly froys vins beu au chault
Vient apostume, sans deffault;
Et le froit vin gele le sang
Ou rent le corps prez impotent.   [fol. 30v]
1460 Cecy fait bien tant que Jeunesse
Vit en France sans Dam Viellesse,
Avec ce que a mire parler
Nulz nen daigne pour soy saigner.[132]
Et vecy tres mortel folie[133]
1465 Que chascun prengne la saignie
Sans parler a nul phisicien.
Chascun qui m'oyt non m'entent bien,
Car je croy de vray, sans faillance,
Que ces fays tuent plus en France

148 The Jacobin replies:

> "My lord, know for certain
> That I am no physician;
> But surely I have read so many books
> 1435   That, if I have understood them correctly,
> He who lives too voluptuously
> Can not live a long life,
> For such a one has a diet
> That makes him incapable of enduring hardship:
> 1440   A little cold will kill him,
> A little heat disturb him.
> And when the French eat frequently
> And drink the same way,
> They find their bodies cannot digest[131]
> 1445   So much drink and so much food.
> The French do not know how to take care of themselves
> When it comes to plunging into hot baths,
> For, if after the hot bath they get cold,
> The two things combine for a single result:
> 1450   Either that they catch their death of something,
> Or have gout forever after.
> Furthermore, after the steaming bath,
> If there is no cold, strong wine to be had,
> A Frenchman thinks all is lost,
> 1455   But through this method he'll find himself stupefied,
> Because cold wine drunk when one is hot
> Brings on carbuncles, and no mistake;
> And the cold wine freezes the blood
> Or makes the body nearly impotent.
> 1460   These practices have made it so that Damoiselle Youth
> Abides in France without Dame Ripe-Old-Age,
> And that whoever needs to speak with a doctor
> Does not hold back from being bled.[132]
> This is an extremely deadly foolishness,[133]
> 1465   That all these people have themselves bled
> Without ever speaking to a physician.
> It seems no one is listening to me on this point,
> Because I believe, without a doubt,
> That this practice kills more people in France

1470 Que coustel, justice ne guerre.[134]
      Je m'en tieng fors sans plus enquerre.
      Encore a dit cilz Sarrazins
      Que les Françoys sont trop aprins
      De deffaire les mariages.
1475 Par ma foy, c'est bien grant dommages
      Que deffaire tel sacrement,
      Car Dieux le fist premierement
      Et bien haultement demonstroit
      Comment ce sacrement amoit,
1480 Quant de vierge sainte et pure
      Vint prendre humaine nature;
      Avec Joseph sans nul oultrage
      L'a donnee par mariage.
      Et se ly roys estoit bien fiers
1485 De chastoyer seulement le tiers
      De ceulx qui rompent mariage,
      Pour quant qu'ilz fussent de parage,
      Les povres auroient leurs fames
      Avecques eulx sans nulz diffames.
1490 Mais pour ce que de sy grant vice
      L'en n'en fait par rigueur justice,
      Aussy legier com de fromage
      Prent on femmes de mariage.   [fol. 31r]
      Des petis hommes oultrageux
1495 Qui portent l'estat com seigneurs,
      Par Dieu, voulentiers m'en riroye,
      Qui les mettroit en basse voye!
      Car porter escarlaste fine
      Appartient a roy et a royne;
1500 Aux grans dames et grans seignours
      Appartiennent tous drapz d'onnours,
      Et fourreures tres notables
      Ne sont aux petis convenables.
      S'ilz ne l'ont de leurs heritages
1505 Je ne scay dont vient telz oultrages,
      Car j'ay doubte, se Dieux me gart,
      Que ne viengne de bonne part.
      On devroit bien vouloir savoir
      Dont telz estas viennent, pour voir,

1470   Than knives, the executioner, or the war [134]
       I hold fast to this conviction, without further inquiry.
       Furthermore, as this Saracen says,
       The French are too well-versed
       At dissolving their own marriages.
1475   By my faith, it is truly pernicious
       To undo such a sacrament,
       Because God made it in the beginning,
       And most resolutely demonstrated
       How He loved this sacrament,
1480   When, from a virgin, holy and pure
       He came to take human nature upon himself;
       To Joseph, without blame,
       She [the Virgin] was given in matrimony.
       And if the king were stern enough
1485   To punish only a third
       Of those who divorce
       Because they aspire to being aristocrats,
       The poor would have their wives
       With them, without any dishonor.
1490   But because this heinous crime
       Is not punished rigorously through our courts,
       As lightly as taking a piece of cheese
       Does one take a woman in matrimony.
       Those puny, scandalous men
1495   Who present themselves as nobles—
       By God, how I would willingly laugh
       If He were to put them back on the low road!
       For wearing the finest fabrics
       Belongs to the king and queen;
1500   To great ladies and great lords
       Belong the robes of honor,
       And the most elegant furs
       Are not suitable for lesser folk.
       Unless they have acquired them through inheritance,
1505   I have no idea how these outrages come to pass,
       But I have my suspicions, God help me,
       That it is not always through lawful means.
       We really should investigate
       How these rich households came to be, in truth,

1510   Et les aucuns sy chastoyer
       Que les autres en l'essayer
       Eussent crainte et paour
       De prendre l'estat de majour.
       Du surplus nen parleray goute,
1515   Mais ce prieur qui nous escoute
       Mette le demourant en glose,
       Ou en vers, ou en clere prose.
       Et puis se ay dit, a Dieu vous dy,
       Car je me vueil partir de cy.
1520   Sur le fait des perescheours:
       Pryez, pour Dieu, a nos seignours
       Que pour l'onneur de Dieu le pere
       Vueillent parler a nostre mere,
       Qu'elle nous vueille par pité
1525   Tenir en bonne charité."   [fol. 31v]

149 Maistre Jehan parle au prieur:

1526   "Prieur, or rapportés en escript
       Quanque ces iiii nous ont dit;
       Et pour le monde ne laissiez
       Que la verité ne escripsiez."

150 Le prieur respont:

Par ma foy, sire, j'ay assés entendu ce que dit est, mais les choses sont
pesantes et sy ay paour qu'elles ne soient notees plus dures qu'elles
ne sont, et que aucuns pour envie[135] ou pour leur melancolie les prengnent
estre escriptes pour entencion d'injurier aucunes gens, en especial les seigneurs
155 de la court de Romme. Mais car je scay [fol. 32r] ma pensee, que non pour eulx ne
autrez injurier je ne le faiz, je rapporteray ce que j'ay ouy, veritablement
a mon pouoir. Et se je puis avoir audience, je m'en delivreray
le plus tost que je pourray. Et bien devotement supplie a tous ceulx qui
les liront, comment ilz vueillent interpreter benignement tout mon escript,

1510 And punish some of them
So that others who think to try the same
Will be apprehensive and afraid
To put on the lifestyle of their betters.
I will say no more about this at all,
1515 But this Prior who is listening to us
Should elucidate the rest for us,
Either in verse or in clear prose.
And now that I have said this, I bid you adieu,
Because I wish to take my leave.
1520 In the matter of the Order of Preachers:
Pray, for God's sake, to our temporal lords,
That for the honor of God the Father
They will wish to speak to our mother the University,
So that she will desire, in her mercy,
1525 To retain us in the spirit of charity."

149 Master Jean speaks to the Prior:

1526 "Prior, now recount in written form
What these four have told us;
And, for the world itself, do not hold back
From writing down the truth."

150 The Prior replies:

By my faith, my lord, I have heard much of what was said, but the criticisms
are weighty and I fear that they could be taken to be more severe than they
really are, and that some people, out of either envy[135] or discontent
might take them
as being written with the intention of harming other people, especially the
155 cardinals in the court of Rome. But I know my heart, and that I do not
do this
to harm them or anyone else; I will but record that which I have heard,
truthfully and to the best of my ability. And if I get an audience, I will
transmit
it as soon as I can. And I fervently implore all those who will read these
comments, that they deign to interpret all I have written in a spirit of
good will,

160 car je n'ay pas mestier d'estre en hayne[136] de personne du monde,[137]
     comme cellui qui suy hors de mon pays, et pour la guerre que maistre
     Remond Rogier[138] a faitte tant longuement en Prouvence contre le jeune
     roy Louys de Cecille.[139] Pour ce que pas ne me plaist d'estre en pays de
     guerre, car ne scay ne doy armes porter, et mon benefice est maintenant
165 de petite value; sy me suy tenus par deça, et m'y tiens tousjours, en
     attendant que Dieu meist remede contre celluy tirant Raymon Rogier. Car
     il n'a tiltre de faire guerre[140] contre cellui a qui il est homme lige, et
     sy lui a fait hommage. Ne appartient point a moy de dire s'il se meffait,
     mais de tant s'avance il par mauvaistié soy faire craindre ou faire parler
170 de luy, car il ne puet par vertu ne par bonnes euvres faire c'om parle de
     luy. Mais j'ay trop grant merveille, comment il puet tant durer en France,
     faisant guerre contre le cousin germain du roy de France nostre seigneur,
     qui est nepveu de tant grans duz, comme de [fol. 32v] nosseigneurs de
     Berry, de Bourgongne, et cousin germain de mon seigneur d'Orliens, et
175 parent de tous ceulx des fleurs de lis. Et sy est li autres venus de lignage
     tel comme l'en scet, mais non mie de hault lignage.[141] Dont j'ay plus de
     merveilles comment il ose tenir tel noyse a un de France. Car je me
     reconforte, car ou temps passé il faisoit entendre au roy et a nos seigneurs
     que la guerre il ne faisoit que contre le pape Clement; et pour ce que fame
180 estoit que aucunement li papes lui avoit tort, ly roys et nos seigneurs
     avoient aucunement pacience. Mais maintenant qu'ilz voyent tout le
     contraire, j'ay esperance que bien briefment il congnoistra
     quel courroucier fait le sang des fleurs de lis, car il ne le fait pas bon
     courroucier. Et pour ce disoit un bien sages homs de Languedoc, quant

160 because I do not need to be hated[136] by anyone in the world,[137] being one who
is now outside of his own country, because of the war that master Raymond
Roger[138] has made for a long time now in Provence against the young king
Louis of Sicily.[139] For I do not like to live in a country at war, because
I neither know how nor am allowed to bear arms, and because my benefice is

165 now of little value; and so I took up residence here, and have remained
here, while
waiting for God to take action against this tyrant Raymond Roger. For
he has no
right to make war[140] against one whose vassal he is, and to whom he has
made homage. It is not at all my place to judge if he has committed a
crime, but he
has succeeded thus far by such evil means, either by intimidation or
forcing people to

170 give testimony about him, for he could not, through virtue or through
good works, have
caused people to say what is spoken of him. But I am exceedingly
amazed how he
manages to survive in France, making war on the first cousin of the
king of France,
our lord, who is the nephew of so many great dukes, such as our lords of
Berry, or Burgundy, and first cousin to my lord of Orléans, and relative
of all the

175 lords of the fleur-de-lys. But this other, Roger, comes from a known lineage,
but by no means from a very high lineage.[141] For this reason, I am even
more
amazed that he should dare to make such trouble with a lord of the house
of France. But I console myself, because in the past he convinced the king
and the dukes that he was making war only against Pope Clement; and since

180 the story was that the pope had done him some wrong, the king and
the dukes had some patience with him. But now that they see that
this is totally false, I hope that very soon he will realize what it means
to anger the blood of the fleurs-de-lys, for one does not do well to
anger them. And for this reason a wise man of Languedoc once said, when

185 l'en parloit de toutes choses, estant en conseil, ou en compaignie ou
autrement: "Sy parlés de ce que vous vouldrés, que que soit, ne touchiez
les fleurs de lis, car les fleurs de leur nature sont nettes et pures
et sans tache, et a toutes gens n'est pas seant de parler d'elles." Mais ce
bon sires Raymon Rogier n'a pas regardé cela, car a son pouoir, il
190 desheritera le roy Louys. [fol. 33r] Car je ose dire que, oultre les dommages qu'il
lui a donnés en Prouvence, il a plus empeschié la conqueste du royaume
de Naples au roy Louys que n'a Lancelot filz de Charles de Duras.[142] Et
je pense que puis que le dit Raymond est subgiez au roy de France et a
nos seigneurs, je verray encores, s'il plaist a Dieu, que le commun
195 parler de Lombardie sera veriffié en Raymond Rogier. Ce dit le Lombart:
"Home de poco retourne en poco." Et ce n'est pas contre nature,
car communement choses qui viennent legierement et en pou de temps,
aussy s'en vont legierement et en pou d'eure. Sy en recite un dotteur un
exemple[143] par moralité, que une foys un datillier estoit en un jardin, et sy
200 avoit pres de cent ans qu'il y estoit, et encores ne portoit fruit, car de sa
nature il ne fructiffie jusques a cent ans et puis dure mil ans en bonne
vertu et tousjours portans fruit. Sy avint que ly jardiniers planta au pié
du datillier une courge, laquelle dedens pou de jours monta a plus hault
du datillier, et avec ses files commença a lyer toutes les branches de ce

185 speaking of things in general, be it in private or in public, or whatever case:
"Speak, therefore, about what you wish, whatever it may be, but do not touch the
fleurs-de-lys, because flowers by their nature are clean and pure and spotless, and it is not fitting that just anybody should speak of them."
But this
good lord Raymond Roger has not abided by this tenet, because he is seeking to
190 deprive King Louis of his inheritance. For I dare to say, the harm he has done
Louis in Provence notwithstanding, that Roger has done more to impede Louis's
conquest of the Kingdom of Sicily than has Lancelot, son of Charles of Durazzo.[142]
And I think that since this Raymond is the subject of the king of France and
of the royal dukes, I will see once again, God willing, that a popular Lombard
195 adage will be personified by Raymond Roger. Thus says the Lombard: "The
insignificant man returns to insignificance." And this is in keeping with the
laws of nature, for it typically happens that things established easily and in little
time disappear easily as well, and in short space. This is what a professor says
in a moral *exemplum*:[143] that once upon a time there was a date palm in a garden that
200 had been there almost one hundred years, and had not yet borne fruit, for it is in its
nature that it does not bear fruit until it has lived one hundred years, and then lasts a
thousand years in good condition, continually bearing fruit. And so it happened that,
at the foot of the date palm, the gardener planted a squash plant, which in a few days
had grown taller than the date palm, and with its tendrils began to tie up all the

205 datillier, et par tous les angles et branches de ce datillier se commença a
espandre. Aprez commença de flourir incontinent, et bien soudainement
vecy venir courjons; et bien tost ilz furent gros et furent courges
[fol. 33v] sy peserent tres malement, tant que les branches de ce datillier
se commencerent a ployer. Mais quant le datillier senty le grans faiz, il
210 regarda Dame Courge et sy lui dist: "Ma dame belle, qui estes vous qui
ainsi m'avez emprisonné et tant d'ennuy me faittes et tant de charge?"
"Compains," fist elle, "je suy Dame Courge." "Ha, dame," fist ly
datilliers, "je vous prie, pour Dieu mercy, que vous ne me vueilliez chargier
ne getter de mon lieu, la ou je me suy nourris, et en suy en
215 saisine et possession paisiblement et de tres long tempz, et sy l'ay
prescript." Lors dist la courge: "Et comment, Datillier, vous en convient
il parler? Par Dieu, je getteray tant de courjons que je vous creveray
dessoubz, ne je ne m'en lairay pour homme qui en parle." Lors ly
datilliers qui bien vit qu'il avoit a faire a personne vilaine, oultrageuse et
220 rigoureuse, et qui avoit tant d'enfans et courges pendans sur luy comme
campanes, mena bien long temps grant dueil, en soupirant et plourant
tousjours demandoit paix a ceste courge. Mais c'estoit pour neant, car
tousjours elle croissoit de courjons et de fleurs et de charge. Et quant ly
datilliers vit que ja paix ne trouveroit avec luy, sy luy dist bien

205 branches of the date palm, and over all the corners and branches of this date palm it

began to spread itself. Then it began to flower all of a sudden, and in no time at all

here come the baby squashes; and soon they were fat and became squashes that weighed more and more, so much so that the date palm's branches began to sag. But when the date palm felt these big things, he looked

210 at Lady Squash and addressed these words to her: "Fair lady, who are you have

thus imprisoned me, and given me so much trouble and such a burden?" "My

friend," she replied, "I am Lady Squash." "Well, milady," replied the

date palm, "I beseech you, for God's sake, that you do not deign to put burdens

upon me, nor to chase me from my place, where I was born and raised, and of which I

215 have been the rightful owner now, in all tranquillity, for a good long time; and so I have

condemned this action." Then the squash said: "And where, Date Palm, do you get the

nerve to tell me about this? By God, I'll pop out so many squashes that I'll

squash you beneath them, and won't stop no matter what anyone says about it."

Then the date palm, who realized that he was dealing with a disreputable, outrageous, and

220 exasperating person, one who had so many baby squashes and squashes hanging all over

her like so many bells—he grieved about this a long time, and, sighing and crying

continually, besought the squash for a peaceful settlement. But this was all for

nought, because she was growing continually in baby squashes, flowers, and weight.

And when the date palm saw he would have no peace with her, he said to her quite

225 humblement: "Je vous prie, belle Dame Courge, pour ce que je ne ouys
oncques parler de vous et sy ay tant d'aage, que vous me dittes combien il
y a que vous [fol. 34r] estes venue cy."—"Certes, Dant Datillier," dist elle, "il y a
bien deux mois et demi." Adont ly datilliers commença a rire tant gran-
dement que ce fut merveilles, et se commença a mocquer, truffer et
230 rigoler de Dame Courge et de faire lui grimaces et grans despis. Sy lui
dist Dame Courge: "Datillier, de quoy vous ryez vous ne menés tel joye?"
— "Par ma foy, Dame Courge," ce dist ly datilliers, "vous m'avez fait
tant grant paour que bien pensoye estre perdus, car oncquez ne vis monter
chose tant hault en sy pou de temps, ne venir en tant grant estat. Mais
235 quant vous dittes qu'en pou de temps estes venue, je ne vous
craing ne riens ne vous prise, et sy m'en rys. Car aussy en un bien pou de
temps vous vous en yrez." Cestuy compte par adventure ne chiet
pas mal au dit Raymond et en pluiseurs autres qui si tost viennent en
haultesse.[144] Car en pou de temps estoit venus trop grans, et je meismes
240 l'ay veu a ce venir; et devant mes yeulx l'en voy aler. Tout aussy les
biens de l'Eglise, selon les decrez, sont biens des povres,[145] et oncques ne
furent ordonnés pour acheter contes, baronnies ne telz haultesses; et
communement font le cours de la courge.

[fol. 34v]

¶ Et se j'ay parlé villainement du dit Remond, nulz ne se esmerveille,
245 car par sa guerre je suy hors de mon pays. Et li bons sirez, car je
le scay bien veritablement, encorez a parlé plus oultrageusement et
plus vilainement du roy nostre sire et de tous nos seigneurs de France.
Et se la guerre fut come jadiz contre Engleterre, il cuidoit courroucier
le royaumes bien a certes. Mais oultre cela que tous les autrez ont dit, ay

225 humbly: "I implore you, my fair Lady Squash, because I have heard no
   one speak

of you and am myself so aged, that you tell me when it is that you came
   to this

place." — "Certainly, Lord Date Palm," she said, "it was a full two
and a half months ago." So then the date palm began to laugh so
loudly that it was a wonder to behold, and began to mock, scoff at, and

230 ridicule Lady Squash, and to make faces at her and treat her with contempt.
   And so

Lady Squash said to him: "Date Palm, why are you laughing and displaying such

glee?" — "By my faith, Lady Squash," said the date palm, "you gave me
such a fright that I thought I might be finished, because I have never
   seen anything

climb so high nor arrive at such prosperity in such a short time. But
   since you

235 say that you came such a short time ago, I neither fear you nor respect
   you one

bit, and that is why I laughed. Because you'll be gone in a very short time as
well." It just so happens that this tale comes very close to the situation of the
aforementioned Raymond, and of many others who come so quickly to
eminence.[144] For in a short time they get too big, and even I have seen
   this happen;

240 and before my eyes I have watched them disappear. In the very same
   way, the

financial assets of the Church, according to the decrees, are the assets
   of the poor,[145]

and were never authorized for the purchase of counties, baronies or
   such eminent

titles; and yet they routinely follow the path of the squash.

¶ And if I have spoken harshly about this Raymond, this should sur-
   prise no

245 one, since because of his war I am outside of my country. And this good
lord—for I know it well and undeniably—has spoken even more scan-
   dalously

and villainously about the king our lord and about all the royal dukes of
   France.

And if open hostilities resume with England, as was the case in the
   past, he will

think about harrying our kingdom. But on top of everything that was
   said by those

250 je veu tant de choses en la commission que fu donnee jadiz a feu sire de
Chevreuse[146] es parties de Languedoc et de Guyenne, en laquelle je fuz
par la voulente du roy, sur lesquelles choses je desire veoir aucuns
bons remedes, que ja ne m'en tairay d'escripre ent aucune chosette en la
fin de cestuy livre.
255 ¶ Et vecy la premiere choses, laquelle aussi le Juif a touchiee.[147] Car
es dis pays les marchans dient, quant l'en leur demande argent a emprunter,
qu'ilz ne sont pas usuriers et qu'ilz n'ont point d'argent. Mais ilz feront
bien chevance de marchandise a cellui qui n'a besoing, et la marchandise
sera vendue pour le terme et pour l'attendre de deux ou de troys moys
260 tres chierement et trop plus qu'elle ne vauldra. En cecy perdra plus que
se ce fust usure. Et certes sur telles chevances seroit une bonne
refformacion bien seant, et que fussent [fol. 35r] aucuns telement chastiez
que les autrez se gardassent de faire le semblable cas. Et se telz
chevances estoient confisquees au roy nostre sire, je m'en ryroye.

265 ¶ La seconde choses sy est que aus diz pays a tant d'excommeniés que
n'est fin ne nombre, et pluiseurs y sont en telz estat par l'espace de dix ou
de vint ans.[148] Certes je desiroye[149] sur ce estre mis ung tel remede que
pas ne l'ose escripre. Mais se l'en m'en demande j'en diray mon adviz,
car les droiz anciennement nen dirent point tant legierement ne pour aussi

250 other four speakers, I saw many things during the commission to which I was

assigned years ago with the lord of Chevreuse[146] in the territories of Languedoc and

Guienne, where I was sent by the command of the king; as regards these matters, I

wish to see some good solutions for them, and will not forbear from writing this

little thing about them here at the close of this book.

255 ¶ And here is the first thing, which the Jew touched upon as well.[147] For in

these countries the merchants say, when one asks to borrow money from them,

that they are not usurers and that they do not have any money. But they will

make a great profit off the sales of merchandise to people who do not need it,

and the merchandise will be paid for in installments with interest, so that in two or

260 three months it will have cost much more than it is worth. In this arrangement,

buyers will lose more than if they had borrowed at interest. And surely, such

profiteering deserves a thorough reform, so that those who employ these practices

be so punished that others will avoid doing the same thing. And if these profits

were to be confiscated by the king our lord, I would have a laugh over it.

265 ¶ The second thing is that in some countries there are so many cases of

excommunication that they are impossible to count, and many have been in this

condition for ten or twenty years.[148] To be sure, the remedy that I wanted[149] to see

implemented in this matter is one I dare not put in writing, but were someone to ask

me, I would give my opinion, because formerly the laws said nothing about

270 petites choses donner escommeniement.

¶ La tierce choses est des peages lesquelz sont d'aucuns petis seigneurs.
Et quant un passant, soit par ignorance ou autrement, puet estre atrappés
de non avoir fait son devoir, les dis seigneurs ou leurs peageurs les em-
prisonnent et prindrent tous leurs biens et marchandises pour confisquees
275 et leur font tant de meschiefz que pluiseurs bonnes personnes en sont
desheritez.[150] Car pleust a Dieu que nulz passans ne fussent tenus de
respondre sur peage brisié, se non que le peage leur eust esté demandé
ou este advisez de le payer et qu'ilz eussent esté reffusés. Et ou cas que debat y
sourvendroit, que cellui a qui seroit [fol. 35v] le peage, se non qu'il fust roy,
280 duc ou prince, ne fust point juge en sa cause ne eust puissance de
emprisonner les passans ne confisquer leurs biens, ains fussent tenus de
demander justice d'icellui passant par devant le seigneurs souverain.
Car selon que j'ay trouvé aux anciens estatus, les peages ne furent trouvez
que pour tenir seurement les passans par tous pays et pour eulx garder de
285 tous larrons. Et se un passant fust desrobé en la terre d'un seigneur qui
eust paage, le seigneur estoit tenus de trouver le larron ou de rendre
tout ce que le passant avoit perdu. Or est venus le temps que je ne dy
pas que les paageurs soient larrons, mais je dy bien que assez petit en y a de
proudommes, et pour bien que s'estudient les passans faire leur

270 excommunication being applied so capriciously or for such petty causes.

¶ The third thing is the toll-booths that belong to certain members of the lesser

nobility. And when a traveler, either through ignorance or whatever, can be

caught for not having paid what is required, these nobles or their toll-collectors

imprison them and confiscate all their goods and merchandise and make so much

275 trouble for them that many good people have lost their inheritances[150] as a result.

For it would be pleasing to God that no travelers be apprehended for violating

toll-gate regulations, unless the toll had been properly requested from them and

they had refused to pay. And in the case of conflicting testimony over whom should

be paid the toll, unless it were the king, a duke, or a prince, there is no one who has

280 the authority to serve as judge in such a case, nor to imprison travelers nor confiscate their property; on the contrary, the toll-collectors would be obliged to

seek justice from this traveler before the sovereign lord. For, according to

what I have found in ancient statutes, the tolls were established only to

ensure the safe passage of travelers in all regions and to protect them from all

285 criminals. And if a traveler were to be waylaid in the territory of a lord who

administered a toll, the lord would be obliged to catch the thief or to

reimburse everything the traveler had lost. Nowadays I would not say that

the toll-collectors are themselves thieves, but I would say that there are certainly

very few of them I would call gentlemen, and that even though travelers take pains to

290 devoir, tousjours trouveront ilz achoyson de prendre sur eulx, soit par
bihaiz ou par traverse. Autretel est ilz des pontonniers et gardes des
passaiges des rivieres, especialment sur la Sone et sur la Roone. Dieux
scet les merveilleux cas que j'en ay veux et ouy dire. Sy prie a Dieu qu'il
mette en cuer au roy nostre sire, et a vous, et a tous ceulx du grant conseil,
295 de prendre aucun bon adviz sur refformacion de telz excez; et vous doint
bonne vie et longue.

Amen.

[fol. 36r]

298 Le prieur en la fin du livre parle a madame d'Orleans:[151]

1530   Belle Susanne[152] par sa grant sainteté
        Fut diffamee sans nulle verité
        Et condempnee par tres faulx jugement
        A souffrir mort assez vilainement;
        Mais Dieu du ciel qui fait vrays jugemans
1535   Tourna la mort sur les faulx accusans.
        Pour quoy tous saiges doit pasciemment porter
        Les mensongiers et leurs faulx diffamer,
        Car ja mensonges non duront longuement:
        Ne sont que songes, ou l'escripture ment.
1540   C'est vraye chose, vraye conclusion
        Que tous baraz sormonte leauté.[153]
        Tres haulte dame, entendés ma chançon
        Aprés yver revendrons en esté.

299 De par vostre povre serviteur, le Prieur de Sallon, dotteur en decret.

290 be aware of tolls they must pay, the collectors will always find some
     reason to rob
them, by hook or by crook. It is the same situation with the pontoniers
     and river
watchmen at ferry-crossings on rivers, especially on the Saône and on
     the Rhône.
God knows the astounding things that I have seen and heard about.
     And so I pray
to God that he put in the heart of the king our lord, and yours, and in
     the hearts of all
295 those on his Great Council, to harken to some good advice concerning
     the reform of
these offenses; and may He grant you a good and long life.

Amen.

298 The Prior speaks, at the end of the book, to the Duchess of Orléans:[151]

1530   The beautiful Susanna,[152] because of her great holiness,
          Was dishonored without any basis in fact,
          And condemned through very deceitful judgment
          To undergo a very ignominious death;
          But God in heaven, who judges truthfully,
1535   Turned the death sentence on to her false accusers.
          This is why all who are wise must patiently endure
          Liars and their truthless slanderers,
          Because lies will never endure for long:
          They are but dreams, or the Scriptures lie.
1540   It is the truth, a believable summation
          That fidelity conquers all corruption.[153]
          Lady most high, hear my song:
          After the winter, we will return to summer.

299 By your poor servant, the Prior of Selonnet, Doctor of Decrees.

NOTES TO THE TEXT

¹ First marginal note in manuscript **P2**:

[P2.1] **P2** 2r
Unum especialiter postulo a legente, quatenus [quod?] recordetur de doctrina quam in epistolis scribit Seneca: "Non gustabit," inquid, "suavitatem lector eorum que legit ex facilitate et transitu." Sensus igitur retinendus est, et non verbum: cap. *Intelligencia, De verborum significacione* [X 5.40.6].

[One thing in particular I require of the reader, that which is called to mind in the teachings written by Seneca in his letters: "The reader" he says, "will not taste the sweetness of these who reads them casually or quickly." The sense, therefore, was retained, and not the word.]

Bovet's citation of both canon law and Roman literature indicates the expectation he has of his readers: he expects them to be intelligent enough to read and understand these sources, and thus to make the intellectual effort to interpret the literal story presented in the French text by way of the learned apparatus provided in the Latin notes. He cautions the reader not to settle for a literal, verbatim interpretation, since the erudite significance of the story can be discerned only after a serious consideration of the great issues raised by the characters of the narrative. Bovet refers to Seneca, but—as will be a pattern throughout these marginal comments—the precise wording of his gloss is not found in any extant works by that author.

The gloss cites, at its end, the *Decretals of Gregory IX: Liber decretalium extravagantium* (otherwise known as "Liber Extra," hereafter referred to as "X") liber 5, titulus 40, entitled *De verborum significatione,* capitulum 6, summarized "Verba sunt intelligenda non secundum quod sonant, sed secundum mentem proferentis" [Friedberg 2:913]. Bovet, however, appears to have been thinking more of the wording of a chapter slightly later in the same titulus, X 5.40.8 *Propterea,* summarized "Sensum, non verba considerare debemus" [Friedberg 2:913–14], which amplifies his point about interpretation:

Propterea, si prolixam epistolam meam ad interpretandum accipere te fortasse contigerit, rogo, non verbum ex verbo, sed sensum ex sensu transferri, quia plerumque, dum proprietas verborum attenditur, sensus veritatis amittitur.

[Therefore, if it should happen that you receive my wordy letter to interpret (translate), I beg that sense for sense be rendered, not word for word, because it often happens that when the specifics of words are attended to the true sense is lost.]

This is a quotation of Gregory the Great, *Registrum Epistolarum* 1.29 (PL 77.482B–483A); ed. D. Norberg, Corpus Christianorum Series Latina [CCSL] 140 (Turnhout: Brepols, 1982), 36 (no. 28). The idea is a commonplace from Jerome (PL 23. 959C).

    2 The first gloss in manuscript **P1** is attached to the opening of Bovet's dedicatory note to Jean de Montaigu:

> [P1.1] **P1** 1r
>
> Unde venit dominium plenius disputavi in libro quem feci pro rege qui vocatur *arbor bellica*. Sed hec est vera conclusio omnium legum, canonum et philosophorum quod homines virtute et racione, sapiencia et discrecione vigentes, aliorum racionabiliter sunt domini et rectores. Ista probantur, cap. *Sit rector,* xliii Dist. [Gratian, *Decretum* D. 43 c. 1]; *Sapiencie,* v [vi] cap.; et in cap. *Grandi, de suplenda neglicencia prelatorum,* Libro vi [Sext 1. 8. 2]

> [I have more fully discussed where lordship comes from in the book that I composed for the king which is called *The Tree of Battles*. But this is the true conclusion of all laws, canons, and philosophers, that men who live by virtue and reason, wisdom and discretion are reasonably the lords and rulers of others. These points are proved in . . .]

Bovet here identifies himself as the author of a text he dedicated to King Charles VI, the *Arbre des Batailles,* another text in which he discourses at length on the origin of lordship. He thus becomes the first *auctoritas* cited in the commentary to his new poem. He then admonishes Jean de Montaigu to do his duty as royal advisor, to speak his mind in defense of the common good, citing first the first line of a canon in Gratian:

> a) Gratian, *Decretum* Distinctio 43, capitulum 1 *Sit rector* [Friedberg 1:153]:
>
> Sit rector discretus in silentio, utilis in verbo, ne aut tacenda proferat, aut proferenda reticescat.

> [Let the leader be discreet in silence, helpful in speech, lest he say things that should be kept silent or be silent about things that should be spoken]

This is a quotation adapted from Gregory's *Pastoral Care* 2.4 (PL 77.30A), itself quoting or alluding to the *Rule* of Benedict.

    Gratian's chapter later cites Isaiah 56:10, in which the Lord complains that his watchmen are asleep, like dogs, neglecting their duty to guard the Lord's house. In the subsequent citations, Bovet raises one of the poem's most urgent concerns, that of the need for virtuous leadership in the West, and cites a line from the book of Wisdom he will use in two subsequent glosses ([P1.6], n. 14 below, and [P2.15], note 69 below):

> b) Wisdom 6:24:
>
> Multitudo autem sapientium sanitas est orbis terrarium:
> et rex sapiens populi stabilimentum est.

> [A great number of wise men is the welfare of the whole world:
> and a wise king is the strong foundation of his people.]

The final citation in this gloss is to the *Liber sextus Bonifacii VIII*, known as "Sext":

> c) Sext 1. 8 ("De supplenda negligentia prelatorum"), cap. 2, beginning "Grandi non immerito," by Innocent IV [Friedberg 2:972–74]. It affirms the duty of the powerful to act responsibly. Johannes Andreae's *Ordinary Gloss* for Sext 1. 8. 2 (*Corpus Canonicum Glossatum* [Lyon: P. Landry, 1606], col. 205), adds:

> Rex Portugalliae negligens erat et remissus circa regnum et subditos eius: prodigus et dissipator erat; permittebat ecclesias, monasteria, et pia loca regni sui et ipsas personas ecclesiasticas aggravari . . . quare papa, supradicto regi et regno et omnibus ibi degentibus providere volens, dedit ipsi regi in coadiutorem nobilem virum, comitem Boloniensem, fratrem praedicti regis, devotum, circumspectum, magnanimum, et potentem, et per quem sperat futuram reformationem ipsius regni . . .

> [The King of Portugal was negligent and remiss concerning his kingdom and subjects; he was prodigal and given to dissipation, permitting churches, monasteries, and holy places of his kingdom and the churchmen themselves to suffer grievances . . . Therefore the pope, wishing to provide for the aforesaid king and kingdom and all living in it, gave the king a noble man as coadjutor, namely, the count of Boulogne, the aforesaid king's brother, a man devout, circumspect, magnanimous, and powerful, through whom he hopes for the future reformation of the kingdom . . .]

The fact that the first part of Sext 1. 8. 2 describes the brother of the king of Portugal as the ideal ruler might be taken to represent Bovet's typical optimism, given the reputations for rapacity of all three brothers of Charles V, uncles of the current king. Bovet also cites this decretal, in the same context, in the "Historical Interpolation" found in some manuscripts of his *Arbre des Batailles* (George W. Coopland, trans., *The Tree of Battles* [Liverpool: Liverpool University Press, 1949], 257).

The last two references—the citation of Wisdom because it extols the benefits of good leadership, and the chapter from the Sext in that it praises someone other than the king who could rule in his place—suggest that Bovet is referring to the disorder in the royal court during Charles VI's recurring periods of mental illness after 1392. The king's instability derailed the program of reforms initiated by the Marmousets and concomitantly strengthened the hand of the royal dukes at court, developments that served to weaken Bovet's already tenuous position at court. In a letter of November 2, 1394, Bovet remarks to his nephew that although Charles VI has been seeking his advice regarding the Schism ("Verum Rex super sisma quesivit meam pauperem opinionem"), since the onset of the king's sickness he has found his position to be "empty" ("Nam ex quo supervenit Regis infirmitas, sum hic, ut ceteri, vacuus"). Given that the above gloss appears in the copy dedicated to Charles VI's grand master of the royal household, Jean de Montaigu—a leading Marmouset who stood to lose his position and even his life due to this turn of events—Bovet's comment could even be taken as consolatory. Bovet's letters (the one cited above and three others) appear in a manuscript of his *Somnium super materia scismatis*, Archivio Segreto Vaticano (hereafter ASV) Armarium 54, vol. 21, fol. 73v; they were first noticed and published by Valois, "Un ouvrage inédit d'Honoré Bonet." See Famiglietti, *Royal Intrigue,* for more on the king's madness and its consequences; see also note 36 below.

3 Arnold (*Apparicion,* 2, n. 2) cites a note in the previous edition of the poem: "D'après le *Livre du roy Modus,* la saison de la chasse à l'épervier durait depuis la sainte Madeleine (22 juillet) jusqu'à la fin de septembre" (*Apparition,* ed. Pichon, xvi).

4 "Le jour des estreines" would be 1 January (Mod. Fr. *étrennes* = "New Year's gifts"); Bovet thus claims to have written the text in midsummer, and to have offered it to his patron on January 1, most likely of 1399. See "Date of the Paris Manuscripts," Introduction.

5 Bovet begins his introduction to Louis of Orléans with an admonition, drawn from Cicero, regarding the behavior expected of those in power:

> [P1.2] **P1** 1v #1
> Princeps quasi "aliis precipiens"; rex quasi "se et alios regens"; imperator, "aliis imperans"; propter virtutem sapiencie taliter nominantur, quia cum stultus sit servus viciorum, quomodo aliis prudentibus imperaret? Quia certum est, ut dicit Tullius: "omnem sapientem liberum esse" ... "Et hoc solum accidit sapienti ut nichil faciat invitus, nichil dolens, nichil coactus, nichil indebite, nichil incongruum." Et subdit, "Quid est libertas nisi potestas vivendi ut volueris?" Sed "Quis vivit prout vult nisi qui recta sequitur, qui racione agit, cui via vivendi in omnibus considerata, atque previsa est?" Et concludit "quomodo igitur imperabit libero qui non potest suis cupiditatibus imperare? Refrenet ergo imperator primum libidines, spernat voluptates, teneat [+ et] occidit [occidat] iracundiam, coherceat avariciam, et ceteras animi labes repellat, ut post juste incipiat aliis imperare."

> [*"Prince" means "giving precepts to others," whereas "king" means "ruling himself and others"; commander or emperor, "ordering others"; they are called such because of the virtue of wisdom, because when a fool is the slave of vices, how can he command others who are prudent? Because it is certain, as Tully says, that "every wise man is free. And this happens only to the wise man, that he never does anything unwillingly, nothing out of deceit, or compelled or unworthy or unsuitable." And he adds: "What is liberty except the power of living as you wish?" But "who is it who lives as he wishes except him who follows what is right, who acts by reason, whose manner of life shows consideration and forethought in all things?" And he concludes, "How then can he command a free man if he cannot command his own desires? Therefore, let the commander or emperor first restrain his own lusts, scorn his pleasures, hold and quell his anger, control his avarice and repel the other faults of his mind, so that then he may begin to rule others rightly."]

This gloss paraphrases some items from Isidore's *Etymologies* 9.3, amd cites several lines from Cicero's *Paradoxae* 5.33–35, beginning with the epigram "Omnes sapientes liberos esse, et stultos omnes, servos." The passage describes the self-restraint, righteousness and dedication to duty that distinguish the wise and free from slaves and fools—characteristics Bovet implies are required of rulers, too. Bovet uses part of the same passage again in gloss [P2.23], note 93 below.

⁶ Manuscript **P1** contains a marginal gloss citing civil- and canon-law sources on various categories of malfeasance:

|P1.3| **P1** 1v #2
Quia si Rex aliquid mali faceret persuasione mea, quis me dubitat non teneri? (ff *Ad legem Acquiliam*, lex *Ita vulneratus* |*Digest* 9.2.51|), et de malo consilio (lxxxvi Dist. cap. *Tanta* |*Decretun* D. 86 c. 24|; ff *De servo corrupto*, lex 1 |*Digest* ll.3.1|). Sic eciam tenetur de peccato qui fert opem peccati |peccanti?| (*C. Si quatuor*, xxiiii |xxiii|, q. finali |*Code* 2.23.8.34|), et ille qui provocat alium ad peccatum tenetur de dolo ut (ff *De dolo C. Eleganter*).

|Because if the king were to do something evil through my counsel, who would doubt that I should be held guilty of it? And concerning evil counsel: Thus also he is held guilty of sin who brings help for the sin, and he who provokes another to sin is held guilty of fraud.|

a) Justinian, *Digest* 9.2.51, tit. *Ad legem Aquiliam*, law *Ita vulneratus* |Mommsen/ Watson 1:291–92|. The law dictates that if one person wounds a slave and another kills him, both are liable, as in the summary provided in the *casus* to this law by Johannes Fehius in his early edition (*Corpus juris civilis Justinianei, cum commentariis* |Lyon: J. Cardon & P. Cavellat, 1627|): "Unus servum meum vulneravit, et alius postea occidit; ambo tenentur de occiso" |One person wounded my slave, and another later killed him; both are held for murder|. Its citation supports Bovet's claim that a counselor who persuades the king to perform an evil deed is also guilty.

Bovet then emphasizes the enormity of "dishonest advice" (*malo consilio*) by citing a canon in Gratian that suggests harsh punishment for evildoers:

b) Gratian, *Decretum* D. 86 c. 24, *Tanta* |Friedberg 1:303|:

Tanta nequitia ad aures meas de tua senectute pervenit, ut eam, nisi humanitus pensaremus, fixa iam maledictione feriremus . . .

|So much wickedness has come to my ears regarding you in your old age, that we would strike it (= you) with an immoveable curse if we did not think to act humanely.|

c) Justinian, *Digest* 11.3.1 tit. *De servo corrupto* |Mommsen/Watson 1:340–341|:

Ait praetor: "Qui servum servam alienum alienam recipisse persuasisseve quid ei dicetur dolo malo, quo eum eam deteriorem faceret, in eum quanti ea res erit in duplum judicium dabo."

|The praetor says: "If a man is alleged to have harbored another man's male or female slave or to have fraudulently persuaded him or her to do anything in order to make him or her worse, I shall give an action against him for double the sum therein involved."|

d) The theme of collective responsibility is also taken up in the next canon cited: Gratian, *Decretum* C. 23 q. 8 c. 34 *Si quatuor* |Friedberg 1:965|.

c) Finally, Bovet refers to a Roman law that holds that if a deceitful slave causes himself to be sold and is thereby manumitted, the slave will be sued: Justinian, *Digest* 4.3.7 tit. *De dolo malo*, para. *Eleganter* [Mommsen/Watson 1:120]. Bovet's point, here tortuously made, is that any fraudulence must be punished.

7 This marginal gloss cites a series of canons extolling the benefits of "true" learning and listing various sorts of "false" learning. The scribe has rendered "philosophi cante" in the last line of the gloss, which I, finding no alternative, have taken to be a neologism, "philosophicante" (= *philosophi*):

[P1.4] **P1** 1v #3

In principio, studium sciendi summe laudabile est, quando non student nisi ut se et subditos sciant discrete Regere (cap. *Duo sunt* xii q. 1 [*Decretum* C. 12 q. 1 c. 7]). Quidam non student ut videantur sapientes, sicut sunt ypocrite, ut cap. *Citius, De penitencia* Distinctio ii [*Decretum, De penitencia* Distinctio 2 c. 44]. Alii student ut sciant, sed non ut bene agant et isti moriuntur in via, ut sunt logici quorum garrulitas dicitur significari signifes [scinifes] et ranas quibus egipti sunt percussi (Exodus 8:16) ut cap. *Legimus* xxxvii *Distinctiones* (*Decretum* D. 37 c. 7). Alii student ut acquirant divicias, sicut legiste et phisici ut in *Autentica* "de Heredibus et Falcidia" in isti. Alii student ut se et alios doceant (Causa viii quaestione i *Licet* [*Decretum* C. 8 q. 1 c. 15, *Licet ergo*]) et isti sunt veri philosophicante [philosophicantes] et theologi.

[First of all, the study of knowledge is most highly praiseworthy when they only study in order to know how to rule both themselves and their subordinates well . . . Some study (only) to appear wise, like hypocrites . . . Others study for knowledge, but not for acting well, and such die along the way, like the logicians whose garrulity is signified by the locusts and frogs with which the Egyptians were stricken . . . Others study to acquire wealth, like the lawyers and physicians . . . Others study to teach themselves and others . . . and they are true philosophers and theologians.]

Once again, Bovet expresses his high expectations of the upper levels of society, here clerics: all should be learned. He cites four chapters from Gratian's *Decretum* and one passage from the *Authentics* of Justinian in support:

a) Gratian C. 12 q. 1 c. 7 *Duo sunt* [Friedberg 1:678]:

Duo sunt genera Christianorum. Est autem genus unum, quod mancipatum divino offitio, et deditum contemplationi et orationi, ab omni strepitu temporalium cessare convenit, ut sunt clerici, et Deo devoti . . .

[There are two kinds of Christians, one of them given over to the divine office and dedicated to contemplation and prayer, (to which) it is proper to cease from all bustle of worldly things, as are, for instance, clerics and those devoted to God . . .]

b) Gratian, *Decretum, De penitencia* D. 2 c. 44 *Citius ad hoc* [Friedberg 1:1207–1209]:

Citius ad hoc respondemus, quia aurum, quod pravis ejus persuasionibus quasi lutum sterni potuerit, aurum ante Dei oculos nunquam fuit . . .

[We replay more swiftly to this, because gold, which can be strewn around like dirt by the arguments of the depraved, was never gold in the eyes of God . . .]

This is a quotation of Gregory the Great, *Moralia in Job* 34.13 (PL 76.734BC). Its language is consistent with the theme of genuineness versus falseness presented in Bovet's gloss, but what is most closely cited here is not the actual canon, but rather Gratian's *dictum* following the previous chapter, and especially its gloss, which continues the quotation from Gregory begun above (PL 76.734C):

V. Pars. §. 1. Illud autem Gregorii: "Qui seduci possunt quandoque non reversuri etc.," non de omnibus generaliter reprobis, sed de ypocritis specialiter intelligendum est.

[Gregory's saying, "Those who can be seduced, sometimes not to return," etc., is not to be taken of all the reprobate, but of hypocrites in particular.]

Johannes Faventinus's gloss on Bartholomew of Brescia's *Ordinary Gloss* to *De penitencia*, Dist. 2 *dictum post* c. 43, ad v. *Illud autem:* "Haec est 5. pars distin. in qua magister loquitur de hypocritis, qui aurum videntur coram populo, sed coram Deo stercus: et hoc probat Gratianus per capitulum sequens" [Here is the fifth part of the distinction, in which the master speaks of hypocrites, who seem to be gold in the eyes of the people but dung before God; and Gratian proves this by the next chapter (viz., 44)].

c) Gratian *Decretum* D. 37 *dictum ante* c. 7 *Legimus de beato* [Friedberg 1:137] (the text preceding these lines is cited below, [P1.37], citation b):

Gratian § 1. Hinc etiam Origenes cyniphes et ranas, quibus Egiptii sunt percussi, vanam dialecticorum garrulitatem et sophistica argumenta intelligit. Ex quibus omnibus colligitur, quod non est ab ecclesiasticis secularium literarum querenda peritia.

[Hence also Origen understands the lice/locusts and frogs by which the Egyptians were struck to be the vain garrulity of the dialecticians and the arguments of the sophists. From all this we gather that skill in secular letters is not to be sought by churchmen.]

The *dictum* goes on to cite the parable of the Prodigal Son (Luke 15:11–32):

Gratian. Hinc etiam filius ille prodigus in evangelio reprehenditur, qui de siliquis, quas porci manducabant, ventrem suum replere cupiebat.

[Hence also the prodigal son in the Gospel is rebuked, who sought to fill his belly with the husks that the swine were eating.]

This *dictum* also cites Origen's *4th Homily on Exodus* §6, in which poets are likened to the pestilential frogs, and dialecticians to the locusts: trans. R. E. Heine, Fathers of the Church 71 (Washington, D.C.: Catholic University of America Press, 1981), 268–69.

d) *Authentics* or *Novellae* of Justinian, *de Heredibus et Falcidia* [Mommsen 3:1–10].

This is the first section of the *Novellae,* dealing with issues of inheritance and the application of the *Lex Falcidia* (*Digest* 35.2.1–96, Mommsen/Watson 3:200–222), which stipulates that no Roman citizen may bequeath more than three-quarters of an estate to anyone other than the rightful heirs. The relevance of these statutes to Bovet's comment is obscure, and the citation may well be to the general principle of greed, and to proverbial associations of specific professions with that vice: that even those whose position ostensibly concerns the public weal, such as lawyers and physicians, are sometimes concerned more with acquiring and bequeathing wealth. The point behind his fifth and final citation, however, is abundantly clear even from its summary:

> c) Gratian C. 8 q. 1 c. 1 5 *Licet ergo* [Friedberg 1:594–95], summarized "Ad sacerdotium non eligatur, nisi qui ceteris et sanctior et doctior habeatur" [Those who are not considered by the others both holier and more learned may not be chosen for the priesthood].

[8] Robert "the Wise," Angevin king of Sicily (r. 1309–1343), was renowned as a scholar and patron of the arts.

[9] Charles II "the Bad," King of Navarre (d.1387), known mainly for his ruthlessness and ambition, nevertheless had a certain reputation as a patron of the arts; Guillaume de Machaut dedicated his *Confort d'ami* to him, and made him the courtly arbitrator of his *Jugement du Roy de Navarre.*

[10] Bernabò Visconti, Lord of Milan, was imprisoned in May 1385 by his nephew Gian Galeazzo, and died mysteriously before the end of that year. Gian Galeazzo was married to Isabelle, daughter of Charles V of France; their daughter Valentina, Duchess of Orléans, was apparently one of Bovet's friends at court, having been offered one of the presentation copies of the *Apparicion* (our manuscript **P2**; see Introduction, § "Manuscripts"). In his analysis of manuscript **P1**, Paulin Paris (*Les manuscrits françois de la Bibliothèque du Roi* [Paris: Techener, 1845], 6: 248), records a traditional reaction to Bernabò's being called a lover of learning: "Il est singulier qu'en s'adressant au duc d'Orléans Bonnet [Bovet] ne parle pas de la passion connue pour les sciences et les arts de Galeas et de Jean Galeas, aïeul et père de Valentine de Milan; tandis qu'il vante les goûts littéraires du grand-oncle de la duchesse d'Orléans, Bernabo, dont les historiens n'ont rappelé que les vices et l'avarice effrénée." In the succeeding lines, however, Bovet's narrator goes on to accuse the duke of precisely that vice Paulin Paris would have expected in a portrait of Bernabò ("il avoit son estude plus en or qu'en science"). Even if Gian Galeazzo was better known for his patronage of the arts than his uncle, however, Bovet's citation of Bernabò here is well taken—especially given this dedication's attempt to praise enlightenment while chiding greed—since Bernabò also had a certain amount of learning, and a considerable library (see E. R. Chamberlin, *The Count of Virtue: Giangaleazzo Visconti, Duke of Milan* [London: Eyre and Spottiswoode, 1965], 27, and Robert A. Pratt, "Chaucer and the Visconti Libraries," *English Literary History* 6 [1939]: 191–99, here 197). But the fact that the Duchess of Orléans is the daughter of Bernabò's murderer, finally, makes his appearance here in Bovet's dedication to the Duke of Orléans seem rather odd. The grouping, moreover, of Charles the Bad

and Bernabò with Robert of Anjou—for whom historians reserve unalloyed praise—deserves more scrutiny than space allows here. For a full and recent consideration of Bernabò as tyrant, see David Wallace, *Chaucerian Polity: Absolutist Lineages and Associational Forms in England and Italy* (Stanford: Stanford University Press, 1997), esp. 319–29.

[11] The first two letters are erased, inexplicably.

[12] The manuscript has "cest chose," but the sense is clearly "si est" (in the mod. Fr. sense of "s'il y a une chose . . .").

[13] As a way of illustrating the incompatibility of greed and learning, in the poetic text Bovet recounts the legend of a "Socrates" who threw his gold in the water in the service of virtue, as it says in the *Decretum* ("our decree"). Although the name is rendered as "Crates" in the modern edition, Friedberg (1:711, n. 859) indicates that two of the authoritative Gratian manuscripts and most of the early printed editions contain the reading "Socrates"; it is thus a common variant, and one Bovet could have seen. Bovet, or at least the scribe responsible for the **P1** glosses, seems to have conflated this Socrates with the Polycrates described in Valerius Maximus (6.9. ext. 5, ed. Karl Kempf, *Valerii Maximii, Factorum et dictorum memorabilium libri novem*, 2nd ed. [Leipzig: Teubner], 1888, 318; ed. J. Briscoe [Stuttgart and Leipzig: Teubner, 1998], 1:431–32), who also flung his treasure (a ring) into the sea, but only "ne omnis incommodi expers esset" [so that he should not be totally immune from distress].

|P1.5| **P1** 2r #3
Unde dicit Policrates "Numipitas non queras cum libricolis; hec duo stare simul non possunt, crede michi," ad hoc cap. *Gloria episcopi* C. xii q. ii.

|Whereby Policrates says "You may not seek the rapacious one with the lover of books; believe me, those two cannot be in the same place."|

The term *numipitas* signifies "one attracted by money," in the same way that the term *Romipetas* (cf. Gratian, *Decretum* C. 24 q. 3 c. 23, *Si quis Romipetas* [Friedberg 1:996]) refers to a pilgrim, one drawn to Rome. More apposite is Richard de Bury's *Philobiblon* 15.194: "Nummipetae cum libricolis nequeunt simul esse" [Misers and bookmen make poor company]: Richard de Bury, *Philobiblon,* ed. E. C. Thomas (London: K. Paul, Trench and Co.,1888; repr. London: Chatto and Windus, 1913). Gratian's Crates seeks to avoid being tarred with this epithet:

Gratian, *Decretum* C. 12. q. 2 c. 71 *Gloria episcopi* |Friedberg 1.711|:

§3. Crates ille Thebanus, homo quondam ditissimus, homo quondam Athenas pergeret, magnum pondus abjecit, nec putavit, se posse et virtutes simul et divicias possidere.

|Crates, that Theban, a man who was one time very rich, a man who once was traveling to Athens, threw a great weight burden overboard; he did not think it was possible to have virtue and riches at the same time.|

[14] A longish gloss, citing one of Bovet's favorite passages ostensibly drawn from Origen, appears at this place in manuscript **P1**:

|P1.6| **P1** 2r #4

Canticorum super omelia quinta |omelie quinte super Canticis| recommendo scientiam et sapientiam. "Ita," inquit, "regnabat igitur in Jherusalem Rex Salomon, gemmis ornatus dÿademate, coronatus serto decorus auro fulgens, septro fungens ministris fultus. Sed plus fulget sapientia quam potentia, plus verbo quam auro, plus moribus |+ quam| rumoribus, plus virtute quam ense, plus fama quam pompa." "Venit igitur Regina Austri ad videndum faciem Salomonis" |1 Kings/Vulgate 3 Kings 10:1, 2 Chron. 9|, sed quare venit? Certe non ut miraretur militum elaces |classes| non ministrancium cultus, non gemmarium |gemmarum| rutilancium gloriam, non cavernarium |cavernarum| effossa metalla, non strepitus hystrionum, sed venit ut audiret sapientiam Salomonis, vidit eum et ait: "Benedictus Dominus Deus, qui constituite |constituit te| super regnum suum Israel" |1 Kings/Vulgate 3 Kings 10:9|. "O," inquit Origenes, "Clarum regnum quod tanto principe pollet, cui Reges tributarii |sunt|, cui principes famulantur, cui aliegene serviunt, cui naciones appropinquant, cui munera offeriuntur |offeruntur|, cui totus favet mundus," nam ut dicit scriptura "Desiderabant omnes Reges terre videre et audire prudentissimum Salomonem" et merito, quia "Rex sapiens stabilimentum est populi" (*Sapientie* cap. quinto).

|I recommend the knowledge and wisdom of Canticles, on the fifth homily. "Thus, therefore," it says, "King Solomon reigned in Jerusalem, adorned with gems, crowned with a diadem, decorous in a garland, shining with gold, wielding a scepter, surrounded by ministers. But he shines more with wisdom than with power, more with word than gold, morals than rumors, virtue than sword, fame than pomp." "Therefore the queen of the south came to see the face of Solomon," but why did she come? Certainly not to admire the battalions of soldiers nor the attention of his ministers, not the glory of shining gems, not the metals mined from caverns, not the clamor of jongleurs; she came rather to hear the wisdom of Salomon; she saw him, and said, "Blessed be the Lord God who set you upon his throne of Israel." "O famous realm," says Origen, "that prospers with such a prince, to whom kings are tributary, whom princes attend and foreigners serve, to whom nations approach, to whom gifts are offered, whom the whole world favors," for, as Holy Writ says, "All the kings of the earth desired to see and hear the most prudent Solomon," and rightly, because, "The wise king is the strong foundation of his people."|

Bovet refers to the same section from a homily by Origen on the *Song of Songs* (which itself cites Matthew 12:42) in his *Somnium super materia scismatis* (ed. Arnold, 99), and in the "Discourse to Wenceslas" (ed. Höfler, 179). He refers here to a *Fifth Homily on the Song of Songs;* however, only two were translated into Latin by St. Jerome—the two now extant—and it is unlikely that Bovet knew any others. See *Origène, Homélies sur le Cantique des Cantiques,* ed. and trans. Dom Olivier Rousseau, O.S.B., Sources Chrétiennes 37bis (Paris: Éditions du Cerf, 1966), which quotes Notker Balbulus (d. 912) as claiming to know of only two homilies on the *Song of Songs* by Origen (47). Athough material referring to the "Queen of the South" (Matthew 12:42) appears several times in both Origen's *Commentary on the Song of Songs* and in the two *Homilies on the Song of Songs* (Origen, The Song of Songs: *Commentary and Homilies,* tran. and annot. R. P. Lawson [New York: Newman

Press, 1957], 67, 93–94, 98–102, 277–78), the text purported to be by Origen in Bovet's gloss here shows little similarity with the texts of these two extant homilies. Curiously, Book 1 of Origen's *Commentary on the Song of Songs* (ed. Lawson, 67) contains a passage presenting more of the biblical text used in Bovet's gloss (1 Kings/Vulgate 3 Kings 10:4–5) than any passage from the two Homilies, but still shows no very close relation to Bovet's citation. The provenance of this quotation, therefore, remains unclear. However, "plus fulget fides quam aurum" is from Augustine, *Sermo* 99 (PL 39. 1936).

Arnold (*Apparicion,* 4, n. 3) observes that the theme is a medieval commonplace, citing similar lines in Deschamps (Ballade 272, "De ceuls qui ont science en despit," *Oeuvres complètes,* ed. A de Queux de Saint-Hilaire and G. Raynaud [Paris: Firmin Didot, 1878–1903], 2.117, lines 6–10):

> Car tresor n'est qui vaille sapience,
> Riens ne se puet comparer a science:
> C est li sieges des Roys et des barons.
> N'orent par lui seignourie et puissance
> Tholomée, David et Salemons?

Bovet actually draws from Wisdom 6:26; the text is also cited in [**P1.1**], note 2 above, and [P2.15], note 69 below.

[15] Bovet's dedication closes cautiously here: he expresses hope that his noble readers will excuse his candor, since it is in the service of the truth. The marginal aphorism, provided as amplification of the sentiment expressed in the body of the text, is not found in the extant works of Seneca. The gloss as it stands contains the word "lubile" ("pleasing," from *lubere,* "to please"), whose peculiarity—especially when compared with Bovet's usual lack of innnovation in Latin—gives rise to the suspicion that the scribe might have miscopied an abbreviation for a more common term such as "notabile" (which would have been abbreviated something like "nōbile"). Nevertheless, "lubile" is what appears in the margin, and since it does make sense in its context I have let the original reading stand, and merely suggested an alternative in brackets.

[P1.7] **P1** 2r #1
Dicit Seneca lubile [notabile?] verbum, "Quod cum potentes habeant omnia, unum deest, quia non habent quem dicant [dicat] eis veritatem. Si enim ad cubiculum potentis homo perveniat, aut veritas tacenda aut amicicia perdenda est."

[Seneca has a pleasing [notable?] saying: "When affluent men have everything, one thing is lacking, because they do not have anyone to tell them the truth. For if one comes to the chamber of a magnate, either truth must be unspoken or friendship lost."]

This text is adapted from Rather of Verona, *Praeloquia,* 1.12: "Si in clientelam felicis hominis potentisque perveneris, aut veritas aut amicitia perdenda est" (PL 136. 173C): termed a proverb.

¹⁶ Bovet addresses a crucial issue very early in his text, exhorting his aristo-cratic audience to use their time on earth well in order to make themselves worthy of salvation, thereby suggesting that eternal punishment will await those leaders who refuse to reform their ways and rule as God intended. Citations from Cicero and Valerius Maximus underline Bovet's theme, proclaiming the great good that can be the legacy of a life well led:

> [P1.8] **P1** 2r #2 (below the poem text in bottom central margin):
> Finis glorie temporalis sunt langor, fletus, dolores, et gemitus, et finaliter ipsa mors cuncta terribilia superans, et non remanet in fine nisi sepulcrum. Et opera virtuosa cetera evanescunt ut supremum ut nubes transeunt velud umbra. Hec de dictis sapientissimi Tullii *Libro de beneficiis,* circa finem. Addit tum quod licet dies hominis pari [pauci] sint et breve tempus, satis tamen longum est ad bene justeque vivendum. Unde Valerius: "Tempus tuum, homo, breve est, sed si eo bene uti volueris, parvum magnum efficies, an-norum numerum multitudine operum superando."

> [The end of temporal glory is languor, tears, sorrows, and groans, and finally death itself, surpassing all terrors, and nothing remains in the end but the grave. And other virtuous works fade away like the end [of the day], as clouds pass by like shadows. This according to the sayings of the wise Tully in his book *On Benefits,* near the end. Then he adds that, although the days of man are few, a short time, still it is long enough to live well and justly. Whence Valerius, "Your time, O man, is short, but if you wish to use it well, you will make the small large, surpassing the number of your years with the multitude of your works."]

> a) Cicero wrote no *Liber de Beneficiis,* although Seneca did; in any case, the text cited here is Cicero's *De Senectute,* c. 70 (trans. Frank O. Copley, *Cicero: On Old Age and On Friendship,* [Ann Arbor: University of Michigan Press, 1967], 35):

> Breve enim tempus aetatis satis longum est ad bene honesteque vivendum; si processerit longius, non magis dolendum est, quam agricolae dolent praeterita verni temporis suavitate aestatem autumnumque venisse.

> [A brief span of years is quite long enough for living a good and honorable life; and if that span should be prolonged, we must not weep and wail about it, any more than farmers weep and wail at the coming of summer and au-tumn, after sweet springtime has passed.]

> b) Valerius Maximus, *Factorum et dictorum memorabilium* 9.12. init. (Kempf. ed., 458; ed. Briscoe, 2:617); trans. D. R. Shackleton Bailey, *Valerius Maximus: Memorable Doing and Sayings* (Cambridge, MA: Harvard University Press, 2000), 2:369:

> . . . nam et si eo bene uti velis, etiam parvum amplissimum efficies, nume-rum annorum multitudine operum superando . . .

> [. . . for if you choose to use it well, you will make even a small span fully ample, surpassing number of years by multitude of achievements . . .]

[17] [P1 9], **P1** 2v–3r

> Pro evidencia materiarum in hoc libello tractatarum . . . et quia pro nunc sum aliis negociis occupatus ulterius non procedam.

At this point in manuscript **P1** appears a long Latin comment treating issues related to the legality of the French church's withdrawal of obedience from Benedict XIII (1398). I designate it [P1.9] in the catalogue of Bovet's glosses; because of its length, the text of this gloss appears later in this volume as Appendix 7.

[18] Identical glosses in the two manuscripts: [P1.10] **P1** 4r #1, [P2.2] **P2** 3r:

> Unde propter metum plures loqui veritatem tacent et maledicit decretum *Quisquis metu;* terrene dignitatis veritatem ocultat, provocat super se iram Dei (cap. *Quis quis* xi q. iii [Gratian C. 11 q. 3 c. 80]).

> [Whence it is that many persons on account of fear keep silent about the truth and speak ill of (or, contradict) the decree, *Quisquis metu;* he hides the truth of earthly dignity, provoking upon himself the wrath of God.]

The text in Gratian cites Isidore, *Sententiae* 3.55.7 (PL 83.727C), lines also cited by pseudo-Alcuin, Rabanus Maurus, Burchard of Worms, and Anselm of Lucca.

> Gratian, *Decretum* C. 11 q. 3 c. 80 *Quisquis metu* [Friedberg 1:665]:

> Quisquis metu cuiuslibet potestatis veritatem occultat, iram Dei super se provocat, quia magis timet hominem quam Deum. Et post pauca: §. 1. Uterque reus est, et qui veritatem occultat, et qui mendacium dicit, quia et ille prodesse non vult, et iste nocere desiderat.

> [Whoever through fear of any power hides the truth calls upon himself the wrath of God. And shortly thereafter: §. 1 Both he who hides the truth and who tells a lie is guilty, because the former is unwilling to help and the latter wishes to harm.]

Bovet, exceptionally, cites not only the title of the canon but some language from the canon text itself. He explains the *Apparicion* as conforming to the demands of Jean de Meun (in the poem) and of canon law (in the gloss) that good people not keep silent on crucial issues.

[19] At the close of his dedication to Louis of Orléans, Bovet continues the deferent stance adopted above in lines Prose 76–Prose 79. He seems to be vacillating between the drive to proclaim the truth and the fear of offending the powerful nobleman to whom he has presented this book. He first calls for God's blessing on all those who uphold this truth wherever possible, qualifying the exhortation with the clause "without offending anyone" (*sans aucun offendre);* he concludes, however, with another qualifying term, "unduly" (*non deuement*). Then, as if regretting this qualification, he reinforces the importance of defending the truth with a marginal gloss that begins by pointing out the rightness in using the term "unduly" (*indebite*), since castigation is certainly justified in many cases, as demonstrated in the law:

|P1.11| **P1** 4r #2
Bene sedit verbum "indebite," quia injustos justi, boni malos, juste et sancte
persequuntur; eos juste diffamant et cum laude Christi condampnant (xxiii
q. iiii cap. *displicet* et quasi per totum. |Gratian C. 23 q. 4 c. 38|)

[The word "unduly" sits well, because the just justly persecute the unjust,
the good blessedly pursue the wicked; they justly speak ill of them and con-
demn them with Christ's approval.]

Gratian, *Decretum* C. 23 q. 4 c. 38 *Displicet* [Friedberg 1:917–19], summarized
"Heretici ad salutem etiam inviti sunt trahendi" [Even when unwilling, heretics are
to be pulled to salvation]. The canon is two full columns long (ca. 800 wds.), and,
as Bovet indicates, almost all of it (*quasi per totum*) contains material in support of
the principle expressed in his marginal comment.

[20] In Bovet's *Somnium super materia scismatis,* the narrator tells an interlocutor
where he has been living: "Venio," dixi, "de extra Parisius, ubi habito in una domo
quasi solitaria que de Tornela vocatur" ["I come," I said, "from outside Paris,
where I live in an isolated house called 'Tournelle.'"(*Somnium,* ed. Arnold, 77)]. A
marginal gloss in the Paris manuscript of this text (BNF MS lat. 14643, fol. 272v)
adds "sita juxta nostram Dominam de Campis" (Notre Dame des Champs). The
manuscript contains blank spaces intended for illustrations that contain instructions
for the illuminator; at this spot, the scribe has inserted "Hic depingatur actor jacens
in domo Tournelle" [Here the character is depicted lying in the Tournelle house"].
See Gilbert Ouy, "Une maquette de manuscrit à peintures (Paris, BNF lat. 14643,
fols. 269–283v, Honoré Bouvet, *Somnium prioris de Sallono super materia Scismatis,*
1394)," *Mélanges d'histoire du livre et des bibliothèques offerts à Monsieur Frantz Calot* (Paris:
Librairie d'Argences, 1960), 43–51.

[21] A marginal gloss here lauds the *Roman de la Rose,* and laments the facile and
ignorant treatment it has been receiving in the author's time. Bovet cites once again
a proverbial saying he attributes to Seneca, but for which no source has been found
(also cited in the first gloss in the Text, [P2.1], note 1 above):

|P1.12| **P1** 4v #1
O benedicte Deus, in quanta scientia et sensu naturali habundat ille liber!
Sed multi multa legunt et sensum non percipiunt, contra quos dicit Seneca:
"Non gustabit dulcedinem eorum que legit lector ex facilitate et transitu."

[O blessed God, in what great knowledge and natural sense does this book
abound! But many people read much but do not understand the sense, and
Seneca says against them, "The reader who reads facilely and fleetingly will
not savor the sweetness of what he reads."]

[22] Bovet refers to the fourteenth-century tradition of apocalyptic prophecy,
which became more popular as the end of the century drew near:

|P1.13| **P1** 4v
In hoc concordant omnis |omnes| secte, vulgaris sententia, sarraceni, Judei
et pagani et varii Christiani, quos |qui| isto tempore mirabilia videbuntur et

in libro sue confessionis magister Arnaldus de Villanova expresse tenet quod Antechristus personaliter tempore istius centenarii regnabit.

[All groups of popular sentiment, Saracens, Jews, pagans and various Christians, agree in this, that in this time wonders will be seen; and in the book of his *Confession,* master Arnald of Villanova expressly holds that Antichrist personally will reign in the time of this centennial year.]

Arnald of Villanova (ca. 1235–1313) was a physician, pharmacist, and alchemist who also wrote much on theology, including texts dealing with the Antichrist and the end of the world. It is impossible to attribute several of these texts to him with any certainty, however, so his role in apocalyptic thought remains difficult to judge.

Bovet makes much use of such prophecies in later notes (46, 81). A general study of this issue is Marjorie Reeves, *The Influence of Prophecy in the Later Middle Ages: A Study in Joachism* (Oxford: Clarendon Press, 1969). See also Hélène Millet, "Écoute et usage des prophéties par les prélats pendant le grand schisme d'Occident," *Mélanges de l'École française de Rome* 102.2 (1990): 425–455. For the prevailing belief in this prophecy and its reference to Arnaldus de Villanova, see Roberto Rusconi, *L'attesa della fine: Crisi della società, profezia ed Apocalisse in Italia al tempo del grande scisma d'Occidente (1378–1417)* (Rome: Istituto storico italiano per il Medio Evo, 1979), 171–84, and cf. Fleming, *The Late Medieval Pope Prophecies.*

23 A reference to the Western defeat at Nicopolis on 25 September 1396. In the margin, an interpretation of the Schism and the disastrous outcome of this battle as signs of God's displeasure:

[P1.14] **P1** 5r #1
Eya, Deus benedicte, que [qui] duo signa magis terrenda potesses [potuisses] nobis ostendere indignacionis tue, quando lumen in capite ecclesie convertisti in tenebras, et regiones nostras coram nostris oculis devorant infideles.

[O blessed God, who may have been able to show two more terrifying signs of your indignation, when you changed light to darkness in the head of the Church, and when infidels devour our lands before our eyes.]

24 Bovet condemns the desertion of monasteries and other religious houses, citing Psalm 21 and a canon from Gratian that itself quotes from Jerome's *Commentary on Titus* (2.15; PL 26.590B–C):

[P1.15] **P1** 5r #2
Certe hodie migravit devocio a monasteriis. Facti sumus "opprobrium populi et abjectio plebis" (Psalm 21:7), deteriores effecti omnibus laÿcis, et hoc est quod Dei ecclesiam destruit, meliores habere Laycos quam clericos (C. viii q. ii [i] cap. *Qualis*).

[Certainly these days devotion has abandoned the monasteries. We have become "the reproach of the populace and the outcast of the common people," brought to a worse condition than all the laity, and this is what destroys the Church of God, to have laypeople who are better than the clerics.]

a) Psalm 21:7: "Ego autem sum vermis et non homo, obprobrium hominum et abjectio plebis."

[But I am a worm, and no man; the reproach of men, and the outcast of people.]

b) Gratian, *Decretum* C. 8. q. 2 c. 1, *Qualis enim ædificatio* [Friedberg 1:597]:

Qualis enim ædificatio erit discipuli, si intelligat se esse majorem magistro? Unde non solum episcopi, presbiteri et diacones magnopere debent providere, et cunctum populum, cui president, conversatione et sermone precant, verum etiam inferior gradus, exorcistae, lectores, editui, acoliti, et omnes omnino, qui domui Dei deserviunt, quia vehementer ecclesiam Christi destruit meliores laicos esse quam clericos.

[For what kind of edification will it be for the disciple, if he sees himself greater than his teacher? Whence not only should bishops, priests, and deacons make great provisions and excel in deed and speech all the people over whom they preside, but so too should the lower grades, the exorcists, lectors, ushers, acolytes, and all others who are in service to the house of God, because it greatly destroys the church of Christ for the laity to be better than the clergy.]

25 Having called attention to the failings of the clergy, Bovet turns to the impertinence of the lay populace, whom he sees as being too quick to take legal action and too little respectful toward their superiors:

[P1.16] **P1** 5r #3
Contra quos dicit Anacletus "nichil impudencius est arrogancia laÿcorum, qui garrulitatem credunt esse auctoritatem." (xlvi Disti. pars i [D. 46, *dictum ante* c. 1])

[Against whom Anacletus says, "There is nothing more impudent than the arrogance of the laity, who take garrulity for authority."]

Gratian, *Decretum* Dist. 46 [Friedberg 1:167], *dictum ante* c. 1; the text is Gratian's, adapting Jerome (Letter 59.9 [PL 22.663]), who has "arrogancia rusticorum"; quoted by Peter Lombard [PL 192.344B]). But Bovet erroneously attributes it to Pope Anacletus, author of the preceding canon (Dist. 45 c.18):

Sequitur: "Non litigiosum." Nichil est enim impudentius arrogantia rusticorum, qui garrulitatem auctoritatem putant, et parati ad lites in subjectos tumide intonant, quod ex arrogancia superbiae provenire manifestum est.

[Next, (St. Paul says, 1 Tim. 3:3, "The bishop should) not be litigious." For nothing is more impudent than the arrogance of rustics, who think that loquaciousness is the same as authority, and who, readied for court battles, pompously sound off against those subject to them, which manifestly comes from the arrogance of pride.]

26 Nearly identical glosses in the two manuscripts justify the punishment, even execution, of the wicked, and thereby exhort the leaders at court to deal more severely with criminals:

|P1.17| **P1** 5r #4; |P2.3| **P2** 4r
De qua loquitur Beatus |**P2**: Unde| Ambrosius in *Libro de Paradiso:* "Cum interficitur impius, Christus infunditur |**P2**: effunditur|, et ubi abhominacio aboletur, sanctificacio consecratur, dicxit Dominus: 'In ea die in qua interfecero omnem primogenitum egypto, sanctificabo michi omnem primogenitum Israel.'" Id est pacem dabo quietis per mortem impiorum (C. xv q. i cap. *Nec his*).

|Of which speaks blessed (**P2** Whence) Ambrose in his book *Of Paradise* says, "When the impious man is killed, Christ is poured inward (**P2**: poured out) and where abomination is abolished, there is a consecration of sanctification. The Lord says, 'In that day in which I shall have slain every firstborn in Egypt, I will sanctify to myself every firstborn of Israel.' That is, I will give the peace of quiet through the death of the impious."|

Gratian *Decretum* C. 15 q. 1 c. 11 *Nec is* ad v. "Illud quoque" [Friedberg 1:749], summarized "Minister Dei est qui invitus homicidium facit" [God's minister is he who, when he slays a man, does so unwillingly]. Idem *de Paradiso in lib.:*

> Illud quoque specta, quia, quum interficitur impius, Christus infunditur, et, ubi abominatio aboletur, sanctificatio consecratur, quia Dominus dixit: "In ea die, qua interfecero omne primogenitum Egypti, sanctificabo michi omnem primogenitum Israel" (Numbers 3:13). Quod non referetur ad unum diem afflictionis Egypti, sed omne tempus.
>
> |Behold that also, because, when the impious person is slain, Christ is poured inward, and, when abomination is abolished, holiness is dedicated, because the Lord has said: "In the day on which I shall have slain every firstborn of Egypt, I shall sanctify to myself every firstborn of Israel." Which would not refer to a single day of the affliction of Egypt, but to all time.|

As the Roman Correctors and Friedberg observe (note 147a), the material from Ambrose comes not from his *De paradiso* but instead from *De Cain et Abel* (PL 14.348C), all but the last sentence; Bovet reproduces the error he finds in Gratian.

²⁷ Arnold (*Apparicion,* 7, n. 3) cites Ernest Lavisse's *Histoire de France* (Paris: Hachette, 1920–1922), 4:428: "Guillebert de Metz . . . dans sa *Description de Paris,* écrite au début du XVe siècle, énumère avec admiration les hôtels princiers de la capitale, récents pour la plupart, ou du moins complètement restaurés, hôtels d'Artois, de Sicile, de Navarre, de Flandre, d'Alençon, de Hollande, etc."

²⁸ The marginal gloss here could well be interpreted as expressing the author's frustration over his failure up to this point to make his voice heard and influence political strategy. To the Prieur's claim of personal insignificance, Bovet attaches an admonition from Ecclesiasticus:

|P1.18| **P1** 5v
Super hoc dicebat Jhesus Cÿrac "non effundas sermonem ubi non es auditus."

Ecclesiasticus (Sirach) 32:6:
Ubi auditus non est non effundas sermonem,
et importune noli extolli in sapientia tua.

[Where there is no hearing, do not pour out speech,
and do not inopportunely wish to be extolled in your wisdom.]

The same text is cited twice by Geoffrey Chaucer in the *Canterbury Tales:* Nun's Priest's Prologue VII.2801–2802, Tale of Melibee VII.1047.

[29] In the text, the Prieur paraphrases a story from Valerius Maximus (7.2 ext. 6, ed. Kempf, 329; ed. Briscoe, 2:446–47; trans. Shackleton Bailey, *Memorable Doing and Sayings,* 2.119): "Quid, Xenocratis responsum, quam laudabile! cum maledico quorundam sermoni summo silentio interesset, uno ex his quaerente cur solus linguam suam cohiberet, 'quia dixisse me,' inquit, 'aliquando paenituit, tacuisse nunquam'" [And again, how laudable was that answer of Xenocrates! Being present at a back-biting conversation between certain persons, he said absolutely nothing. When one of them asked why he alone held his tongue, he said: "Because I have sometimes been sorry I spoke, never that I kept silent"]. Arnold (*Apparicion,* 8, n. 2) cites an earlier edition of Valerius Maximus. The same proverb is contained in the *Disticha Catonis* 1.12, and cited in Langland, *Piers Plowman* (C-text), Passus XIII, line 223a (ed. Derek Pearsall [York: Edward Arnold, 1978], 232).

In the margins of the two manuscripts are similar glosses expressing a wish for governments more just than that described in Valerius Maximus:

[P1.19] **P1** 5v # 2
Hoc fuit quando Res publica habuit tales tyrannos ut contra dictes [dictos] innocentes falsa accusacio criminalis quacumque via querebatur, [ita] quod per eam mortem paterentur ut sic fisco eorum bona confiscarentur. Ergo tunc non quoad personas sed quoad divicias crimina imponebantur. A tali maligno enim regimine libera nos, domine.

[This happened at a time when the Republic had the sort of tyrants that a false criminal accusation would be sought in whatever way against such innocent persons, so that through it they would suffer death and thus their goods would be confiscated to public treasury. Therefore at that time crimes were imputed not with reference to persons but riches. Therefore from such a malign rule deliver us, O Lord!]

[P2.4] **P2** 4v #1
Hoc fuit quando Res publica habuit talem tirannum imperatorem ut etiam contra innocentes quereretur falsa accusacio criminalis, talis quod per eam mortem paterentur et bona eorum fisco applicarentur. Et sic contra eorum divicias, non contra personas crimen inveniebatur, licet falso. a tali maligno Regimine libera nos, Domine.

[This was when the Republic had such a tyrant for emperor that even against innocent citizens a false criminal accusation would be sought, such that through it they would suffer death and their goods be applied to the public treasury. And so the crime was found against their riches, not against their persons, though falsely. From such an evil rule deliver us, O Lord.]

[30] Cf. *Somnium,* ed. Arnold, 70: "Et quoniam dies mali sunt, valde grandia patent pericula de veritatibus offerre parabolas, in quibus quandoque magnorum et potentum redarguatur oblivio et negligentia reprehendatur."

[31] Similar glosses in the two manuscripts:

> |P1.20| **P1** 5v
> Contra diffamatores scribens doctorum locutus est ille venerabilis Tullius, in *Libro de Morte,* qui postquam scripserat septem libros, sic dixit: "Non libet michi deplorare vitam, sicut multi indocti fecerunt, quoniam sic me vixisse, cognosco ut non me frustra natum existimem, |et| ex hac vita ita discedo non tanquam ex hospicio sed tanquam a domo."

> |Writing against the detractors of the learned, the venerable Tully spoke out in his book *On Death.* After he had written seven books, he said thus: "I am not inclined to weep over life, as many uneducated men have done, because I know that I have lived in such a way that I do not think that I was born in vain, and I depart from this life not as from a hotel but as from my own home."|

> |P2.5| **P2** 4v #2
> Contra eos qui dampnant scriptores librorum loquebatur Tullius, in *Libro de Morte* postquam scripserat septem libros, dicens "Non libet michi deplorare vitam sicut varii indocti fecerunt. Sed neque me vicxisse penitet quoniam ita vicxi ut non me frustra natum existimem, |et| ex hac vita ita dicedo |discedo| non tanquam ex hospicio sed tanquam a domo."

> |Tully, after he had written seven books, spoke out in his book *On Death* against those who condemned the writers of books, saying: "It gives me no pleasure to deplore life, as various unlearned men have done. But neither do I have any regret for having lived, because I have lived in such a way that I do not think that I was born in vain, |and| I depart from this life thus, not like leaving a guest-house but rather like leaving my own home."|

The gloss attributes this material to the lost *Liber de Morte* by Cicero, although the text actually comes from *De senectute* c. 84 (trans. Copley, *Cicero: On Old Age and On Friendship,* 41); note how Bovet reverses the sense of the original:

> . . . Non libet enim mihi deplorare vitam, quod multi, et ei docti, saepe fecerunt, neque me vixisse paenitet, quoniam ita vixi ut non frustra me natum existimem, et ex vita ita discedo tamquam ex hospitio, non tamquam e domo.

> |I have no inclination to sob and sigh over life, as many men—and men of cultivation, at that—have done, again and again. I'm not sorry that I have lived, either; after all, I have lived in such manner that I need not consider my birth to have been a waste of effort, and I am departing from life as from a temporary lodging, not as from a home.|

Neal Wood, *Cicero's Social and Political Thought* (Berkeley: University of California Press, 1988), 56, observes that the "*Liber de Morte* is the text otherwise known as the *Consolatio;* it is listed in the *De Divinatione* along with two other lost works, the *Hortensius* and *Cato.*"

[32] Arnold (*Apparicion,* 9, n. 1) identifies this as a Provençal form, and suggests the translation *quoique* [although]; the reading makes sense here.

[33] Bovet's gloss exhorts his readers not to recoil from God's work, whatever the consequences; it cites three different texts:

> |P1.21| **P1** 6r
>
> "Nichil enim," ut dicit Augustinus in libro *De civitate Dei,* "est curandum de vili morte illius cuius bona vita precessit." Ad hoc i, q. iii, cap. *Salvator (Decretum* C. 1 q. 3 c. 8) principio. "Nichil miserius est quam propter mundum deserere Deum" xii, q. i, cap. *Duo (Decretum* C. 12 q. 1 c. 7).
>
> |"For no concern is to be taken," as Augustine says in his *City of God,* "about a sordid death suffered by one whose good life has preceded it." The canon *Salvator,* in the first part, speaks to this, as does the canon *Duo:* "Nothing is more miserable than to abandon God because of the world."|

> a) St. Augustine, *De civitate Dei* 1.11 (*The City of God Against the Pagans,* Loeb Classical Library, trans. George E. McCracken |Cambridge, MA: Harvard University Press, 1957|, 1:56–57:

> Nec ignoro quam citius eligatur diu vivere sub timore tot mortium quam semel moriendo nullam deinceps formidare. Sed aliud est quod carnis sensus infirmiter pavidus refugit, aliud quod mentis ratio diligenter enucleata convincit. Mala mors putanda non est, quam bona vita praecesserit.

> |I am not unaware how much sooner a man would choose to live long under the menace of so many deaths rather than by dying once to fear none of them henceforth, but it is one menace that the apprehension of the flesh weakly seeks to escape and quite another that the carefully analyzed calculation of the mind pins down. That death should not be judged an evil which follows a good life.|

See also Augustine's *De disciplina Christiana* 12.13, "Mors bona, si vita bona praecessit" (PL 40.676).

> b) Gratian, *Decretum* C. 1 q. 3 c. 8 *Salvator* |Friedberg 1:413–15|, *principio* |at the beginning|:

> Salvator predicit in evangelio, circa finem seculi pseudochristos et pseudoprophetas surgere et multos seducere, et fideles suos in mundo multas habituros pressuras, sed tamen portas inferi non prevalituras. Proinde (ut ait Apostolus, oportet esse hereses, ut qui probati sunt manifesti fiant) oportet nos cum propheta ex adverso consurgere, et murum pro domo Israel opponere, et cum Apostolo per multas tribulationes intrare in regnum Dei quoniam non sunt condignae passiones huius temporis ad futuram gloriam, que revelabitur in nobis.

> |The Savior in the Gospel predicts that near the end of the world false prophets will arise and seduce many (Matthew 24:24. Mark 13:22), and those in the world who are faithful to him will experience many pressures, but nevertheless the gates of hell will not prevail against them (Matthew 16:18). Therefore (since, as the Apostle says, "heresies must needs be, so

that those who are proven may be made manifest" [1 Corinthians 11:19], it is necessary for us, with the Prophet, to rise up in opposition and build "a wall in front of the house of Israel" [Ezekiel 13:5], and with the Apostle through many tribulations enter into the kingdom of God (Acts 14:21), because the sufferings of this time are not worthy to be compared to the glory that is to come, which will be revealed in us (Romans 8:18).]

c) Gratian, *Decretum* C. 12 q. 1 c. 7 *Duo sunt* [Friedberg 1:678]; see [P1.4], note 7 above:

§. 1. Aliud vero est genus Christianorum, ut sunt laici. *Laos* enim est populus. His licet temporalia possidere, sed non nisi ad usum. Nichil enim miserius est quam propter nummum Deum contempnere.

[But there are other kinds of Christians, like the laicty. For "laos" means "people." They are allowed to possess temporal things, but only to use them. For there is nothing more wretched than to contemn God because of money.]

For the latter, cf. Lupus, *Regula monachorum* 5, "De utilitate paupertatis" (PL 30.336C), attributing it to Jerome.

[34] In **P1**, this line follows the rubric "Maistre Jehan parle au phisicien"; for clarity, I have reversed them, following their order in **P2**. The "iiii dessus nommés" are, of course, the Physicien, the Juif, the Sarrazin, and the Jacobin.

[35] A marginal gloss in **P1** cites Justinian's *Digest* as a proof of the danger the Physicien has subjected himself to in his quest to proclaim the truth. As with [P1.21] (note 33 above), the language is not precisely the same in the law as in Bovet's gloss, but the two texts agree in calling attention to the bravery of the Physicien: his current unpopularity reduces him to sneaking about by night, and yet in doing so he risks his life (as does a thief) to come "testify" in secret against the stupidity of the French people. The Prieur's initial reluctance to raise his voice against injustice compares poorly with this example of righteous courage:

[P1.22] **P1** 7r
Qui vadit per noctem in domo aliena magis presumitur velle occidere quam furare, et ideo impugne [impune], occiditur a domino domus ut *De sicariis et veneficiis.*

[Whoever enters another's house at night is presumed to be a killer rather than a thief, and therefore he can be killed with impunity by the master of the house, as in *De sicariis et veneficiis.*]

Justinian, *Digest* 48.8 tit. *Ad legem Corneliam de sicariis et veneficiis* ("*Lex Cornelia* On Murderers and Poisoners") c. 9 [Mommsen/Watson 4:820]:

Furem nocturnum si quis occidit, ita demum impune feret, si parcere ei sine periculo suo non potuit.

[If anyone kills a thief by night, he shall do so unpunished if and only if he could not have spared the man('s life) without risk to his own.]

[36] Similar glosses in both manuscripts provide a vehement and learned defense for the opening argument in the Physicien's long diatribe against discord (ll. 90–228), which begins by condemning the Parisian public for their willingness to believe the accusations of sorcery made against practitioners of his art in the case of King Charles VI's illness, and against the Duchess of Orléans, Valentina Visconti, as well (see note 49 below). The gloss cites the examples of two sinners, King Nebuchadnezzar (Daniel 4) and Elisha's servant Gehazi (2 Kings/Vulgate 4 Kings 5), whose sufferings come about not through the machinations of humans (as the Physicien sees being assumed in the case of Charles) but as the result of divine justice:

|P1.23| **P1** 7v #1; |P2.6| **P2** 6r

|**P2**: Ymo| Propter peccatum Rex potentissimus Nabugodonozor conversus fuit in sensum bovis, ita ut erraret septem annis per montes et nemora herbas pascendo sicut jumenta cap. *Nabugodonozor* C.. xxiii q iiii (*Decretum* C. 23 q. 4 c. 22). Eciam propter peccatum parentum aliquando corporaliter affliguntur sequentes generationis |generationes; **P2**: generis| ut apparet in |*missing in* **P2**: in . . . generis| Geizi cuius propter peccatum lepra transivit ad omnis |omnes| posteros sui generis, eciam |**P2**: et| peccato patrum |**P2**: parentum| percusit Deus omnem primogenitum Egypti, "ab homine usque ad pecus" |Psalm 134:8|; ymo et etiam terram peccato hominum "conversa est in salsuginem a malicia |**P2**: mali| habitancium in ea" (Psalm 107:34). Hec omnia in cap. *Ecclesia,* 1 q iiii.

|Because of his sin the most powerful king Nebuchadnezzar was transformed into a bovine mentality, so that he wandered seven years through the mountains and woods, eating vegetation like cattle . . . Also because of the sin of their parents sometimes following generations are afflicted, as appears in Gehazi, on account of whose sin leprosy passed on to all following generations of his race, and likewise because of the sins of the fathers that God struck the firstborn of Egypt, "both man and beast"; no, what is more, through the sins of men the land "was converted into a wasteland, because of the wickedness of those who live there." (See) all these in cap. *Ecclesia* . . .|

a) Gratian, *Decretum* C. 23 q. 4 c. 22 *Nabuchodonosor* |Friedberg 1:906–07|:

Nabuchodonosor penitenciam meruit fructuosam. Nonne post innumeras inpietates flagellatus penituit, et regnum, quod perdiderat, rursus accepit?

|Nebuchadnezzar deserved to have a fruitful penitence. Did he not, after innumerable impieties, being chastized, repent, and once again recover his kingdom, which he had lost?

Nebuchadnezzar is chastised, but then recovers both his senses and his kingdom, precisely the outcome Bovet wishes for his King. "Geizi" (Gehazi) wrongfully accepts the gifts offered by the leper Naaman but refused by Elisha; his master punishes him by afflicting him and his descendants with Naaman's leprosy: "Sed et lepra Naaman adherebit tibi et semini tuo in sempiternum et egressus est ab eo leprosus quasi nix" [Just as also for the sin of Achor the ark of the covenant was handed over to the Philistines, and for the sin of Gehazi leprosy passed on to his descendants; 2 Kings/Vulgate 4 Kings 5.27]. Bovet also refers to the story of Gehazi in his *Somnium super materia scismatis* (Arnold, ed., 82): "Sicut etiam pro peccato Achor, arca federis tradita est in manibus Filistinorum, et pro peccato Gyezi lepra transivit ad posteros." For that matter, Gratian uses this story in two places, the canon *Cito* (*Decretum* C. 1 q. 1 c. 16 [Friedberg 1:362])—where Gehazi appears as the type of the simoniac clergyman—and in the *dictum* cited here by Bovet:

b) Gratian, *Decretum, C.* 1 q. 4. *dictum post* c. 11 *Ecclesia que* [Friedberg 1:420–22]:

Gratian. § 2. Item peccato Egyptiorum possessiones eorum grandini traditae, jumenta et primogenita eorum morte consumpta sunt.
III Pars. § 10. . . . Pariter etiam demonstratum est, peccatis parentum parvulos aliquando corporaliter flagellari.
§ 11. Item Cam peccante Chanaam filius eius maledicitur (Genesis 9:22–25); Iezi delinquente lepra transmittitur ad posteros . . .

[Gratian. § 2. Likewise, the possessions of the Egyptians because of their sin were given over to hail, their livestock and firstborn consumed by death.
III Pars. § 10 . . . Similarly it has been shown that sometimes children are corporally scourged because of the sins of their parents.
§ 11. Also, when Cham sinned his son Chanaan was cursed; and when Gehazi sinned leprosy was transmitted to his posterity. . . .]

The Physicien goes on to maintain that the attribution to sorcery is nothing less than the influence of the devil (l. 163); Bovet supports this point by showing that disasters such as the king's illness should be interpreted instead as the result of divine judgment (cf. [P1.14], note 23 above). Nebuchadnezzar was punished properly for his own sin, as sinful France is punished through the disorder brought on by Charles's madness; and innocent Charles suffers along with his wicked subjects, as did the innocents of Egypt for the intransigence of Pharaoh, and the descendants of Gehazi for his sin. See the discussion of Charles VI's illness and the resultant public outrage against physicians in note 2 above.

[37] Bovet amplifies his citations of canon law in the previous gloss ([P1.23], [P2.6]; note 36 above) by insisting here that anyone who ignores these canons sins against the Holy Spirit:

[P1.24] **P1** 7v
Periculum est canones non servare quia qui voluntarie contra canones faciunt videntur spiritum sanctum blasphemare (xxv q i cap. *Violators. [Decretum* C. 25 q. 1 c. 5]).

[There is danger in not observing the canons, because those who willingly act against the canons appear to blaspheme against the Holy Ghost.]

Bovet's note very closely follows Gratian's summary to *Decretum* C. 25 q. 1 c. 5 *Violatores* [Friedberg 1:1008]: "In Spiritum sanctum blasphemant qui sacros canones violant."

[38] A brief marginal gloss corroborates Bovet's claim regarding the sanctity and divine origin of medicine:

[P1.25] **P1** 7v
Altissimus de celo creavit medicinam et vir sapiens non aborrebit illam.

[God in the highest heaven created medicine, and the wise man should not scorn it.]

The line is nearly identical to Ecclesiasticus (Sirach) 38:4. It is also cited by (ps.-) Augustine, *Speculum de Scriptura*, on Ecclesiasticus (Sirach) 38 (PL 34.968).

[39] In order to demonstrate the sinfulness of divination, Bovet here cites a canon and the subsequent *dictum* by Gratian:

> [P2.7] **P2** 6v
> Devinare res occultas vel futuras nunquam potest capi in bonam partem, quia devinacio est diabolica et hoc probat Jheronimus super Mathiam [Michaeam] et est textus prima (q. i cap. *Judices* ¶ *Cum ergo*.|*Decretum* C. 1 q. 1 *dictum post* c. 24, *Cum ergo*])
>
> [The divination of occult or future things can never be considered favorably because it is diabolical, as Jerome demonstrates . . .]

The first part of his gloss refers to the text of the canon itself:

> Gratian *Decretum* C. 1 q. 1 c. 24 *Numquam divinatio* [Friedberg 1:368]:
> Numquam divinatio in bonam partem accipitur. Videbantur sibi quidem esse prophetae, sed quia pecuniam accipiebant, prophetia eorum facta est divinatio.
>
> [Divination never has a favorable interpretation, Some men seemed to be prophets, but because they took money, their prophecy became divination.]

The second part refers to Gratian *Decretum* C. 1 q. 1 *dictum post* c. 24, *Cum ergo* [Friedberg 1:368]; in earlier editions, cap. 24 was part of cap. 23, which is entitled *Duces* in Friedberg [1:367] but *Judices* in previous versions (= q. i cap. *Judices* ¶ *Cum ergo*). Bovet indicates that Gratian will apply teachings from Jerome's *In Michaeam* (Jheronimus super Mathiam) 1.2, PL 25.1180A, 1182D–1184B.

> Gratian. Cum ergo secundum Jeronimum boni prophetae non munera prophetiae accipiebant, sed stipes tabernaculi, malis autem, qui accipiebant, prophetia, que donum Dei videbatur in divinationem, que diabolica est, convertebatur, quid aliud colligitur, nisi quod symoniacis (quod superius dictum est) nulla spiritualis gratia cooperatur?
>
> [Since therefore according to Jerome good prophets did not accept payments for their prophecy but only tabernacle stipends, for the wicked prophets, who were accepting payment, their prophecy, which seemed to be a gift of God, was converted into divination, which is diabolical, what else can be concluded except, as noted above, that for simoniacs no spiritual grace is at work?]

The "meschans devins, sorceliers, arquimans" et "coquins" mentioned in the text certainly refer to widespread quackery in the courts of France, but Bovet could also have in mind the specific case of the two Augustinian friars who tried and failed to cure Charles VI's illness and then accused others of sorcery (see note 48 below): their incompetence and subsequent fraud, the Physicien could be saying, put a blot on the reputations of all physicians, and could be responsible as well for some of the accusations leveled at Valentina Visconti.

⁴⁰ Bovet condemns dishonest physicians by providing a very close paraphrase of the first line of a canon in the *Decretum:*

> [P1.26] **P1** 8r #1
> Contra taliter condempnatam medicinam dicit decretum: Qui sine salvatore salutem vult habere, et sine vera sciencia credit se prudentem fieri posse, non sanus, sed eger, nec prudens, sed stultus in anxietate perpetuo permanebit, et demens et fatuus perpetuo laborabit C. xxvi. q. ii cap. *Qui sine.*

> [Against such condemned medical practices, the *Decretum* says: Whoever wishes to have health without the savior, and who without true knowledge thinks himself able to be prudent, is not healthy, but sick; nor prudent, but foolish; in perpetual anxiety he will remain, and, mad and idiotic, he will always labor.]

The canon cites a line from Rabanus Maurus (*De magicis artibus*, PL 110.1097A–B) that is also quoted by Burchard of Worms and Ivo of Chartres; the summary is an adapted continuation of the Rabanus text, PL 100.1097B:

> Gratian, *Decretum* C. 26 q. 2. c. 7 [Friedberg 1:1022–1023], summarized "Non est vita, sed mors inquisitio vel curatio, que a divinis vel magis expetitur" [The enterprise or practice in which divination or magic are sought is not life but death]:

> Qui sine salvatore salutem vult habere, et sine vera sapientia estimat prudentem se fieri posse, non sanus, sed eger, non prudens, sed stultus in egritudine assidua laborabit, et in cecitate noxia stultus et demens permanebit.

> [Whoever wishes to have health without the savior, and who without true wisdom thinks himself able to be prudent, is not healthy, but sick; not prudent, but foolish, in constant sickness he will labor, and in noxious blindness he will remain foolish and mad.]

⁴¹ The reference to the innocent Susanna (Daniel 13) in a marginal gloss in **P1** alludes to the recent slanders suffered at court by the Duchess of Orléans, Valentina Visconti (see note 49 below). The gloss amplifies the Physicien's denunciation of slanderers with a citation from Christ's attack on his detractors in John's gospel, and a *dictum Gratiani* providing a corollary to the same verse:

> [P1.27] **P1** 8r #2
> Hic venit directe istoria de Susanna que per falsum testimonum malorum periisset, nisi Deus per Daniellem illius veritatem revelasset, de quibus similibus dicitur: "Vos ex patre diabolo estis, quia opera patris vestri facere vultis" (cap. *Qui odit De pe.* Di. i).

> [Immediately at this point comes the history of Susanna, who would have perished by the false testimony of evil men, if God had not revealed her truth, through Daniel. Of these and similar [evil men] it is said: "You are of your father, the devil, because you are willing do to the works of your father."]

De penitentia Distinctio 1, *dictum ante* c. 36 *Qui natus est* |Friedberg 1:1167|, ad
v. "qui odit":

Item, ut Christus ait: "Omnis, qui odit malum, in luce agit" |John 3:20| . . .
Item: "Vos ex patre diabolo estis, quia opera patris vestri vultis facere."
Nemo autem filius Dei et diaboli simul esse potest" |John 8:44|.

|In the same, as Christ said "Everyone who hates evil acts in the light" . . .
and in the same: "You are of your father, the devil, because you wish to do
the works of your father."|

⁴² Similar citations at this place in the two manuscripts denounce the use of
poison:

|P1.28| **P1** 8r #2
Detestabilius et inhostius |= inhonestus| est veneno occidere quam gladium
(cap. *Certe* C. xii q. i c. iii |xviii| glossa et para. *De male.* l|lex| i) et idem dice-
bat Valerius, quod nobilitas Romanorum occidere veneno penitus ignorabat.

|It is more detestable and disgraceful to kill with poison than by the sword,
and Valerius says the same, that the Roman nobility knew nothing of killing
by poison.|

I have found no strictly relevant passages in the text of Valerius Maximus's *Factorum et dictorum memorabilium.*

|P2.8| **P2** 6v
Quia magis homicidium est et gravior culpa et offensa magis inhonesta apud
Deum et homines occidere veneno quam gladio (cap. *Certe* C. xii q. i c. iii
|xviii| glossa et para. *De male.* l|lex|. i).

|Because it is a greater and a more serious crime and an offense worse be-
fore God and men to kill with poison than with the sword.|

Gratian, *Decretum* C. 12 q. 1 c. 18 *Certe ego* [Friedberg 1:683]; the *Ordinary Gloss*
(col. 974) refers to Justinian, *Code* 9.18, *De maleficis et mathematicis et ceteris similibus,*
law 1: "Plus est hominem veneno extinguere quam occidere gladio" [It is worse to
kill a man with poison than to slay him with the sword].

⁴³ Bovet refers to the evil power of the devil as expressed in canon law. His use of
this canon here differs from the more legalistic application he gives it in an identical
gloss in manuscript **P1** ([P1.30, note 47 below]: here, he focuses only on the word *insidiator* (one who lays an ambush) as a synonym for the devil, who is mentioned in the
poem text (163–64) as chief of liars and source of the world's discord:

|P2.9| **P2** 7r
Quia ut dicit decretum, "insidiator humani generis bona sepissime solet
convertere in malum, et in electis ponere maculam" (C. ii q. vii c. i).

|Because, as the Decree says, "the enemy of the human race often changes
good to evil and plants faults in the elect."|

Gratian, *Decretum* C. 2 q. 7 c. 1 *Non est a plebe* [Friedberg 1:483]:

Non est a plebe aut vulgaribus hominibus arguendus vel accusandus episco-
pus, licet sit inordinatus, quia pro meritis subditorum disponitur a Deo vita
rectorum. Ideo ista dico, quia insidiator bona sepissime solet convertere in
malum, et in electis ponit maculam.

[A bishop should not be impugned or accused by the people or the common folk, even if he is at variance with divine law, because the manner of
living of the rulers is arranged by God on the basis of the merits of their
subordinates. I say this because the enemy often changes good to evil and
plants faults in the elect.]

44 The only apparent sense to be made of this expression is that discord now
bedevils even monastic institutions, whose rituals were long ordered by the daily
reading of and meditation upon the Psalms; perhaps the author felt a consideration
of the "Seven Penitential Psalms" to be in order, given the need for penance made
apparent by Christian society's disarray.

45 On the conflict between papal partisans in Flanders in the 1380s and '90s,
see Valois, *La France et le grand schisme d'Occident*, 3:235–71.

46 Bovet inserts the following twelve lines of Latin goliardic and Leonine verse
in the margin at this point, and while the general context of the verses (the sickness
of the king, exacerbated through the evil of the "sorcerers," which has spawned
further discord and menaces the general stability of the realm) seems clear enough,
several lines are incomprehensible, and the poem's provenance remains enigmatic:

[P1.29] **P1** 8v
Multa mala evenient deffuncta gallina;
Gallus cito moritur, carens medicina;
Pulli desolabuntur hora vespertina;
Vertetur post paululum totum in ruina.

Unus potentatus si fuerit dominatus
Erit status manens incontaminatus;
Dividens flatus si fuerit implicatus
Ponci affatus patebit deificatus.

Patenter visa fuit mors in gallo previsa
Ac per insanem pullorum est desolamen.
Non compleatur cauda ponci. Deus, o quero, queratur
Morbi medela, orbem inficiens assequela.

[Many evils will occur when the hen is dead;
The cock dies soon, lacking medicine;
The chicks are deserted at the hour of vespers;
Everything is transformed shortly into ruins.

Even if one powerful one will have been overcome,
He will remain in unsullied condition;
If the dividing breath will have been involved,
The bridge's address will appear deified.

Clearly it is seen, the death in France foreseen,
And through the madman is the devastation of the chicks.
The tail of the bridge is not filled in. O God, I ask, may healing of the sickness
Be sought, stabilizing the world by its result.|

Neither of the previous editors succeeded in solving the mystery of these quatrains, which Pichon (69, note V) describes as "fort obscurs" and Arnold (*Apparicion*, 13, n. 4) simply transcribes. The current editor, in his turn, despairing before both translation and exegesis, has assembled but a few scraps of context for the poem. It bears certain resemblances to an eleven-line prophetic poem noted by Marjorie Reeves, *The Influence of Prophecy in the Later Middle Ages*, 312. Reeves observes that "In the period which saw the downfall of the Hohenstaufen prophetic oracles circulated briskly. A second Ghibelline prophecy attributed to Joachim had a wide distribution. Its opening lines reveal an anti-French bias: 'Gallorum levitas Germanos justificabit, Et tribus adjunctis consurget aquila grandis' [The inconstancy of the cocks [= French] will vindicate the Germans, and the great eagle will rise up against the three neighbors]; while the Imperial triumph is expressed thus: 'Papa cito moritur, Caesar regnabit ubique'" [The pope dies quickly, Caesar will reign everywhere]. She cites Bartholomew Cotton (*Historica Anglicana (A.D. 449–1298),* ed. Henry R. Luard [London: Longman, Green, Longman, and Roberts, 1859]), whose chronicle (239) reproduces verses supposed to have been inscribed on a tomb at Rome in 1293 and destined for an English friend. Bovet's lines, however, share with this text only the prophetic mode, their reference to the French [Gallus], and the phrase "cito moritur." Reeves (op. cit.) refers to a number of Vatican manuscripts containing this or similar texts, to which list I can add one with a variant version of this prophecy by Jean de Roquetaillade: Vatican City, ASV Armarium 54/31 fols. 7r–8r, "Fragmentum pseudo-prophetiae alicuius auctoris qui frater Johannes de Rupa Cissa nominatur, ex libro primo conscriptorum secretorum archanorum invisi Dei, de electione Urbani VI et Clementi VII" [Fragment of a false prophecy of a certain author named Brother John of Rupescissa, from the first book of written arcane secrets of the unseen God concerning the elections of Urvan VI and Clement VI]. See Johannes de Rupescissa (ca. 1300–ca. 1365), *Liber secretorum eventuum,* ed. Robert E. Lerner and Christine Morerod-Fattebert (Fribourg, Switzerland: Editions Universitaires, 1994). None of this explains fully the difficult lines Bovet inserts at this point in his poem, nor does it suggest a source for the lines more definitive than his basic familiarity with the medieval prophetic tradition. See notes 78 and 79 below, for another use of prophetic material by Bovet.

47 Bovet here repeats the identical gloss he uses in manuscript **P2** at line 164 (see gloss [P2.9], note 43 above) for service in a different context. By citing a canon that outlaws accusations of bishops by laypeople, Bovet calls attention to the danger posed to society by reckless and malicious allegations such as those made against the physicians of Paris and Valentina Visconti:

|P1.30| **P1** 9r #1
Quia ut dicit decretum, "Insidiator humani generis bona sepissime solet convertere in malum et in electis ponere maculam (C. ii q. vii c. i).

[Because as the *Decretum* says, "the enemy of the human race is very often in the habit of turning all the good into bad, and of putting stains on the chosen ones."]

[48] The word *maillés* (line 226), to which a marginal gloss is attached, refers to a episode of civil unrest sixteen years before the writing of this poem, one brought about by criminal activity: the March 1382 rebellion of tradespeople and artisans now known as the "Maillotins." The insurgents, protesting an increase in taxes, had armed themselves with lead hammers found in the arsenal at the Hôtel de Ville and caused great panic among the upper class (see Autrand, *Charles VI*, 93–98; Frédéric Godefroy (*Dictionnaire de l'ancienne langue française* [Paris: Librairie de sciences et des arts, 1937–1938], 5:3–74, s.v. *maillé* and *maillet*) shows that the term became synonymous with "evildoer." At this point in the poetic text, and in identical glosses at this point in the two manuscripts, Bovet refers to the potential for violence inherent in the acts of contemporary malefactors, and the commentary is exceptional in that it presents a historical aside instead of the usual elucidation drawn from Scripture or from canon or civil law. The glosses treat the affair of two apostate Augustinian friars who had been engaged to cure the king of his mental illness (lines 135–168, above, seem to refer, in general terms, to the iniquities of this pair). They apparently began their efforts early in 1397. Charles recovered for a time, then relapsed; the two apparently feared that they would be held responsible for the king's worsening condition, and so attempted to attribute their failure to the sorcery of various magnates at the court of France. Their two-part strategy, Bovet observes, was to insist upon being closely protected, saying that *magni viri* (cf. "nos seigneurs les plus grans," l. 154) would try to kill the king's healers; they then spread the rumor that many people were casting spells upon the king, and that they would continue until arrested; the culmination would be an uprising by the people, who would be furious until the aristocrats who caused the monks' failure had been brought to justice:

[P1.31] **P1** 9r #2; [P2.10] **P2** 7v
Audivi quod duos modos tenuerunt valde mirabiles ad faciendam maximam commocionem in populo. Primus fuit quod petebant se multum curiose custodiri, dicentes quod magni viri tenebant manum in ista infirmitate principis, qui procurarent occidi facere illos qui eum vellent curare. Secundus fuit quod dicebant per sortilegia semper multos operari contra infirmum, et quod semper ita facerent nisi fieret una magna justicia; et quia credebant in suo proposito deficere quoad curationem, quando populus (**P2**: ~~populus~~) audiret illam impeditam quia Justicia non fiebat de magnis, sperabant ex hoc fieri tumultum et sedicionem in populo.

[I heard that they held (employed) two truly marvelous methods of making the greatest disturbance among the people. The first was that they petitioned to be guarded very carefully, saying that great men, who were trying to have those killed who wanted to cure him, had a hand in this infirmity of the king. The second was that they claimed that many were constantly working by sorcery against the ailing king, and that they would always continue to do so unless a great act of justice were brought about [= a tribunal convened against them?],

> and because they believed that their undertaking to cure the king was failing, when the people heard [their claim] that the cure was being impeded because justice was not being done against the magnates, they hoped that this would cause tumult and sedition among the people.]

Louis of Orléans had the two arrested; they were tried by an ecclesiastical court, condemned, and beheaded on 30 October 1398. Apparently this comment was composed between their arrest and execution (see Introduction, § Manuscripts): at this point, manuscript **V** (fol. 48v) adds two lines announcing that justice had been carried out by the time of Bovet's revision of the text for presentation to the Duke of Burgundy:

> Maiz ia en ont leur paiement
> Aulcuns receu villainnement
>
> [But now they have received their comeuppance, in disgraceful fashion]

This episode is recorded in the *Chronicle* of the Monk of St.-Denis (ed. Bellaguet, 2.542–47, 662–69). See also Pichon's very full historical contextualization (n. 4, 67–68), and Famiglietti, *Royal Intrigue*, 209, n. 26.

[49] The prompt "Maistre Jehan parle" appears at this point in manuscript **P1**; since Prose 124–125 already introduce Jean de Meun's ensuing speech, an introduction already recapitulated by Prose 126, I have chosen to omit this extraneous line.

Immediately following Prose 125 in manuscript **P2** (fol. 8r), an entire page is dedicated to a fourteen-line consolatory poem presenting Valentina Visconti as the wronged Susanna of Daniel 13 (see gloss [P1.27], note 41 above), framed by two miniatures: on one side the Physicien presents his book, and on the other stands Valentina with a lady-in-waiting (see figure 7). Following the 14 lines of verse, a red rubric identifies the intended speaker of these lines: "Son physicien parle a madame d'Orliens." Manuscript **P1**, although not dedicated to the Duchess, includes the accompanying dedicatory lines after the conclusion of the text proper, and this edition follows that format (see lines 1530–1543). These verses have been thought by some scholars to refer to Valentina's supposed banishment from the court after being accused of poisoning the king. Sandra Hindman, for example (*"Epistre Othea,"* 166) follows Froissart in contending that Valentina had been banished from the court three years earlier on charges of exacerbating the king's illness through sorcery. Valentina's husband Louis of Orléans, whom the mad Charles had tried to kill at one point, had been accused of poisoning the king; the Duchess herself, one of the few persons the king would allow in his presence, became an obvious object for slander as his condition worsened. R. C. Famiglietti, however (*Royal Intrigue* 238–39, n. 183), presents compelling evidence that Valentina, pregnant at the time, left the court for her own health. Nevertheless, Bovet appears to imply a certain popular antipathy toward Valentina, as reflected in his marginal gloss mentioning Susanna [P1.27], the consolatory verses above, and in the Physicien's references to the slander against members of the highest nobility (ll. 141, 154–158, 210–212).

[50] Different glosses condemning both usury and its toleration appear at this point in both manuscripts (see note 53 for the **P2** version, [P2.11]). In **P1** (see fig-

ure 6), the gloss is executed in a hand different from that found in the text or glosses, whose sloppiness suggests the work of one not trained as a scribe. It is the same hand as the first three lines of the gloss on **P1** 25v [P1.34]. Gilbert Ouy recognizes this script as the autograph of Honorat Bovet, an attribution which would suggest a very close cooperation between the author and the atelier that produced these dedication copies.

|P1.32| **P1** 9v

Usure dampnate sunt utroque testamento, et ideo nec rex nec imperator ymo ipse vicarius Jhesus Christi super eis posset dispensare (*Extra De usuris* cap. *Quia in omnibus*). Caveant ergo reges ne dent privilegium fenerandi, nam ipsi acrius quam feneratores peccarent (C xxiiii q. iii cap. *Qui aliorum*).

|Usuries are condemned in both Testaments, and therefore neither king nor emperor nor even the vicar of Jesus Christ himself can give dispensations in this matter . . . Therefore let kings take care not to grant the right of lending money, for in doing so they would sin more grievously than the lenders themselves.|

a) X 5.19 tit. *De usuris* cap. 3 *Quia in omnibus* |Friedberg 2:812|:

Quia in omnibus fere locis ita crimen usurarum invaluit, ut multi, aliis negotiis praetermissis, quasi licite usuras exerceant, et qualiter utriusque testamenti pagina condemnentur, nequaquam attendant: ideo constituimus quid usurarii manifesti nec ad communionem admittantur altaris, nec Christianum, si in hoc peccato decesserint, accipiant sepulturam, sed nec oblationes eorum quisquam accipiat.

|Since almost everywhere the crime of usury is so dominant that many men have abandoned other businesses and practice usury as if it were a legitimate enterprise, paying no attention to how it is condemned in the text of both Testaments, therefore we have decreed that openly practicing usurers are not to be admitted to communion at the altar, nor are they to receive Christian burial, if they should die in this sin, and furthermore no one is to accept their offerings.|

b) Gratian, *Decretum* C. 24 q. 3 c. 32 *Qui aliorum* |Friedberg 1:999|:

Qui aliorum defendit errorem multo est damnabilior illis, qui errant, quia non solum ille errat, sed etiam aliis offendicula preparat erroris et confirmat. Unde quia magister erroris est, non tantum hereticus, sed etiam heresiarcha dicendus est.

|Whoever has supported the errors of many is more to be blamed than they who transgress, because not only does he himself transgress, but also prepares and confirms the stumbling-block of error for others. Therefore because he is the master of transgression, he is called not only a heretic, but also a founder of heresy.|

Bovet's contemporary Philippe de Mézières also comments on usury: George W. Coopland, ed., *Le Songe du Vieil Pelerin of Philippe de Mézières, Chancellor of Cyprus* (Cambridge: Cambridge University Press, 1969), 2:285–92.

   51 In 1394; see the account in the Monk of St.-Denis (ed. Bellaguet, 2:118–22), and Introduction, § "Bovet and Islam."

   52 This practice is decried again during the Prieur's concluding harangue, lines Prose 255–264, below.

   53 The Juif makes it clear that his definition of usury includes the sort of chicanery he describes (ll. 257–274) as being currently practiced by Christians. An attached gloss is **P2**'s version of the proscription on usury we have seen in [P1.32], note 50 above, and repeats that gloss's first citation in observing that usuries are condemned in both OT and NT. In the ensuing five, Bovet refers to chapters in canon law expressing the limitations in the power of king, emperor, and pope to grant licenses to lend money at interest:

> |P2.11| **P2** 9r
> Quia usure sunt utroque testamento dampnate (*Extra De usuris* cap. *Quia in omnibus;* x–c–vii–q). Rex non poterit super eis dispensare, quia psaltem |saltem| Rex Jus divinum sibi recognoscit dominari, et eciam ecclesiasticum, ut dico cap. *Per venerabilem,* cum sua materia; ymo nec imperator habet illam potestatem dandi licensiam fenerandi, qui tantum est lex animata in terris (in *Autenticis De consili.* coll. iiii); ymo nec etiam vicarius Christi in spiritualibus, papa, cum non possit dare licenciam peccandi, nec ipsimet est peccandi auctoritas atributa (xl Di. cap. *Si papa* et cap. *Non nos* |et| C. ix q. iiii |iiii| cap. *Facta*).
>
> |Since usury is condemned in both Testaments, the king cannot grant dispensations in the matter, because the king, at least, recognizes that he is under the domination of divine law and also church law, as I point out concerning the chapter *Per venerabilem* and its apparatus; nor does the Emperor have such a power of licensing usury, for he is nothing more than the embodiment of the law on earth; and not even Christ's spiritual vicar, the pope (has such power), since he cannot give license to sin, nor is the authority to sin one of his attributes.|

a) X 5.19 |tit. *De usuris*|.3 |Friedberg 2:812|—see |P1.32|, note 50 above. The stricken citation "x–c–vii–q" that follows reverses the usual order (*quaestio* before *capitulum*), and may well have been crossed out for that reason; and if indeed it does refer to a particular canon in the *titulus* X 5.19 *De usuris*, it is not *Quia in omnibus* (cap. 3) but rather cap. 7, *Praeterea parochianis* |Friedberg 2:813|, another pronouncement on usury, summarized "Usurarius monitus, non desistens, si clericus est, ab officio et beneficio suspenditur; si laicus, excommunicatur" |The usurer, once warned and not desisting, if a cleric, is suspended from office and benefice; if a layman, he is excommunicated.|

b) X 4.17.13 *Per venerabilem* |Friedberg 2:714|, summarized "In terris ecclesiae Papa potest libere illegitimos legitimare, in terris vero alienis non, nisi ex causis multum arduis, vel nisi in spiritualibus . . ." |In the lands of the Church, the pope can freely legitimate the illegitimate, but not so in others' lands, except for extremely grave reasons, or only in spiritual matters . . .|. Bovet refers not to any specific language from this decretal, but rather to its general significance in the discussion of papal power; see end of note, below.

c) Bovet mistakenly cites the title *De consili* from the *Authentics (Novels)* of Justinian, *collatio* 4; the correct reference is to *De consulibus, Auth.* Coll. 8 (= *Novel* 105), cap. 2. par. 4, ad v. *legem animatam* [Mommsen 3:507], where the gloss reads "Nota principem esse ipsam legem animatam in terris" [Note that the prince is the very law itself embodied on earth]: *Corpus juris civilis Justinianei, cum commentariis* (Lyon: J. & P. Cavellat, 1627), col. 468. The Greek original is νόμος ἔμψυχος, ensouled law.

d) Gratian, *Decretum* D. 40 c. 6 [Friedberg 1:146]; first commented upon by Ivo, as per PL 161.329D–330.A:

[III. Pars.] Si Papa suae et fraternae salutis negligens deprehenditur inutilis et remissus in operibus suis, et insuper a bono taciturnus, quod magis officit sibi et omnibus, nichilominus innumerabiles populos catervatim secum ducit, primo mancipio gehennae cum ipso plagis multis in aeternum vapulaturus . . .

[If the pope is detected of being negligent of his own and his brother's salvation, being useless and remiss in his deeds, and moreover reticent about what is good, which is more offensive to himself and to everyone, in spite of all he leads innumerable peoples with him, as first serf, to Gehenna, to be punished along with him by many lashes . . .]

e) Gratian, *Decretum* D. 40 c. 1 *Non nos* [Friedberg 1:145], is summarized "Offitium sacerdoti non confert, sed adimit licentiam delinquendi" [A priest's office does not confer but rather removes the license to sin]. Cf. Gregory VII, *Letters* 9.9, PL 148.614C.

f) Gratian, *Decretum* C. 9 q. 3 c. 15 *Facta subditorum* [Friedberg 1:610–11]; the first part is from Isidore, *Sententiae* 3.42.2, PL 83.711C, the latter from *Sent.* 3.38.5, PL 83.709B:
Facta subditorum judicantur a nobis: nostra vero a Domino judicantur. §. 1. Deteriores sunt qui vitam moresque bonorum corrumpunt his, qui substantias aliorum prediaque diripiunt.

[The deeds of our subordinates are judged by us; but God judges ours. § 1. Those who corrupt the life and morals of the good are worse than those who seize and despoil the substance of others.]

Facta subditorum is also cited by Bovet in his *Arbre des Batailles* (ed. Nys, 92, bk. 4, chap. 6) during a discussion of the comparative rights of pope and emperor. Bovet claims to have argued this matter of royal responsibility in a commentary, now lost, on *Per venerabilem* with its gloss (*dico . . . cum sua materia*). *Per venerabilem* is cited along with Innocent III's gloss on that canon in Bovet's *Arbre des Batailles* (ed. Nys, 189, 4.83) in support of the papal stance regarding the comparative powers of the King of France and the Holy Roman Emperor; it became the locus for discussing the dispensing power of the pope. See H. A. Kelly, "Canonical Implications of Richard III's Plan to Marry His Niece," *Traditio* 23 (1967): 269–311, esp. 281–83.

⁵⁴ King Muhammad VI of Granada (r. 1395–1405).

⁵⁵ The Sarrazin here insinuates that the existence of two popes and the resulting antagonism between their followers must signify an essential error in Christian doctrine. Bovet replies by citing a canon and its gloss: the law is one and unblemished even if contemporary prelates defy it, and mutual abdication can be the solution to the papal schism:

> [P2.12] **P2** 11r
> Pro tanto est error, quia etiam ex causa necessitatis duo pape esse non possunt (C. vii q. i cap. *Non autem* et ibi in glossa largissime).
>
> [This error is so great, because even in case of necessity there cannot be two popes.]

Gratian, *Decretum* C. 7 q. 1 c. 12 *Non autem* [Friedberg 1:571] is summarized "Augustinus non tam successit quam accessit" [Augustine is more an addition to [to the bishopric] than a successor]. The canon deals with the fact that St. Augustine was appointed bishop of Hippo while the current bishop was in still in place. A good portion of the gloss ("in glossa largissime") attached to this canon can be brought to bear on this case. The gloss (cols. 822–823), s.v. "et non succederet," raises the problems inherent in having two bishops of one see, and suggests potential solutions. It then raises the question of whether there could not be two "apostles" [i.e., popes] in the same way: "Item, nunquid eodem modo possunt esse duo apostoli?" [Now, in the same way can there be two popes?]. The glossator then argues in the negative, saying "Dominus tantum unum constituit" [Christ instituted only one], and then that the Church is one and catholic, and has only one head; and though we read of several emperors at once, it is different with the Church, because it would violate the article of the Creed, "Unam, sanctam, catholicam," etc. ["Preterea, quia una est ecclesia catholica, et unum caput; et tamen plures imperatores fuisse legimus . . . ; sed hoc non est ita, quia offenderetur illa regula, 'unam, sanctam, catholicam,'" etc.]. The gloss adds that the pope could renounce his office, a timely notion given the strength of support for the *via cessionis* at the time of Bovet's writing. See note 123 below.

⁵⁶ Lines 387–388 represent a variant from Manuscript **V** (fol. 52r). **P1** and **P2** provide identical readings for these lines:

> C'est trop grant debat que de loy.
> La ou n'a loy n'a bonne foy . . .

This version, however, forces line 387 to be considered in isolation, in which case it makes little sense. As Arnold (*Apparicion*, 20, n. 1) observes, however, the **V** variant allows 387 and 388 to function as a couplet, its sense consistent with the Sarrazin's subsequent argument.

⁵⁷ Bovet presents the pagan Virgil as the "master" of the Moslems and Christ as that of Christians; given the respect shown the character of the Sarrazin up to this point, the association slights neither Virgil nor Islam. For the reputation of Virgil in medieval legend see Domenico Comparetti, *Vergil in the Middle Ages,* trans. E. F. M. Benecke (London: Sonnenschein, 1908; repr. Hamden, CT: Archon

Books, 1966). Virgil had in fact been known in the eastern Roman provinces later conquered by Islam: see L. Casson and E. L. Hettich, *Excavations at Nessana* 2: *Literary Papyri* (Princeton: Princeton University Press, 1950).

[58] To amplify the theme of aristocratic excess and ostentation being sounded by the Sarrazin, Bovet enlists the help of a canon that repeats the moral principles regarding gluttony found in the homilies of St. John Chrysostom:

> [P2.13] **P2** 12r
> Contra istam habundanciam loquebatur beatus Johannes Os Aureum, dicent [dicens] "Nichil sic jocundum est sicut cibus bene dictus sanctus [bene digestus et decoctus]. Nichil sic salutem vel sensuum accumen operatur, nichil sic egritudinem fugat, sicut moderata refectio; quia quod solum ad vitam sufficit sanitatem generat et producit etiam voluptatem; nimia vero habundancia ciborum molestias ingerit et egritudinem generat. Quod enim facit extrema fames, hoc facit eciam plenitudo ciborum, ymo eciam facit pejora. Fames quippe in paucis diebus aufert hominem ex hac vita penali; excessus vero ciborum consumit et putrefacere facit corpus, et morte crudeli consumit (Dist. vi [v] cap. *Nichil De Cons.* [Gratian, *Decretum, De consecratione* D. 5 c. 28 *Nihil enim*]).

> [Against such abundance Blessed John Golden-Mouth spoke, saying: "Nothing is as pleasant as food, well called 'holy' [Gratian: well prepared and cooked]. Nothing supports health so well, and the acumen of the senses, nothing so puts illness to flight as does moderate eating, because what only suffices for wholeness generates and produces pleasure as well. But too much abundance of food brings in troubles and produces disease. For plenitude of food causes the same thing as extreme famine—in fact, even worse. For famine within a few days takes one away from this painful life; but an excess of food consumes the body and makes it putrefy, consuming it with a cruel death."

The entire gloss follows very closely after the language of Gratian, *Decretum, De consecratione* D. 5 c. 28 *Nichil enim* [Friedberg 1:1419], which itself cites John Chrysostom's 29th Homily on the Epistle to the Hebrews (PG 63. 201–208 [§4]). A similar theme is sounded in a gloss later in the same manuscript [P2.22] (note 91 below).

[59] Jean of Nevers—known to history as "Jean sans Peur" for his audacity in the later civil war—was the son and heir of Philip of Burgundy. Through his father's influence Jean (then aged 24) was given nominal command of the Christian army at Nicopolis, against the wishes of many experienced knights (Bovet deals with the problem of young men in command below, lines 623–630). Jean was held prisoner by the Turks for nine months after Nicopolis, until June 1397. See Introduction, § "Bovet and Islam," and note 84. Arnold, *Apparicion*, 22, n. 1, calls attention to Deschamps' poem on the same topic (Ballade 876, "Sur son désir de rentrer en France, après la guerre de Flandres," *Oeuvres* 5:58, lines 7–9), referring, however, to the 1383 campaign against the Flemish:

> Gesir vestu, boire eaue, et en la fin
> Avoir pou pain, soy tout le jour armer,
> Je suis perduz quant on ne boit de vin.

[60] Arnold (*Apparicion*, 22, n. 2) provides the following explanation to this line: "'S'il en trouve, que ce soit à son avantage!' Bonet doit vouloir dire que toute viande est bonne au Sarrasin, mais la phrase est peu claire."

[61] Arnold (*Apparicion*, 22 n. 3) reproduces the recipes for these dishes he finds in Pichon's 1845 edition (70), which come from the *Menagier de Paris* and the Viandier de Guillaume Tirel, also known as Taillevent.

[62] Bovet takes up the same theme in his *Arbre des Batailles:* ". . . nous disons que la chevalerie du jour d'huy n'est mie de la prouesse qu'elle fut du temps passé, car selon les loix anciennes les chevaliers mengoient feves et lart de porc et viandes grosses. Ils gesoient dur et portoient le harnois le plus du temps. Aussi ils demuouroient au dehors des citez et goustoient l'air de la champaigne en eulx retraiant en bastilles et forteresses et voulontiers tenoient les champs. Si ne disputoient pas de coustume des vins lequel estoit le meilleur, ainçois beuvoient de l'eaue clere pour ce que toute paine et traveil sceussent endurer" (ed. Nys 255, 4.132). Also cited by Arnold, *Apparicion*, 23, n. 1.

The decadence of the Western warrior, a popular theme in the later Middle Ages, endures in later centuries as well: see Octavius Caesar's rebuke to Antony in Shakespeare's *Antony and Cleopatra*, 1.4.55–71 (*The Riverside Shakespeare* [Boston: Houghton Mifflin, 1974] 1352–1353):

> Antony,
> Leave thy lascivious [wassails]. When thou once
> Wast beaten from Modena, where thou slew'st
> Hirtius and Pansa, consuls, at thy heel
> Did famine follow, whom thou fought'st against,
> (Though daintily brought up) with patience more
> Than savages could suffer. thou didst drink
> The stale of horses and the gilded puddle
> Which beasts would cough at:; thy palate then did deign
> The roughest berry on the rudest hedge;
> Yea, like the stag, when snow the pasture sheets,
> The barks of trees thou brows'd. On the Alps
> It is reported thou didst eat strange flesh,
> Which some did die to look on: and all this
> (It wounds thine honour that I speak it now)
> Was borne so like a soldier, that thy cheek
> So much as lank'd not.

[63] In a note to lines 470–472, Pichon (71 n. 8) makes the following comment: "Il me paroit manquer ici deux vers dont le sens seroit: "On acquière la force nécessaire pour suivre le métier des armes." Since Pichon did not know of the existence of the Vatican manuscript, his observation takes on prophetic significance given the fact that these two lines from **V** I have inserted here (472a, 472b), missing in **P1** and **P2**, seem to complete this phrase. Arnold makes this emendation as well (*Apparicion*, 24, n. 1).

[64] Valerius Maximus expresses very similar ideas in speaking of Cato the Elder (4.3.11, ed. Kempf 183; ed. Briscoe, 7:250–51; trans. Bailey, *Memorable Doing and Sayings*, 1:377, 379):

> Age, si quis hoc saeculo vir inluster pellibus haedinis pro stragulis utatur tribusque servis comitatus Hispaniam regat et quingentorum assium sumptu transmarinam provinciam petat, eodem cibo eodemque vino quo nautae contentus sit, nonne miserabilis existimetur? Atqui ista patientissime superior Cato toleravit, quia illum grata frugalitatis consuetudo in hoc genere vitae cum summa dulcedine continebat

> [And now, if in this day and age a celebrated person were to use goatskin coverlets and govern Spain accompanied by three slaves and go to an overseas province at a cost of five hundred asses and be content with the same food and wine as the sailors had, would he not be thought a sad fellow? And yet the elder Cato tolerated all this quite uncomplainingly because the frugal habits he loved kept him in this way of life which he thoroughly enjoyed].

Arnold (*Apparicion*, 24, n. 2) once again cites another edition.

[65] Bovet's gloss cites Cicero's praise of Cato (actually his speaker Cato the Elder's adulation of his departed son, Cato):

> [P2.14] **P2** 12v
> De isto Cathone dicit Tullius in *Libro de morte,* quod in mundo eo [nemo] melior natus est.

> [Concerning this Cato, Tully says, in his book *On Death*, that (no one) has been born in the world better than he.]

On the lost *Liber de Morte*, see commentary on [P1.20] and [P2.5] (note 31 above). Bovet once again attributes this material to this lost text by Cicero, when the text actually comes from *De senectute* c. 84, just several lines after the passage cited in the above-mentioned glosses.

[66] This is a **V** reading; both **P1** and **P2** offer the following couplet at lines 485–6, which Pichon (74, n. 9) rightly terms "fort obscur":

> Car sa vice vraye et certaine
> Par grant vertu fut vie vaine.

[67] Arnold's line 490 reads "Nen pour robes *ne* vanités"; the "nen" occurs in **P2**, his base text, and the "ne" in **V**, which provides the following couplet in the same place in the text (489–490) in **P1** and **P2**:

> Au monde plais pour tes bontés,
> Non pour robes ne vanités.

Arnold insists that "plaisir" (l. 489) is an infinitive, and cites (25 n. 1) the following paraphrase from St. Bernard in Deschamps's *Miroir de Mariage* (*Oeuvres* 9.137, lines 4149–4153):

> Et dit oultre [St. Bernard], si com j'entens,
> Que riche vesteure est pou sens

Et gendre a ses voisins envie:
On doit plaire par bonne envie,
Non par robes ne par orgueil.

The text paraphrased is Bernard's Letter 113.4, PL 182.258B–C. I remain unconvinced, and have therefore retained the **P1** reading and translated it as an ironic gibe, which fits better with the Sarrazin's next statement than would a pious declaration.

[68] In **P1**, the "ne" is superscript in a similar hand, indicating a contemporary correction.

[69] The passage from Origen and the line from Wisdom cited in this gloss appear in [P1.6], n. 14 above; the biblical passage is cited in [P1.1], n. 2, as well. In both previous appearances, these texts were mustered in support of broad theoretical statements regarding the duties of kingship and the public good provided by stable leadership. This comment seems slightly out of place in this context, given that the point being made here in the poetic text is that Christian generals send the wrong people into battle:

[P2.15] **P2** 13r

Inter ceteras virtutes per sapienciam principes regnant. Est eis, ut dicit Origenes, "Gloria regni in rege prudente"; *Quanticorum super omelia quinta* [*Homilia quinta super libro Canticorum*]; et alibi "Rex sapiens stabilimentum est populi" (*Sapientie* cap. v [vi]).

[Among other virtues princes reign through wisdom. As Origen says, "The glory of the kingdom consists for them in a prudent king"; and, elsewhere, "The wise king is the foundation of his people."]

[70] This is another jab at the ostentation many found responsible for the failure of the Christian forces at Nicopolis. In his *Chevalerie de la Passion de Jésus-Christ*, written in the same year the Western army left for Nicopolis, Philippe de Mézières indicates that he had no illusions about how this army was going to proceed: the French, English and German knights were too much in love with one of the most beautiful women in the world, "Dame Vaine Gloire" (Paris, Bibliothèque de l'Arsenal, MS 2251, fols. 31–32v; cited in Nicolae Jorga, *Philippe de Mézières et la croisade au XIVe siècle* [Paris: Bouillon, 1896], 489). Their behavior indicated neither humility nor military discipline: "les menistreulx et les hyraux precedens à grans pourpes et à grans paremens, en robes et en vaisselle d'argent, faisans les grans disners des viandes oultrageuses" (Arsenal, MS 2251, fol. 31v). Mézières's book, intended as a warning, unfortunately ended up being prophetic. In his *Chronique*, Froissart (in idem, *Oeuvres*, ed. H. Kervyn de Lettenhove, 25 vols. [Brussels: Devaux, 1867–1877], 15:332–37) talks about the knights' folly in rejoicing before they had even joined battle with the enemy. The Monk of St.-Denis (ed. Bellaguet, 2:484) notes that the army arrived at Nicopolis in spectacular luxury, and that Nevers' troops had been pillaging everywhere they went; clerics were reminding them of the holy purpose for this mission, and warning them, unavailingly, of God's impending wrath.

[71] Arnold (*Apparicion*, 26 n. 2) cites a passage in the Monk of Saint-Denis (ed. Bellaguet, 1:661) recording Louis de Bourbon's "crusade" against Mahdia (Tunis) in 1390 that describes the Muslim light cavalry charge in action against heavily armored Christian knights: barefoot and wearing only silk-stuff tunics for armor, they nimbly avoided the heavy fire of Christian archers, retreating in different directions on their speedy horses, later regrouping to counterattack and drive the Christians back to their ships, killing many. The strategy recalls Muslim light-cavalry tactics against heavy Byzantine cataphracts in the seventh century.

[72] Bovet's gloss seconds the Sarrazin's critique of Western extravagance, a theme echoed later by the Jacobin (line 1444; see [P1.37], note 131 below). The citation praising moderation in eating that Bovet attributes to Seneca is not found in his extant works, though it is reminiscent of the *Formula Honesta Vitae* § 3, *De continentia*, PL 72.25C:

> |P2.16| **P2 13v**
> Humana natura, pro vita levi et corporis sanitate sienciam quocorum |coquorum| non querit, nec tantam exquisicionem ciborum, nec talem inflammacionem salsarum, unde Seneca in quadam epistola: "O dii boni, quam de modico vera femes |fames| et vera sitis extinguitur."

> |Human nature does not seek out the expertise of cooks in order to have a calm life and bodily health, nor such great refinement of food or such biting sauces; whence Seneca in one of his epistles says, "O good gods, with what little |food and drink| are real hunger and thirst quenched!"|

[73] Bovet here refers to the Battle of Aljubarrota (in west-central Portugal, between Porto and Lisbon), 14 August 1385, where the mixed forces of King João I of Portugal defeated Juan II of Castile's numerically superior force. The citizenry of local towns rose up in support of João and his knights, led by Nuno Álvares Pereira, and a cohort of English longbowmen apparently turned the tide of battle. This encounter is described by Froissart in his *Chroniques* (ed. Kervyn de Lettenhove, 11:179–81). The outcome effectively ended the Castilian threat to Portuguese independence, and led to the Treaty of Windsor being signed in the following year, an alliance between England and Portugal that endures to this day.

João's triumph may be regarded, in the expression used by a recent encyclopedia article, as "a victory of the national spirit against the feudal attachment to established order" (*Encyclopedia Britannica*, 15th ed. [1993], vol. 25, s.v. "History of Portugal, The House of Aviz, 1383–1580," 25:1054–55). Later Portuguese historians made much of the contributions of the common folk to preserving their freedom, even if contemporary chroniclers—as was their wont—gave more attention to the achievements of the aristocratic commanders than to other participants. English employment of commoner bowmen in the battle line was revolutionary in the fourteenth century, and the fact that Bovet cites this episode as illustrative of the military capacity of simple folk indicates the popular reception of the battle's significance in the few years after it took place. Nevertheless, I have yet to find any support for the colorful legend recorded by Pichon (71, n. 10) and cited by Arnold (*Apparicion*, 27, n. 1): "M. le vicomte de Santarem, ancien ministre des affaires etrangeres de Portugal, qui connoît si bien l'histoire de son pays, m'apprend (ce qu'Honore Bonet savoit évidemment) que les paysans portugais se levèrent en masse à cette occasion et prirent les armes contre les Castillans. Ils avoient à leur tête une boulangère armée d'une pelle et d'une épée. On conserve encore aujourd'hui à Aljubarrota, parmi les trophées de cette celebre bataille, la pelle et l'épée dont se servoit cette héroïne."

[74] Like Arnold (*Apparicion*, 28, n. 1), I find nothing in Valerius Maximus dealing with the desirability of sending peasants into combat. Arnold, however, offers this pertinent citation from Jean de Meun's French translation of Vegetius: Ulysse Robert, ed., *L'art de chevalerie, traduction du De re militari de Vegees par Jean de Meun*, SATF 39 (Paris: Firmin Didot, 1900), 7:

> Si ensicut a enquerre li quel homme sont plus pourfitable a estre chevalier, ou cil des chans ou cil des cités; mais je ne croi pas que de ceste partie puissons nous douter que li pueples champestres ne soit plus convenables que cil des cités, car il sont norri hors des delis as chans, a l'air, es painnes et es travaus, et seuffrent le soulail et despitent les umbres, ne ne sevent riens de biangni [bains] ne de delices, et sont de simple corage et se tiennent a paie de peu et ont les menbres endurcis a souffrir toutes manieres de travaus et sont coustumier de porter fais et de faire fosses ai chans.

[75] The Sarrazin's lines paraphrase a passage from Cicero's *De Senectute* c. 20 (trans. Copley, *Cicero: On Old Age and On Friendship*, 12): "Quod si legere aut audire voletis externa, maximas res publicas ab adulescentibus labefactatas, a senibus sustentatas et restitutas reperietis" [But if you care to read or listen to the history of peoples other than ourselves, you will discover that it is young men who have sent the most powerful governments crashing to ruin, and the old who have either kept them strong or restored their strength]. Also noted by Arnold, *Apparicion*, 30, n. 2.

The Monk of Saint-Denis (ed. Bellaguet, 2:486) comments upon the Western leadership during the battle at Nicopolis, noting that Marshal Boucicaut and Nevers rejected the cautious proposals of the experienced King of Hungary as cowardly and insisted on a fatal cavalry charge, expressing a sentiment similar to the that of Bovet's *Sarrazin*: ". . . sed juniorum oculis, qui cor facile sequebantur, sermo regis dignus accepcione dignus visus non est" [but in the opinion of the younger ones, who are easily led by their passions, the king's advice was seen as unworthy].

[76] Aziz S. Atiya, *Crusade, Commerce and Culture* (Bloomington: Indiana University Press, 1962), 110–11, notes that Muslim losses in the battle of Nicopolis were estimated at nearly 30,000, and that the Turkish commander, the Sultan Bāyazīd (Bajazet), was sufficiently infuriated to order the massacre of some 3,000 Christians on the next day. The Sarrazin continues (ll. 640–666) with a condemnation of the French abandonment of a great number of nobles who were spared execution but imprisoned or sold into slavery in Turkey after the battle. See also Atiya, *The Crusade of Nicopolis* (London: Methuen, 1934), and his broader study, *The Crusade in the Later Middle Ages* (London: Methuen, 1938); more recently, A.-M. Talbot, "Nikopolis, Crusade of," in *Oxford Dictionary of Byzantium*, 3 vols. (New York: Oxford University Press, 1991), 3:1486, with bibliography.

[77] At Nicopolis.

[78] Nearly identical glosses in the two Paris manuscripts record a prophecy current in the late fourteenth century which held that a French force [*gallus*] would cross the Alps, engage an evil enemy, and be destroyed in battle, but that the enemy dominance would be short-lived, and French power would ultimately prevail. The "prophecy" is one comment, but is divided into two stanzas, the first of which prophesies the French defeat, and the second France's eventual revenge. The two parts are attached to separate verses in both manuscripts. In **P1** the first part is attached to l. 691, "Car une prophecie disoit," the second to l. 696. It seems Bovet divides the prophetic text in half to take advantage of the threat in the later poetic line, "Que mal en sera vostre pance": Jean de Meun here answers the Sarrazin's trenchant critique with the promise of vengeance for the Christian defeat at Nicopolis (see Introduction, § "Bovet and Islam"). The second and sixth lines in the first stanza refer to Jean de Nevers, leader of the ill-fated expedition, himself the son of the fourth son of the House of France, Philip of Burgundy (*quartus Gallus*, line 2). In order to retain its place of appearance in the manuscripts, I have put the second part of this prophecy and the conclusion of the accompanying commentary in the succeeding note (79).

[P1.33A] **P1** 17r #1, attached to line 691; [P2.17A] **P2** 15v, attached to line 692:

Precedens prophecia Ganimedis: [rubric; only in **P1**]

Futurum est ut ad instigacionem
filii quarti Galli magna gens
contra barbaros congregetur
et illa in bello peribit. Sed   **P2**: et illa in bello peribit, et bene.
qui bene intelligens dominus   **P2**: intelligens clare videt quod dominus
Nivernensis est filius quarti galli.

[Presented first, the prophecy of Ganymede:
In the future, at the instigation
Of the fourth son of the cock, a great nation
Will gather against the barbarians
And will perish in the battle. But   **P2**: . . . and rightly so.
Who understands well: the Lord   **P2**: Who understands clearly sees that the Lord
Of Nevers is the son of the fourth cock.]

[79] Continuation of the prophecy begun in the previous note:

[P1.33B] **P1** 17r #2; [P2.17B] **P2** 16r; both attached to line 696:

Sequens prophecia que fuit [fecit] Prothey: [rubric; only in **P1**]

Gallus per Lacium transmissis
Alpibus, ingens ibit, et expensis [expansis]
obstabit nubibus alis. Gallus
sternet avem Jovis, armaque
sacrataque jura arripiet, victa
et dominabitur urbe.

[Next, the prophecy made by Protheus:
After crossing the Alps, the cock,
Huge, will progress through Latium,
And with expanded wings will oppose the clouds.
The cock flattens Jove's bird, he will seize his arms
And sacred laws, and, with the city conquered,
Will hold dominion.]

Eustache Deschamps's Ballade 1117 (in *Oeuvres*, 6:29) also refers to these prophecies:

Selon aucuns tresanciens poetes
Faingnans d'oyseaulx et de bestes leurs fables,
De Protheus, de Ganimedès fectes,
Et de pluseurs qui sont mal entendables
Aux gens communs, sont les diz recitables.
Ou le coq doit les Alpes transvoler,
L'aigle et poucins d'icelle subjuguer,
Et si rongnier les ongles, queue et eles
Qu'en cheant lors, sanz pouoir relever,
Perdra du tout ses ailes natureles.

Jean-Patrice Boudet and Hélène Millet, *Eustache Deschamps en son temps* (Paris: Publications de la Sorbonne, 1997), 136, point out this connection, and place it in the context of late-fourteenth-century prophecies of "the Second Charlemagne" (see note 81 below). Deschamps's ballade, however, does not suggest any necessary linkage between the prophecies and Nicopolis, and focuses more on France's conflict with imperial Italy. Arnold (*Apparicion*, 32, n. 2) observes that this prophecy was known well before 1398, and also cites the Deschamps ballade. Notes 22 and 46 above also treat Bovet's references to prophecy.

[80] "Nobles" refers to the antecedent "ilz" in line 715.

In the *Arbre des Batailles*, Bovet makes the following observation: "Mais je vous demande qui a gaignié le Daulphiné, le principat d'Orenge, de Vienne et de Aragon, le royaulme d'Arle et celui de Narbonne et de Carcassone, les parties de Thouloze, de Guyenne, de Bordeaulx, de Garonne, de Barselonne, de Navarre, des regions de Mons Perrous, et de toutes les isles d'Espaigne. Certes ce ont faict le roy Charlemaigne et ses successeurs, se les histoires n'ont menty, car ils les ont conquis au trenchant de l'espee sur les Sarrasins ennemis de la foy qui pour lors tenoient ces royaulmes et seignories" (ed. Nys, 189, 4.83; cited in Arnold, *Apparicion*, 33, n. 1).

[81] Manuscript **V** (fol. 59v) provides a closer translation of the name and, keeping with the reviser's usual procedure, expands the reference:

Car nous avons la prophecie
Ou la prenostication
D'ung cordelier qui ot a nom
Frere Jehan de Roche Taillie
Auquel moult fort je me talie . . .

As Arnold (*Apparicion*, 34, n. 1) observes, the **P1** and **P2** readings of this name are due to Bovet's French rendering of the Latin *Johannes de Rupescissa,* which the **V** scribe then corrected.

The Sarrazin is referring to the prophecies of Jean de Roquetaillade, a French Franciscan whose interpretations of the writings of Joachim of Fiore helped spread the influence of Joachim's prophecy regarding the "Second Charlemagne" (see Marjorie Reeves, *The Influence of Prophecy in the Later Middle Ages,* esp. ch. 2). In Roquetaillade's version, the secular ruler who would join with the angelic pope to reform the world under Christianity was the King of France. Reeves (*Influence of Prophecy,* 324) notes that this idea spread so quickly that the *Diario d'Anonimo Fiorentino* (ed. A. Gherardi, in *Documenti di storia italiana* 6 [Florence: Sansoni, 1876], 389–90) records a prophecy supposedly made "per uno Frate minore nel 1368" in which the Angelic Pope would rise after 1378 and, together with "lo Re di Francia, imperadore di Roma," bring a new world order. Arnold cites Froissart (ed. Kervyn de Lettenhove, 6:262–63) for the following details: "En ce tamps (vers 1350) avoit un Frère-Meneur, plain de grant clergie et de grant entendement en Avignon, qui s'appelloit frère Jehans de Rochetaillade, lequel Frère-Meneur li pappes Ynnocens VIe faissoit tenir en prisson ou castiel de Baignolles, pour les grandes merveilles qu'il disoit qui devoient avenir, meysmement et princhipaument sus les prélas et présidens de Sainte-Eglise pour les supperfluités et leur grant orgoeil qu'il demainnent, et ossi sus le royaumme de Franche et sus les grans seigneurs des crestiennetés, pour les impressions qu'il font sus le commun peuple."

[82] Belamary: Banum Marin, the fourteenth-century Berber dynasty that controlled present-day Morocco; the region is here called by the dynasty's name. Cf. Chaucer's portrait of the Knight in the General Prologue of the *Canterbury Tales:* in his list of martial exploits appears that claim that he has "riden in Belmarye" (Larry D. Benson et al., eds., *The Riverside Chaucer,* 3rd ed. [Boston: Houghton Mifflin, 1987], I.57). Jamil M. Abun-Nasr, *A History of the Maghrib* (Cambridge: Cambridge University Press, 1971), 127–28, describes a series of attacks in the period on Marinid towns by Christian privateers; these escapades could be what Chaucer had in mind (cited by Vincent di Marco in his notes to the General Prologue, *Riverside Chaucer,* 801). See detailed discussion by Malcolm Andrew in his commentary (vol. 2) on the General Prologue, *A Variorum Edition of the Works of Geoffrey Chaucer,* Volume Two [*The Canterbury Tales*], Part A: The General Prologue, 2 vols. (Norman, OK: University of Oklahoma Press, 1993), 66–68. Chaucer, incidentally, mentions *Gernade* (Moslem Granada)—a city also mentioned by the Sarrazin (l. 723 above)—among the Knight's campaigns (l. 56).

[83] Sultan Bāyazīd (Bajazet) I (r. 1389–1402), victor at Nicopolis (1396); see note 76 above.

[84] A marginal comment in **P2** quotes Ecclesiasticus in condemning the contemporary vogue of swearing:

[P2.18] **P2** 17r #1
Unde Salamon: "Vir nimis jurans replebitur iniquitate et ad [a] domo eius non dissedet plaga" [Ecclesiasticus 23:12].

[Whence Solomon: "A man who swears much will be filled with iniquity and a scourge shall not depart from his house."]

Ecclesiasticus (Sirach) 23:12:
Vir multum jurans implebitur iniquitate, et non discedet a domo illius plaga.

Note how the Sarrazin ironically goes on himself to swear, by Muhammad, in l. 759.

[85] Another gloss in **P2**, drawn from Gratian via the Fourth Council of Toledo, A.D. 633 (PL 130.477C), amplifies the Sarrazin's ongoing critique of contemporary Christian practices, censuring those who make and break oaths:

[P2.19] P2 17r #2
Non potest, ut dicit scriptura, apud homines esse fidelis qui Deo fuerit infidelis (C. secunda q. vii cap. *Non potest*).

[As it is written, one cannot be faithful among men who is unfaithful to God.]

Gratian, *Decretum* C. 2 q. 7 c. 24 *Non potest erga* [Friedberg 1:488], is summarized "Christianos accusare vel in eos testificari non possunt qui fidem acceptam deserverunt" [They cannot accuse Christians or testify against them who have deserted the faith] and begins "Non potest erga homines esse fidelis qui Deo exstiterit infidus" [They who are unfaithful to God cannot be faithful towards men].

[86] Bovet's gloss inserts a personal message to Valentina Visconti:

[P2.20] **P2** 17v
Utinam domina mea Aurelianensis laborare dignetur, pro Relevamento totius pauperi ~~Regni~~ populi Regni Francie, ad diminucionem tantorum servientum sive sergentulorum, quia vere comedunt populum Domini sicut cibum panis.

[Would that my lady of Orleans would deign to labor to decrease the great number of servants [= functionaries] or little sergeants, thereby relieving all the poor people of the kingdom of France, for, truly, they devour the Lord's people like eating bread (Psalm 52:5).]

The office of sergeant, like that of bailiff, provosts etc., was created near the beginning of the fourteenth century. The number and venality of sergeants grew despite the passage during the century of several ordinances intended to limit both; the reign of Charles VI, as witnessed by Bovet, saw another increase. His choice of the diminutive form ("sergentulorum") in this gloss seems a token of his distaste for these figures. Ferdinand Lot and Robert Fawtier, *Histoire des institutions françaises au Moyen Age*, vol. 2, Institutions royales (Paris: Presses universitaires de France, 1958), discuss the establishment of these offices and the frequent royal ordinances that were necessary to curb abuses committed by royal officers, and describe the corruption of sergeants in particular:

Ce qui pousse baillies, sénéchaux, prévôts, viguiers, sergents, à empiéter sans cesse, c'est intérêt, l'orgueil, la propension de tout fonctionnaire à donner de l'extension à son service, à manifester son autorité . . . Ils sont enivrés de leur puissance . . . Plus que baillis et sénéchaux, leurs subordonnés et surtout les sergents, étaient haïs, et justement semble-t-il, pour leur cupidité, leur insolence, leur tyrannie. La répétition même des règlements pour réprimer leurs excès prouve l'innullité de ces tentatives (153–54).

Agents d'exécution des sentences, gardiens de la sécurité publique, les sergents sont comme la cheville ouvrière du Châtelet . . . Ils sont puissants et redoutés. Leur fonction est enviée, car, outre leur salaire régulier, ils touchent de toutes mains, sans qu'il soit possible de remédier à leurs extorsions (380–81).

[87] Arnold, *Apparicion*, 37, n. 1: "*Envalée*, mot inconnu au dictionnaire de Godefroy, doit etre construit sur *enval*. Le sens parait être: 'que les affaires (du seigneur) aillent bien ou mal.'"

[88] In a marginal gloss, Bovet takes up the cause of prisoners in French jails, a group that was subjected to a number of outrageous abuses in this time. His point is not only to inspire the sympathy of Duchess Valentina, to whom he appealed directly in the previous note regarding abuses by royal officers: by citing three examples from canon law, he argues that the same principles of propriety and honesty specified in the law ought to be observed in any case involving the king's subjects.

|P2.21| **P2** 18r

O Deus, quantum peccatum et quanta tirannia regnat in carceribus Francie! Non sum ausus plane loqui; unde pleniores sermones super hac materia relinquo confessoribus dominorum, quia clarum est quod secundum leges et decreta, jurisdicio et potestas dominandi quocumque modo vendi non debent ("Ne prelati vices suas" cap. *Preterea* |X 5.4,|; C. i q. iii cap. *Ex multis;* et cap. *Vendentes*)

|O God, how much sin and how much tyranny reign in the jails of France! I have not dared to speak plainly; wherefore I leave fuller discussions about this material to the confessors of noblemen, because according to the laws and decrees, it is clear that jurisdiction and authority should in no way be sold.|

The gloss describes the corruption rampant among royal officers in French jails; citations of canon law here all deal with analogous abuses of ecclesiastical office. The first bars clerics from accepting payments for the performance of their duties, the second forbids the taking of bribes, and the third condemns simony:

a) X 5.4, tit. *Ne praelati vices suas vel ecclesias sub annuo censu concedant*, c. 1 *Preterea* |Friedberg 2:767–68|: "Prelates shall not sell their jurisdiction in return for annual payment." The decretal itself refers to rural archpriests who are not to be required to pay the bishop money in return for being able to exercise jurisdiction.

b) Gratian, *Decretum* C. 1 q. 3 c. 9 *Ex multis* |Friedberg 1:415–16|, from a letter of Pope Alexander II, PL 146.1390D–1391A, summarized "Ministri et servitores ecclesiae absque ulla venalitate ab episcopis ordinentur" |Let ministers and servants of the church be ordained by the bishops without venality|.

c) Gratian, *Decretum* C. 1 q. 3 c. 10 *Vendentes* |Friedberg 1:416–17|, an adaptation of Gregory the Great, *Homilia in Evangelia* 39.6, PL 76.1297D; ed. R.

Étaix, CCSL 141 (Turnhout: Brepols, 1999), 386. The chapter is summarized "Qui dona Dei vendunt vel emunt, pariter a Deo damnantur" [Whoever sells or buys the gifts of God is equally condemned by God].

Bovet's concern with jail abuses in this time was well founded. An ordinance of Charles VI from August 1394 describes a few of the injustices the French court was attempting to reform. It dictates that the offices responsible for oversight for prisons, those of royal judge and consul, will be given to honest people; no men and women will be allowed in same cell; prisoners will be allowed to purchase their food from the outside, not forced to buy it from jailers; and those unjustly imprisoned will not be liable for *clavagium* (payments to the jailer), which cannot in any case exceed 12 deniers de Cahors. See D. F. Secousse, *Ordonnances des Rois de France de la troisième race* 9 vols. (Paris: Imprimerie Royale, 1723–1755); 7 (1745): 668, no.. 46 (at Figeac, Cahors).

[89] These two lines were reversed by the scribe, who added a tiny "b" before line 825 and an "a" before 826 in the left margin to indicate his mistake; I have emended their order accordingly.

[90] Pope Boniface IX (r. 1389–1404), the Roman contender for the papacy.

[91] Returning to a theme he has treated previously in the same manuscript ([P2.13], note 58 above), Bovet disparages the extravagant aristocratic lifestyle, this time among the leaders of the clergy, in a gloss taken almost verbatim from a canon in Gratian's *Decretum:*

[P2.22] **P2** 18v

Dubitandum [non] est de scriptura que dicit "Ecclesie principes, qui deliciis effluunt [affluunt], et inter epulas pudicitiam servare credunt," apostolicus [propheticus] sermo describit "quod deiciendi sunt de spaciosis domibus, lautisque cunviviis et multo labore epulis conquisitis" [Micah 2], "in tenebras exteriores ubi erit fletus et stridor dentium"[Matthew 8:12, 22:13]. "An non confusio est Jhesum pauperem crucifixum, farsis predicare corporibus?" Et infra iii [iv] cap. *Ecclesie principes* xxxv distinctio [*Decretum* D. 35 c. 4].

[One should have (no) doubt about the writing that says, "A prophetic dictum describes the leaders of the Church who abound in delicacies and who are confident of being able to preserve modesty in the midst of rich foods, saying that 'they are to be cast out of their spacious homes and away from their splendid banquets and rare foods that have been acquired with great effort' [Micheas 2] 'into outer darkness, where there will be weeping and the gnashing of teeth' [Matthew 8:12, 22:13; see Jerome, *In Michaeam* 2.9–10, PL 25.1172A–B for the entire quotation]. "Is this not a confused state of affairs, for gluttons to preach the poor and crucified Jesus?" And so on [= the rest of Gratian] D. 35 c. 4, *Ecclesie principes*.

Gratian, *Decretum* D. 35 c. 4 *Ecclesiae principes* [Friedberg 1:131–32]:

Ecclesiae principes, qui deliciis affluunt, et inter epulas atque lascivias pudicitiam servare se credunt, propheticus sermo describit, "quod eiciendi sint de spatiosis domibus lautisque conviviis et multo labore conquisitis epulis propter malas cogitationes et opera sua." [Micah 2]. Et si vis scire, quo ejiciendi sunt, evangelium lege: "in tenebras scilicet exteriores, ubi erit fletus et stridor dentium"

|Matthew 8:12, 22:13.| An non confusio et ignominia est Jesum crucifixum, magistrum pauperem atque esurientem, farsis predicare corporibus?

|The prophet's word speaks of the leaders of the church, etc., |saying| "that they are to be thrown out of their spacious homes and away from their splendid banquets and rare foods that have been acquired with great effort because of their own evil thoughts and deeds." And if you wish to know whither they are to be thrown, read the Gospel: that is, "into outer darkness, where there will be weeping and gnashing of teeth." Is this not a matter of confusion and ignominy, for gluttons to preach the crucified Christ, the master poor and hungry?|

Gratian's canon draws from the general sense of Micah 2; the closest verbal similarity is in verse 9, "Mulieres populi mei ejectis de domo deliciarum suarum . . ." [You have cast out the women of my people from their houses, in which they took delight . . .]; he is directly citing Jerome's Commentary on Micah 2, as cited above.

    [92] Arnold, *Apparicion*, 39 n. 1, cites M. A. Delboulle (*Romania* 33 [1908]: 600), who himself cites Léopold Delisle, *Actes normands de la Chambre des comptes sous Philippe de Valois* (1328–1350) (Rouen: A. Le Brument: 1871), 261 and 262, for the following early uses of *preuves:* "1340. Vingt plates de prove et demie prove. — Cinquante plates, dont il en i a .xxx. d'Allemaigne et les autres de prove." The glossary in Pichon's edition refers to *preuve* as a "pièce de vaisselle dans laquelle l'ecuyer du prince essayoit le mets ou la boisson, c'est à dire en prenoit une portion pour prouver qu'elle n'étoit pas empoisonnée."

    Naux, in the same line, is the Provençal equivalent of the Middle French *nefz:* here, a silver dish in the form of a boat, for serving sauces, etc.

    [93] Quoting from the same section in Cicero's *Paradoxa* 5 cited in the introduction to Montaigu's copy of the *Apparicion* ([P1.2], note 5 above), this gloss applies to ecclesiastics the same standards for virtue that Bovet, in that manuscript's introduction, required of secular rulers:

|P2.23| **P2 19r**
Qui imperator vult videri nomine et eciam opere primo debet sue voluptati scire dominari, ut possit postmodum subditis imperare. Unde Tullius in *Libro de Beneficiis,* "ut princeps nomine principantis dignus putetur: Quomodo tandem libero homini imperabit qui non potest suis cupiditatibus imperare? Refrenet igitur suas primum libidines spernat voluptates, iracundiam reprimat, coerceat avariciam, et ceteras animi labes repellat, et tunc incipiat |regere| aliis presse, cum ipse improbis actibus et turpitudini et nequicie parere desierit."

|Whoever wishes to be seen as an emperor in name and also in deed should first know how to rule his own desires, so that he can subsequently rule subordinates. Whence Tully in the book *On Benefits,* says, "in order that the prince be deemed worthy of the name of rulership: How, finally, can he command a free man, who cannot command his own lusts? Therefore let him first curb his own concupiscences, spurn his desires, repress his ire, coerce his avarice, and repel other blemishes of the mind, and then let him begin to rule others firmly, when he himself has ceased to obey bad acts and foulness and wickedness."|

[94] Arnold, *Apparicion*, 40 n. 1, observes that Bovet here alludes to *De Consolatione Philosophiae* 1 m. 6, "Memoriam moeror hebetavit," and compares 1 m. 4, "sensus nostros moeror hebetavit."

[95] The Jacobin here refers to the controversy over the denial of the Immaculate Conception of the Blessed Virgin Mary that had been preached by the Aragonese Dominican Juan de Monzon (line 927). In defending his theses for his master's degree in May 1387, Monzon not only reaffirmed St. Thomas Aquinas's contention that Mary had been conceived in sin but purified in the womb, but insisted that to hold the contrary position was against the faith. His propositions were condemned by the University of Paris on July 6, and the bishop of Paris excommunicated Monzon and any who held his beliefs publicly or privately. Perhaps perceiving an attack on their prestige, the Dominican Order rallied behind Monzon during his appeal to Pope Clement VII at Avignon in the next year, and many even loudly proclaimed his doctrines from the pulpit while the case was being argued. The Monk of St.-Denis (ed. Bellaguet, 1:577) describes their audacity and confidence in their political power. The cardinals at Avignon excommunicated Monzon as contumacious and ordered him to present himself at Paris, but he escaped to Aragon. The Dominicans were summarily disbarred from the University of Paris, and all those who would not swear obedience to the bishop of Paris were denied graduation. Many fled Paris, many were jailed, and even those who recanted were told the Order was to be given the last place in any University functions. Reconciliation did not take place until 1403. See William A Hinnebusch, O.P., *The History of the Dominican Order* (New York: Alba House, 1973), 2:171–76.

[96] A much later (eighteenth-century?) hand places an "x" before the word "Mouzon" and in the margin notes "Jean de Monteson, Dominicain en 1387."

[97] St. Thomas Aquinas, here described as the "son" of the University of Paris, taught there from 1252 to 1259.

[98] Saint Peter of Verona (or St. Peter Martyr) (b. 1205), Dominican preacher and inquisitor, was assassinated by proponents of the Manichaean heresy near Milan in 1252, and canonized in the following year (*New Catholic Encyclopedia* [New York: McGraw-Hill, 1967–1989], 11:223).

Bovet's marginal comment examines the issue of dying for one's faith, a topic only tangential to the major theme of this section, the ancient honor of the Dominican order:

[P2.24] **P2 20r**
Istud Martirium est summum, quando pro fide, pro qua sustinenda quando impugnatur, debet mors oblata non timeri. Idem eciam quando castitas corporis queritur corrupi. Idem quando aliquis compellitur ad quodcumque peccatum mortale, xxiii v cap. *Non est* [C. 23 q. 5 c. 11] et q. viii *Convenior* [C. 23 q. 8 c. 21], et eciam pro sustinendis juribus ecclesie, cap. *Sicut dignum de homicidi* [X 5.12.6] et ibi per doctores. Nullus autem debet sibi mortem inferre, sed ab alio sustinere (cap. *Neque* xxiii v [C. 23 q. 5 c. 11 *Non est nostrum*]). Sed numquid est dicendus martir qui per tormenta negat Christum et mente adorat? Dicit *Decretum* quod qui fragilitate carnis per vim negat non perdit gloriam martirii (cap. *Potest fieri De pen.* Di. prima [*De penitentia* D. 1 c. 52]).

[That martyrdom is the highest when death, which is proffered for the up-holding of the faith when that faith is impugned, should not be feared. Likewise also when bodily chastity is threatened with corruption. Likewise when one is compelled to commit any mortal sin, and also for the uphold-ing of the laws of the Church. However, no one should bring death upon oneself, but only endure it from another. But is not he to be called a martyr who because of torture denies Christ while continuing to adore him in his mind? The *Decree* says that one who because of the frailty of the flesh through the use of force denies does not lose the glory of martyrdom.]

a) Gratian, *Decretum* C. 23 q. 5 c. 11 *Non est nostrum* [Friedberg 1:934–35]. Jerome's canon argues that no one, if persecuted, is permitted take his own life, but may only submit his neck to the executioner. Jerome makes an exception where chastity is being threatened, but the *Ordinary Gloss* (col. 1341) disagrees.

b) Gratian, *Decretum* C. 23 q. 8 c. 21 *Convenior* [Friedberg 1:959–61]. This canon, culled from St. Ambrose's letters to his sister Marcellina (Letter 20, PL 16.994A–1002C), defends the general principle that the good man will prefer death to be-ing coerced into mortal sin, as would be the case were the Emperor to demand that a church be given to him, and as was the case (§. 5) with the holy man Naboth (1 Kings/Vulgate 3 Kings 21), who permitted himself to be killed rather sell his patrimony to King Ahab. See Ambrose, *Exhortatio ad Virginitatem* 5.30, PL 16.344D–345A.

c) X 5.12.6 *Sicut dignum* [Friedberg 2:794–95], tit. "De homicidio voluntario vel casuali" [Of homicide, voluntary or accidental]. Bovet's comment has noted the righteousness of dying in defense of the rights of the Church; the decretal cited here concerns the punishments for the murderers of St. Tho-mas Becket, as well as for those who cooperated or failed to intervene.

d) Gratian, *Decretum* C. 23 q. 5 c. 11 *Non est nostrum* [Friedberg 1:934–35]. This is a mistaken citation of a canon Bovet has already used once in this gloss. It begins with the instruction "De eodem" (from the same canon as before), which is summarized "Nemini licet sibi manus injicere" [No one is permitted to lay hands on himself]. That canon (*Tu dixisti*) ends with a sentence drawn from Augustine's *Contra litteras Petiliani* (2.114, PL 43.299), "Neque enim vene-ramur nomine martirum eos, qui sibi collum ligaverunt" [For neither do we venerate with the name of martyr those who bound their own neck]; its first word likely caused Bovet's misattribution.

e) Gratian, *De penitentia* D. 1 c. 52 *Potest fieri* [Friedberg 1:1171], from Ambrose's *De penitencia* 1.4, 18–19, PL 16.472A–B:

IV. Pars. "Potest fieri, ut aliquis victus suppliciis sermone neget, et corde adoret. Numquid eadem causa eius, qui sponte negat, et eius, quem tor-menta inclinaverunt ad sacrilegium? Non. . . . Et Christus athletas suos, quos viderit gravibus paulisper cessisse suppliciis, sine venia patietur manere?"

[It can happen that someone overcome by tortures will deny in words and adore in his heart. Is it the same thing for one to freely deny as for one whom torments have moved to sacrilege? No. . . . And will Christ allow his athletes, whom he sees to have yielded somewhat because of grave tortures, to remain without forgiveness?]

[99] The Dominican St. Raymond of Peñafort (1175–1275) compiled a new collection of laws, the *Decretals of Gregory IX* (1234), named for the pope who issued the work. He is also the author of a *Summa de casibus penitentiae* (ca. 1225), to which was later appended a revision of Tancred's *Summa de matrimonio;* the combined text bore the name *Summa de penitentia et matrimonio.* See Hinnebusch, *The History of the Dominican Order,* 2:248–50 (as in note 95 above).

[100] John of Freiburg (d. 1314), Dominican, moralist, canonist, and lector at Freiburg im Breisgau (sometimes inexplicably confused with Johannes Teutonicus [d. ca. 1245], author of the *Glossa ordinaria* [1215–1217] to Gratian's *Decretum*), wrote an index to Raymond of Peñafort's *Summa* and its gloss, an original work on moral problems entitled *Liber de quaestionibus casualibus,* and a monument in canon law, the *Summa confessorum* (1280–1298). See Hinnebusch, *The History of the Dominican Order,* 2:252–254, and his article on this author in the *New Catholic Encyclopedia,* 7:1051. Arnold (*Apparicion,* 42, n. 4) finds it curious that Bovet "aurait inséré [line 957] entre ces deux ouvrages un troisieme, le Questionnari (*Quæstionarius super quinque libros decretalium*), qui est de la main du dominicain Jacques de Tonnerre." It is possible, however, that Bovet uses the name *Questionari* here to represent the title of John of Freiburg's *Liber de questionibus.*

[101] Vincent of Beauvais (ca. 1190–ca. 1264), a Dominican, was author of the *Speculum maius,* a work containing 80 books in 9885 chapters, and divided into three major parts: *Speculum naturale, Speculum doctrinale,* and *Speculum historiale.*

[102] Bovet names the wrong king here. Philip III did not ascend the throne until 1270, whereas Vincent died by 1264; his patron was Louis IX (r. 1226–1270).

[103] The Dominican Bernard Gui (1261–1331; Latin *Guidonis*), the inquisitor at Toulouse against the Albigensians and a prolific historian, wrote the *Flores Chronicorum,* which covered the history of the world from the time of Christ to 1331. See Hinnebusch, *The History of the Dominican Order,* 2:411–16. The *Historia Tripartita,* however, is the work of another Dominican, Tolomeo (or Bartholomew, sometimes called "Ptolemy") of Lucca (ca. 1236–ca. 1327), who is best known for his *Annales* (covering 1061–1303), *Historia ecclesiastica nova* (twenty-four books, up to 1294), and for his completion of Thomas Aquinas's *De regimine principum* (see Introduction, § "Bovet and Islam"). The *Historia Tripartita* is known only from citations in other works by Tolomeo, who is also cited quite frequently by Bovet in the *Arbre des Batailles.* See also Hinnebusch 2:416–20.

[104] The French Dominican William Peraldus (d. 1270?), also known as Perault, is best known for his *Summa de virtutibus et vitiis,* the combined form of two separate works, a *Summa de virtutibus* (ca. 1236) that circulated independently before the appearance of the *Summa de vitiis* (ca. 1249). On Peraldus, see the *New Catholic Encyclopedia* 14:956b, and Siegfried Wenzel, "The Source for the 'Remedia' of the Parson's Tale," *Traditio* 27 (1971): 433–53. Arnold (*Apparicion,* 43, n. 5) asserts that "Le confesseur de Philippe III, frère Laurent, écrivit sur l'ordre du roi un *Livre des vices et des*

vertus." Laurent d'Orléans, another French Dominican, was indeed the confessor to Philip III (r. 1270–1285), and the author of the *Somme le Roi,* also a treatise on vice and virtue (see the introduction in W. Nelson Francis, ed., *The Book of Vices and Virtues,* EETS O.S. 217 [London: Early English Text Society, 1942], ix–xxviii). Laurent's work, however, shows no sign of having been composed in two parts, as is the case with the text described by Bovet's Jacobin, and Peraldus's work as well.

[105] The fiftieth tale of the *Gesta Romanorum* recounts the advocacy of a father for a wicked son, a rapist who should lose both eyes but is saved by his father's offer to have his own right eye put out instead (Charles Swan, trans., *Gesta Romanorum* [London: G. Routledge & Sons, 1905], 148.) Bovet cites the very similar tale of Zaleucus from Valerius Maximus (6.5 ext. 3; ed. Kempf, 301–02; ed. Briscoe, 1:409) in his *Arbre des Batailles* (ed. Nys, 253–54, 4.132).

[106] During the schism, the opposing papal courts of Rome and Avignon strove always to outdo the other in splendor, but each had to make do with much less revenue than was available to the unified papacy; the Jacobin is suggesting that, had the Sarrazin visited the Holy See before the onset of the schism, he would have observed even greater luxury than he has just described.

[107] The gloss refers to the misfortunes suffered by the physically frail Pope Gregory XI after he moved the papal court back to Rome (January 1377); he met tremendous political resistance from the Romans, and died there on 28 March, 1378. The papal schism ensued. See Richard C. Trexler, "Rome on the Eve of the Great Schism," in idem, *Religion in Social Context in Europe and America, 1200–1700,* MRTS 238 (Tempe: MRTS, 2002), 42–69. Although historians do not normally consider Gregory's court to have been as extravagant as that of his Avignon predecessor Clement VI (r. 1342–1352), the Jacobin presents him as the pinnacle of ostentation, and Bovet's attached gloss uses Gregory's career as an exemplum of the vagaries of fortune:

> [P2.25] **P2** 21v
>
> Hec est natura fortune que semper gaudet inferiora superioribus superiora infimis commutare, ut dicit Philosophus in libro Ethiquorum. Unde Seneca in Epistola: "Neminem sic Fortuna provexit ut non sibi tantum comminetur quantum promiserat," et sic fuit de isto Gregorio qui circa viam ad Romam et prope mortem habuit multa contraria cum prodicxerat [predicxerat] Joachim: "Dulce principium habuisti; finem expectabis amarum. Rubigo te consumet; hoc est dilectio propincorum."
>
> [This is the nature of Fortune, who always rejoices in flipping lower with higher and higher with lowest, as the Philosopher says in the book of *Ethics.* Whence Seneca says in his epistle: "Thus Fortune has never raised up anyone such that she does not threaten him as much as she had promised." And so it was with that Gregory, who experienced many contrary things in connection with his return to Rome near the time of his death, as Joachim had predicted: "You have had a sweet beginning; you can expect a bitter end; rust—that is, the affection of your neighbors/relatives—will consume you."]

The three citations in this comment are all puzzling. Bovet attributes the first to Aristotle's *Ethics,* and while its description of capriciousness seem roughly similar to descriptions in *Ethics* (Book 4) of the serenity with which the magnanimous man faces fortune, the sentiments seem closer to Boethius's *Consolation of Philosophy*. The similar ideas expressed in the next citation are not found as such in Seneca's letters, but may derive from his *De Constantia Sapientis* 5.4: "Nihil eripit fortuna nisi quod dedit" (in *Moral Essays*, ed. and trans. John W. Basore, 3 vols., Loeb Classical Library [Cambridge, MA: Harvard University Press, 1958], 1:60–61). It seems to be traceable in this form to Marbod of Rennes, Letter 1, PL 171.1471B: "Neminem eo fortuna provexit, ut non tantumdem illi minetur quantum permisit." A very similar citation appears in gloss [P1.40]; see note 144 below. The reference to Joachim of Fiore's prediction of a bitter end for one who had previously enjoyed much sweetness, finally, has not been found in published works by that author. The reference to the deleterious effects brought on by the affection of Gregory's relatives (*dilectio propincorum*) could well be a muted version of the vehement denunciations he makes elsewhere of the fruits of Gregory's nepotism, i.e. the swift ascent of the Rogier family (see esp. note 139 below).

[108] Bovet's *Arbre des Batailles* (ed. Nys, 12, §1.5) describes the Donation of Constantine, the document thought to have been the fountainhead of ecclesiastical privilege: "Il [Pope Silvester I, 314–335] fist tant que l'empereur Constantin receut le saint sacrement de baptesme, lequel empereur aima tant devotement sainte Eglise et tant de beaulx privileges lui donna avec grant plenté de rentes que longue chose seroit de les toutes raconter." This financial language comes from Bovet's day, however: annuities were "assigned" on "real property" (as opposed to "personal property"), but the assignment was often not carried out at the time of the grant of the annuity; and sometimes the annuities were not "assigned" for a long time. Many thanks to Richard C. Famiglietti for this explanation.

[109] The term "dignity" refers to an especially lucrative ecclesiastical position; its holder would be a "dignitary," "a member of a chapter, cathedral or collegiate, possessed not only of a foremost place, but also of a certain jurisdiction" (*New Catholic Encyclopedia*, 1:192, s. v. *beneficium*).

[110] A reference to the reform of papal elections undertaken by Pope Nicholas II in 1059. The Holy Roman Emperor, with the consultation of the Roman people and clergy, had heretofore been empowered to elect the new pontiff; Nicholas II's Lateran Synod produced a document (Gratian, *Decretum* D. 23 c. 1, *In nomine Domini* [Friedberg 1:77–79]) that Brian Tierney calls "a declaration of independence by the reformed papacy directed against both the imperial power and the factions of the Roman nobility that had often manipulated papal elections in the past" (*The Crisis of Church and State, 1050–1300* [Englewood Cliffs, NJ: Prentice Hall, 1964], 36). Bovet concerns himself with the actions of the Roman nobles, and ignores the role of the emperor in this episode.

[111] Bovet's gloss here refers the reader to the discussion of papal rights contained in the lost copy of the *Apparicion* he dedicated to Louis of Orléans, a matter he also treats at length in manuscript **P1**; see note 17, above, and Appendix 7 below.

|P2.26| **P2** 22v
In libro domini mei Aurelianensis tractavi materiam istam plenissime, et idcirco in isto, causa brevitatis, omitto.

|I dealt fully with this material in the book of my lord of Orleans, and therefore, for the sake of brevity, I omit it in this book.|

[112] A reference to the practice of *annates* or "first fruits," by which those named to a benefice or see would give the pope a full year's revenue upon appointment. Pichon (76 n. 17) observes that the first pope to raise *annates* was Clement V in 1305, and that Clement VII's enforcement of this policy led to a royal edict of 1385 forbidding French clergy to pay them. Bovet, therefore, seems to comment on contemporary abuses via a discussion of the origins of the Byzantine Schism in the eleventh century (see also note 108 above). Given the author's usual outspokenness, Pichon rightly finds it curious that Bovet should seek to mask these criticisms of ecclesiastical practices by raising them in a distant historical context (see also the following two notes).

[113] This note, dealing with the lawfulness of raising tithes, was erroneously inserted later in manuscript **P2**, at line 1229; for the purposes of this edition, I have transferred it to its appropriate location in the text, the equivalent of 9 lines above gloss [P2.27] on the same folio (**P2** 23r), while retaining here its actual location and sequential identification number:

|P2.28| **P2** 24v
Utrum sit pape obediendum volenti decimas levare super ecclesiis sine justa causa: hanc questionem plene posui in libro domini mei Aurelianensis.

|Whether a pope is to be obeyed who wishes to levy tithes on churches without a just cause is a question that I treated fully in the book of my lord of Orleans.|

The presentation copy of the *Apparicion* dedicated to Louis of Orléans, of course, is lost.

[114] Bovet provides a brief marginal note here in manuscript **P2** referring the reader to a historical text by Tolomeo of Lucca:

|P2.27| **P2** 23r
De ista maligna tirannia et casu orribili vide in Tholomeo libro XI et ibi plene.

|Concerning this evil tyranny and horrible event, see Tolomeo, book 11, where it is fully treated.|

See the extended discussion of the issue of tyranny in the Introduction, § "Bovet and Islam," and notes 99, 102, 104, and 105. The relevant lines actually occur in Tholomeo's Bk. 12 rather than Bk. 11. Interestingly, a marginal gloss in Simon de Cramaud's *De substractione obediencie* cites the same passages from Tholomeo of Lucca's *Historia Ecclesiastica* that Bovet refers to in this gloss in a very similar context. See Howard Kaminsky, ed., *Simon de Cramaud's "De substractione obediencie"* (Cambridge, MA: Medieval Academy of America, 1984), Appendix III (228–229), gloss attached to ll. 1801–1804, 128. On Cramaud, see note 123 below.

[115] Arnold's glossary (*Apparicion,* 125) suggests a Provençal origint for the word *pron,* and adds that the idiom in line 1152 should be translated as "agir dans son propre intérêt"; however, a modern Provençal dictionary notes that the Provençal expression carries more a sense of duty than of self-interest: "cadun a fa soun proun" means "chacun a fait ce qu'il a pu, son devoir" (F. Mistral, *Lou tresor dóu Felibrige ou Dictionnaire Provençal-Français* [Barcelona: Berenguié, 1968], 2:655, s.v. *proun*).

[116] The Byzantine emperor Bovet has in mind can be neither Justin I or II, nor one of the Justinians; it is rather Heraclius. See the Introduction, § "Bovet and Islam."

[117] The first nine words of the marginal note that appears at this point in **P1** (Dicit . . . Mulierarius) are in the hand that executed gloss [P1.32] (note 50 above), a very untidy script that Gilbert Ouy identifies as that of Honorat Bovet. The handwriting compels a conjectural reading of the last word it renders; I take this to be *mulierarius,* as in Isidore, *Etymologiae,* ed. W.M. Lindsay, 2 vols., Oxford Classical Texts (Oxford: Clarendon Press, 1911, repr. 1957) 10.107: [Femellarius, feminis deditus, quem antiqui mulierarium appellabant]: "A 'femaler,' one given to females/women, whom the ancients called a 'womanizer.'" An alternate reading would be *Milesius,* an adjective referring to the city of Miletus in Caria (Asia Minor), whose inhabitants were known, through the scandalous reputation of the lost "Milesian Tales," for their luxury and wantonness. Both terms make sense in the context of the description of Muhammad's vices that ensues; the gloss text appearing below contains the first conjectural reading mentioned:

> |P1.34| **P1** 25v
> Dicit Guido in *Mari istoriarum* quod Macometus fuit Mulierarius et Christianus sed valde luxuriosus ebreus [ebrius] et gullosus, et ideo in lege sua omnia facilia et carnalia permitebat, sicut pluralitatem uxorum feminarum seu concubinarum et Reliqua dampnata judicio racionis, et idcirco quia in disputacione non posset stare lex precepit quemcumque contradicentem legi vel predicantem contrarium sine misericordia mori.
>
> [Guido says in his *Sea of Histories* that Mahomet was a womanizer, and a Christian but very lecherous, drunken, and gluttonous, and therefore in his law he allowed all things to be easy and carnal, like the multiplicity of wives, women, or concubines, and the other things condemned by the judgment of reason, and therefore, because his law could not prevail in disputations, he prescribed death without mercy for anyone who contradicted the law or preached the contrary.]

For a discussion of medieval Christian representations of Muhammad as libertine and epicurean, see Daniel, *Islam and the West,* 96, 246, and *passim;* and Iogna-Prat, *Order and Exclusion,* 342–43.

The Dominican Giovanni Colonna (Johannes de Columpna; ca. 1300–1343/44) and not Guido (Bovet was likely thinking of the author of the *Historia Troiana,* 1287) is the author of the *Mare Historiarum* (c. 1340) mentioned here (a recent biography appears in the *Dizionario biografico degli Italiani* 27 [Rome: Istituto della Enciclopedia Italiana, 1982], 337–338). This compilation, divided into seven books and seven hundred thirty-two chapters, was intended to chronicle all of history, from the beginning of the world until the time of the author, but at Colonna's death it had reached only to the year 1250. Although the complete work has never been published, excerpts appear in G. Waitz, ed., *Monumenta Germaniae Historica, Scriptores* (Hannover: Hahn, 1879), 24:266–84; the passage cited by Bovet does not appear there. Indeed, despite his frequent verbatim renderings of cited material, Bovet here seems only to paraphrase his source, since the section of the *Mare Historiarum* dealing with the origins of Islam in a Paris manuscript—although it also presents Muhammad as an arch-heretic who disseminates a pernicious doctrine through violence and conquest—nowhere repeats the phraseology of Bovet's note. What is more, its opprobium goes further than Bovet's, presenting Muhammad as "primogenitus Sathane" (fol. 234v), the firstborn of Satan. Nevertheless, like Bovet's gloss, the *Mare Historiarum* description does present Muhammad as a libertine and a drunkard:

> Paris, BNF, MS fonds latin 4914, fols. 234v–235r, no. 234, rubric "De Mahumeto seductore et qualiter variis deceptoribus quandam matronam seductam accepit uexorem et qualiter velut magus homines illius regionis simplices ut sibi adhererent variis prestigiis seduxit" [Concerning Mohamet as a seducer, and how he received as his wife a matron seduced by various deceivers, and how like a magician he persuaded simple men of that region with various tricks to become his adherents]:

> Regnante Heraclio imperatore Machometus primogenitus Sathane primo legem illam, ymo perfidiam spargere cepit cuius doctrina pestilens, et disseminatus langor ita universas occupant provincias ut exhortacionibus et predicacionibus insuper gladio et violencia in suum errorem populos descendere compelleret inimicos . . . [During the reign of the emperor Heraclius, Mahomet, the firstborn of Satan, first began to spread that law, or rather perfidy, whose pestilential teaching and widespread torpor took over the provinces to such an extent that he compelled enemy peoples to accept his error, by means of exhortations and preachings and, in addition, resorting to the sword and violence . . .]

The passage goes on to describe Muhammad as "this miserable man, given over to wine and the belly" [hic . . . homo miserabilis, vino deditus et ventri]. See Introduction, § "Bovet and Islam."

[118] A marginal comment ([P2.28]; see note 113 above) appears out of place here in manuscript **P2**.

Pichon (77 n. 20) considers this passage an allusion to the nepotism practiced by the popes of the Rogier family, specifically that which benefited Bovet's enemy Raymond de Turenne (note 139 below).

[119] Arnold (*Apparicion*, 52, notes 1 and 2) points out that Bovet invokes the same concepts in this section as he had earlier in the *Arbre des Batailles* (ed. Nys, 27, 1.11): compare line 1248 with the *Arbre*'s "A ceste estoile, c'est à scavoir celui Barthelemy lequel est tombé du ciel de l'Eglise, a esté donnée la clef du puys d'abysme, c'est à entendre, d'avarice," and line 1251 with "De avarice viennent tous maulx et tous pechiez, comme l'Escripture le tesmoigne: *Avaritia radix omnium malorum.*"

[120] I accept Arnold's emendation (*Apparicion*, 53, n. 1) here, replacing *dira* with *dire*. If we retain the reading in both **P1** and **P2**—*dira*—then the subject must be "l'Université" (l. 1277), since that noun is given another verb in the future tense (*monstrera*, l. 1278). This reading would make nonsense of the direct discourse that follows (lines 1281–1283). Substituting *dire* for *dira* however, allows for the previous sentence to end at line 1279, and for 1280 to become a new phrase, introducing the direct discourse, and working in parallel with a later verse that comments on the quoted statement (1284), and with still another (1297) that introduces another two lines of direct discourse immediately following.

[121] This gloss amplifies the Jacobin's arguments against the folly of those who seek to know the future by demonstrating the unlawful nature of divination, as expressed in two canons:

[P2.29] **P2** 25v
In speculo divino vident angeli plura futura, et quantum Deo placuerit (C. xxvi q. v cap. *in principio* [= *dictum ante* cap. 1]). Eciam angeli sciunt ea quo [que] fiunt hic, quia praesto nobiscum sunt (C. xiii q. ii cap. Fatendum).

[The angels see many future things in the divine mirror, and how much (that) pleases God. Angels also know those things that happen here, because they are present here with us.]

a) Gratian, *Decretum* C. 26 q. 5 *dictum ante* c. 1 [Friedberg 1:1027]:
Quod autem sortilegi et divini, si cessare noluerint, excommunicandi sint, ratione et auctoritate probatur. Est enim quoddam genus culturae ydolorum, ex demonum consultationibus futura predicere . . . Futura enim prescire solius Dei est, qui in sui contemplatione etiam angelos illa prescire facit.

[That sorcerers and diviners are to be excommunicated if they are unwilling to cease their activity is demonstrated both by reason and authority. For there is a certain kind of worship of idols that consists of predicting the future by consulting demons. For knowing the future is something for God alone, who in contemplating himself also makes his angels foreknow the same.]

b) Gratian, *Decretum* C. 13 q. 2 c. 29 *Fatendum est* [Friedberg 1:730–31]:
Fatendum est, nescire quidem mortuos quid hic agatur, sed dum hic agitur; postea vero audire ab eis, qui hinc ad eos moriendo pergunt, non quidem omnia, sed que sinuntur etiam isti meminisse et que illos quibus hec indicant, oportet audire. Possunt et ab angelis, qui rebus, que hic aguntur, presto sunt, audire aliquid mortui, quod unumquemque illorum audire debere judicat cui cuncta subjecta sunt.

[It must be admitted that, while the dead do not know what happens here while it is happening, they do hear about it later from those who go to them after they die; not everything, however, but only those things that they are allowed to remember and what those to whom they impart it should know. The dead can also hear something from angels, who are present to things that happen here, what(ever) each one of them should hear, according to the judgment of Him to whom all things are subject.]

This citation is from the Commentary on Kings in PL 50.1203D (attribution uncertain; CPPMA 2188, 2:493–94).

[122] Note this wording in the *Chronicle* by the Monk of St.-Denis (ed. Bellaguet, 2.510), where the author bewails the wrath of God visited upon Christianity at Nicopolis: "judicia tua abyssus multa" (Psalm 35.7: "justitia tua sicut montes Dei, judicia tua abyssus multa" [Your justice is like the mountains of God; your judgments are a great deep].

[123] Bovet refers here to the General Assembly of the French clergy, which voted on 23 July 1398 to withdraw the French Church's obedience from Benedict XIII: the canon in Gratian comes from a section dealing with the transgressions of prelates, and calls for the removal of those who mislead the flock of Christ and foment division in the church. See Hélène Millet and Emmanuel Poulle, eds., *Le vote de la soustraction d'obédience en 1398*, vol. 1: Introduction, Édition et facsimiles des bulletins de vote (Paris: CNRS, 1988), and two works by Howard Kaminsky, *Simon de Cramaud and the Great Schism* (New Brunswick: Rutgers University Press, 1983), and *Simon de Cramaud's "De substractione obedientie"* (Cambridge, MA: Medieval Academy of America, 1984). The Withdrawal of Obedience is the occasion for Bovet's long comment ([P1.9]) mentioned in note 17 above, and included here as Appendix 7.

As Arnold (*Apparicion*, 55, n. 1) observes, Bovet himself was sent by the court of France to defend the *via cessionis* and the French assembly's decision before the Holy Roman Emperor at Prague. The text of his oration is published in K. Höfler, ed., *Geschichtsschreiber der Husitischen Bewegung in Böhmen;* see Introduction, note 43.

In the margin:

|P2.30| **P2** 26r
Videtur impletum quod scriptum est: "Nunc in occidente sol justicie oritur, in oriente autem Lucifer ille, qui secidit [ceciderat], supra sidera posuit tronum suum" (C. xxiiii q prima cap. *Quoniam vetusto*).

[What was written seems to be fulfilled: "Now in the West the sun of justice rises, while in the East that Lucifer (Morning Star) who fell has placed his throne above the stars."]

The gloss cites verbatim a sentence from Gratian, *Decretum* C. 24. q. 1 c. 25 *Quoniam vetus* [Friedberg 1:975], drawn from St. Jerome's Letter 25 to Pope Damasus (PL 22.355; the last clause is an allusion to Isaiah 14:13). As for Bovet's use of *vetus* for *vetusto*: the Roman Correctors, in a note, indicate that while *vetusto* is the original reading, they have changed it to *vetus*, which is the reading in the *Ordinary Gloss* as well. Bovet's manuscript of the *Decretum*, therefore, reads *vetus;* the editorial change was made in printed editions long after his time.

[124] An episode from Valerius Maximus here serves to underline Bovet's scorn for those who rise in the world through flattery:

|P1.35| **P1** 28v
Contra tales flatatores dicebat Valerius, quod cum vidisset Aruspus Diogenem lavantem olera dixit ei "Nequaquam ista ederes si velles imperatori Dionysio adulari." Quem Diogenes torruo [torvo] vultu respiciens, valde contempsit dicens, "Ymo," inquit, "si tu ista ederes Dionysio non adulares."

Et subdit Valerius, "Veridicus nunciator malleus |malens| oleribus sustentari quod magnatibus adulari."

|Against such flatterers Valerius said that, when Aruspus |Aristippus| saw Diogenes washing vegetables, he said to him, "Don't eat those, if you wish to flatter the Emperor Dionysius." Diogenes, regarding him sternly, held him in great contempt, and responded: "Rather, if you eat them you will not flatter Dionysius." "Being a teller of the truth," Valerius adds, "he preferred living on vegetables to flattering the great."|

Valerius Maximus, *Factorum et dictorum memorabilium* 4.3 ext. 4, ed. Kempf, 187; ed. Briscoe, 1:255 (trans. Shackleton Bailey, *Memorable Doing and Sayings*, 1:385):

Idem Syracusis, cum holera ei lavanti Aristippus dixisset, si 'Dionysium adulari velles, ista non esses,' 'immo,' |Diogenes| inquit 'si tu ista esse velles, non adularere Dionysium.'

[The same (Diogenes) in Syracuse was washing vegetables when Aristippus said to him, "If you would flatter Dionysius, you wouldn't be eating those." "On the contrary," said Diogenes, "if you would eat these, you wouldn't be flattering Dionysius."|

The second passage is not found in Valerius Maximus.

[125] Arnold (*Apparicion*, 56, n. 1) points out that Deschamps's ballade 69 "Contre les flatteurs" (in *Oeuvres* 1:167, lines 9–10) uses the expression "plumer le pelisson" [to pluck feathers out of a furry coat] in the sense of "to flatter":

Tel consenteur ont honni maint enfant
Desquelz ont plumé le pelisson.

Pichon's glossary (83) provides the following entry: "*desplumer*, ôter de la robe les petites plumes, les petits duvets qui peuvent s'y trouver. Le flatteur, dans les *Caractères de Théophraste*, *déplume* la robe de celui qu'il adule. Bonet, parlant dans son *Arbre des Batailles* de l'indépendance du Roi de France à l'égard de l'Empereur, ajoute: 'Et si ne dis pas cecy par flatterie, ne pour oster la plume du chaperon au roy de France.' C'est l'expression *desplumer* decomposée."

The passage from Theophrastus cited runs: "With these and the like words, he will remove a morsel of wood from his patron's coat . . ." *The Characters of Theophrastus*, trans. R. C. Jebb; new ed. J. E. Sandys (London: Macmillan, 1909), 39, §1.9–10.

[126] At this point in the "Burgundy" manuscripts (V fol. 75r–76r, L fols. 212r col. B-212v col. B) appears an inserted story, a 62-line *exemplum* illustrating the theme the Jacobin has been treating since line 1338: the injustice he has perceived at courts, where base-born flatterers are given great rewards and ask for more, while loyal knights would rather go hungry than make such requests, even after having risked their lives on the king's behalf. See Appendix 3 below for the complete text.

[127] *Camelin:* a fabric made from wool and silk mixed with other fibres, sometimes goat hair. It is also mentioned in *Roman de la Rose* 12045, and in Chaucer's *Romaunt* C 7365.

[128] A marginal gloss at this point contains an aphoristic comment on the ideal of cooperation between the clerical and chivalric estates:

|P2.31| V 27r

Vulgare dictum est clericorum quod ibi versatur manus, ubi respicit oculus. Et communi cursu ubi scientia viget, illam sociatur milicia, et quod videt oculo clerus manu operatur potencia militaris.

|It is a common saying of clerks that the hand is busy where the eye gazes, and, generally speaking, where knowledge flourishes chivalry is there with it, and what the cleric sees with eye the force of arms works by hand.|

¹²⁹ A marginal comment in **P1** assembles six citations from canon and civil law in support of the theme expressed by the Jacobin: the decline of learning among the clergy will pose grave dangers to Christianity. Bovet's six citations attack the poverty imposed on students, insist that they should not be reduced to begging, and demand that they be provided with food, clothing, and books:

|P1.36| **P1** 29r

Vere timendum est quod istis diebus scientia evanescat quia pausi |pauci| prelati diligunt litteratos, et dabuntur beneficia servitoribus et consanguineis et forsan indignis; unde litterati videntes se contempni, de studio non curabunt, quia licet paupertas non sit de genere malorum (cap. *Illa* C. xv q. i), tamen mendicitas reprobatur (C. xxiii Dist. cap. *Diaconi*), et saltem studens debet |+ habere| victum et vestitum (cap. *Clericus* xii q. i) et libros per sequelam ~~quia~~ per clausulam "quia omnia sine quibus," cap. i *De officiis dele*. Sed quis non miseratur studentibus? in *Autentica* "Habita" *Ne filius pro patre; Super specula* xx^a *De privilegiis* cum adjunctis.

|It is truly to be feared that these days knowledge is fading away, because few prelates love the literate, and benefices will be given to their servants and relatives, and possibly unworthy ones; whence the men of letters, seeing thmselves held in contempt, will take no further care about study, because, though poverty is not categorized as an evil, still begging is reproved, and the student should at least |have| food and clothing, and books, as follows from the clause "Quia omnia sine quibus." But who would not pity students?—as in the *Authentic* "Habita" (and in) X . . . |

a) Gratian, *Decretum* C. 15 q. 1 c. 6 *Illa cavenda* |Friedberg 1:747–48|, from Ambrose, *Hexaemeron* 1.8.31, PL 14.141A:

. . . Mala enim non sunt, que nec crimine mentem inplicant, nec conscientiam ligant. Unde paupertatem et ignobilitatem, egritudinem, mortem, nemo sapiens mala dixerit, nec in malorum sorte numeraverit.

|For that is not evil which does not entangle the mind in crime or tie up the conscience. Therefore, no wise man will call poverty and low birth, or sickness or death, evil, or number them in the lot of evil.|

b) Gratian, *Decretum* D. 93 c. 23, *Diaconi sunt* |Friedberg 1:326–27|, from (ps.-) Jerome, *De septem ordinibus ecclesiae* 5, PL 30.154B:

§.5 . . . Mendicat infelix in plateis clerus, et servili operi mancipatus publicam de quolibet deposcit elemosinam. Qui ex eo magis despicitur a cunctis, quo misere desolatus juste putatur ad hanc ignominiam devenisse.

[The unhappy cleric begs in the crossroads, and, delivered over to servile work, demands alms from everyone, and, the more he in his miserable desolation is seen to have deservingly descended to this ignominy, the more he is despised.]

c) Gratian, *Decretum* C. 12 q. 1 c. 5 *Clericus, qui Christi* [Friedberg 1:678], from Jerome, Letter 52.5, PL 22.531:

. . . Si autem ego pars Domini sum, et funiculus hereditatis eius, non accipio partes inter ceteras tribus, sed quasi Levita et sacerdos vivo de decimis, et altari serviens altaris oblatione sustentor. Habens victum et vestitum, his contentus ero, et nudam crucem nudus sequor.

[But since my portion is the Lord's and I am the measure of his heritage, I do not receive portions among the other tribes, but as Levite and priest I live from tithes, and as a server at the altar, from the altar offerings. Having food and clothing, I will be content with them, and, naked, follow the naked cross.]

d) *Glos. ord.* to X 1.29, tit. *De officio et potestate judici delegati*, c. 1 *Quia quesitum*, summarized "Delegatus Papae potestatem habet non solum in partes, sed etiam in alios, qui suam jurisdictionem impediunt" (The Pope's delegated judge has jurisdiction not only over the parties of the trial but also over others who impede his jurisdiction), ad. v. *impedire:*

. . . hoc contingit quia impedit ipsam jurisdictionem et judex omnia potest, quae ad ipsam jurisdictionem pertinent et sine quibus causa expediri non potest.

[. . . This happens because it impedes his jurisdiction, and a judge can do everything that pertains to the jurisdiction itself and without which the case cannot be carried on.]

Bovet cites this text to justify his statement that a student ought to have books "as a consequence of the clause 'that all things without which [one cannot do the job are to be supplied]'" (*per sequelam per clausulam, "quia omnia sine quibus"*). Bovet's exact citation led me to expect to find this clause verbatim in the decretal, but no such clause appears there. Nevertheless, the overall conclusion of the cited lines can be applied, by extension, to the argument being made by Bovet about the students: that their advancement should not be impeded either in whole or in part.

e) *Auth.* "Habita" (new constitution of Frederick Barbarossa) post Cod. 4.41.5 (*Ne filius pro patre*), *Corpus juris civilis Justinianei, cum commentariis,* ed. Fehius (Lyon, 1627), vol. 4 (*Code*), cols. 824–26. *Authenticae* such as this one (not to be confused with the collection of *Novels* by Justinian known as the *Authenticum*) do not appear in the Mommsen-Krueger edition. See James A. Brundage, *Medieval Canon Law* (New York: Longman, 1995), 204–5, for a concise review.

Frederick's *constitutio* placed students under imperial protection and commanded authorities to treat students properly; halfway through (middle col. 825), the author asks "Quis enim eorum non misereatur, qui amore scientiae exules facti, de divitibus pauperes, semetipsos exinaniunt, vitam suam multis periculis exponunt, et a vilissimis saepe hominibus (quod graviter ferendum est) corporales injurias sine causa perferunt?" [For who would not have pity upon those who, because of their love of knowledge having become exiles, and poor after being rich, exhaust themselves, expose their lives to many dangers, and endure bodily injuries without cause from often the vilest kind of men, a grievous thing to bear?].

> f) Bovet's reference is puzzling. His abbreviation refers to the chapter *Super specula* from the title *De privilegiis et excessibus privilegiatorum* (X 5.33.28, Friedberg 2:868), with associated material (*cum adjunctis*). This chapter is one of three embedded excerpts in X from Honorius III's decretal *Super specula* of 22 November 1219. However, the particular matter being raised in Bovet's gloss—the welfare of students—is actually taken up in another section of *Super specula*, X 5.5.770–71, tit. *De magistris.* The notation "xxᵃ," finally, remains inexplicable.

¹³⁰ The word "sera" is inserted atop an obvious erasure.

¹³¹ Bovet's gloss amplifies the Jacobin's recapitulation of the theme of aristocratic immoderation, a critique first offered by the Sarrazin. He begins with a proverb he again attributes to Seneca (but which is not found in his extant works) that claims moderation as the way to dispel true hunger and thirst; the same text appears in [P2.16] (note 72 above). He then presents a saying he attributes to St. Jerome (but which is not found in his works) concerning the threat to health represented by gluttony, and concludes with two citations of the *Decretum* that draw from Jerome's *Adversus Jovinianum:*

> [P1.37] **P1** 30r
> Unde Seneca "O dii boni, quam de modico vera fames et vera sitis extinguitur"; et Jheronimus dicit "Pro penis facit habundancia magna ciborum quod faciat fames, quia ex ipsa proveniunt morbi, potraga et guta generantur, et putrefacit corpus humanum" (*De Consecratione* Di. v cap. *Ne tales*); sed per vitam tenuem pauperem et frugalem curabitur [curavuntur] predicta (eodem Dist. iii [v] cap. *Legimus*).

> [Whence Seneca: "O good gods, with what little [food and drink] are real hunger and thirst quenched!" And Jerome says, "As punishment, great abundance of food brings it about that it creates famine, because disease comes from it, gout and ulcers are produced, and the human body putrifies." But by a strait, poor, and frugal life, the aforesaid thing will be healed.]

> a) Gratian, *Decretum De cons.* D. 5 c. 29 *Ne tales* [Friedberg 1:1419]; the chapter begins with a citation from St. Jerome, *Adversus Jovinianum* 2.10 (PL 23.299C–D):

> Ne tales accipiamus cibos, quos aut difficulter digerere, aut comestos partos magno et perditos labore doleamus.

> [We should not take such food that we later complain is difficult to digest or that, once eaten, was obtained and then lost with great labor.]

The canon goes on to cite Galen and Hippocrates in support of this theme, very similar to that expressed in [P2.22] (note 91) and [P2.13] (note 58) above; the latter, in fact, draws from the preceding chapter (3.5.28 *Nichil enim*). Bovet concludes by citing the next canon in *De consecratione:*

> b) Gratian *De cons.* D. 5 c. 30 *Legimus* [Friedberg 1:137], citing *Adversus Jovinianum* 2.12 (PL 23.301C-302A):

> Legimus quosdam, morbo articulari et podagrae humoribus laborantes, proscriptione bonorum ad simplicem mensam et pauperes cibos redactos convaluisse. Caruerant enim sollicitudine dispensandae domus et epularum largitate, que et corpus frangunt et animam.

> [We read that certain persons, laboring under arthritis and the humors of gout, regained their health by proscribing "good" food and being reduced to a simple table and poor foods. For they were without the cares of managing a household and supplying an abundance of fine foods, which break both body and soul.]

132 Both manuscripts include a marginal comment at this point in the text. In **P1** there is one long gloss, presented here; **P2** has two shorter ones ([P2.32] at line 1464 and [P2.33] at line 1470, **P2** 28r nos. 1 and 2) containing almost identical material:

> [P1.38] **P1** 30v
> Unus potens homo secundum consilium Aristotelis non debet flobothomari, nisi de consilio plurium medicorum et debent in unam oppinionem concordare. Una tamen est flobothomia que fuit per angelum revelata et fit XIII^a mensis februarii. Et faciens illam de illo anno non debet mori per distemperanciam in febris, prout dicunt Vincencius et Johannem [Johannes] in cap. *Cum ad monasterium, De statu monachorum.*

> [A powerful man, according to the advice of Aristotle, should not be bled except on the advice of a number of physicians, who should all be of one opinion. Nevertheless, one kind of phlebotomy there is that was revealed by an angel, and it is done on the 13th of February. And the one doing it should not die that year because of distemper in fever, as Vincent and John say . . .].

The "Aristotle" reference is apparently to the *Secretum secretorum*, although some of the facts are wrong; the alteration could result from an editorial choice by Bovet, a variant in the available manuscript, or a simple failure of memory. Roger Bacon's translation (ed. Robert Steele [Oxford: Clarendon Press, 1920], 108, Part 2, cap. 30) advises Alexander to seek the counsel of astrologers, not physicians.

Bovet's gloss refers to Johannes Andreae's commentary on the *Decretales* of Gregory IX, *Novella in Decretales Gregorii IX* (1338; ed. Venice, 1581; repr. Turin: Bottega d'Erasmo, 1963); the chapter cited by Andreae is X 3.35.6, *De statu monachorum* cap. 6, *Quum ad monasterium* [Friedberg 2:599–600]. In it, he is ostensibly citing an earlier commentator on X, Vincentius Hispanus (d. 1248), whose commentary remains unedited. Andreae's comment (vol. 3, fol. 178a, no. 11) deals with the word "minutione" [bloodletting] in the decretal text:

Nota quod qui minuit 13 die februari, ab initio mensis computando, non
morietur illo anno ex febrili distemperantia. Et hec est salubris minutio per
angelum revelata Vincentio. Dicebat etiam, quod minuenti imputatur im-
peritia, non eventus mortalitatis . . .

[Note that one who is bled on the 13th day of February, counting from the
beginning of the month, will not die that year from fever distemper. And
this is a salutary bleeding revealed by an angel to Vincent. He also said that
lack of skill is attributed to a bloodletter, not the outcome of death . . .]

Although angelic revelation is not the usual source for canon-law commentators, it
is nevertheless impossible to say whom Andreae refers to at this point. Most likely
he would not have referred to St. Vincent—whose story in the *Legenda aurea* includes an angel welcoming the dying martyr into heaven—simply as "Vincentio,"
but more formally as "Sancto Vincentio"; furthermore, there is no direct mention
there (or in Prudentius's story of Vincent, *Peristephanon* 5, which de Voragine cites)
of bloodletting or its benefits.

[133] Two glosses in **P2** (the second attached to line 1470; see following note,
134) combine to present a text almost identical to the parallel comment in **P1**
([P1.38], previous note):

[P2.32] **P2** 28r #1
Aristotiles dicebat Alexandro quod Rex non debet facere flobothomiam sine
consilio plurium medicorum concordancium in una oppinionem.

[134] [P2.33] **P2** 28r #2:

Una tamen est flobothomia que dicitur fuisse per angelum revelata ut dicunt
Vincencius et Johannes Andree nec morietur illo anno qui eam fecerit ex
distemperancia febris, et fit XIII[a] • die februarii vide in cap. *Cum ad
monasterium, De statu monachorum.*

[135] Two very similar glosses (see also following note) appear in this section in
both manuscripts, illustrating Bovet's defense of the purity of his intentions; his
precarious political status as an exile from his native Provence (see note 139 below)
makes this appeal all the more urgent. The gloss cites an aphoristic condemnation
of spiteful prattle (note how he accuses the hated Raymond de Turenne of this very
crime in ll. Prose 221–224). The lines, however, do not appear in any of the extant
works of Seneca, but are adapted instead from Pseudo-Caecilius Balbus (who attributes the line to Socrates), *De nugis philosophorum*, 5.10.3.; also cited by Albertanus
of Brescia, *De amore*, c. 5:

[P2.34] **P2** 29v
Contra tales invidos dicebat Seneca: "O utinam invidi oculos in omnibus fe-
licitatibus torquerentur, nam quanta sunt felicium gaudia tanti invidorum
sunt gemitus."

[Against such envious persons Seneca said, "O, would that the envious
would turn their eyes upon all felicities, for the groans of the envious are as
great as the joys of the happy."]

[136] See previous note (135); **P1** provides a gloss very similar to **P2**'s offering at nearly the same line in the poetic text:

|P1.39| **P1** 32r

Magis dubito invidiam et loquacitatem detractionis, contra quam dicit Seneca: "O utinam quod omnis |omnes| invidi oculos in omnibus civitatibus haberent ut de omnibus felicitatibus torquerentur, quia quanta sunt felicium gaudia tanti invidorum sunt gemitus."

|I have more doubt over the envy and gossip of back-biting, against which Seneca says, "O would that all envious persons would have eyes in all cities, so that they |= their eyes| would be wrenched away from the sight of all happiness, for the groans of the envious are as great as the joys of the happy."|

[137] The sense of this clause is "I do not need any more enemies" (*avoir mestier de*, to have need of), in the spirit of the demotic "I need all the help I can get": the author is already in de facto exile from his own country owing to the aggression of a powerful baron, and can ill afford the wrath of those in power.

[138] A much later hand (apparently the same as the one that executed the marginal gloss at l. 926; see note 96) inserts a caret next to the name "Rogier" and adds "de Turenne" in the margin.

[139] Bovet's almost fanatical hatred of this obscure Provençal nobleman can be explained by the Roger family's meteoric rise to importance (cf. Bovet's repeated criticism of *parvenus,* especially his tale of "la Courge et le Datilier," ll. Prose 198–243), the papal nepotism exercised on their behalf (cf. esp. Bovet's condemnation of this practice in ll. 1225–1233), and the war carried out by this family against the pope and the count of Provence, a conflict that reduced the value of Bovet's benefice and effectively kept him out of his native country for a long period (Prose 141–143). Raymond Roger de Beaufort, viscount of Turenne, between 1388 and 1399 made war on the pope and the Duke of Anjou (who was also Count of Provence) under pretext of defending his rights. His family had profited much from the generosity of Turenne's great-uncle Pope Clement VI (Pierre Roger) and his uncle Pope Gregory XI (Pierre Roger de Beaufort). When Gregory died in 1378, the new pope at Avignon, Clement VII, granted a petition by the members of the House of Anjou allowing them to take possession of certain Provençal lands; this decision deprived the Roger family, longtime Angevin partisans, of some castles and terrains. His pleas for restitution ignored, Raymond went to war against the pope and the Angevins, bringing in Italian brigands and doing great damage for more than a decade: an Italian merchant in Avignon said Turenne "kept the territory in darkness" (Maurice Agulhon and Noël Coulet, *Histoire de Provence* [Paris: Presses Universitaires de France, 1987], 43–44). Turenne, obviously no believer in half-measures, went so far as to support the Roman papacy against Avignon, and the house of Durazzo against Anjou in their struggle over the Kingdom of Naples. See long notes by Pichon (77–80) and Arnold (*Apparicion,* 62, n. 1) for more details.

[140] The last gloss in **P2** comments on the theory of the "Just War".

[P2.35] **P2** 30r
Titulum belli judicare non potest nisi sit princeps (cap. *Dominus noster C.* xxiii
q. i [ii])

[One cannot adjudge a title of war unless one is a prince.]

Bovet cites Gratian, *Decretum* C. 23 q. 2. cap. 2 *Dominus Deus noster jubet* [Friedberg 1:894–95], summarized "Nichil interest ad justiciam, sive aperte sive ex insidiis aliquis pugnet" [From the viewpoint of justice it does not matter whether a battle is fought openly or from ambush]. However, *Dominus Deus noster jubet* does not correspond to the argument of this canon; it explains rather that not everyone is allowed to fight, and defines what a just war is, while not saying exactly who can declare the war. Closer to the sentiment aimed at by Bovet is the previous canon, C. 23 q. 2. cap. 2 *Justum est bellum*, inc. "Justum est bellum, quod ex edicto geritur"—that is, to be just, a war must be decreed by edict. This concept is picked up by Gratian in his *dictum post* c. 2 [Friedberg 1:895]: "Cum ergo justum bellum sit, quod ex edicto geritur, vel quo injuriae ulciscuntur, queritur, quomodo a filiis Israel justa bella gerebantur" [Since therefore a war is just which is waged by edict, or by which injuries are avenged, the question is, in what way were just wars waged by the children of Israel?]. All of Causa 23 deals with the issue of just war, as does much of Bovet's *Arbre des Batailles*, where Bovet expresses a precept that reappears in the gloss above: "Aultre personne qui ne soit prince ne peut commander guerre générale . . . toutefois aujourd'huy chascun veult commander guerre, et mesme ung simple chevalier contre ung aultre" (ed. Nys, 90–91, 4.4).

Frederick H. Russell (*The Just War in the Middle Ages* [Cambridge: Cambridge University Press, 1975], 62) notes that "The texts in [Causa 23] quaestio 2, in asserting that a just war must be waged on authority, set in motion the whole sequence of legal consequences and moral cautions attendant upon the just war." Referring in particular to this canon, Russell adds that "Only legitimate authorities and soldiers under their command were capable of undertaking a just war." Clearly Bovet sees Raymond de Turenne's case as falling outside the provisions of this law.

[141] Arnold (*Apparicion*, 63, n. 1) points out that Raymond held the title of viscount of Turenne because his father, Guillaume-Roger, had married Eléonor de Comminges, and then purchased Turenne from her sister; this seems a questionable claim to "hault lignage" in Bovet's eyes.

[142] Charles of Durazzo was the grandson of Jean, eighth son of Charles II of Anjou, King of Naples, and by right of marriage to a niece of Giovanna I, Queen of Naples, had expected to assume the throne after her death. However, in 1380 she took up the Clementist (French) cause and adopted Louis I, Duke of Anjou— the brother of French king Charles V—as her heir. Thus began a long struggle between these two branches of the House of Anjou. See Michael Hanly, *Beauvau, Boccaccio, Chaucer: "Troilus and Criseyde": Four Perspectives on Influence* (Norman, OK: Pilgrim Books, 1990), 40–43, for a summary of the politics of the adoption. Charles had Giovanna poisoned in 1382, and then opposed Louis I's invasion of Italy in 1384; Louis died there in September of that year, and Charles himself in 1386. Louis II of Anjou took up the Angevin claim, and occupied Naples in 1392, but

was chased out in 1399 by the Durazzo heir, Ladislas (whom Bovet calls "Lancelot"). For a thorough treatment of these complex issues, see Émile Léonard, *Les Angevins de Naples* (Paris: Presses Universitaires de France, 1954).

143 The origin of this exemplary tale has not been traced.

144 The last gloss in **P1** enlists a wealth of sources in a lengthy denunciation of those who have risen too quickly to prominence and political power; of course, he has Raymond de Turenne in mind (see note 139 above). Bovet's marginal comment ruminates over the role of humankind in the acquisition and practice of earthly power, ranging through citations of canon law, Scripture, popular proverbs, and, ostensibly, philosophy (including the dropping of some famous names not cited here). The thread linking these desultory citations is, of course, Bovet's great resentment of the upstart Turenne, who, according to the author's account, arose from nowhere and then showed none of the virtue or restraint called for by the texts cited here.

|P1.40| **P1** 34r

Aliquando per gloriam Dei aliqui vocantur ad alta eciam sine merito presedente |precedente|, sicut Jheremias sanctificatus in utero matris. Aliquando propter meritum, sicut David quem de pastore ovium vocavit Deus ad Regnum; aliquando vocantur ad alta quia mali sunt, ut per eorum malignitatem plures mali pugnientur |pugnentur|, sicut Saul (C. viii, q. 1. cap. *Adacter* |*Adaucter*|, et cap. *Remittuntur*, xxiii, q. 8 |5|); eciam Deus totum hoc facit, qui cito pauperem ditat, qui cito divitem pauperem facit. "Sucitat |Suscitat|," inquid Scriptura, "de pulvere egenum et de stercore elevat pauperem, ut sedeat cum principibus et solium glorie teneat" |1 Samuel/Vulgate 1 Kings 2:7–8|. Et prout eum sublimavit ita cadere faciet cum placebit. Unde Seneca: "Neminem sic fortuna provexit quin tantum ei minaretur quantum promiserat." Cato sapiens: "Indulget fortuna quandoque, ut ledere possit," quoniam ut ipsa levis cito facit pauperes esse beatos, sic fortunatos deprimit hora brevis. Quare Philosophus |= Aristoteles| prebuit documentum: "Sapientis," inquit, "est nec in prosperis effluere nec in adversis merore sepeliri." Et, nisi Boetius, Valerius, Tullius, et secasses |sequaces| omnino menciantur, plures pereunt et periclitant in prosperis quam in adversis, et concordat philosophia cum dicit "homo cum in honore esset non intellexit conparatus est jumentis incipientibus |insipientibus|," etc. |Psalm 48:13|. Istud verebatur et timebat sapiens Salomon cum dicebat "Extollencia oculorum meorum ne dederis michi;" |Ecclesiasticus 23:5| "Ne forte impinguatus et dilatatus, evomam nomen tuum" |Deuteronomy 32:15|; "Divicias ergo et paupertates ne dederis michi, sed tantum victui meo tribue necessaria" |Proverbs 30:8|.

|Sometimes through the glory of God some people are called to high things even without a preceding merit, like Jeremias, who was sanctified in his mother's womb. Sometimes because of merit, like David, whom God called from being a herder of sheep to |rule| a kingdom. Sometimes persons are called to heights because they are bad, so that through their malice other bad persons will be warred against, like Saul. Even all this God does, who suddenly enriches the pauper, who suddenly makes the rich man poor. Scripture says, "The Lord makes poor and makes rich; he humbles and he exalts. He raises up the needy from the dust, and lifts up the poor from the

dunghill, that he may sit with princes, and hold the throne of glory." And just as he elevated him, just so he will make him fall, when it pleases him. Whence Seneca says, "Fortune has not raised up anyone so much as not to threaten him as much as she had promised." Cato the Wise says, "fortune will sometimes be indulgent so that she can inflict injuries," because, being the capricious thing that she is, as she suddenly makes the poor to be happy, just so in a brief hour thrusts down those favored by Fortune. Therefore the Philosopher adduced the lesson: he said that "it is characteristic of the wise man neither to dissipate in prosperity nor, when in adversity, to be buried in sorrow." And, unless Boethius, Valerius, Tully, and their followers are complete liars, more people are perishing and endangering themselves in prosperity than in adversity, and philosophy agrees when it says that "Man, when he was in honor, did not understand; he is compared to senseless beasts," etc. The wise Solomon was apprehensive and fearful of this, when he said, "Do not give me haughtiness of my eyes," "lest perhaps, being fattened and broadened, I shall vomit out your name." "Therefore, give me neither beggary nor riches, but only the necessities of life."|

a) Gratian, *Decretum* C. 8 q. 1 c. 18 *Audacter* |Friedberg 1:596|, summarized "Non ex arbitrio Dei aliquando datur princeps ecclesiae" |Sometimes a head is given to the Church who is not God's choice|:

Audacter fortassis aliquid dicimus, tamen quod scriptum est dicimus. Non semper princeps populi et judex ecclesiae per Dei arbitrium datur, sed prout merita nostra deposcunt. Si mali sunt actus nostri et operamur malignum in conspectu Dei, dantur nobis principes secundum cor nostrum. Et hoc tibi de scripturis probabo. Audi namque quid dicat Dominus: "Fecerunt sibi regem, et non per me; principem, et non per consilium meum" |Hosea 8:4|. Et hoc dictum videtur de Saule |Saulo| illo, quem utique ipse Dominus elegerat, et regem fieri jusserat. Sed quoniam non secundum Dei voluntatem, sed secundum peccatoris populi meritum fuerat electus, negat eum cum sua voluntate vel consilio constitutum . . .

|We say something perhaps boldly, but which is nevertheless written. A leader of the people and a judge of the Church is not always given according to the best judgment of God, but rather in accord with what our merits demand. If our deeds are bad and we perform what is evil in the sight of God, leaders are given to us after our own hearts. And this I will prove to you from the Scriptures, for listen to what the Lord says: "They made themselves a king, and not through me; a prince, and not by my counsel." And this seems to be said about Saul, whom, it is true, the Lord chose and ordered to be made king, but because he was elected not according to the will of God but according to the merit of the sinful people, He denied that that he was instituted by His will or counsel . . .|

The second citation amplifies the first:

b) Gratian, *Decretum,* C. 23 q. 5 c. 49 *Remittuntur* |Friedberg 1:945|, summarized "Aliquando puniuntur peccata per populos divino jussu excitatos" |Sometimes sins are punished by peoples |= invading hordes| mobilized by God's command|:

... Puniuntur quoque peccata per homines, sicut per judices, qui potestate ad tempus utuntur. § 1. Puniuntur peccata etiam per populos, sicut legimus, quia sepe ab alienigenis, Dei jussu excitatis propter divinae majestatis offensam, subactus est populus Judeorum.

[Sins are also punished by means of men, such as, for instance, judges, who exert power in the temporal sphere. § 1. Sins are likewise punished through peoples, as we read, because the people of the Jews were often subjugated by foreigners raised up by God's command because of an offense against the divine majesty.]

c) 1 Samuel/Vulgate 1 Kings 2:7–8: "Dominus pauperem facit et ditat humiliat et sublevat suscitat de pulvere egenum et de stercore elevat pauperem ut sedeat cum principibus et solium gloriae teneat" [The Lord makes poor and makes rich; he humbles and he exalts. He raises up the needy from the dust, and lifts up the poor from the dunghill, that he may sit with princes, and hold the throne of glory].

d) This passage is not found in this form in the extant works of Seneca, but may derive from him; Bovet uses it in [P2.25] (note 107 above) as well.

e) *Disticha Catonis* 2.23:

Noli successus indignos ferre moleste;
Indulget fortuna malis, ut laedere possit.

[Do not bear undeserved successes with an ill grace;
Fortune favors the wicked in order to savage them.]

f) Bovet assumed this passage to be from the works of Aristotle, and indeed the ultimate source is *Nicomachean Ethics* 4.3.18 (1124a 15–16); the Latin text of that passage (trans. Grosseteste, ed. R. A. Gauthier, Aristoteles Latinus 26 [Leiden: Brill, 1973], 440–41) runs "neque bene fortunatus gaudiosus erit, neque infortunatus tristis." Bovet's citation is also found in this form in the works of Hildebert of Lavardin (Hildebertus Cenomanensis, ca. 1036–1133/4), a consolatory epistle (bk. 1, letter 12, dated 1121) addressed to King Henry I of England upon the death of his son William in a shipwreck (1120), PL 171.173C:

Sapientia enim est, nec in prosperis effluere, nec in adversis moerore sepeliri.

[For it is wisdom not to be expansive when prosperous nor, when in adversity, to bury oneself in sorrow.]

Cf. also Ambrose, Letter 37.5, PL 16.1085A: "Sapiens ... non attollitur prosperis, non tristibus mergitur."

g) Psalm 48:13: "Et homo, cum in honore esset, non intellexit; conparatus est jumentis insipientibus ..." [And man, when he was in honor, did not understand; he is compared to senseless beasts ...].

h) Ecclesiasticus (Sirach) 23:5: ". . . extollentiam oculorum meorum ne dederis mihi, et omne desiderium averte a me . . ." [Give me not haughtiness of my eyes, and turn away from me all coveting].

i) The previous comment is amplified by language from Deuteronomy 32:15: ". . . incrassatus, inpinguatus, dilatatus; dereliquit Deum factorem suum; et recessit a Deo salutari suo" [(The beloved grew fat, and kicked;) he grew fat, and thick, and gross. He forsook God who made him, and departed from God his savior].

j) Proverbs 30:8: "Vanitatem et verba mendacia longe fac a me; mendicitatem et divitias ne dederis mihi; tribue tantum victui meo necessaria" [Remove far from me vanity and lying words. Give me neither beggary nor riches. Give me only the necessities of life].

[145] The maxim "Bonae ecclesiae bona pauperum" is adapted from Gregory the Great, *Registrum Epistolarum* 3.21 (PL 77.620D) and Chrysostom's *Homily 86 on Matthew;* also (ps.-) Augustine, *Sermo ad fratres in eremo* 21, PL 40.1269 (= CPPMA 1148, 1:247).

[146] See Introduction, § "Life and Works," and note 34, and also § "Bovet and Islam," note 94.

[147] See lines 252–279, above.

[148] The Great Schism began in 1378, twenty years before the writing of the *Apparicion.*

[149] As Arnold (*Apparicion,* 66, n. 2) suggests, the use of the imperfect here could suggest a reform Bovet had already envisioned during the time of the Languedoc commission (1390) mentioned in line Prose 228, above.

[150] Bovet implores his dedicatees to address the abuse of "péages": travelers were frequently allowed to cross bridges, but were pursued and fined after the fact. Paulin Paris, *Les manuscrits françois de la Bibliothèque du Roi* (Paris: Techener, 1845), 6:269, n. 1, cites the *Traité des Peages* by Mathieu de Vauzelles, published by Jean de Tournes at Lyon in 1550: "J'ay veu, dit-il, certains vieux cartulaires produits par ceulx qui tiennent le peage de Trevous; et au preambule y a ces propres mots: 'Fuerunt statuta pedagia ad conservationem rerum per aquas conductarum et ad evitandum pericula quæ per aliquos raptores et latrones multis modis committebantur'" [There were traveler statutes for the maintenance of water cargo and for guarding against dangers variously perpetrated by certain pillagers and robbers].

[151] The succeeding verses appear here in **P1**, but in **P2** are inserted into the text at fol. 8r, at the end of the speech by the Physicien (line 228), under the rubric "Madame d'Orliens." After "Amen" in **P2** appears the following *ex libris:* "Ce livre est a Charles duc d'Orliens etc.," followed by his autograph signature.

[152] Daniel 13.

[153] Arnold (*Apparicion,* 68, n. 1) accepts without reservation an unsupported claim made by the editors of Deschamps's collected works (A. de Queux de Saint-Hilaire and G. Raynaud, eds., *Oeuvres complètes* [Paris: Firmin Didot, 1878–1903], 11:76, n. 7) that the heraldic device "Loyaulté passe tout" was used by Valentina Visconti. R. C. Famiglietti, however, notes that although the words

Loyaulté passe tout appeared on a belt owned by Valentina, "the motto was not specifically said to be hers . . ." (*Tales of the Marriage Bed from Medieval France [1300–1500]* [Providence, RI: Picardy Press, 1992], 269). Famiglietti cites Claude Paradin, *Devises héroiques* (Lyon: Tournes & Gazeau, 1557), 91–92, and F. M. Graves, *Quelques pièces relatives à la vie de Louis I, duc d'Orléans et de Valentine Visconti, sa femme* (Paris: Champion, 1913), 45.

APPENDICES

Appendix 1
The Artois Redactor's Introduction and Dedication of his Work to the Bishop of Arras

Manuscript **V**, Vatican City, BAV, MS Reg. lat.1683, fols. 39r line 25–40v line 1 [this text is not found in manuscript **L**, which begins with the material found in Appendix 2]

    A reverend et venerable
    Noble de meurs de sens estable
    Prestre de la plus noble eglise
    Qui soit dedens Artoys assise
5   Homme enluminé de science
    Honneur service et reverence
    Pere reverend j'ay visé   [fol. 39v]
    Du livret et bien avisé
    A grant deliberation
10   Qui se dit *l'apparition*
    De maistre Jeham de Meun
    Qui n'est mie encor au commun
    Qu'a ung pouvre rude bergier
    Vous pleust chargier de corriger
15   Aucuns mesfais ou aucuns vices
    Qui par aucuns escripvains nices
    Estoient fais en transcripvant
    Ainsy que pluseurs vont faisant
    Or m'a semblé diverse chose
20   Pour ce qu'a la fois est en prose
    Et quant la prose se terminnent
    Il commence a parler par rime
    Trop pou me plaist ceste
    Car mauvais chantre hait muance
25   Aussy mutation soudainne
    Aux courages fait souvent peine
    Et les esmeut aucunement
    Se Boece de ce ne ment
    Et pour ceste muance oster

Appendix 1

The Artois Redactor's Introduction and Dedication of his Work to the Bishop of Arras

TO the reverend and venerable,
Virtuous and rational
Priest of the most exalted church
That exists within Artois,

5 An enlightened man of knowledge,
Honor, service and reverence.
[39v] Reverend father, I have examined
And analyzed this book
With great perspicacity;

10 It is called *The Apparition*
Of Master Jean de Meun,
Who is is not among us any more.
Although it pleased you that a poor, rustic shepherd
Be charged with correcting

15 Whatever mistakes or lapses
Have been committed by foolish scribes
During its copying,
As well as several others
It now seems to me a different matter,

20 Since some passages are in prose,
And when the prose breaks off
It begins to speak in rhyme.
This pleases me but little;
For a poor poet abhors variety,

25 And sudden change
Disturbs the spirits of many,
And upsets them greatly,
If Boethius does not lie about this.
Then to alleviate this variety

30 Affin qu'il soit a l'escouter
    Plus gracieux et plus plaisans
    Aux escoutans et aux lysans
    La prose j'ay mué en ryme
    Puis consonant, puis leonime
35 Et qui ma rime veult blasmer
    Je luy respons par saint Aumer
    Ad ce et dy en excusant   [fol. 40r]
    Que trop iroit souvent musant
    Qui tout vouldroit ouvrer a lime
40 Pour ce leur fai ceste maxime.
    Mais sans plante oster ne mettre
    Je vouldray ensuivre la lettre
    Que l'acteur sy a mis en prose
    Sans faire ne mettre grant glose
45 Selon mon pouvre entendement
    Qui n'est pas mis parfondement
    Et moy [read *mon*] pouvre engin gros et rude
    Car pou ay pousieuvy l'estude
    Qui les gens rudes fait soubtiz
50 Et villains nobles et gentiz
    Mais besoing fait vielle troter
    Besoing me fist l'estude hoster
    Pour ce qu'en jennesse n'avoie
    Blanc argent ne aultre monnoye
55 Si vous suppli que m'ignorance
    Soit par vous mis en excusance
    Et se vous amés mieulx la prose
    Que la rime que je propose
    Prenes la je vous renvoye
60 Car point ne l'ay gettee en voye
    Mais le maistre corrige ay
    Selon le petit sens que ay
    Sans en rien muer la sentence
    Or est il temps que je commence
65 Ainçois que je face aultre chose
    A rimer la premiere prose.

    [40v] *Actor* [rubric]
    Or en entendez la teneur

30 So that the poem be to the ear
    Sweeter and more pleasant—
    Both for those who hear it and those who read it—
    I have changed the prose into rhyme,
    First finding consonance, then forming rhymed couplets.
35 And whoever wants to criticize my rhymes
    I reply to him, by St. Omer,
    [40r] Regarding this, and say, by way of excuse,
    That he would spend too much time in thought
    Who sought to file and polish every verse.
40 For such folk I declare this principle.
    But neither adding nor omitting a thing,
    I would like to follow the letter
    That the author has written in prose
    Without expanding or adding anything,
45 As permitted by my feeble intellect,
    Which is not very keen,
    And by my deficient talents,
    For I have but little of the learning
    That makes rustic folks refined,
50 And turns peasants into gentlemen.
    But need causes old people to scurry,
    And need forced me to abandon my studies
    Because in youth I had no
    White silver or other money.
55 I pray, therefore, that my ignorance
    Be excused by you
    And that, if you prefer the prose
    To the rhymes I have proposed:
    Here, please have another look,
60 For I omitted nothing along the way,
    But have corrected the master's work
    As much as my feeble intellect allowed,
    Without changing the meaning at all.
    Now it is time for me to begin—
65 Before I undertake another task—
    To versify the first prose lines.

[40v] *Actor*
Now you shall hear the contents [of this work]

Appendix 2

*The Artois Redactor's Transcription of Bovet's Dedication of the Appari-
cion to Philip of Burgundy*

(immediately following the text of Appendix 1, above, in manuscript **V**)

This introduction also appears in **L** (London, BL, MS Lansdowne 214)
at fol. 201 5 col. A ll. 1–41); the text reproduced here is that of the Vatican
manuscript, **V**.

V 40v l. 2–41r l. 14

[*Actor*]
      A mon tres redoubté seigneur
      Monseigneur le duc de Bourgongne
      Que Dieu gard de mal et d'ensoigne
      S'il se voit de son bien liez
5   Soit ce petit livret bailles.

[*Predicator*]
      Monseigneur plaise vous entendre
      Que depuis qu'il vous pleust aprendre
      Ung petit livre que je feis
      Auquel le titre et le nom je mis
10   Et nommez l'*abre des batailles*
      J'ay eu grant mal en mes entrailles
      Et pourtant mon corps ensement
      Dont j'ay jeü moult longuement.
      Si n'ay vespree ne matin
15   Riens escript fors que en latin
      Et pour ce que guaires n'usez
      De livres latin vous n'avez
      De puis riens eu que j'ay escript
      Vous ay ce petit cy transcript
20   Lequel vous envoye briefment
      Et vous suppli benignement
      Et en l'onneur de dieu qui pendre
      Voult pour nous qu'il vous plaise prendre
      En bon gré ce petit present

Appendix 2

The Artois Redactor's Transcription of Bovet's Dedication of the Apparicion to Philip of Burgundy

[*Actor*]
To my mighty lord
The Duke of Burgundy:
In the hope that God will preserve him from evil and from distress,
And grant him well-being and happiness,
5   This little book is sent.

[*Predicator*]
My lord, may it please you to hear this,
Just as once it pleased you to accept
A little book that I composed
To which I gave the name
10   *The Tree of Battles.*
I had a serious illness in my stomach
And in my whole body, as well,
From which I suffered for a very long time.
Thus, in the evening and morning both,
15   I wrote nothing except in Latin;
And since you have little use
For Latin books, you have
Since that time received nothing I have written.
This little copy here
20   I sent you as soon as I could,
And implore you eagerly,
And for the honor of God, who upon on the cross
Agreed to hang for us, that you deign to accept
And that you delight in this little gift,

25 Que je pouvres homes vous present
   Si suppli au saint esperit
   Que d'encombrier et de peril
   Vous veulle garder par sa grace   [fol. 41r]
   Et vivre vous doint longue espace
30 En honneur en en bonne vie
   Et vous guarde des dangiers d'envie
   Et faire telz euvres que France
   Peust vivre en paiz et en plaisance
   Et vostre ame en ait sauvement
35 En gloire perpetuelment
   Le livre en bonne intencion
   Ay mis mon [read *nom*] apparicion
   De maistre Jehan de Meum
   Qui point ne s'appert au commun
40 Des ors veul au traicte entendre
   Or les veulles chescun entendre.

25 Which I, a poor man, present to you.
And so I pray the Holy Spirit
That all anguish and danger
[41r] Be spared you, through his mercy,
And that he give you long life
30 In honor and in comfort,
And that he protect you from the pitfalls of envy,
And cause such works that France
Will be able to live in peace and happiness,
And that he will then have your soul
35 In glory for all eternity.
To this book, with good intent,
I have given the name "Apparition
Of Master Jean de Meun,"
Who no longer appears among us.
40 From this point on, whoever wishes to hear this work:
May it please you that everyone comprehend it.

Appendix 3
Bovet's "Charles de Napples" Story, in Version Dedicated to
Philip of Burgundy

Bovet's exemplum, in the "Burgundy" manuscripts, amplifying the argument that princes should avoid flatterers and reward their loyal vassals; it immediately follows line 1365 in the edited text (see note 126).

The text reproduced here is that of the Vatican manuscript, **V**. In manuscript **L** (London, BL, MS Lansdowne 214), the story appears at fols. 212r col. B (l. 34)–212v col. B (l. 5).

Vatican City, BAV Reg. lat. 1683, fols. 75r (l. 14)–76r (l. 15)

. . . Portant roys
Charles, qui de Napples fut roys
Si en ouvra moult vaillaument;
Se l'istoire de luy ne ment
5   Laquelle est digne de memoire
Au propos dont nous sommes oire.
Du temps qu'il fust roy, dont je dis,
De Napples, au temps que jadis
Une conte luy eschay
10 Dont tost les nouvelles oy,
Ung chevallier ot en sa court
Qui au jour le tint fort de court
De luy conter, de luy preschier,
Affin qu'il luy voulsist donner
15 La conte par son sermonner,
Qu'il l'en tint jusqu'a son couchier.
Le roy qui moult saige estoit,
Qui vers son lit se desvetoit,   [fol. 75v]
Si dist: "Alles, et revenés
20 Demain quant je seray levés;
De ce responce vous donray."
Lors le chevallier sans delay
Se partit de la, mes anciois
Fist tant aux chamberlans courtois

Appendix 3
Bovet's "Charles de Napples" Story, in Version Dedicated to
Philip of Burgundy

. . . However, King
Charles, who was king of Naples,
Proceeded quite valiantly in this case;
If the history does not lie,
5   That story is worthy of remembering
Which, on this subject, we are gathered to hear.
When he was king, as I said,
Of Naples, in days gone by,
A county reverted to his possession,
10 And soon the news was known
By a knight of his court,
Who all day watched him closely,
Wishing to speak with him, to sway him
So that he would wish to give him
15 That county, through his insistence;
He observed the king thus, right through to bedtime.
The king, a very wise man,
[75v] Who was undressing himself near his bed,
Then said: "Go now, and come back
20 Tomorrow when I arise;
I shall answer you about this at that time."
Then the knight promptly
Left that place, but before he did,
He made the court chamberlains

25 Qu'ilz luy promirent, sans desroy,
   Que nulz ne parleroit au roy,
   Si seroit il vers luy venus.
   Cil, au matin, ancois que nulz
   Peust veir le roy ne parler,
30 Revint a luy pour demander
   La conte qui estoit vacant.
   Le roy qui respondit errant:
   "Certes Jehannes de Veniz—
   Que de Dieu soit son corps beneiz—
35 Ne me laissa dormir ennuit.
   Pour ce demander ne t'ennuit,
   Car, pour voir, je luy ay donnee
   La conte que m'as demandee."
   Adont cil qui fut a son destre
40 Luy dist: "Sire, ce ne peult estre;
   Car il a bien trois moys passés
   Qu'il ne fust au pays assés.
   En Tarente est, je le say bien."
   "Tu dis voir; je ne mesprens rien.
45 En Tarente est, bien le savoie,
   Pour moy a bien faire s'anoie
   Et nuit et jour pour moy servir
   Se mest en peril de morir.
   Mainte griefte et mainte peine
50 Ha pour moy chescune sepmaine,
   Et de moy servir n'est point nices.
   Et pour ce cest noble services,
   Les grans perilz et les travaulx
   Qu'il seuffre, es mons et es vaulx,
55 Pour moy aient tout ce bien fait,
   M'ont mieulx prie que tu n'as fait.
   Toute nuit ont crié a my:
   'Souviengne vous de vostre amy.
   De noz souldoiers cappitainnes,
60 Pour Dieu, ne retenés leurs peines.'
   Si que je luy ay octroyé,
   Car il l'avoit bien desservié."

[76r]

25 Promise that, without fail,
  No one would speak to the king
  Until he had come to him.
  This man, in the morning, before anyone
  Could see the king or speak to him,
30 Came back to him to ask for
  The county which was now available.
  The king answered him curtly:
  "Surely, John of Venice—
  May God bless him—
35 Never let me sleep last night.
  For this request, do not trouble yourself:
  For, verily, I gave to him
  The county you have asked to have."
  Then the one who stood at his right
40 Said to him: "My lord, this could not be;
  For it is fully three months now
  That he has hardly been in this country at all.
  He is in Taranto; that I know well."
  "You speak the truth; I deny nothing.
45 He is in Taranto, I knew it well,
  Facing adversity on my behalf,
  And, day and night, in order to serve me,
  [76r] Placing himself in danger of death.
  Many griefs and many pains
50 He endures for me every week,
  And does nothing foolish while on duty.
  And because these stalwart services,
  These great perils and exertions
  That he undertakes by hill and dale,
55 Have all been done on my behalf—
  These services have swayed me more than you have.
  Every night they have cried out to me:
  'Remember your friend!
  Our soldiers and captains—
60 For God's sake, do not forget their sufferings!'
  Therefore, I gave it to him,
  Because he had deserved it."

Appendix 4
Comparison of Bovet's Original Prose with the Artois Redactor's Versification of a Prose Passage, Manuscripts **L** and **V**

Edition, lines Prose 83–85, immediately following the dedicatory introductions and preceding the beginning of the narrative proper:

> A tous ceulx qui vouldront ouyr parler de verite soit de par Dieu donnee bonne perseverance de la soustenir et de la dire, quant lieu sera et proffit, sans aucun offendre non deuement.

[**L** fol. 201r A.41—201v B.6]   [**V** fol. 41r ll. 16–25]

A tous ceulx qui aront plaisir   A tous ceulx qui auront plaisir
D'entendre, d'escouter, d'oir   D'entendre, d'escouter, d'ouir
Parler de Dieu en verité   Parler de droitte verité
Soit de par Dieu de deité   Soit de Dieu de deité
[201vA] Donnee en bien perseverance   Donnee en bien perseverance
Et de la dire aient plaisance   Et de la dire aie plaisance
Et de soustenir ensement   Et de soustenir ensement
Sans homme offendre indeuement   Sans homme offendre indeuement
Quant le temps et le lieu sera   Quant le temps et le lieu sera
Que au dire elle prouffit ara.   Qu'a dire elle prouffitera.

Appendix 5
Comparison of Bovet's Original Prose with the Artois Redactor's Versification of a Prose Passage, Manuscripts **L** and **V**

Edition, lines Prose 117–119, immediately following Jean de Meun's opening harangue: the narrator's introduction to the Jacobin.

> . . . par derrieres venoit un Jacobin qui par samblant menoit grant dueil, sy sambloit il bonne personne et tresgrant clerc en toutes sciences.

L 202v A.15–23   **V** 45r l. 22–45v l. 1

Apres un Jarennin aloit   Apres un Jacobin alloit
Qui menoit grant deul par semblant   Qui menoit grant deuil par semblant
N'aloit ne courant ne amblant   N'alloit ne courant ne amblant
Mais a douche et simple aleure   Mais a doulce et simple alleure
Bien samblant saincte creature   Bien sembloit simple creature
Et clers plain de toutes sciences   Et clerc plain de toutes sciences
Fors que des sophismes d'elienches   Fors que des sophismes de lenches
Ancor ne say s'il les savoit   Encor ne say s'il les savoit
Car moult simple visaige avoit   [45v] Car moult simple visage avoit

*Comparison of Bovet's Original Prose with the Artois Redactor's Versifi-
cation of a Prose Passage, Manuscripts **L** and **V***

Edition, lines Prose 244–254, immediately following the exemplum of
the "Courge et Datillier":

¶   Et se j'ay parlé villainement du dit Remond, nulz ne se esmerveille,
245 car par sa guerre je suy hors de mon pays. Et li bons sirez, car je
le scay bien veritablement, encorez a parlé plus oultrageusement et
plus vilainement du roy nostre sire et de tous nos seigneurs de France.
Et se la guerre fut come jadiz contre Engleterre, il cuidoit courroucier
le royaumes bien a certes. Mais oultre cela que tous les autrez ont dit, ay
250 je veu tant de choses en la commission que fu donnee jadiz a feu sire de
Chevreuse es parties de Languedoc et de Guyenne, en laquelle je fuz
par la voulente du roy, sur lesquelles choses je desire veoir aucuns
bons remedes, que ja ne m'en tairay d'escripre ent aucune chosette
en la fin de cestuy livre.

[**L** fol. 214v A.44—215v B.26]   [**V** fol. 84v l. 26–fol. 85r l. 23]

Si vous suppli tres humblement	Si vous suppli treshumblement
Tresnoblez princes que briefment	Tresnobles princes que briefment
[215v B] Ad ce cy soit remede mys	A ce cy soit remede mis
Ad ce que cilz grans ennemis	Affin que cil grans ennemis
Ca Remond Rogier de Touraine	Ce Raymond roger de turaine
Soit mis a tourment et a paine	[85r] Soit mis a tourment et a peine
Ad fin que puist estre la guerre	Affin que puist estre la guerre
Mise jusqu'au pais et terre	En paix au pais et terre
De Loys le vostre nepveu	De Loys le vostre nepveu
Lequel com monseigneur ay veu	De quel com monseigneur ay veu
Et dieu vous en doist le puissance	Et dieu vous en doint le puissance
Je pri Dieu et la virge france	J'en pry dieu et la vierge france
Car il ne carent Dieu ne sa mere	Car il ne croit dieu ne sa mere
Tant a le conscience amere	Tant a sa voullente amere
Et oultre plus que plusieurs dient	Et oultre ce que plusieurs dient
Du tirant et qui le maudient	Du tirant et qui le maudient
Le commission vi jadis	Le commission vy jadis
Donnee si com je le lis	Donnee sy com je le dis
A feu le seigneur de chevreuse	A feu le seigneur de chevreuse

De ne me contrevue n'abuse

En languedoc et en guyenne

Ou en son temps fu capitaine

En ces lieux fu o gens abuser

Envoyez du Roy no seigneur

Plusieurs choses sans fiction

Icy dont feray mencion

En livre s'il ne me meschiet

De le premiere a cy touchiet . . .

De ce ne nontrevue n'abeuse

En languedoc et en guienne

Qui en son temps fut cappitanne

En ce lieu fust aux gens d'onneur

Envoye du roy nosseigneur

Plusieurs choses sans fiction

Je vy dont feray mencion

En l'eure s'il ne me meschiet

De le premiere ay cy touchet . . .

Appendix 7
Bovet's Commentary on the French Church's Obedience to the Pope

[P1.9] manuscript **P1**—Paris, BNF, manuscrit français 810, fols. 2v–3r

Following the two dedications in manuscript **P1**, Bovet inserts a learned Latin disquisition (catalogued as [P1.9]—see Text, note 17 above) that covers two full folio sides (fols. 2v–3r). The comment ends with the statement "et quia pro nunc sum aliis negociis occupatus ulterius non procedam" [And because for the time being I am occupied with other business, I will not proceed further]. His leaving off at this point could represent a last-minute change of plan by the author, since the subsequent folio, 3v, is blank, apparently intended for more writing. Furthermore, Bovet claims to have covered the topic at length elsewhere, in the lost manuscript presented to Louis of Orléans: a reference in the other Paris manuscript ([P2.26], Text, note 111) describes a "very full" discussion in the Orléans manuscript of some matters not covered in **P2**. The note begins "Pro evidencia materiarum in hoc libello tractatarum et etiam pro eo quia per dominum patriarcham super eis scribere fui, diu non est, requisitus, videntur necessario disputande questiones subsequentes" [For examining the materials to be treated in this book, and also because I was requested not long ago by the Lord Patriarch, it seems necessary to discuss the following questions]. Bovet claims to have been consulted by Simon de Cramaud, titular Latin Patriarch of Alexandria and leader of French bishops, on a delicate legal problem that arose during the Third Paris Council in 1398. The French prelates were charged with deciding whether or not to continue their allegiance to Pope Benedict XIII, and among the matters under discussion would have been the one raised here by Bovet: could the French church appeal a decision by the pope? In an ingenious response covering sixty-seven long lines, Bovet assembles forty citations from canon and civil law and commentaries in deciding in the affirmative. In good scholastic fashion, Bovet first presents opposing arguments, and then (section 14, beginning "Sed in contrarium") turns to arguments supporting the affirmative case. The manuscript text breaks only twice, after the "introduction" ("Pro evidencia . . . questiones subsequentes"), and at "Sed in contrarium." In the interests of clarity, however, I have broken the text into blocks corresponding to individual topics, and numbered them (bold face, in brackets). While emblematic of the author's scholarly practice, this long note is extraneous to the poetic text, and for that reason appears here as an appendix.

[1] Pro evidencia materiarum in hoc libello tractatarum et etiam pro eo quia per dominum patriarcham super eis scribere fui, diu non est, requisitus, videntur necessario disputande questiones subsequentes.

[For examining the materials to be treated in this book, and also because I was requested not long ago by the Lord Patriarch, it seems necessary to discuss the following questions.]

[2] Prima est, utrum a papa qui verisimiliter creditur velle regem gravare, stantibus terminis juris communis, posit licite appellari.

[The first is, whether, given the boundaries of common law, one can licitly appeal from a pope who apparently wishes to inflict a grievance upon a king.]

[3] Et primo movet dubium quod non; quia pape ab omnibus est obediendum, [D.] 21 cc. 2–3, cap. *In novo* et cap. *Quamvis* [Gratian, *Decretum* D. 21 c. 2 *In novo* and c. 3 *Quamvis uniuersae*, Friedberg 1:69–70] et cap. *Se* cap. *Nulli* 19 Distinctio [D. 19 c. 1 *Si Romanorum* and c. 5 *Nulli fas est*, Friedberg 1:58, 61]. Et ab obediencia non appellatur a subjecto, cap. 3, *Ad nostram, De appellationibus* [X 2.28 *De appellationibus*, c. 3 *Ad nostram*, Friedberg 2:410] et *Cum a speciali* [c. 61 *Cum speciali*, Friedberg 2:437–438], et cap. *Reprehensibilis* [c. 26, Friedberg 2:418–419], et cap. *De priore* [c. 31, Friedberg 2:420]; et cap. *Super, De officio delegati* [X 1.29 *De officio delegati*, c. 25 *Super eo* or 27 *Super questionum*, Friedberg 2:171]; Igitur, etc.

[And first a doubt arises against it; because the pope is to be obeyed by all, as in the canons *In novo, Quamvis, Si,* and *Nulli.* And no appeal from obedience is to be made by a subject; see the decretals *Ad nostram, Cum speciali, Reprehensibilis, De priori,* and *Super.* Therefore, that which was meant to be proven has been proven.][107]

[4] Confirmatur superiori eciam malo, et male agenti non debet obediencia denegari, cap. *Judicet* [C. 3 q. 7 c. 4 *Judicet ille*, Friedberg 1:527] et cap. *Sacerdotes* [C.] 2 q. 7 [C. 2 q. 7 c. 51 *Sacerdotes*, Friedberg 1:500]; ergo, si gravat vel gravaret, appellandum non esset, ymmo negas obedienciam, quam maxime papa probatur infidelis, [C.] 8 q. 1 cap. *Sciendum* [C. 8 q. 1 c. 10 *Sciendum est summopere*, Friedberg 1:593], quia meritum fidei sola obediencia possidet. Appellans ergo ab illa extra fidem esse probatur, ut ibi dicitur, quam filius Dei super omnia elegit in se ipso servare, [C.] 11 q. 3 c. 99 *Quid ergo* [C. 11 q. 3 c. 99 *Quid ergo mirum*, Friedberg 1:671].

---

[107] This formula is repeated at the end of section 12.

[This is confirmed even for a wicked superior, and obedience should not be denied to one who acts badly, as in the canons *Judicet* and *Sacerdotes;* therefore, if he aggrieves or should aggrieve you, you should not appeal, for you are denying obedience, however much the pope proves unfaithful, as in the canon *Sciendum,* because only obedience possesses the merit of faith. Therefore, appealing from it is shown to be outside of faith, as is said there, which the Son of God chose above all things to preserve in himself, as in the canon *Quid ergo.*]

[5] Confirmatur quia ecclesia propter nullum majus bonum posset appellare; ergo nec rex consequencia tenet, quia nullum majus bonum posset super obedienciam inveniri, cum illa excedat bona cetera in virtute, ut clare patet in allegato capitulo, *Quid ergo* [C. 11 q. 3 c. 99; see above, section 4].

[This is confirmed, because the Church could not appeal on account of any greater good; therefore neither does the king have these results, because no greater good than obedience could be found, since it exceeds all other good things in virtue, as is clear in the cited chapter, *Quid ergo.*]

[6] Fortius confirmatur quia istud querere, quod a papa qui est lex viva appelletur omni juri repugnat, quia jure communi ab ipso non appellatur. *De restitucione in integrum* cap. *Tum ex litteris* [X 1.41.4 *Tum ex litteris,* Friedberg 2:225–26][108]; *De re judicata* c. *Cum olim* [X 2.27.12 *Quum olim,* Friedberg 2:396–398]; c. *Veniam* et capitulis sequentibus [C.] 25 [lege 35] q. 9 [c. 5 *Veniam nunc,* c. 6 *Sententiam Romanae,* c. 7. *Gregorius,* c. 8 *Grave non,* and c. 9 *Sicut ergo,* Friedberg 1:1284–1286].

---

[108] The decretal *Tum ex litteris,* written by Innocent III in 1220, holds that the sentence of a pope can be reversed, and so affirms the opposite of what Bovet is seeking to prove here. The headnote (Friedberg 2:225) explains "Etiam contra sententiam papae restituitur ecclesia" [A church is restored even against the sentence of a pope]; later in the decretal (Friedberg 2:226), the pope says "Sententiam Romanae sedis non negatur posse in melius commutari, cum aut surreptum aliquid fuerit, aut ipsa pro consideratione aetatum et temporum seu gravium necessitatum dispensative quicquam ordinare decrevit" [it is not denied that a sentence of the Roman See can be changed for the better, either when something has been surreptitious, or when it decreed to ordain something by way of dispensation because of the age or times or grave necessity]. However, Bovet does argue below (sections 14–16) that the pope can be wrong, and that measures can be taken to respond to his errors. His insistence on *jus commune* could explain this seeming contradiction; he maintains that by *common law* there is no appeal, but that one can indeed address a later pope directly, and ask him to reconsider.

[A stronger confirmation is that this querying about making an appeal from the pope, who is the "living law," is repugnant to all law, for by common law there is no appeal from him. See the decretals *Tum ex litteris*, *Cum olim*, and the canon *Veniam* and the following chapters.]

[7] Et racio est quia cum a sentencia canonis vel legis mortue non appellatur, ut lege *Si qua pena* ff. *De verborum significatione* [*Digest* 50.16 *De verborum significatione* c. 244 *Si qua poena*, Mommsen 1:867–868] cap. *Cupientes, de electione*, in 6 [Sext. 1.6.16.6 *De electione et electi potestate*, c. 16 *Cupientes*, Friedberg 2:954–956] quantum minus appellabitur a principe legi mortue prebente auctorem [lege auctoritatem] prout placet et auctoritatem detrahente. *Puelle.*[109] [D.] 19 c. *Nulli* [D. 19 c. 5, Friedberg 1:61; see above, section 3].

[And the reason is that, since there is no appeal from the sentence of a canon or a dead law, as in the law *Si qua pena* and the decretal *Cupientes*, far less can one appeal from the prince who gives authority to a dead law as he pleases and takes it away. See the canons *Puelle* and *Nulli*.]

[8] Adhuc arguo fortius quia modus querendi videtur contradicere racioni juris communis, quo clare patet quod in causa appellationis requeritur major judex illo a quo appellatur ut lege *Prefecti* ff. *De minoribus* [*Digest* 4.4. *De minoribus*, c. 17 *Praefecti*, Mommsen 1.59]; cap. *Ad Romanam* [C.] 2 q. 7 [C. 2 q. 6 c. 8 *Ad Romanam*, Friedberg 1:468, or c. 6 *Ad Romanam ecclesiam omnes*, Friedberg 1:467–468] et cap. *Omnis oppressus* [C. 2 q. 6 c. 3 *Omnis oppressus*, Friedberg 1:467]; cap. *Non putamus, De consuetudine* libro 6 [Sext. 1.4 *De consuetudine* c. 2 *Non putamus*, Friedberg 2:944].

[Moreover, I argue more strongly that this kind of query appears to contradict common law, by which it is clear that in a case of appeal one needs a judge greater than the judge from whom the appeal is made as in the law *Prefecti*, the canons *Ad Romanam* and *Omnis oppressus*, and the decretal *Non putamus*.]

[9] Sed cum papa nullum habeat superiorem nec se majorem preter Deum cujus solius judicio reservatur? cap. *Facta* [C.] 9 q. 3 et cap. *Aliorum* [C. 9

---

[109] The canon *Puelle* (Gratian *Decretum* C. 20 q. 1 c. 8, Friedberg 1:845) deals with a girl's vow of virginity; Bovet's citation of the chapter is inexplicable, given its irrelevance to the matter at hand. As for his citation of *Nulli fas est* (D. 19 c. 5 *Nulli fas est*, Friedberg 1:61): Bovet has already cited it once above, when it is used to confirm that one cannot appeal from the pope; here, it seems rather superfluous, even out of place.

q. 3. c. 15 *Facta subditorum* and c. 14 *Aliorum hominum,* Friedberg 1:610–611], quomodo poterit ista opinio sustineri? Quis erit judex istius appellationis nisi solus Deus, et quis inhibebit ne ligent ipsum sententie et processus qui ligabunt donec fuerit inhibitur? ut cap. *Eum, De dolo et contumacia* libro 6 [Sext. 2.6 *De dolo et contumacia,* c. 2 *Eum,* Friedberg 2:1000].

[But since the pope has no superior nor anyone greater than himself except God, to whose judgment alone he is reserved? See the canons *Facta subditorum* and *Aliorum hominum.* How can this opinion be sustained? Who will be the judge of this appeal except God alone, and who will inhibit the sentences and processes from binding the one they bind until they are inhibited? As in the decretal *Eum.*]

[10] Et quomodo habebuntur apostoli, sine quibus appellando a gravamine appellacio erit nulla? ut cap. *Ab eo, De appellationibus,* eodem libro [Sext. 2.15 *De appellationibus,* c. 6 *Ab eo,* Friedberg 2:1017].

[And how will "apostles"[110] be had, without which an appeal from a grievance is null? See the decretal *Ab eo.*]

[11] Et si dicas quod ad consilium generale, replicatur quod papa est major omni consilio, ymmo contra quatuor consilia et contra apostolum ipse dispensat, ut cap. *Lector* 34 Distinctio [D. 34 c. 18 *Lector si viduam,* Friedberg 1:130]; 82 Distinctio cap. *Presbyter* [D. 82 c. 5 *Presbyter,* Friedberg 1:292–293]; et cap. *Sunt quidam* 25 q. 1 [C. 25 q. 1 c. 6 *Sunt quidam,* Friedberg 1:1008].

[And if you say, "to a general council," the reply is that the pope is greater than any council; in fact, he dispenses from the Four Councils and from the Apostle. See the canons *Lector si viduam, Presbyter,* and *Sunt quidam.*]

[12] Fortius confirmatur quia hoc est privilegium sedis apostolice ut ab ipso [lege ipsa] non appelletur; sed suis privilegiis detrahere est heresis, 22 Distinctio cap. 1 [D. 22 c. 1 *Omnes, sive patriarchae,* Friedberg 1:73]. Igitur, etc.

[A stronger confirmation is that this is a privilege of the Holy See, from which there is no appeal; but to detract from its privileges is heresy. See the canon *Omnes, sive patriarchae.* Therefore, etc.]

---

[110] The non-ecclesiastical Latin use of *apostolus,* found in Roman law: a short statement of the case, sent up by a lower to a higher court, when an appeal is made.

[13] Ultra hoc esset dubitare de potestate sedis et sic incurreretur sacrilegium cap. *Si quis* [C.] 17 q. 4 [C. 17 q. 4 c. 14 *Si quis ecclesiam,* Friedberg
1:818] quia ad solam voluntatem videtur posse, quod placet,
[fol. 3r]
cum nullus mortalium sibi dicat cui ita paris, [C.] 9 q. 3 cap. *Aliorum* [C.
9 q. 3 c. 14 *Aliorum hominum,* Friedberg 1:610; cited above, section 9].

[Moreover, it would be to doubt the power of the Holy See and
thus incur the sin of sacrilege, because power seems to belong to its
will alone, which is fitting, since no mortal man says to himself
"This is what you should thus obey." See the canons *Si quis ecclesiam*
and *Aliorum hominum.*]

[14] Sed, in contrarium, videtur Paulus pro insistendo. Pone enim quod,
vacante sede Parisiensi, currente guerra Anglie contra Franciam, nepo-
tem regis Anglie creat episcopum Parisiensem, jure communi princeps
potest episcopum recusare ut notorium hostem; et dicit hoc pape; papa
non vult hec audire. Queritur an debite appelletur ab eo? et clare probatur quod sic. Papa subest evangelio et legi Christi, a qua nullus fidelis
est exemptus, *De judiciis* cap. *Novit ille* [X 2.1 *De judiciis,* cap. 13 *Novit ille,*
Friedberg 2:242–243] cum adjunctis.

[But, on the other side, Paul seems to favor the affirmative. For if
we posit that the see of Paris is vacant and the war of England
against France continues, and that the pope creates the nephew of
the king of England as bishop of Paris, by common law the prince
can recuse him as a notorious enemy. If he says this to the pope,
and the pope does not wish to hear it, the question is: can an appeal be properly made from him? It is clearly proved that it can: the
pope is subject to the Gospel and the law of Christ, from which
none of the faithful is exempt. See the decretal *Novit ille* and adja-
cent canons.]

[15] Igitur subest doctrine superioris sui: "Si peccaverit in te frater tuus,
corripe eum," etc. [Matt. 18:15]. Quia dicere quod papa esset extra fini-
tatem fidelium esset absurdus. Si ergo non vult reges audire cum de
ipso conqueritur, debet dicere rex istud ecclesie [Matt. 18.17]. Et que
erit ista ecclesia, nisi collegium, vel ecclesia gallicana cum ecclesia anglicana? ([si] istam ad monicionem canonicam non audiret . . .)[111] Et si

---

[111] Bovet clearly revised the end of this sentence, which can be translated as
"[if] the pope should not hear that church, after a canonical admonition." The
word *ad* is careted in, and the letters *cam* appear in the space above the final letters

audire recusat papa ecclesiam gallicanam, numquid rex papam habebit "sicut ethnicus et publicanus" [Matt. 18:17]? Certe, sic. Quia licet papa habeant clavem potestatis, illa tantum debet regi et gubernari per clavem discrecionis; alias si indiscrete regem ligaret sua sententia nichil esset, sicut si regem excommunicaret quia elemosinam facit vel quia visitat in hospitali infirmos.

[Therefore, he is subject to the teaching of his superior: "If thy brother shall offend against thee, go and rebuke him," etc. Because to say that the pope is out of the bounds of the faithful would be absurd. If therefore he is unwilling to listen to kings when there is a complaint against him, the king should say it to the Church. And what will that church be, except a "college," that is, the Gallican church along with the English church? ... And if the pope refuses to hear the Gallican church, should not the king hold him "as the heathen and publican"? Certainly, yes. For though the pope holds the key of power, it should be ruled and wielded through the key of discretion; otherwise, if he were to bind a king without discretion, his sentence would be null; if, for instance, he excommunicated a king for giving alms or for visiting the sick in a hospital.]

[16] Item pone quod papa citat regem ad locum sibi inimicum et de morte periculosum, non[ne] quis rex teneretur obedire? Certe clarus est quod non, per cap. *Pastoralis, De re judicata* in *Clementinis* [*Constitutione Clementinae* 2.11 *De re judicata* c. 2 *Pastoralis*, Friedberg 2:1151–1153]. Et si tu dicas quod papa non ligatur illa decretali, et ego dico contrarium, quia ipsa est fundata in jure naturali cui papa et omnis princeps est subjectus, pro eo quia immobile perseverat, lege *Jus naturale, Digesto, De justitia et jure* [*Digest* 1.1.1.3: *De justicia et jure* cap. 3 *Jus naturale*, Mommsen 1:1] et cap. *Jus naturale* 1 Distinctio [Gratian, *Decretum* D. 1 c. 7 *Jus naturale*, Friedberg 1:2]. Et idcirco dicunt doctores quod quantum decretum vel decretalis de[s]cendit per modum declaracionis vel diffinicionis a lege divina naturali vel morali, papa ligatur; vel si aliquid contra facit indiscrete vel ignoranter non ligat animam contra quam procedit, per doctores in cap. *Litteras, De restititione spoliatorum* [X 2.13 *De restititione spoliatorum*, c. 13 *Litteras*, Friedberg 2.286–287], cap. *A nobis, De sentencia excommunicationis* [X 5.39 *De sententia excommunicationis*, c. 21 *A nobis*,

---

in the sentence, *can;* the two symbols combine to form an abbreviation for *canonicam*. I surmise that Bovet would have deleted the line had he not been hurried (note his hasty concluding line, section 17), and therefore read the sentence as ending with the word *anglicana*.

Friedberg 2:896], et per Johannem de Bolonia in *Clementina Dispendiosam* [*Constitutiones Clementinae* 2.1.2, *Dispendiosam*, Friedberg 2:1143], et per Guillermum de Montelauduno in *Sacramentali*,[112] titulo *De indulgentiis*, et per antiquos, [C.] 11 q. 3 in cap. *Si Dominus* et cap. *Julianus* [C. 11 q. 3 c. 93 *Si dominus* and c. 94 *Julianus*, Friedberg 1:669].

[Again, let us say that the pope summons a king to a place hostile to him, where he would be in danger of death, would any king be bound to obey? It is certainly clear that the answer is no, according to the Clementine constitution *Pastoralis*. And if you were to hold that the pope is not bound by that decretal, I say the contrary, because it is founded on natural law, to which the pope and every prince is subject, because it remains unchanged, as is stated in the law *Jus naturale* in the *Digest* and in the canon *Jus naturale* in Gratian. And therefore doctors say that insofar as a decree or decretal descends from the divine law, natural law, or the moral law, by way of declaration or definition, the pope is bound by it; or if he does anything against it, through lack of discretion or ignorance, he does not bind the soul against whom he proceeds, as the doctors say in the decretals *Litteras* and *A nobis*, and as John of Bologna [Johannes Andreae] says in the *Clementine Dispendiosam* and William of Mont-

---

[112] Guilelmus de Monte Laudano (Guillermus de Montelao, Guillaume de Montlauzun; d. 1343), O.S.B., was a professor of canon law at Toulouse. His works included an *Apparatus* on the Clementines (ed. 1517), an *Apparatus* on the Extravagantes of John XXII, a commentary on the Sext (ed. 1524), and a *Sacramentale* (ca. 1319), a canonist's manual on theological sacramental doctrine that contains a section entitled *De indulgentiis;* the text, extant in several manuscripts, remains unpublished. Cited in R. Naz, *Dictionnaire de Droit Canonique*, 7 vols. (Paris: Letouzey et Ané, 1935–1965), 4 (1944): 639. A fuller biography and list of printed editions and manuscripts of Guilelmus's works appears on a website prepared by Kenneth Pennington, http://faculty.cua.edu/pennington/1298c-g.htm.

lauzun in his *Sacramental,* in the title *Indulgences,* and the older doctors on the canons *Si Dominus* and *Julianus.*]

[17] Et quia pro nunc sum aliis negociis occupatus, ulterius non procedam.

[And because for the time being I am occupied with other business, I will not proceed further.]

CRITICAL APPARATUS

Numerals in bold print indicate prose line numbers.

33 ennemis **83** oyr **85** prouffit **86** rubric *missing in* **P2** 1 faittes. 2 ny temps . . . moine 5 ennuit 7 mains 9 veez 10 Prins . . . souhez 12 Aprés 15 prouffit. 21 jadis 22 advis 24 faulsete 27 Car vecy 29–30: *missing in both* **P2** *and* **V** 31 verrez 35 oultrecuidee 37 couraige 39 Moynes 40 Sont devenus 41 eulx 43–46: *missing in* **P2**, *included in* **V**. 55 seigneurz 58 plus s'y met 60a Le prieur respont **86** Le prieur parle: *missing in* **P1 87** m'en alay **93** Maistre Jehan de Meun parle au prieur et lui dist **95** Lors que tins . . . esbahis, je puez **96** oys **97** se lui **100** feistes jadiz **101** escoutés . . . feistes **102–103** Et ne scay **105** doctrines . . . l'opinion **106** tressaige . . . lequel **107** voulu **109** jamaiz 61 parolles . . . vilen 69 faiz 72 parillier 75 noble guerredon 79 laisse **113** Lors maistre Jehan de Meun se courrouça, sy dist au prieur **115** je lui **116** Juif **118** derrieres **120** parle au prieur **121** Sy pris a dire aux quatre dessus nommés [*see note 34*] 89 de nuyt 90 vueillies 92 Quer je . . . m'aures 94 puys 97 puys 102 vrayement 105 trayson 111 Ce c'est . . . parmission 113 D'oyr 117 decres 118 tout ce. 131 saige 132 los . . . lui 134 honnourree 135 venus 137 Qui cuident 144 saiges 147 l'instance 149 pluiseurz 153 doulans 155 cuydoit 158 loyaulx 161 luy 162 chestiveté 163 soutilté 173 royaulmes 174 Les abbayes, les sept seaulmes 175 annemy 180 A mis l'Eglise a turbacion. 189 colompne 196 Saiges . . . loyaulx 200 Mais non 207 flourist 212 netz 218 haulce 223 supply **124** Lors quant **125** luy 230 ordonnance 231 venes 232 jadis 233 vostres . . . iniquités 234 usurez 236 L'en 238 ne usez 239 prouffis 242 honnouree 243 paradiz 244 Orez, dittez 245 estez 252 ouy 257 gaige 259 gaige 260 perles 263 perles . . . lui 275 disoie 276 orryez 277 Pires usurez oncquez 284 ducz 286 gracioux 289 nuyt 293 le Juif 295 dist 303 trossimant 304 Sarrasisme 306 paraige 308 m'entens 316 Sus 319 venuz 323 puys 331 finye **130** Maistre Jehan luy repliqua 333 asert 335 saige 340 faittes 345 faittes 347 villonnie 348 compaignie 349 dittez quanques 351 puys 354 fu jadis 356 renvironde 361 scismatiques 365 diz 368 descort 370 Crestianté 379 En une loy vit en charite [en: *superscript in* **P2**; the emendation ignores the syntax of the passage] 383 laissiee 384 pitie 387–388 [*emendation; see note 56*] 395 ayderay 409 douleur 411 usaige 418 doubtez 420 gent 425 et: *missing*

in **P1** 428 annuy 430 foulez 442 treuve 449 saulce 450 fyne 452 attendre 456
vrayes 460 donoient fevez 465 ordonné 466 prestz 467 usaige 468 usaige
. . . tristre 473 Sy dist Valere 474 saige 475 mauvais 476 bevraige . . . reffusa
477 luy 479 sale 480 male 484 tel 485–86 **P1, P2** Car sa vice vraye et certaine, Par grant vertu fut vie vaine [*see note 66*] 489 au monde 490 Nen pour
491 tendres 492 soudayers 493 tenez 494 doulz . . . fryans 495 vestus 496
P1 il 497 chault 501 doulx 505 chaperon . . . barrette 507 saiges 508
passaiges 509 paiens 511 **P1** regarde 518 annemis 522 perduz 525 armez
529 d'armez 531 **P1** escouffez 532 vostres . . . armez 533 Ayes . . . vostres
534 **P1** ameures 536 couraige 539 apris 547 frommaige 548 chapons gens de
paraige 549 jamaiz 550 tenez 554 Angleterre 557 Prenez exemple 561 soit
en Espaigne 562 Alemaigne 563 Cyppre 566 prouffiteux 569 faittes 577
coupz 580 harnoys porter 584 Quant de 588 leurs corpz 589 Crestians
dommaige 590 paraige 593 **P1** ses 598 bien 600 savatier 605 fyne 615 Encores 618 bouillent 621 meureté 641 Ne voy nullui qui en souspire 644 veuz
649 laboures 650 quinze . . . soutes 651 **P1** est noe 653 chappel 658
chezaulx 662 vengence 666 pitie 669 boubance 673 femenye 674 paiennie
675 **P1** S'il tenissent 677 Pour dessourdre **134** Maistre Jehan parle 682 faiz
. . . doulant 692 **P1** frans 693 compaignie 694 mesmes 697 puys que vas 702
vueullent 704 Et les 707 quelconques 708 adviz 711 puys . . . traitter 716 De
recouvrer . . . heritaige 718 ocuppa 721 Seiche 723 Puys . . . Grenade 725
adviz 727 combien il aura 728 Apris les armes 731 Aprez 734 midy 736 Se
en 738 yres 739 eue compaignie 743 veu 745 advisez 749 mauvais usaige
750 couraige 754 sauroyent 762 usaige 764 n'y esperit 765 puys 767
congnoiz 772 Tel 775 voisin 781 perler 783 gaiges 784 dommaiges 786 Encores 788 chapeaulx de bievre 790 bien pluiseurz 791 Adont n'avoye mal
aux dens 793 pryer 795 Encores 797 gaiges 798 vueullent . . . oultraiges 799
chascune annee 801 heritaige 802 soufist . . . gaige 808 Que s'officier 811
paier 816 Se present 819 dit 821 ne or ne 823 dit 825 on lui vent chier 827
c'on 830a Maistre Jehan parle: 831 n'empartirez 832 direz 833 Puys 836
Eustace 837 l'avez 839 adviz 842 chappez 844 chapellains . . . escuyers 846
sales 850 m'en pourra on croyre 853 vostres [*scribe corrected from* nostres] 857
veisse . . . tynel 860 nefz 862 tripplez 865 Puys 872 Bonniface 885 Encorez.
887 hommes 891 deliz 893 **P1** qu'il ilz sont 898a Lors maistre Jehan regarda
vers le Jacobin, sy luy dist 899 oy 902 saurez 904 empesche scavoir 910
puys 911 Mais l'en 914 **P1** emprison 916 fais 918 telz debaz 919 **P1** Il n'aura
927 Mouzon 942 je ne dy 946 puys 947 decretales 948 ditees 950 Puys 955
decrez 956 aprez 957 Celluy qu'on dit le Questionnari 958 exemplari 967
maint 971 Guydon 973 hystoires 976 grant 983 Puys nostre mere ot passe
temps 985 luy 991 Mouzon . . . sonne 996 puys 998 fais 1002 compaignie
1006 traittre 1009 ducz **142** Cy respont le Sarrazin aux questions du Jacobin

1016 Quant tu 1018 Tu t'es esbays. 1020 Fusses 1023 long temps 1026 tout rien 1029 sormontant 1034 haulx 1036 seur 1037 cuyde . . . yster 1039 saiges 1040 aprint 1047 ces 1049 **P1** Et s'ilz sont il 1052 Quant a l'estat ne l'ay leu 1054 chapellains 1056 preudommes 1057 Sy estoit . . . preudomie 1058 Honouree . . . compaignie 1063 papes . . . mittres 1066 **P1** com 1070 empettrer 1074 ystement 1075 Rommains 1077 vacquant 1078 Rommains 1082 commencerent 1084 depuys 1087 chapel 1094 Tant eglises, tant prevostes 1095 Tant chanoinyes, tant priores 1096 quanques 1097 papes 1103 prins 1115 vacqant 1121 Aprez 1125 disme: **P1** Xme; **P2** diziesme 1133 **P1** Patoutes 1138 debaz 1140 douleur 1144 **P1** frant 1150 senz 1153 moittye 1157 puys 1160 Amoit 1168 compaignie 1172 le champ 1173 Constantin 1179 **P1** Qui; **P2** luy 1180 luy 1187 luy 1191 laissier; **P1**: non 1192 **P1**: non 1193 dommaige 1195 amendrye 1202 puent bien tenir 1204 crestiante 1209 auroyent 1215 abbayés 1216 couventuelz 1217 moynes despouillés 1220 **P1** sevent 1222 ocupper 1223 **P1** diin [*scribe omitted abbreviation for "v"*]; **P2** Quant s'en pert le divin services 1224 qui: *missing in* **P1**; douerent 1229 baronnyes 233 mesprisee 1234 dam 1237 Qu'ilz n'en 1241 puys 1245 Qui tousjours **143** Maistre Jehan parle: 1257 estez 1262 **P1** gent que sachant non 1264 ly 1266 clergaux 1271 secres 1274 garir 1275 eresie 1276 d'anfidelite 1280 *Both manuscripts:* dira [*See note 120*] 1282 dens 1283 Celluy 1286 mais cilz 1287 quanques 1294 Pour non 1299 Et se fera **145** Maistre Jehan parle: 1306 encorez 1314 scisme 1318 qu'une 1326 commence 1330 autres 1338 ly 1344 Quant d'avoir 1346 Luy faulsist paier 1349 luy . . . luy 1351 saiges 1352 sauroient 1353 ces 1354 baz 1355 vueullent 1363 pres 1369 onques leur pere n'ot 1370 paier 1371 Aprez 1372 salez 1373 ducz 1376 vueillent . . . homes 1377 *Both manuscripts:* ses 1378 Ly mondes 1382 teille 1385 Ne se 1388 sauroient aider 1393 prelaz n'ayment 1394 ne saura 1402 Se c'est 1405 tel qui 1406 droys 1407 diz 1410 domaige 1411 sy 1412 officier 1417 le pueple povre 1420 doint 1423 puys **147** Maistre Jehan parle: 1424 gracious 1427 n'en soit 1430 vueillent 1431 soyés 1432 certain 1433 suy pas 1434 livres 1435 entendus 1437 Nen 1441 chaut 1447 vueullent 1448 estuves 1453 froys 1469 **P1** Que ses fais 1475 dommaiges 1479 ay moit 1482 oultraige 1483 mariaige 1489 Avecquez 1491 L'en ne 1492 frommage 1500 seigneurs 1501 onneurs 1518 Et puys ay dit 1520 prescheours 1521 Pryés **149** Le prieur: Lors maistre Jehan regarda vers moy et sy me prist a dire; Maistre Jehan parle au prieur 1526 Pryeur, rapportes 1527 quatre **151** assez **152** paour que soient. **153** par . . . par **156** autres . . . fays . . . j'ay veu **157** puys . . . deliveray **159** **P1** interpeter **161** celluy . . . pays pour **162** en Prouvence *missing in* **P2** **163** Louys *missing in* **P2** **166** Dieux . . . celluy . . . Remon **167** guerre *missing in* **P1** **169–170** *entire passage between* mais de tant *and* c'om parle de luy *missing in* **P1** **173** dus . . . Bourgoigne **175** liz . . . ly **177** Mais je

178 ou temps *repeated in* **P2 180** ly . . . luy **181** pascience **182** congnoistera **184** courroucer . . . saiges **185** conseil, en compagnie **186** parlez . . . vouldrez **187** de lis *missing in* **P1**; leurs nature **188** sans tache, a toutes **189** Remon **192** Napples . . . fils **193** Remond **194** qui plaist **195** Raymond . . . dist **199** datilier **200** prez . . . encorez **201** puys **202** portant . . . advint **203** datilier . . . au plus **205** datilier **208** et peserent . . . datilier **209** datilier . . . grant fays **211** ainsy . . . annuy **213** datiliers **216** datilier **219** datiliers **220** luy **224** datiliers . . . luy . . . luy **225** oys **226** oncquez . . . eage **227** y *missing in* **P1**; Certez; elle *missing in* **P1 228** moys . . . demy **230** rigoüler . . . luy . . . luy **231** ryés **232** datiliers **233** perduz **236** ris . . . en bien **238** Remon . . . sy **239 P1**: grans, car je **240** ad ce **241** oncquez **242** baronys **244** vilainement . . . nulz ne s'en doit merveillier **245** ly . . . sires **248** fust comme . . . Angleterre **249** le royaume . . . ad certes . . . autres **250** qui fu jadis donnee a **251** Chevereuse **253 P1**: que jay non m'en **255** chose . . . aussy . . . touchee **256** es diz **258** celluy **262** que aucuns fussent tellement **263** samblable **264** ryroie **265** chose **266** tel **267** Certez . . . un **269** aussy **271** chose . . . paiages **272** atrappez **273** diz . . . paageurs **274** prendent **275** tant *missing in* **P1 276** desherités . . . Et pleust **279** survendroit . . . celluy **281 P1**: confiquer **282** d'icelluy . . . le seigneur **283 P1**: peages qui furent; trouvés **286** peage **287 P1**: avoir **288** peageurs **289** preudommes, et pour bien pou qui s'estudient des passans **290** achoison **291** pontoniers et gardez **292** le Roone **293** oy **1530** saintite **1531** Fut accusee **1533 P1**: A prendre **1534** Dieux . . . jugemens **1536** Par quoy **1537 P1**: leur **1539** Non sont **1540** C'est verite . . . vraye **1541** loyaulte **298** Son phisicien parle a madame d'Orliens

BIBLIOGRAPHY

Manuscript Sources

Works by Honorat Bovet

Apparicion maistre Jehan de Meun: Paris, BNF MSS français 810 (**P1**) and 811 (**P2**); Vatican City, BAV, MS Vat. Reg. 1683, fols. 39r–87v (**V**); London, BL, MS Lansdowne 214, fols. 201r–216v (**L**).

Somnium super materia scismatis (contains at end four letters by Bovet): Paris, BNF, MS lat. 14643, fols. 269r–283r; Vatican City, ASV, MS Armarium 54, vol. 21 (*De schismate Urbani*), fols. 73r–90r.

Discourse to Wenceslas ("Oratio legati Caroli VI Francorum regis ad Wenceslaum Romanorum et Bohemiae regem"). Prague, Karls Universität MS XIII. F. 16, fols. 125r–131v.

Verses in the "Cronique dels comtes de Foix et Senhors de Bearn." Pau, Archives départementales des Pyrénées Atlantiques, MS E392, fols. 1–26; Paris, BNF, MS Doat 164, fols. 1r–50v.

Bovet: Biographical Evidence

BNF fr. 21145, fol. 93 (1392: royal grant of annual pension)

BNF *Dossiers Bleus* 650 (MS français 30,195), "Titres du Château de Lavardin," dossier 17265 (Tussé), fol. 30v (March 1405: in service of Louis II of Anjou)

BNF, Pièces originales 2626 (MS fr. 29110), dossier 58417 (Sanglier), #7 (1391: royal service in Armagnac)

BAV, MS Vat. lat. 4000, fol. 102v (1409: representative of Abbey of Ile-Barbe at Pisa)

Lyon, Archives départementales du Rhône, dossier 10 G 3146, pièces i & ii (1400: mission to Imperial court)

Marseille, Archives départementales des Bouches du Rhône, dossier B9, fol. 138 (1406: on Louis II's royal council)

Other Works

BNF manuscrit fonds français 5015: Journal of Jean le Fèvre, Bishop of Chartres and Chancellor of Louis I of Anjou, 1380–1388.

BNF MS français 603: Christine de Pizan, *Livre des faits d'armes et de chevalerie.*

Brussels, Koninklijke Bibliotheek, MS 9009–9011, fol. 181v: Christine de Pizan, *Livre des faits d'armes et de chevalerie;* illumination depicting Honorat Bovet appearing to Christine.

Printed Works

A. Primary Sources

Abelard, Peter. *Petrus Abaelardus, Dialogus inter Philosophum, Iudaeum et Christianum.* Ed. Rudolf Thomas. Stuttgart: Bad Cannstatt, 1970.

――――. *Peter Abelard, A Dialogue of a Philosopher with a Jew and a Christian.* Trans. Pierre J. Payer. Toronto: Pontifical Institute of Medieval Studies, 1979.

Andreae, Johannes. *Novella in Decretales Gregorii IX* [1338]. Venice: F. Franciscum, 1581. Repr. Turin: Bottega d'Erasmo, 1963.

Augustine of Hippo, Saint. *The City of God Against the Pagans.* Trans. George E. McCracken. 7 vols. Loeb Classical Library. Cambridge, MA: Harvard University Press, 1957.

Bédier, Joseph ed. *"La chanson de Roland," publiee d'apres le manuscrit d'Oxford.* Paris: H. Piazza, 1966.

Bellaguet, Louis, ed. *Chronique du Religieux de Saint-Denys, contenant le règne de Charles VI, de 1380 à 1422.* 6 vols. Paris: Crapelet, 1840.

Bernis, Michel de. "Cronique dels comtes de Foix e Senhors de Bearn, feyt l'an de l'Incarnacion de N.-S. 1445." In *Panthéon Littéraire. Choix de Chroniques et Mémoires sur l'Histoire de France,* ed. J. A. C.Buchon, 575–600. Paris: Mairet et Fournier, 1841.

Blythe, James M., trans. *On the Government of Rulers: "De Regimine Principum"* *by Ptolemy of Lucca*, with portions attributed to Thomas Aquinas. Philadelphia: University of Pennsylvania Press, 1997.

Bovet, Honorat. *L'arbre des Batailles d'Honoré Bonet*. Ed. Ernest Nys. Brussels: C. Muquardt, 1883.

_____. *The Tree of Battles*. Trans. George W. Coopland. Liverpool: Liverpool University Press, 1949.

_____. *L'apparicion Maistre Jehan de Meun et le Somnium super materia scismatis*. Ed. Ivor Arnold. Publications de la Faculté des lettres de l'Université de Strasbourg 28. Paris: Les Belles Lettres, 1926.

_____. *L'Apparition de Jehan de Meun ou le Songe du Prieur de Salon par Honoré Bonet, Prieur de Salon, Docteur en Décret (1398)*. Ed. Jérome [Baron] Pichon. Paris: Silvestre, 1845.

_____. "Oratio legati Caroli VI Francorum regis ad Wenceslaum Romanorum et Bohemiae regem." Ed. Karl A. C. Höfler. In *Geschichtsschreiber der Husitischen Bewegung in Böhmen*, Fontes rerum Austriacarum 1 [Scriptores], 6.2:174–87. Vienna: Kaiserliche Akademie der Wissenschaften, 1865.

[Pseudo-]Caecilium Balbus. *Caecilii Balbi De Nugis Philosophorum quae supersunt*. Ed. Eduard Wölfflin. Basel: Schweighauser, 1855.

Cicero, Marcus Tullius. *Cicero: On Old Age and On Friendship*. Trans. Frank O. Copley. Ann Arbor: University of Michigan Press, 1967.

Corpus Canonicum Glossatum. 3 vols. Lyon: P. Landry, 1606.

Deschamps, Eustache. *Oeuvres complètes*. Ed. Auguste Henry Édouard Marquis de Queux de Saint-Hilaire and Gaston Raynaud. 11 vols. Paris: Firmin Didot, 1878–1903.

Fehius, Johannes, ed. *Corpus juris civilis Justinianei, cum commentariis*. 6 vols. Lyon: Jacques Cardon & Pierre Cavellat, 1627.

Froissart, Jean. *Oeuvres de Jean Froissart*. Ed. Henri Kervyn de Lettenhove. 25 vols. Brussels: V. Devaux, 1867–1877. Repr. Osnabruck: Biblio Verlag, 1967.

Gherardi, Alessandro, ed. *Diario d'Anonimo Fiorentino*. Documenti di storia italiana 6, Cronache dei secoli XIII e XIV. Florence: Tipi di M. Cellini, 1876.

Guibert of Nogent. *Dei Gesta per Francos*. Ed. R. B. C. Huygens. Corpus Christianorum: Continuatio Medievalis 127A. Turnhout: Brepols, 1996.

Isidore of Seville, Saint. *Etymologiae*. Ed. W.M. Lindsay. 2 vols. Oxford Classical Texts. Oxford: Clarendon Press, 1911. Repr. 1957.

Mézières, Philippe de. *"Le Songe du Vieil Pelerin" of Philippe de Mézières, Chancellor of Cyprus*. Ed. George W. Coopland. 2 vols. Cambridge: Cambridge University Press, 1969.

Migne, J.-P., ed. *Patrologiae cursus completus . . . Series Latina*. 221 vols. Paris: Migne, 1844–1864.

_____, ed. *Patrologiae cursus completus . . . Series Graeca*. 161 in 166 vols. Paris: Migne, 1857–1866.

Mommsen, Theodore, and Paul Krueger, eds. *The Digest of Justinian*. Trans. Alan Watson. 4 vols. Philadelphia: University of Pennsylvania Press, 1985.

_____, Paul Krueger, and Rudolf Schoell, eds. *Corpus juris civilis*. 3 vols. Berlin: Weidmann, 1904–1908.

Moranvillé, Henri, ed. *Journal de Jean le Fèvre, évêque de Chartres et Chancelier des Rois de Sicile Louis I et II d'Anjou, 1380–1388*. Paris: A. Picard, 1887.

Origen. *Homélies sur le Cantique des Cantiques*. Ed. and trans. Dom Olivier Rousseau, O.S.B. Sources Chrétiennes 37bis. Paris: Éditions du Cerf, 1966.

_____. *The Song of Songs: Commentary and Homilies*. Trans. and annnot. R. P. Lawson. New York: Newman Press, 1957.

_____. *Homilies on Genesis and Exodus*. Trans. R. E. Heine. Fathers of the Church 71. Washington, D.C.: Catholic University of America Press, 1981.

Richard de Bury. *Philobiblon*. Ed. E. C. Thomas London: K. Paul, Trench and Co., 1888.

Robert, Ulysse, ed. *L'art de chevalerie, traduction du De re militari de Vegees par Jean de Meun*. SATF 39. Paris: Firmin Didot, 1900.

Rupescissa, Johannes de. *Liber secretorum eventuum*. Ed. Robert E. Lerner and Christine Morerod-Fattebert. Fribourg: Éditions universitaires, 1994.

Sandys, J. E., ed., and R. C. Jebb, trans. *The Characters of Theophrastus*. London: Macmillan, 1909.

Secousse, Denis-François. *Ordonnances des Rois de France de la troisième race*. 9 vols. Paris, Imprimerie Royale, 1723–1755.

Seneca, Lucius Annaeus, *Moral Essays*. Ed. And trans. John W. Basore. 3 vols. Loeb Classical Library 214, 254, 310. Cambridge, MA: Harvard University Press, 1958.

Steele, Robert, ed. *Secretum secretorum*. Oxford: Clarendon Press, 1920.

Swan, Charles, trans. *Gesta Romanorum*. London: G. Routledge & Sons, 1905.

Tolomeo [Ptolemy] of Lucca. *Historia Ecclesiastica*. Ed. Lodovico Muratori. Vol. 11 (1728) in Rerum Italicarum Scriptores. 25 vols. Milan: Societatis Palatinae, 1723–1751.

Valerius Maximus. *Facta et dicta memorabilia*. Ed. Karl Kempf. 2nd ed. Leipzig: Teubner, 1888; repr. Stuttgart: Teubner, 1966.

_____. *Facta et dicta memorabilia*. Ed. John Briscoe. 2 vols. Stuttgart and Leipzig: Teubner, 1998.

_____. *Factorum et dictorum memorabilium libri IX: Memorable Doings and Sayings*. Ed. and trans.D. R. Shackleton Bailey. 2 vols. Loeb Classical Library. Cambridge, MA: Harvard University Press, 2000.

B. Secondary Works

Abun-Nasr, Jamil M. *A History of the Maghrib*. Cambridge: Cambridge University Press, 1971.

Agulhon, Maurice, and Noël Coulet. *Histoire de Provence*. Paris: Presses Universitaires de France, 1987.

Allmand, Christopher T. "Changing Views of the Soldier in Late-Medieval France." In *Guerre et société en France, en Angleterre et en Bourgogne (XIVe–XVe siècle)*, ed. Philippe Contamine, Charles Giry-Deloison and Maurice H. Keen, 171–188. Villeneuve d'Ascq: Centre d'histoire de la région du Nord et de l'Europe du Nord-Ouest, Université Charles de Gaulle, 1991.

Arnold, Ivor. "Notice sur un manuscrit de la traduction des *Annales du Hainaut* de Jacques de Guise par Jean Wauquelin (British Museum Lansdowne 214)." *Romania* 55 (1929): 382–400.

Atiya, Aziz S. *Crusade, Commerce and Culture*. Bloomington: Indiana University Press, 1962.

_____. *The Crusade in the Later Middle Ages*. London: Methuen, 1938.

_____. *The Crusade of Nicopolis*. London: Methuen, 1934.

Autrand, Françoise. *Charles VI: la folie du roi*. Paris: Fayard, 1986.

Avril, François. *Manuscript Painting at the Court of France: the Fourteenth Century, 1310–1380.* Trans. Ursule Molinaro and Bruce Benderson. New York: G. Braziller, 1978.

Bartos, Frantisek Michálek, ed. *Autograf M. Jana Husi.* Bibliothecae Clementinae Analecta 4. Prague: Státní pedagogické Nakladatelstri, 1954.

_____, and Pavel Spunar. *Soupis pramenù k literární literární cinnosti M. Jana Husa a M. Jeronyma Prazského.* Prague: Historicky ústav CSAV, 1965.

Batany, Jean. "Un Usbek au XIV^c siècle: le Sarrasin juge des Français dans l'Apparicion Jehan de Meun." In *Images et signes de l'Orient dans l'Occident médiéval: littérature et civilisation,* ed. Jean Arrouye, 41–58. Actes du colloque du CUER MA, février 1981. Sénéfiance 11. Aix–en–Provence: Publications de CUER MA, 1982.

Benson, Larry D., et al., eds. *The Riverside Chaucer.* 3rd ed. Boston: Houghton Mifflin, 1987.

Boudet, Jean-Patrice, and Hélène Millet. *Eustache Deschamps en son temps.* Paris: Publications de la Sorbonne, 1997.

Brundage, James A. *Medieval Canon Law.* New York: Longman, 1995.

Camille, Michael. *The Master of Death: The Lifeless Art of Pierre Remiet, Illuminator.* New Haven: Yale University Press, 1996.

Chamberlin, E. R.. *The Count of Virtue: Giangaleazzo Visconti, Duke of Milan* London: Eyre and Spottiswoode, 1965.

Collas, Émile. *Valentine de Milan, Duchesse d'Orléans.* 2nd ed. Paris: Plon, 1911.

Comparetti, Domenico. *Vergil in the Middle Ages.* Trans. E. F. M. Benecke. London: Sonnenschein & Co., 1908. Repr. Hamden, CT: Archon Books, 1966.

Contamine, Philippe. *La Guerre au moyen âge.* Paris: Presses Universitaires de France, 1980.

Cortez, Fernand. *Les grands officiers royaux de Provence au Moyen Age.* Aix–en–Provence: Secrétariat de la Société d'études provençales: A. Dragon, 1921.

Daniel, Norman A. *Islam and the West: the Making of an Image.* Edinburgh: The University Press, 1960; rev. ed. Oxford: Oneworld, 1993.

Delaville le Roulx, Joseph Marie Antoine. *La France en Orient au XIV^c siècle: Expéditions du Maréchal Boucicaut.* 2 vols. Bibliothèque des Écoles francaises d'Athènes et de Rome 44–45. Paris: Ernest Thorin, 1886.

Delisle, Léopold. *Actes normands de la Chambre des comptes sous Philippe de Valois (1328–1350)*. Rouen: A. Le Brument, 1871.

Dizionario biografico degli Italiani. 54 vols. Rome: Istituto della Enciclopedia Italiana, 1960–2000.

Doutrepont, Georges. *La littérature française à la cour des Ducs de Bourgogne*. Paris: Champion, 1909.

Emmerson, Richard K. *Antichrist in the Middle Ages: A Study of Medieval Apocalypticism, Art, and Literature*. Seattle: University of Washington Press, 1981.

Encyclopedia Britannica. 15th ed. 28 vols. Chicago: Encyclopedia Britannica, Inc., 1993.

Evans, G. Blakemore, et al., eds. *The Riverside Shakespeare*. 1st ed. Boston: Houghton Mifflin, 1974.

Famiglietti, Richard C. *Tales of the Marriage Bed from Medieval France (1300–1500)*. Providence, RI: Picardy Press, 1992.

_____. *Royal Intrigue: Crisis at the Court of Charles VI (1392–1420)*. New York: AMS Press, 1986.

Fleming, Martha. *The Late Medieval Pope Prophecies*. MRTS 204. Tempe: MRTS, 1999.

Fleury, Edouard. *Les manuscrits à miniatures de la Bibliothèque de Soissons, étudiés au point de vue de leur illustration*. Paris: Dumoulin, 1865.

Foulet, Alfred, and Mary Blakely Speer. *On Editing Old French Texts*. Lawrence, KS: Regents Press of Kansas, 1979.

Godefroy, Frédéric. *Dictionnaire de l'ancienne langue française*. 10 vols. Paris: Librairie de sciences et des arts, 1937–1938.

Hanly, Michael. "Courtiers and Poets: An International Network of Literary Exchange." *Viator: Medieval and Renaissance Studies* 28 (1997): 305–32.

_____. "'Et prendre nom de Sarrazin:' Islam as Symptom of Western Iniquity in Honorat Bovet's *L'apparicion maistre Jehan de Meun*." In *Cultures in Contact: Essays in Honor of Paul Beekman Taylor*, ed. Margaret E. Bridges, Special issue of *Multilingua* 18 (1999): 227–49. Berlin and New York: Mouton de Gruyter.

_____. *Beauvau, Boccaccio, Chaucer: "Troilus and Criseyde": Four Perspectives on Influence*. Norman, OK: Pilgrim Books, 1990.

_____, and Hélène Millet. "Les Batailles d'Honorat Bovet: Essai de biographie." *Romania* 114 (1996): 135–81.

_____. "Marriage, War, and Good Government in Late-14th-Century Europe: the *De Regimine Principum* Tradition in Langland, Mézières, and Bovet," in *Chaucer and the Challenges of Medievalism: Studies in Honor of Henry Ansgar Kelly*, ed. Donka Minkova and Theresa Tinkle (Frankfurt am Main: Peter Lang), 2003, 327–49.

Hasenohr, Geneviève. "Discours vernaculaire et autorités latines." In *Mise en page et mise en texte du livre manuscrit,* ed. Henri-Jean Martin and Jean Vezin, 289–316. Paris: Editions du Cercle de la Librairie-Promodis, 1990.

Hayez, Anne-Marie, ed., with Janine Mathieu and Marie-France Yvan. *Grégoire XI (1370–1378): Lettres Communes (analysées d'après les Registres dits d'Avignon et du Vatican).* 2 vols. Bibliothèque des Écoles françaises d'Athènes et de Rome, 3e Série, 6bis: *Lettres Communes des Papes du XIV^c siècle.* Rome: École française de Rome, 1992.

Hayez, Michel, Anne-Marie Hayez, and Pierre Gasnault, eds., with Janine Mathieu and Marie-France Yvan. *Urbain V (1362–1370): Lettres Communes (analysées d'après les Registres dits d'Avignon et du Vatican).* 11 vols. Bibliothèque des Écoles françaises d'Athènes et de Rome, 3e Série, 5: *Lettres Communes des Papes du XIV^c siècle.* Rome: École française de Rome, 1954–1986.

Henneman, John Bell. *Olivier de Clisson and Political Society in France Under Charles V and Charles VI.* Philadelphia: University of Pennsylvania Press, 1996.

Hindman, Sandra. *Christine de Pizan's "Epistre Othea": Painting and Politics at the Court of Charles VI.* Toronto: Pontifical Institute of Mediaeval Studies, 1986.

Hinnebusch, William A., O.P. *The History of the Dominican Order.* 2 vols. New York: Alba House, 1973.

Iogna-Prat, Dominique. *Order and Exclusion: Cluny and Christendom Face Heresy, Judaism, and Islam (1000–1150).* Trans. G. R. Edwards Ithaca: Cornell University Press, 2002.

Jorga, Nicolae. *Philippe de Mézières et la croisade au XIV^c siècle.* Paris: Bouillon, 1896.

Jarry, Eugène. *La vie politique de Louis de France, duc d'Orléans (1372–1407).* Orléans: Herluison, 1889.

Jenkins, Romilly. *Byzantium: the Imperial Centuries, A.D. 610–1071*. New York: Random House, 1966.

Jodogne, Omer. "Povoir ou pouoir? Le cas phonétique de l'ancien verbe povoir." *Travaux de linguistique et de littérature* 4 (1996): 257–66.

Jorga, Nicolae. *Philippe de Mézières et la croisade au XIVᵉ siècle*. Paris: Bouillon, 1896.

Kaegi, Walter E. "Problems of Cohesion: the Battle of Jābiya-Yarmuk Reconsidered." In *Byzantium and the Early Islamic Conquests*. Cambridge: Cambridge University Press, 1992, 112–146.

Kaminsky, Howard. *Simon de Cramaud and the Great Schism*. New Brunswick NJ: Rutgers University Press, 1983

_____. *Simon de Cramaud's "De substraccione obediencie."* Cambridge, MA: Medieval Academy of America, 1984.

Keen, Maurice H. *The Laws of War in the Middle Ages*. London: Routledge & Kegan Paul, 1965.

Kelly, H. A. "Canonical Implications of Richard III's Plan to Marry His Niece." *Traditio* 23 (1967): 269–311.

Krynen, Jacques. *Idéal du prince et pouvoir royal en France à la fin du Moyen Âge (1380–1440): Étude de la littérature politique du temps*. Paris: A. et J. Picard, 1981.

Laennec, Christine M. "Christine 'Antygrafe': Authorship and Self in the Prose Works of Christine de Pizan with an Edition of BN manuscript 603 *Le livre des fais d'armes et de chevallerie*" (vols. 1 and 2). Ph.D. diss., Yale University, 1988.

Langlois, Ernest. "Notice des manuscrits français et provençaux de Rome antérieurs au XVIᵉ siècle." In *Notices et extraits des manuscits de la Bibliothèque nationale et autres bibliothèques, publiés par l'Institut national de France,* [faisant suite aux Notices et extraits lus au comité établi dan l'Academie des Inscriptions et Belles-Lettres] 33.2, "Notice des manuscrits français et provençaux de Rome antérieurs au XVIᵉ siècle," 208–17. Paris: Imprimerie Nationale, 1890.

Lavisse, Ernest. *Histoire de France depuis les origines jusqu'à la révolution*. 9 vols. Paris: Hachette, 1900–1911.

Lemaire, Jacques. "L'*Apparicion Maistre Jean de Meun* d'Honoré Bouvet et les *Lettres Persanes* de Montesquieu: Points de convergence." *Études sur le XVIIIe siècle* 5 (1978): 59–71.

Léonard, Émile. *Les Angevins de Naples.* Paris: Presses Universitaires de France, 1954.

Lewis, Bernard. *Race and Color in Islam.* New York: Harper and Row, 1970.

Llull, Ramon. *Llibre del Gentil e dels tres savis.* Trans. Armand Llinarès. Paris: Éditions du Cerf, 1993.

Lot, Ferdinand, and Robert Fawtier. *Histoire des institutions françaises au Moyen Age.* 5 vols. Paris: Presses universitaires de France, 1957–1958.

Marti, Kevin. "Dream Vision." In *A Companion to Old and Middle English Literature,* ed. L. C. Lambdin and R. T. Lambdin. Westport, CT: Greenwood Press, 2002, 178–209.

McGrady, Deborah. "What is a Patron? Benefactors and Authorship in Harley 4431, Christine de Pizan's Collected Works." In *Christine de Pizan and the Categories of Difference,* ed. Marilynn Desmond. Minneapolis: University of Minnesota Press, 1998, 195–214.

Millet, Hélène. "Écoute et usage des prophéties par les prélats pendant le grand schisme d'Occident." *Mélanges de l'École française de Rome* 102 (1990): 425–55.

_____. "Les français du royaume au Concile de Pise (1409)." In *Crises et réformes dans l'Église de la réforme grégorienne à la préréforme,* 259–85. Actes du 115e Congrès national des sociétés savantes, Avignon, 1990. Paris: Éditions du CTHS, 1991.

_____, and Emmanuel Poulle, eds. *Le vote de la soustraction d'obédience en 1398.* Tome I: Introduction, Édition et facsimiles des bulletins de vote. Documents, Études et Répertoires publiés par l'Institut de Recherche et d'Histoire des Textes. Paris: CNRS, 1988.

Mirot, Léon. "Bonaccorso Pitti: aventurier, joueur, diplomate et mémorialiste." *Annuaire-Bulletin de la Société de l'Histoire de France* 60 (1930): 183–252.

Mistral, Frédéric. *Lou tresor dou Felibrige ou Dictionnaire Provençal-Français.* 2 vols. Barcelona: Berenguié, 1968.

Mittler, Elmar, et al., eds. *Bibliotheca Palatina: Katalog zur Ausstellung vom 8. Juli bis 2. November 1986, Heiliggeistkirche Heidelberg.* Heidelberger Bibliotheks-schriften 24: herausgegeben von Elmar Mittler in Zusammenarbeit mit

Walter Berschin, Jürgen Miethke, Gottfried Seebass, Vera Trost, Wilfried Werner. 2 vols.: 1: Textband; 2: Bildband. Heidelberg: Braus, 1986.

The New Catholic Encyclopedia. 18 vols. New York: McGraw-Hill, 1967–1989.

Ouy, Gilbert. "Honoré Bouvet (appelé à tort Bonet), prieur de Selonnet." *Romania* 85 (1959): 255–59.

⸺. "Une maquette de manuscrit à peintures (Paris, BN lat. 14643, fols. 269–283v, Honoré Bouvet, *Somnium prioris de Sallono super materia Scismatis*, 1394)." In *Mélanges d'histoire du livre et des bibliothèques offerts à Monsieur Frantz Calot*, 43–51. Bibliothèque elzévirienne, nouvelle série: Études et documents. Paris: Librairie d'Argences, 1960.

Oxford Dictionary of Byzantium. Ed.-in-chief Alexander P. Kazhdan. 3 vols. New York: Oxford University Press, 1991.

Paris, Paulin. *Les manuscrits françois de la Bibliothèque du Roi*. 7 vols. Paris: Techener, 1846–1848.

Pennington, Kenneth. "Guilelmus de Monte Laudano." In "Medieval Canonists. A Bio-Bibliographical Listing," Collections and Jurists, Part Two (1298–1500), C-G, http://faculty.cua.edu/pennington/1298c-g.htm.

Perroy, Edouard. *L'Angleterre et le grand schisme d'Occident: Étude sur la politique religieuse de l'Angleterre sous Richard II (1378–1399)*. Paris: Monnier, 1933.

Petkov, Kiril. "The Rotten Apple and the Good: Orthodox, Catholics, and Turks in Philippe de Mézières's Crusading Propaganda." *Journal of Medieval History* 23 (1997): 255–70.

Pratt, Robert A. "Chaucer and the Visconti Libraries." *English Literary History* 6 (1939): 191–99.

Randall, Lilian M. C., ed. *Medieval and Renaissance Manuscripts in the Walters Art Gallery*. Vol. 1: France, 875–1420. Baltimore: Johns Hopkins University Press, 1989.

Reeves, Marjorie. *The Influence of Prophecy in the Later Middle Ages: A Study in Joachism*. Oxford: Clarendon Press, 1969.

Ruggiers, Paul, and Daniel Ransom, eds. *A Variorum Edition of the Works of Geoffrey Chaucer*. Volume Two [*The Canterbury Tales*]. Part A: The General Prologue. 2 vols. Norman, OK: University of Oklahoma Press, 1993.

Rusconi, Roberto. *L'attesa della fine: Crisi della società, profezia ed Apocalisse in Italia al tempo del grande scisma d'Occidente (1378–1417)*. Rome: Istituto storico italiano per il Medio Evo, 1979.

Russell, Frederick H. *The Just War in the Middle Ages*. Cambridge: Cambridge University Press, 1975.

Said, Edward. *Orientalism*. New York: Vintage Books, 1978.

Schaefer, Lucie. "Die Illustrationen zu den Handschriften der Christine de Pisan." *Marburger Jahrbuch für Kunstwissenschaft* 10 (1937): 119–208.

Shahîd, Irfan. *Byzantium and the Arabs in the Sixth Century*. Washington, D.C.: Dumbarton Oaks, 1995.

Tierney, Brian. *The Crisis of Church and State, 1050–1300*. Englewood Cliffs, NJ: Prentice Hall, 1964.

Treadgold, Warren. *A History of the Byzantine State and Society*. Stanford: Stanford University Press, 1997.

Valois, Noël. "Un ouvrage inédit d'Honoré Bonet, Prieur de Salon." *Annuaire-Bulletin de la Société de l'Histoire de France* 27 (1890): 193–228.

_____. *La France et le grand schisme d'Occident*. 4 vols. Paris: A. Picard et fils, 1896–1903. Repr. Hildesheim: Georg Olms, 1967.

Vasiliev, Alexander A. *History of the Byzantine Empire, 324–1453* 2nd English ed., revised. Madison: University of Wisconsin Press, 1952.

Vincke, Johannes. *Briefe zum Pisaner Konzil*. Beiträge zur Kirchen- und Rechtgeschichte 1. Bonn: Hanstein, 1940.

_____. *Schriftstücke zum Pisaner Konzil: ein Kampf um die öffentliche Meinung*. Beiträge zur Kirchen- und Rechtgeschichte 3. Bonn: Hanstein, 1940.

Wallace, David. *Chaucerian Polity: Absolutist Lineages and Associational Forms in England and Italy*. Stanford: Stanford University Press, 1997.

Wallace-Hadrill, J. M., trans. *The Fourth Book of the Chronicle of Fredegar*. London and New York: Nelson, 1960.

Wenzel, Siegfried. "The Source for the 'Remedia' of the Parson's Tale." *Traditio* 27 (1971): 433–53.

Wood, Neal. *Cicero's Social and Political Thought*. Berkeley: University of California Press, 1988.

Wright, N. A. R. "The *Tree of Battles* of Honoré Bouvet and the Laws of War." In *War, Literature and Politics in the Late Middle Ages,* ed. C. T. Allmand. New York: Barnes & Noble, 1976), 12–31.

INDEX